P9-CQV-686

SANDRA BAO
BRIDGET GLEESON

BUENOS AIRES
CITY GUIDE

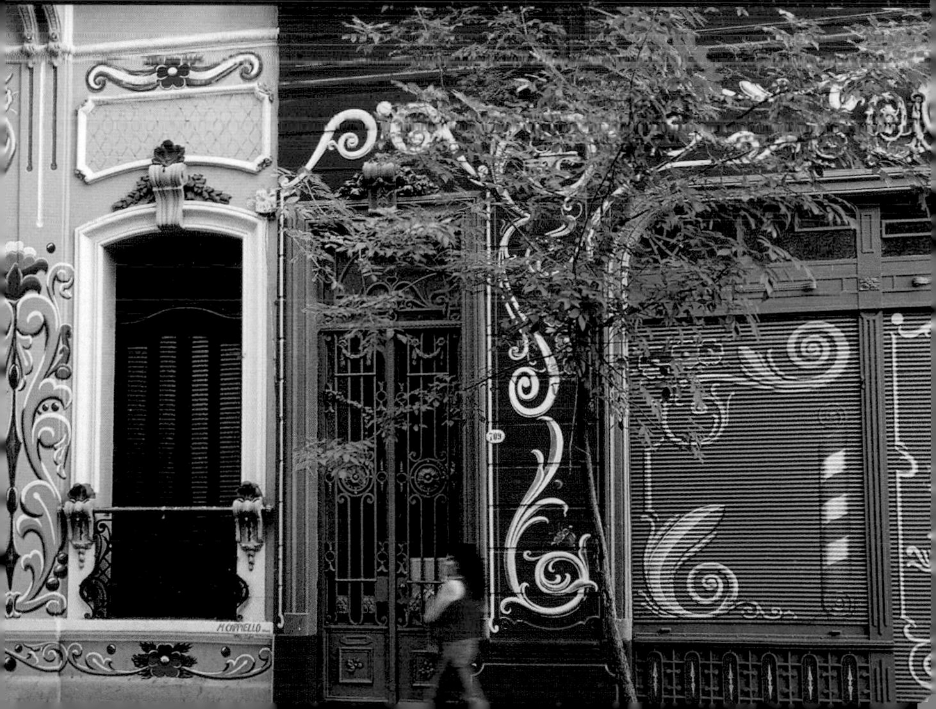

INTRODUCING BUENOS AIRES

BA's impressive cafe culture, part of its European heritage, adds to the colorful street life

MICHAEL COY

Sexy, alive and supremely confident, this beautiful city gets under your skin. Like Europe with a melancholic twist, Buenos Aires is unforgettable.

Built by Europeans, this vibrant city overflows with energy and brims with attractive residents called porteños. The food is fresh and innovative, the shopping ranges from designer labels to street hawkers, and nightlife will keep you swinging all night long. Don't miss attending a super passionate *fútbol* game, snatching a quick tango lesson or downing a juicy steak – it's all top-drawer here. And despite a wobbly economy and pesky inflation, Buenos Aires can still be a reasonable deal for anyone with hard currency.

Scratch beneath the surface and you'll find a wealth of old-world cafés, colonial architecture, outdoor markets and diverse communities. Rub shoulders with Recoleta's rich and famous while you visit its fascinating necropolis. Hunt for that antique gem in a dusty San Telmo shop, and wander Boedo's bohemian streets. Rollerblade around Palermo's green parks with the Sunday crowd.

BA is elegant, old-world languor blended with contemporary slickness, whipped together into a unique and seductive city. Come and you'll understand why so many travelers are setting foot in this incredible place. More and more are loving it so much they've even decided to stay – you might be one of them.

BUENOS AIRES LIFE

Glistening humidity, sultry stares and that insanely sexy Spanish – you're in Buenos Aires now and sensuality drips down every corner. Sure, it's a bit of a stereotype, but there's some truth to every generalization.

> Buenos Aires has two faces; it's a city that harbors both decline and prosperity.

Porteños are famous for their attractiveness; they are a proud people with a heightened sense of style and self-image. Because of their reputation they may seem a bit glamorized, but they're like most other big-city denizens – they live a typically modern lifestyle, most of them commuting by public transport to their city-center jobs, then they'll spend weekends with family and friends. Try to meet a few – after you get to know them they can be incredibly friendly and open, and once you're in their hearts they'll love you forever.

Buenos Aires has two faces; it's a city that harbors both decline and prosperity. You'll see dirty, neglected buildings even in the bustling heart of the city – yet a definite rebirth has taken hold. Millions of dollars have been sunk into Puerto Madero, while Palermo Viejo's upscale restaurants fill up every weekend. Shopping streets are jammed with people, yet everyone complains about not being able to make ends meet. There's definitely a rich-getting-richer-and-poor-getting-poorer phenomenon going on, so take a good look beneath the surface to get at the truth.

Porteño confidence is always going up and down, but it's hardly out. The economic disaster of 2001 is a fading memory now; the manufacturing industry has awakened with a vengeance, and along with a massive influx of foreign tourists has helped Argentina's economy get on the rebound.

This city is rough, refined and being reborn all at once. The steaks are really that good, the night life is really that rockin', the politicians are really that corrupt and life really does go on – even when everyone thinks they can't handle another pay cut. Porteños are resilient people, and will survive whatever crisis is tossed their way; after all, they've been dealing with uncertainty all their lives. But most importantly, they'll look their damn best doing it.

MICHAEL TAYLOR

Get friendly with all kinds of characters at a street fair (p118) in Caminito, La Boca

HIGHLIGHTS

HOLGER LE

THE CENTER

Whether it's the striking European architecture, jam-packed sidewalks, gorgeous porteño residents or speeding buses spewing more than their share of carbon footprints, Buenos Aires' center will leave you breathless – and pleasantly surprised.

ROBERTO GEROMET

❶ Plaza de Mayo
Get an eyeful of sights in this historic plaza (p63)

❷ Galerías Pacífico
Shop in top style at BA's French-style mall (p61)

❸ Av 9 de Julio
Dare to cross the daunting expanse of 9 de Julio (p71)

❹ Casa Rosada
Visit Evita's old offices in BA's pink palace (p64)

❺ Calle Florida
Mingle with the masses on the main artery of the Microcentro (p60)

LIVER STREWE

MICHAEL TAYLOR

KRZYSZTOF DYDYNSKI

HOLGER LEUE

PUERTO MADERO

Throw millions and millions of dollars into an old dockside area and shiny new buildings are bound to spring up like mushrooms. Stroll over cobbled lanes, stop for dinner at one of dozens of swish restaurants and take a walk in a nature reserve.

KRZYSZTOF DYDYNSKI

❶ Puente de la Mujer
Snap photos of this modern, harplike bridge (p68), designed by Santiago Calatrava

❷ Dikes
Stroll alongside the picturesque *diques* (dikes) (p68)

❸ Reserva Ecológica Costanera Sur
Explore the dirt paths in this ecological reserve (p70)

❹ Colección de Arte Amalia Lacroze de Fortabat
Pop into this Rafael Viñoly–designed museum for a dose of high art (p68)

RICHARD WAREHAM FOTOGRAFIE / ALAMY

INIGO BUJEDO AGUIRRE / PHOTOLIBRARY

KRZYSZTOF DYDYNSKI

❶ Teatro Colón
Don't miss the backstage tours of the Teatro Colón (p71)

❷ Palacio del Congreso
Feed the pigeons in front of Palacio del Congreso (p74)

❸ Obelisco
Check out BA's most prominent (and phallic) landmark (p71), designed by Alberto Prebisch

❹ Avenida Corrientes
Take in a play on BA's theater strip (p170)

CRAIG PERSHOUSE

CONGRESO & TRIBUNALES

Brush elbows (or wingtips) with the legal eagles in Buenos Aires' judicial neighborhood, where key landmarks pop up here and there and theatrical culture lights up the night.

MICHAEL TAYLOR

DAVID R. FRAZIER PHOTOLIBRARY, INC. / ALAMY

SAN TELMO

Tripping back into the past has never been so much fun. San Telmo delivers with its colonial buildings, cobbled streets, tango themes and antique shops. On Sunday see the barrio's famous antiques street fair, which is so much more than just old stuff.

TERRY CARTER

1

TERRY CARTER

2

MICHAEL TAYLOR

1 Classic Eateries
Go back in time at one of San Telmo's many atmospheric hangouts (p129)

2 Feria de San Pedro Telmo
Browse the antiques fair, watch the buskers or just sit at a sidewalk café (p118)

3 Colonial Buildings
Wander along San Telmo's streets and admire its colonial buildings (p75)

4 Tango Shows
Be amazed by high kicks at a tango show (p164)

4

KRZYSZTOF DYDYNSKI

TERRY CARTER

LA BOCA

Bright, brash and blue-collar, La Boca stuns with its unusual architecture and outlandish color schemes. Wander through El Caminito, check out some street tango or attend a passion-fueled fútbol *(soccer) game at La Bombonera stadium.*

ROBERTO GEROMETTA

ANDREW BAIN

❶ Fútbol Games
Watch a superpassionate *fútbol* (soccer) game at La Bombonera (p174)

❷ Street Tango
Pause to watch a donation tango show (p164)

❸ El Caminito
Walk through El Caminito enjoying the streetscape of colorful buildings (p79)

1 Plaza San Martín
Enjoy some midday sun in pleasant Plaza San Martín (p82)

2 Museo de Arte Hispanoamericano Isaac Fernández Blanco
Wander through this exceptional museum, located in a historic mansion (p83)

3 Downtown Retiro
Take a stroll in one of Buenos Aires' ritziest neighborhoods (p82)

BRIDGET GLEESON

RETIRO

Upscale Retiro is a fine sight, boasting impressive buildings full of aristocrats and a beautiful park dotted with sunbathers on a hot day. Retiro is BA's transportation hub and is home to the city's main train and bus stations.

KRZYSZTOF DYDYNSKI

JON HICKS / CORBIS

RECOLETA & BARRIO NORTE

Spiff up your threads and ready that bank account; it's time to visit Recoleta. Mingle with BA's richest inhabitants on Av Alvear's high-class boutiques, but whatever you do don't miss the Cementerio de la Recoleta – an astounding miniature city of the dead.

MICHAEL COYNE

KRZYSZTOF DYDYNSKI

KRZYSZTOF DYDYNSKI

MICHAEL COYNE

TERRY CARTER

KRZYSZTOF DYDYNSKI

❶ Recoleta Cemetery
Find that perfect sarcophagus shot at Cementerio de la Recoleta (p86)

❷ La Biela
Sit with Recoleta's royalty at this café (p153)

❸ Avenida Alvear
Window-shop or spend up big on this avenue (p111)

❹ Feria Plaza Francia
Shop your way between the hippies at this street market (p118)

❺ Museo Nacional de Bellas Artes
Wander past the works of European masters and well-known 19th- and 20th-century Argentine artists (p88)

❻ Floralis Genérica
Be impressed by this huge metal flower (p86) by architect Eduardo Catalano

PALERMO

Palermo is awesome. It has large grassy parks where you can kick a ball, good museums and great entertainment: sleep in BA's slickest hotels, eat at spectacular restaurants, shop at cutting-edge boutiques and stay up all night at trendy bars.

TERRY CARTER

1

❶ Jardín Zoológico
Talk to all the animals at the zoo (p95)

❷ Top-Notch Restaurants
Eat your way into heaven at Palermo's restaurants (p134)

❸ Parque 3 de Febrero
Walk, jog, bike or picnic in Palermo's green park (p90)

❹ Museo de Arte Latinoamericano de Buenos Aires (Malba)
Gaze at top-drawer art in this beautiful and slick museum (p90)

2

TERRY CARTER

MICHAEL COYNE

3

TERRY CARTER

4

MARGIE POLITZER

1 Tigre
Take a break from busy BA and visit this peaceful delta region on a boat tour (p200)

2 Basílica Nuestra Señora de Luján
Gather with the faithful at the basilica in Lújan (p205)

3 Punta del Este
See *La Mano en la Arena* sculpture by Mario Irarrázabal at this famous beach resort (p215)

4 Colonia
Stroll Colonia's peaceful cobbled streets and charming buildings (p209)

DAY TRIPS

Ready to escape the big city lights? Then head north to Tigre, where you can cruise the nearby delta channels. And across the Río de la Plata there's cute Colonia and intriguing Montevideo; both just a boat-ride away in Uruguay.

KRZYSZTOF DYDYNSKI

KRZYSZTOF DYDYNSKI

VIVIANE PONT

CONTENTS

Continued from previous page.

THE AUTHORS

Sandra Bao

Sandra's mom and her family escaped China's communist regime, eventually boarding a freighter bound for Argentina in 1952. After months at sea they arrived in Buenos Aires - just two days after the death of Evita Perón. Sandra's dad came over from England in 1955, where he'd been studying.

Sandra's parents met and married in Montevideo, Uruguay, and moved to Buenos Aires, where they raised Sandra and her brother Daniel. They lived the carefree porteño life (with *asados* every Sunday) until 1974, when the Baos emigrated to greener pastures – this time the USA – and got into California real estate at just the right time.

Sandra is proud to be a porteña and has regularly returned to her homeland as an adult. As well as writing most of the chapters of this book, over the last decade Sandra has contributed to Lonely Planet's *Argentina* and *South America on a Shoestring*.

SANDRA'S TOP BUENOS AIRES DAY

It's Sunday morning, so like most other porteños I get up around noon – not bad for having stayed up till 5am the night before. I nurse my hangover with *té negro* (black tea) and a couple of *medialunas* (croissants) at the local corner café, then deal with the crazy crowds bustling through San Telmo's antiques market. A refreshing walk sounds perfect on this glorious spring day, so I head over to the Reserva Ecológica Costanera Sur for some bird-watching. After my clearing dose of nature, a visit to Plaza de Mayo and its impressive Casa Rosada is in order. Strolling up Calle Florida means avoiding traffic, so this is what I do, window-shopping all the way (and grabbing a luscious ice-cream cone, too). When I reach the stunning Galerías Pacífico I pop inside for a quick peep at the gorgeous ceiling murals (and take a bathroom break downstairs). Plaza San Martín invites a restful sit-down and makes for some great people-watching on the grassy lawns. Then I head up Av Alvear into upscale Recoleta, where I wander the crafts stalls before ducking into the cemetery for some quiet reflection and awesome photo ops. After catching the 59 bus to Palermo Viejo I find the stores still open, and go on a shopping spree at clothing boutiques. Soon it's 10pm and time for dinner, so I meet some friends at one of the dozens of fine restaurants in this neighborhood – and start a long night out all over again.

Contributing Author

BRIDGET GLEESON

Bridget is a Buenos Aires–based travel writer who's been up to the highest cliffs of the Andes and down to the sandy floor of the Brazilian Atlantic in the name of journalism. She's contributed to several Lonely Planet titles and writes for *Budget Travel, Delta Sky, Mr & Mrs Smith* and *Afar*.

LONELY PLANET AUTHORS

Why is our travel information the best in the world? It's simple: our authors are passionate, dedicated travelers. They don't take freebies in exchange for positive coverage so you can be sure the advice you're given is impartial. They travel widely to all the popular spots, and off the beaten track. They don't research using just the internet or phone. They discover new places not included in any other guidebook. They personally visit thousands of hotels, restaurants, palaces, trails, galleries, temples and more. They speak with dozens of locals every day to make sure you get the kind of insider knowledge only a local could tell you. They take pride in getting all the details right, and in telling it how it is. Think you can do it? Find out how at **lonelyplanet.com**.

GETTING STARTED

Buenos Aires is a cosmopolitan city (population: over 13 million people in the greater metropolitan area), and you can expect to find pretty much all the modern conveniences and services you're used to. There's a plethora of accommodations in nearly all neighborhoods that are popular with tourists, and they range from countless hostels to five-star hotels such as the Four Seasons. There are also dozens of lovely guesthouses and boutique hotels to choose from. It's always a good idea to reserve ahead of time – especially during the busier November to March and July to August seasons. At other times there are usually a few rooms available at all but the most popular places. That said, don't come to BA during major holidays such as Christmas or Easter without reservations.

BA eateries cater to all budgets – you can nab a *choripán* (spicy sausage sandwich) for just a few pesos, or pay international prices at the most expensive restaurants. As a whole, Argentine cuisine isn't hugely creative – typical fare consists of steak or pasta. Buenos Aires, however, has a fairly good range of (pricier) exotic cuisines, especially in its Palermo Viejo neighborhood.

Most traveler services are easily found in the center, including internet cafes, telephone offices and laundries. It's easy to get from one area to another using the Subte, buses or taxis. Many people speak some English, especially those in the tourist sectors.

WHEN TO GO

In terms of weather, spring (September to November) and fall (March to May) are the best seasons to visit Buenos Aires. Also, most festivals take place during these months, as do a good chunk of sporting events. Winter can be cold but not freezing, and a fine time to visit the city's theaters, museums and cafés.

Many tourists come during the late spring and summer (November to March), though the hottest months of January and February are usually unpleasantly humid. Porteños who can afford it leave the city for the coasts, so some places – like museums and entertainment venues – close down in the capital (January and February are also the worst months to be doing business here). However, no matter what time of year you visit, BA will have something exciting to offer.

FESTIVALS

There are festivals happening in Buenos Aires all the time, and they celebrate nearly everything – tango, horses, gauchos, cinema, art, wine, fashion and books. Check with tourist offices (p232) for exact dates as some vary from year to year; they can also tell you of other goings-on (or check www.festivales.gov.ar). See p226 for a list of national holidays.

ADVANCE PLANNING

Buenos Aires has become a popular destination, so book your hotel in advance to ensure a roof above your head. In fancier hotels you'll also save a few bucks off those outrageous rack rates.

Most restaurants don't require advance reservations, but if you want to eat at a popular place (especially on weekends) then be sure to call ahead. We note in individual reviews whether reservations are recommended at a particular place; in general, the fancier a restaurant the more likely you'll need a reservation.

Some websites can help you plan ahead and catch special events: Visit www.whatsupbuenosaires.com for hip music happenings, or www.bue.gov.ar for general information and upcoming events. To find reviewed restaurants see www.saltshaker.net (or www.guiaoleo.com.ar if you read Spanish).

If you're a do-it-yourselfer with an MP3 player and don't need a tour guide but would still appreciate some guidance, check out www.mptours.com. You can download unique self-guided tours and maps of BA neighborhoods for US$4.99 each, walking, stopping and listening at your leisure. The city website (www.bue.gov.ar/audioguia; both in English and Spanish) also has free downloads.

Finally, pack some smart clothing in your bag. Porteños are a well-dressed and well-groomed lot, and you'll definitely stick out as a tourist in loud shirt, shorts and flip-flops (in fact, porteños hardly ever wear shorts at all unless they're working out). Especially if you're going out at night, dress nicely – everyone else will.

February

CARNAVAL

Usually occurring in February, Buenos Aires' Carnaval is a tiny affair compared to Rio's or Bahia's, but there's still a chance to be clobbered by water balloons and canned foam. This is a great time to catch some Brazilian-flavored *murga* groups (traditional Carnaval ensembles), with dancing and drumming around Plaza de Mayo. If you want something with more oomph, head to Gualeguaychú in Entre Ríos province. Montevideo (p212) in Uruguay also has a good Carnaval. Future dates are February 18-21, 2012 and February 9-12, 2013.

CHINESE NEW YEAR

Yes, Buenos Aires has a Chinatown, but blink and you'll miss it. Check it out in Belgrano on Arribeños street; it's only about four blocks long and fairly tame as far as big-city Chinatowns go, but New Year's is a lively time and worth heading up here for food, firecrackers and festivities. Dates depend on the lunar calendar; it'll be on January 23 in 2012 and February 10 in 2013.

BUENOS AIRES FASHION WEEK

www.bafweek.com

Buenos Aires' fashion-design scene has skyrocketed in the last decade, and these four days of clothing stalls and catwalk action show off the city's latest threads and their makers. It takes place at Palermo's La Rural in late February (fall collection) and in mid-late August (spring collection). Plenty of models and other beautiful people of BA attend – bring out the voyeur in yourself.

April

FERIA DEL LIBRO

www.el-libro.org.ar

Buenos Aires' annual book fair is one of the top book expos in the world, attracting tens of thousands of book lovers for three weeks in April and May. It features famous authors doing readings and signing books; many books are also sold at a discount. Most exhibitors (publishers) come from Latin America, but there are also displays from countries like England, China, France, Ukraine, Norway and Armenia. Look for it at the La Rural building in Palermo.

FESTIVAL INTERNACIONAL DE CINE INDEPENDIENTE

www.bafici.gov.ar

This mid-to-late-April independent film festival highlights both national and international independent films, with awards given out in separate categories; guest directors and actors are invited. Over a hundred films are screened in the city's cinemas, with a main venue being the Abasto shopping mall (p97).

May

ARTE BA

www.arteba.com

This exciting event held in mid to late May features exhibitions from hundreds of art galleries, dealers, institutions and organizations in Buenos Aires, with both national and international contemporary art on display. Conferences, presentations and discussions make the rounds, and young new artists get key exposure. It all takes place at Palermo's La Rural building.

July

EXPOSICIÒN DE GANADERÌA, AGRICULTURA E INDUSTRIA INTERNACIONAL (LA RURAL)

www.exposicionrural.com.ar

This is the mother of all livestock fairs, where prize cows, sheep, goats, horses and – most especially – bulls, all strut their stuff. Agricultural machinery is also highlighted, and gaucho shows provide entertainment. It takes place for two weeks in late July to early August at Palermo's La Rural building.

August

FESTIVAL Y MUNDIAL DE TANGO

www.mundialdetango.gob.ar

Taking place in mid-August, this two-week-long tango festival is spread out geographically all over the city and offers a great way to see some of the country's best tango dancers and musicians do their thing. There's a world-class dance competition, where international couples compete fiercely for this most prestigious trophy and title to 'the world's best tango dancers'. Plenty of classes and workshops also take place.

September

VINOS Y BODEGAS

www.expovinosybodegas.com.ar

A can't-miss event for wine aficionados, with vintages from dozens of Argentine *bodegas* (wineries). Mix with thousands of sommeliers, restaurateurs, journalists and general wine-lovers at Palermo's La Rural building. Occurs in mid-late September; expect cooking demonstrations and live music too.

LA SEMANA DEL ARTE EN BUENOS AIRES

www.lasemanadelarte.com.ar

In late September dozens of cultural centers, museums and art galleries all over BA open their doors for a mega-event that highlights some of the best contemporary artists in the country. Mediums include everything from etchings to photographs to paintings, while conferences, concerts and special gallery nights also come with the package. All activities are free of charge.

CASA FOA

www.casafoa.com

This is the city's top-notch architecture, design and landscape fair, which runs from October through November and showcases local and international trends. Each year a different dilapidated location is picked and rehabbed into an amazing venue; in 2010 it was a three-storey building in San Telmo.

October

FESTIVAL BUENOS AIRES DANZA CONTEPORÀNEA

www.buenosairesdanza.gov.ar

Contemporary dance gets four days to shine in Buenos Aires at this biennial celebration (every even-numbered year), with productions by Argentine choreographers and dancers and including some international guest artists. Performances, seminars and workshops take place in the city's cultural centers and theaters.

MARATÓN DE BUENOS AIRES

www.maratondebuenosaires.com

In October long-distance runners can go the whole 42km, passing many of BA's famous landmarks and neighborhoods along the way. Parque Roca, north of the center, marks the start and finish line; there's a half-marathon option also.

PEPSI MUSIC FESTIVAL

www.pepsimundo.com/argentina/pepsimusic

Hugely popular, 10-day-long international music festival showcasing dozens of bands from Argentina and beyond; in 2010 the front headliners were Green Day and Rage against the Machine. Expect several kinds of music – rock, Argentine rock, indie, punk, reggae and even possibly a little electronica.

November

GRAN PREMIO NACIONAL

www.palermo.com.ar

In mid-November the country's biggest horse race takes place in Palermo's opulent and French-styled hipódromo (p176). First held in 1884, this is a fine event that not only attracts the well-to-do and celebrity-watchers, but regular families as well. Watch for the *granaderos* (presidential horseback guards) in their impressive outfits, marching around for the crowds.

MARCHA DEL ORGULLO GAY

www.marchadelorgullo.org.ar

It's nothing like San Francisco's or Sydney's, but BA has its own gay pride march. Each year on the first Saturday in November, thousands of BA's gays, lesbians, transgenders and more strut their way from Plaza de Mayo to the Congreso. They use this high-profile event to promote their rights, and each year the colorful party gets bigger – the march was first held in 1992. Gay Pride Week follows later in November.

DÍA DE LA TRADICIÓN

This is the closest thing to traditional gaucho culture you'll probably witness, with folk music and dancing, traditional foods and feats of horsemanship. The best place to be during these mid-November festivities is San Antonio de Areco (p206), Argentina's ground zero for gauchos and a day trip away from BA. If you can't get away, head to the Feria de Mataderos (p118), way west of center in the barrio of Mataderos. For exact dates (they change yearly) call Areco's tourist office (p208).

LA NOCHE DE LOS MUSEOS

www.lanochedelosmuseos.com.ar

This one-night, mid-November sees over a hundred museums, galleries and cultural spaces open their doors for free from 7pm to around 3am; there are guided tours, special shows, music festivities and even free buses that whisk visitors between the venues.

December

CAMPEONATO ABIERTO ARGENTINO DE POLO

Argentina boasts the world's best polo (see p176), and the Abierto is the world's premier polo event. This series of matches also marks the culmination of the spring polo season. It takes place at Palermo's Campo Argentino de Polo. For exact dates and details, contact the Asociación Argentina de Polo (☎ 4777-6444; www.aapolo.com).

CAMPEONATO ABIERTO ARGENTINO DE PATO

Steeped in gaucho culture, *pato* (see p176) is still not quite the national sport of Argentina it claims to be. A six-handled, leather-covered ball (originally a dead duck) is the center of attention. Don't miss this spectacle; it's cool and quirky as hell. For details, contact the Federación Argentina de Pato (☎ 4372-0180; www.fedpato.com.ar).

BUENOS AIRES JAZZ FESTIVAL INTERNACIONAL

www.buenosairesjazz.gob.ar

BA's biggest jazz festival takes place over five days all over the city, attracting over 35,000 spectators. Jazz musicians of all kinds are featured – emerging and established, avant-garde and traditional, national and international. Concerts and films also take place.

COSTS

In the last 10 years Argentina has gone from being a very expensive country to a sudden bargain destination to a not-as-cheap-as-it-was kind of place. Today the peso hovers around four to one US dollar, but Argentina is an economically volatile country and things could change quickly. It's always wise to check what that pesky peso is doing (see www.xe.com).

Despite a steep rise in inflation the past few years, Buenos Aires remains a decent deal for visitors with hard currency. Dorm beds can be had for US$12, and cheap hotel rooms go for around US$60. Three-star hotels are US$90, and if you book online you might be able find a five-star one for under US$200.

Dinners at upscale restaurants, including appetizer, main course and drinks, often cost under US$25; lunches are cheaper, especially when you order the *menu ejecutivo* (set lunch). Bus or Subte tickets are US$0.30 and short taxi rides under US$8. Entry to museums, theaters, nightclubs and special events is just a few bucks. You could spend US$125 per day and be quite comfortable. So while BA isn't the bargain it once was, it's still a big exciting city and an affordable place to visit.

HOW MUCH?

Cup of coffee at café AR$10-12

Glass of chopp (draft beer) AR$14

Empanada (meat pie) AR$4

Steak dinner AR$50

Internet use per hour AR$5

Average taxi ride AR$30

Liter of gasoline AR$4

Movie ticket AR$20-25

Group tango class AR$35

Fancy tango show ticket with dinner AR$400

INTERNET RESOURCES

The following are just a sampling of websites devoted to Argentina; all are in English or have an English link:

www.argentinaindependent.com Great well-written articles on Argentina current affairs and culture, plus online directory, events listing and musings about expat life.

www.argentinepost Useful wide-ranging articles on BA and Argentina.

www.baexpats.org & www.bainnewcomers.org Popular expat websites.

www.bainsidermag.com Reviews and the essentials about expat life in BA.

www.bue.gov.ar The city's official website.

www.buenosaires.en.craigslist.org Find an apartment, a job and/or a lover.

www.buenosairesherald.com The *Buenos Aires Herald*'s view of the country and the world.

www.landingpadba.com Fun insider facts on living in Buenos Aires, plus all the basic info and a booking service as well.

www.lonelyplanet.com Forums, travel news, recent updates, postcards from other travelers and lots more.

www.saltshaker.net Best for its detailed restaurant reviews.

www.thegayguide.com.ar All things gay in BA.

www.whatsupbuenosaires.com Current happenings, especially for music.

BACKGROUND

HISTORY

Ask anyone from Buenos Aires and they will tell you that the business, history and politics of the city are the business, history and politics of Argentina. As the capital of the country and home to one-third of the national population, Buenos Aires is the epicenter of every major Argentine drama – from triumph to defeat and back.

THE SPANISH ARRIVE

Although the banks of the Río de la Plata (River Plate) had been populated for tens of thousands of years by nomadic hunter-gatherers, the first attempt at establishing a permanent settlement was made by Spanish aristocrat Pedro de Mendoza in 1536. His verbose name for the outpost, Puerto Nuestra Señora Santa María del Buen Aire (Port Our Lady Saint Mary of the Good Wind) was matched only by his extravagant expedition of 16 ships and nearly 1600 men – almost three times the size of Hernán Cortés' forces that conquered the Aztecs. In spite of his resources and planning, Mendoza unfortunately arrived too late in the season to plant adequate crops. The Spanish soon found themselves short on food and in typical colonialist fashion tried to bully the local Querandí indigenous groups into feeding them. A bitter fight and four years of struggle ensued, which led to such an acute shortage of supplies that some of the Spanish resorted to cannibalism. Mendoza himself fled back to Spain, while a detachment of troops who were left behind retreated upriver to Asunción (now the capital of Paraguay).

With Francisco Pizarro's conquest of the Inca empire in present-day Peru as the focus of the Spanish Crown, Buenos Aires was largely ignored for the next four decades. In 1580 Juan de Garay returned with an expedition from Asunción and attempted to rebuild Buenos Aires. The Spanish had not only improved their colonizing skills since Mendoza's ill-fated endeavor but also had some backup from the cities of Asunción and Santa Fe.

Still, Buenos Aires remained a backwater in comparison to Andean settlements such as Tucumán, Córdoba, Salta, La Rioja and Jujuy. With the development of mines in the Andes and the incessant warfare in the Spanish empire swelling the demand for both cattle and horses, ranching became the core of the city's early economy. Spain maintained harsh restrictions on trade out of Buenos Aires and the increasingly frustrated locals turned to smuggling contraband.

The city continued to flourish and the crown was eventually forced to relax its restrictions and co-opt the growing international trade in the region. In 1776 Madrid made Buenos Aires the capital of the new Viceroyalty of the Río de la Plata, which included the world's largest silver mine in Potosí (in present-day Bolivia). For many of its residents, the new status was recognition that the adolescent city was outgrowing Spain's parental authority.

Although the new viceroyalty had internal squabbles over trade and control issues, when the British raided the city twice, in 1806 and 1807, the response was unified. Locals rallied against

TIMELINE

1536

Spanish aristocrat Pedro de Mendoza reaches the Río de la Plata and attempts to set up a permanent settlement, only to return to Spain within four years.

1580

Buenos Aires is reestablished by Spanish forces, but the city remains a backwater for years, in comparison to growing strongholds in central and northwestern Argentina.

1660

Buenos Aires' population is around 4000; it would take another century for it to double.

SMUGGLING IN BUENOS AIRES

It's not a coincidence that one of the most popular whiskeys served in Buenos Aires is called Old Smuggler. The city's history of trading in contraband goes all the way back to its founding. Some argue that the culture of corruption, so pervasive until the economic collapse of 2001, was tolerated because the historical role of smuggling in Buenos Aires led to a 'tradition' of rule-bending.

The Spanish empire kept tight regulations on its ports and only certain cities were allowed to trade goods with other countries. Buenos Aires, originally on the periphery of the empire, was hard to monitor and therefore not allowed to buy from or sell to other Europeans. Located at the mouth of the Río de la Plata, the settlement was an ideal point of entry to the continent for traders. Buenos Aires merchants turned to smuggling everything from textiles and precious metals to weapons and slaves. Portuguese manufactured goods flooded the city and made their way inland to present-day Bolivia, Paraguay and even Peru.

Later, the British and high-seas pirates found a ready and willing trading partner in Buenos Aires (and also introduced a taste for fine whiskeys). An increasing amount of wealth passed through the city and much of the initial growth of Buenos Aires was fuelled by the trade in contraband. As smuggling was an open game, without favored imperial merchants, it offered a chance for upward social mobility and gave birth to a commercially oriented middle class in Buenos Aires.

Although smuggling has died down in recent years it is never that far away. There have been a series of recent government incidents, including what has been called 'the suitcase scandal': in August 2007, a Venezuelan businessman tried to sneak US$800,000 into Argentina on a plane chartered by the government's national energy company. In the same year Cristina Kirchner's economy minister was forced to step down over US$64,000 found stashed in a bag in her office toilet.

the invaders without Spanish help and chased them out of town. These two battles gave the city's inhabitants confidence and an understanding of their self-reliance. It was just a matter of time until they broke with Spain.

INDEPENDENCE

When Napoleon conquered Spain and put his brother on the throne in 1808, Buenos Aires became further estranged from Madrid and finally declared its independence on May 25, 1810.

Six years later, on July 9, 1816, outlying areas of the viceroyalty also broke with Spain and founded the United Provinces of the River Plate. Almost immediately a power struggle arose between Buenos Aires and the provincial strongmen: the Federalist landowners of the interior provinces were concerned with preserving their autonomy while the Unitarist businessmen of Buenos Aires tried to consolidate power in the city with an outward orientation toward overseas commerce and European ideas. Some of the interior provinces decided to go their own way, forming Paraguay in 1814, Bolivia in 1825 and Uruguay in 1828.

After more than a decade of violence and uncertainty, Juan Manuel de Rosas become governor of Buenos Aires in 1829. Although he swore that he was a Federalist, Rosas was more of an opportunist – a Federalist when it suited him and a Unitarist once he controlled the city. He required that all international trade be funneled through Buenos Aires, rather than proceeding directly to the provinces, and set ominous political precedents, creating the *mazorca* (his ruthless political police) and institutionalizing torture.

1776

Buenos Aires becomes capital city of the new Spanish Viceroyalty of the Río de la Plata, which included what are today Bolivia, Argentina, Paraguay and Uruguay.

1806 & 1807

British troops raid the city but are beaten back by the people of Buenos Aires in two battles, now celebrated as La Reconquista (the Reconquest) and La Defensa (the Defense).

May 25, 1810

In a huge public protest, Buenos Aires declares its independence from Spain and renames the city's main square Plaza de Mayo to commemorate the occasion.

THE FLEETING GOLDEN YEARS

Rosas' overthrow came in 1852 at the hands of Justo José de Urquiza, a rival governor who tried to transfer power to his home province of Entre Rios. In protest, Buenos Aires briefly seceded from the union, but was reestablished as the capital when Bartolomé Mitre crushed Urquiza's forces in 1861. From there, Buenos Aires never looked back and became the undisputed power center of the country.

The economy boomed and Buenos Aires became a port town of 90,000 people in the late 1860s. Immigrants poured in from Spain, Italy and Germany, followed by waves of newcomers from Croatia, Ireland, Poland and Ukraine. Its population grew nearly seven-fold from 1869 to 1895, to over 670,000 people. The new residents worked in the port, lived tightly in crammed tenement buildings, developed tango and jump-started the leftist labor movement. The onslaught of Europeans not only expanded Buenos Aires into a major international capital but gave the city its rich multicultural heritage, famous idiosyncrasies and sharp political differences.

By Argentina's centennial in 1910, Buenos Aires was a veritable metropolis. The following years witnessed the construction of the subway, while British companies built modern gas, electrical and sewer systems. Buenos Aires was at the height of a Golden Age, its bustling streets full of New World businesses, art, architecture and fashion. Argentina grew rich during this time based on its meat production. Advances in refrigeration and the country's ability to ship cow meat to distant lands was key to its economic success. In fact, by the beginning of WWI, Argentina was one of the world's 10 richest countries, and ahead of France and Germany.

Conservative forces dominated the political sphere until 1916 when the Radical Party leader Hipólito Yrigoyen took control of the government in a move that stressed fair and democratic elections. After a prolonged period of elite rule, this was the first time Argentina's burgeoning middle class obtained a political voice.

It was also at this time that Argentina's fortune started to change, but unfortunately not for the better. Export prices dropped off, wages stagnated and workers became increasingly frustrated and militant. La Semana Trágica (Tragic Week), when over a hundred protesters were killed during a metalworkers' strike, was the culmination of these tensions; some say this radical reaction was due to the government being pressured by moneyed interests. The Wall Street crash of 1929 dealt the final blow to the export markets and a few months later the military took over the country. The Golden Age rapidly became a distant memory. It was the first of many military coups that blemished the rest of the century and served to shackle the progress of the nation. Scholars have argued that the events that culminated in the 2001 economic collapse can be traced back to the military coup led by General José Félix Uribiru in 1930.

THE AGE OF THE PERÓNS

During WWII the rural poor migrated into Buenos Aires in search of work. The number of people living in the city nearly tripled and it soon held a third of the national population (which is in fact similar to the percentage today). The growing strength of these urban working classes swept populist Lieutenant-General Juan Domingo Perón into the presidency in 1946. Perón had been stationed for a time in Italy and developed his own brand of

1829

Federalist caudillo Juan Manuel de Rosas takes control of Buenos Aires and becomes its governor; the influence of BA increases dramatically during his 23-year reign, before he is overthrown by José de Urquiza.

1861

Bartolomé Mitre, the governor of Buenos Aires province, poet and founder of *La Nación* newspaper, becomes president after defeating Urquiza's federal forces.

1871

Serious shortage of water and adequate sewage systems leads to a severe outbreak of yellow fever that kills more than 10% of the city's population.

watered-down Mussolini-style fascism. He quickly nationalized large industry, including the railways, and created Argentina's first welfare state. Borrowing from Fascist Italy and Germany, Perón carefully cultivated his iconic image and held massive popular rallies in the Plaza de 25 de Mayo.

The glamorous Eva Duarte, a onetime radio soap-opera star, became the consummate celebrity first lady upon marrying Perón, and an icon who would eclipse Perón himself. Known as Evita, her powerful social-assistance foundation reached out to lower-class women through giveaways of such things as baby bottles and strollers, and the construction of schools and hospitals. The masses felt a certain empathy with Evita, who was also born into the working class. Her premature death in 1952 came just before things went sour and her husband's political power plummeted.

After Evita's death Perón financed payouts to workers by simply printing new money, bungled the economy, censored the press and cracked down on opposition. He was strikingly less popular without Evita, and was deposed by the military in 1955 after two terms in office. Perón lived in exile in Spain while a series of military coups ailed the nation. When he returned in 1973, there were escalating tensions from left and right parties; even if he'd lived to serve his term of re-election, Perón would have had much on his plate. His successor, his hapless third wife Isabelita, had even less staying power and her overthrow by a military junta in 1976 came as no surprise.

Although the effects of Perón's personal political achievements are debatable, the Peronist party, based largely on his ideals, has endured.

THE DIRTY WAR

The new military rulers instituted the Process of National Reorganisation, known as El Proceso and this was headed by the notorious Jorge Rafael Videla. Ostensibly an effort to remake Argentina's political culture and modernize the flagging economy, El Proceso was little more than a Cold War–era attempt to kill off or intimidate all leftist political opposition in the country.

Based in Buenos Aires, a left-wing guerrilla group known as the Montoneros bombed foreign buildings, kidnapped executives for ransom and robbed banks to finance their armed struggle against the government. The Montoneros were composed mainly of educated, middle-class youths who were hunted down by the military government in a campaign known as La Guerra Sucia (the Dirty War). Somewhere between 10,000 and 30,000 civilians died; many of them simply 'disappeared' while walking down the street or sleeping in their beds. Most were tortured to death, or sedated and dropped from planes into the Río de la Plata. Anyone who seemed even sympathetic to the Montoneros could be whisked off the streets and detained, tortured or killed. A great number of the 'disappeared' are still unaccounted for today.

The military leaders let numerous aspects of the country's well-being slip into decay along with the entire national economy. When Ronald Reagan took power in the USA in 1981, he reversed Jimmy Carter's condemnation of the junta's human-rights abuses and even invited the generals to visit Washington, DC. Backed by this relationship with the USA, the military were able to solicit development loans from international lenders, but endemic corruption quickly drained the coffers into their Swiss bank accounts.

1916

Hipólito Yrigoyen, leader of the Radical Party popular with the middle classes, is elected president and introduces minimum wage to counter inflation; he's re-elected in 1928.

1930

Hipólito Yrigoyen is overthrown in a military coup led by General José Félix Uriburu, who stays in power for two years, after which civilian rule is restored.

1946

Populist Lieutenant-General Juan Domingo Perón is elected president; Perón and his young wife Evita introduce higher wages and welfare campaigns, and make sweeping changes to the political structure.

ESMA: ARGENTINA'S AUSCHWITZ

Along a busy road in the BA neighborhood of Nuñez is an imposing building officially called the Naval Mechanics School but better known as ESMA. During Argentina's 1976-83 military rule it served as an infamous detention center where some 5000 people were brutally tortured and killed. Truckloads of blindfolded prisoners were unloaded outside the building, taken to the basement, sedated and killed. Some were murdered by firing squads and others were drugged and dropped from planes into the Río de la Plata on twice-weekly 'death flights.' The building also served as a clandestine maternity center that housed babies taken from their mothers (many of whom were subsequently killed) to be given to police and military couples without children.

In 2004, as part of Kirchner's effort to revisit the Dirty War crimes, the building was designated as a memorial museum, handed over to a human rights group and named the Space for Memory & Promotion and Defense of Human Rights. But reviving the memory was like opening Pandora's box and a public debate ensued on how to tackle the museum – whether to make it educational, poignant, moralizing or realistic. This debate has delayed the museum launch; what also caused the delay was the insistence of the human rights groups that all campus buildings, some of which were still occupied by the Navy, be vacated. The Navy finally did move to another locale.

Eventually, it was agreed that it's best to leave the space bare, with few explanatory signs, and so commemorate the victims. On the public tours (see www.derhuman.jus.gov.ar/espacioparalamemoria) through the bleak rooms, guides tell the stories of detainees' tragic lives. According to photographer Marcelo Brodsky, whose brother disappeared in ESMA, 'The site is charged with torture sessions, muffled screams, odors and sounds.' This reminder of Argentina's state terror allows visitors to ponder the frailty of democracy and contemplate the evil of military dictatorships not only in Argentina but around the world.

In 2007 La Marca Editora published an excellent book on the public debate that surrounded the opening of ESMA. Compiled by Marcelo Brodsky, *Memoria en Construcción* features over 65 artists and artists' collectives, and their reflections on this sensitive issue.

Another more easily accessed ex-torture site are the exposed basement chambers of the old Club Atlético building in San Telmo (the building was torn down and is no longer there); it's ill-located under a freeway, however. See the Historical Saunter walking tour on p105.

THE RETURN TO DEMOCRACY

The military dictatorship that ruled the country with an iron fist lasted from 1976 to 1983. General Leopoldo Galtieri took the reins of the draconian military junta in 1981 but its power was unraveling: the economy was in recession, interest rates skyrocketed and protesters took to the streets of Buenos Aires. A year later, Galtieri tried to divert national attention by goading the UK into a war over control of the Falkland Islands (known in Argentina as Las Islas Malvinas). The British had more resolve than the junta had imagined and Argentina was easily defeated. The greatest blow came when the British nuclear submarine *Conqueror* torpedoed the Argentine heavy cruiser *General Belgrano,* killing 323 men. Argentina still holds that the ship was returning to harbor.

Embarrassed and proven ineffectual, the military regime fell apart and a new civilian government under Raúl Alfonsín took control in 1983. Alfonsín enjoyed a small amount of success and was able to negotiate a few international loans, but he could not limit inflation or constrain public spending. By 1989 inflation was out of control and Alfonsín left office five months early, when Carlos Menem took power.

1955

On June 15, 1955, anti-Peronists within the army use navy aircraft to bomb Peron supporters at Plaza de Mayo, killing 350 people. Some consider this crushed coup d'état a prelude to the Dirty War.

1976

The military junta led by Jorge Rafael Videla replaces Isabelita Perón; this marks the beginning of the Dirty War that involved harsh repression and eradication of civilian government.

1982

General Leopoldo Galtieri provokes the UK into a war over control of the Falkland Islands (Las Islas Malvinas), but Argentina is easily defeated by the British.

MENEM & THE BOOM YEARS

Under the guidance of his shrewd economy minister, Domingo Cavallo, the skillfully slick Carlos Menem introduced free-market reforms to stall Argentina's economic slide. Many of the state-run industries were privatized and, most importantly, the peso was fixed by law at an equal rate to the American dollar. Foreign investment poured into the country. Buenos Aires began to thrive again: buildings were restored and new businesses boomed. The capital's Puerto Madero docks were redeveloped into an upscale leisure district, tourism increased and optimism was in the air. People in Buenos Aires bought new cars, talked on cell phones and took international vacations.

Although the Argentinine economy seemed robust to the casual observer, by Menem's second term (1995–99) things were already amiss. The inflexibility imposed by the economic reforms made it difficult for the country to respond to foreign competition, and Mexico's 1995 currency collapse jolted a number of banks in Buenos Aires. Not only did Menem fail to reform public spending, but corruption was so widespread that it dominated daily newspaper headlines.

THE ECONOMIC CRISIS

As an economic slowdown deepened into a recession, voters turned to the mayor of Buenos Aires, Fernando de la Rúa, and elected him president in 1999. He was faced with the need to cut public spending and hike taxes during the recession.

The economy stagnated further, investors panicked, the bond market teetered on the brink of oblivion and the country seemed unable to service its increasingly heavy international debt. Cavallo was brought back in as the economy minister and in January 2001, rather than declaring a debt default, he sought over US$20 million more in loans from the IMF.

Argentina had been living on credit and it could no longer sustain its lifestyle. The facade of a successful economy had been ripped away, and the indebted, weak inner workings were exposed. As the storm clouds gathered, there was a run on the banks. Between July and November, Argentines withdrew around US$20 billion from the banks, hiding it under their mattresses or sending it abroad. In a last-ditch effort to keep money in the country, the government imposed a limit of US$1000 a month on bank withdrawals. Called the *corralito* (little corral), the strategy crushed many informal sectors of the economy that function on cash (taxis, food markets), and rioters and looters inevitably took to the streets. As the government tried to hoard the remaining hard currency, all bank savings were converted to pesos and any remaining trust in the government was broken. Middle-class protesters joined the fray in a series of pot-and-pan banging protests, and both Cavallo and, then, de la Rua bowed to the inevitable and resigned.

Two new presidents came and went in the same week and the world's greatest default on public debt was declared. The third presidential successor, former Buenos Aires province governor Eduardo Duhalde, was able to hold onto power. In order to have more flexibility, he dismantled the currency-board system that had pegged the peso to the American dollar for a decade. The peso devalued rapidly and people's savings were reduced to a fraction of their earlier value. In January 2002 the banks were only open for a total of six days and confidence in the government was virtually nonexistent. The economy ceased to function: cash became scarce, imports stopped and demand for nonessential items flat-lined. More

1983

The military regime collapses, bringing the Dirty War to an end; civilian government is restored under Radical leader Raúl Alfonsín but he leaves office five months early due to rising inflation problems.

1989

Perónist Carlos Menem succeeds Alfonsín as president and overcomes the hyperinflation that reached 197% per month by instituting free-market reforms and triggering an economic boom.

1992 & 1994

In 1992 a bomb attack at the Israeli embassy in Buenos Aires kills 29 and injures over 200; in 1994, 85 people are killed and over a hundred wounded at a Jewish community center.

TAKING IT TO THE STREETS

Just like the tango and *dulce de leche* (a creamy filling found in many Argentine desserts), street protests are a well-known pastime of the people of Buenos Aires. Whether the city is booming or in the midst of a depression, unless there's martial law, someone is out on the street demonstrating against something. Plaza de Mayo has long been the focal point of protests.

The best-known voices of dissent are the famed Madres de la Plaza de Mayo (the Mothers of Plaza de Mayo). On April 30, 1977, 14 mothers whose children had disappeared in the Dirty War marched on the Plaza de Mayo. They demanded to know what had happened to their missing children. The military government dismissed them, claiming that their children had simply moved abroad, but the women continued to march in their iconic white handkerchiefs every Thursday. They played an essential historical role as the first group to openly oppose the military junta and opened the doors for later protests. In 1986 the Madres split into two groups – Asociación Madres de Plaza de Mayo is presided over by Hebe de Bonafini, the outspoken and oftentimes controversial activist who in 2006 announced that her group will stop participating in *la marcha de la resistencia* around Plaza de Mayo as they no longer viewed the Kirchner government as responsible for the disappearances. The other group, Madres de Plaza de Mayo Línea Fundadora, headed by Nora Cortiñas, still marches every Thursday as a way to further social causes in Argentina.

Even in 1996 when the economy was good and the country was under civilian control, a number of protests broke out against corruption and for the reform of pensions. Senior citizens hurled eggs at government buildings and were chased by trucks mounted with water cannons. The protests after the economic collapse in 2001 were particularly large and vociferous. Thousands of people – both in the poorer areas as well as middle-class neighborhoods – spontaneously gathered in public parks in Buenos Aires. To the shouts of *'¡Qué se vayan todos!'* (get rid of them all), they banged pots and pans – an act known as a *cacerolazo*. Both the economy minister and the president eventually stepped down, and some of the politicians who hadn't fled the country were beaten in the streets. People felt betrayed by the government and they made sure that this was known.

There are still occasional grievances expressed on Plaza de Mayo, whether it's to protest the price of beef and tomatoes, or the closure of a hospital. You can always count on them being loud, but these days they're usually peaceful.

than half of the fiercely proud Argentine people found themselves below the national poverty line: the once comfortable middle class woke up in the lower classes and the former lower classes were plunged into destitution. Businesspeople ate at soup kitchens and homelessness became rampant.

ENTER NÉSTOR KIRCHNER

Duhalde, to his credit, was able to use his deep political party roots to keep the country together through to elections in April 2003. Numerous candidates entered the contest; the top two finishers were Menem (making a foray out of retirement for the campaign) and Néstor Kirchner, a little-known governor of the thinly populated Patagonian province of Santa Cruz. Menem bowed out of the runoff election and Kirchner became president.

Kirchner was the antidote to the slick and dishonest Buenos Aires establishment politicians. He was an outsider, with his entire career in the provinces and a personal air of sincerity and austerity. The people were looking for a fresh start and someone to believe in – and they found that in Kirchner.

1999

The mayor of Buenos Aires, Fernando de la Rúa, is voted president of Argentina as a result of dissatisfaction with the corrupt Menem administration; he inherits $114 billion in public debt.

2001

Argentina commits the largest debt default in world history; Argentina's economy is totally ruined, which sparks massive riots and lootings around the country.

2003

Néstor Kirchner – a governor from Patagonia's province of Santa Cruz – is sworn in with 22% of the vote as Argentina's president.

During his term Kirchner defined himself as a hard-nosed fighter. In 2003 he managed to negotiate a debt-refinancing deal with the IMF under which Argentina would only pay interest on its loans. In 2006 Argentina repaid its $9.5 billion debt, not a small feat, which drove his approval rates up to 80%. The annual economic growth was averaging an impressive 8%, the poverty rate dropped to about 25% and unemployment nose-dived. A side effect of the 2001 collapse was a boom in international tourism, as foreigners enjoyed cosmopolitan Buenos Aires at bargain prices, injecting tourist money into the economy.

But not everything was bread and roses. The fact that Argentina repaid its debts was fantastic news indeed but economic stability didn't necessarily follow by design. In fact, a series of problems ensued during Kirchner's presidency – high inflation rates caused by a growing energy shortage, the unequal distribution of wealth and the rising breach between the rich and the poor that was slowly obliterating the middle class. It's likely that the official inflation figures had been (and still are being) manipulated to mask the government's failure at reining in inflation.

On the foreign policy front, Kirchner's belligerence became aimed at outside forces. In November 2005, when George Bush flew in for the 34-nation Summit of the Americas, his presence sparked massive demonstrations around the country. Although anti-US sentiment unites most Argentines, some feared that Kirchner's schmoozing with Chavez alienated potential investors in the United States and Europe.

Kirchner made admirable strides toward addressing the human rights abuses of the military dictatorship. In 2005 the Supreme Court lifted an amnesty law that protected former military officers suspected of Dirty War crimes, and this led to a succession of trials that put several of them away for life.

THE TRIALS & TRIBULATIONS OF CRISTINA

When Néstor Kirchner stepped aside in July 2007 in favor of his wife's candidacy for the presidential race, many started wondering: would 'Queen Cristina' (as she's often called due to her regal comportment) be just a puppet for her husband who intended to rule behind the scenes?

In the October 2007 Argentine presidential election, Cristina Fernández de Kirchner succeed in her ambition to move from being first lady to president. The weak opposition and her husband's enduring clout were some of the reasons cited for Cristina's clear-cut victory, despite the lack of straightforward policies during her campaign. While this was not the first time Argentina has had a female head of state (Isabel Perón held a brief presidency by inheriting her husband's term), Cristina is the first woman president to become elected by popular vote in Argentina. As a lawyer and senator she has often been compared to Hillary Clinton; as a fashion-conscious political figure with a penchant for chic dresses and designer bags, she also evokes memories of Evita.

Cristina's tumultuous presidency has been laced with scandals, unpopular decisions, high inflation and roller-coaster approval ratings. During her first days as president, a Venezuelan-American entering Argentina from Venezuela was found with almost US$800,000 cash in his suitcase, and lied about its origins (it was thought this was Hugo Chavez' way of helping Cristina's election campaign). In March 2008 Kirchner significantly raised the export tax on soybeans, infuriating farmers who soon went on strike and blockaded highways. In June 2009,

2007

A lawyer, senator and former first lady, Cristina Fernández de Kirchner becomes Argentina's first woman president elected by popular vote.

2010

Argentina celebrates its bicentennial in May with a big bang; Buenos Aires' Av 9 de Julio shuts down for many colorful festivities, and the Teatro Colón finally opens after four years of restoration.

2011

Her husband Néstor Kirchner's untimely death in late 2010 leaves Cristina Kirchner in a lurch, but she's likely to seek presidential re-election in October.

Cristina's power base was shattered during the mid-term elections, when her ruling party lost its majority in both houses of Congress. Soon after, she enacted an unpopular law set to break apart Clarín, a media conglomerate that often shone unfavorably on her presidency. All the while, Argentina has been hounded by inflation that has been unofficially estimated at up to 25%.

Still not everything in Argentina has been bad news. The economy has grown strongly during her tenure, bolstered by high consumer spending and a strong demand for the country's agricultural exports and manufactured goods. In a true Peronist vein, Cristina has implemented a wide range of social programs to beef up the pension system, benefit impoverished children and help fight cases related to crimes against humanity. And in July 2010 she also signed a bill that legalized same-sex marriage in Argentina – Latin America's first country to do so.

But on October 27, 2010, Cristina's presidency was dealt a serious blow when Néstor Kirchner died suddenly of an apparent heart attack. As Néstor was expected to run for the presidency in 2011, this was widely seen as a disaster for the Kirchner Dynasty. The country rallied around Cristina's sorrow, but at the same time many thought this might be the end to her power – and any possible re-election ambitions. Her popularity in early 2011 remained fairly high, however, and despite opposition from Ricardo Alfonsín (a center-left congressman and ex-president Raúl Alfonsín's son) and Mauricio Macri (Buenos Aires' current mayor) – both of whom intend to run in October 2011 – Cristina has a good chance at winning re-election. This would undoubtedly be quite an accomplishment for her. Something even her popular husband, unfortunately, couldn't live long enough to achieve or witness himself.

ARTS

The arts scene in Buenos Aires has always been lively but in the decade following the economic crisis of 2001, there has been an outburst of creative energy in Buenos Aires' art circles. The woes that ensued seemed to be as big a stimulant to creativity as the military dictatorship was a terrible drag on it. Gone was the booming '90s dominance of snooty galleries, lavish films and over-hyped plays. A refreshing, make-do approach was born out of the troubles, particularly in cinema, theater and the visual arts. Filmmakers began producing quality works on shoestring budgets, artists showcased their work in funky storefront galleries, and drama troupes performed in private homes and other unconventional venues. Today, the unconventional has become mainstream bringing about a boom in artistic activity that's easily accessible and diverse enough to please all tastes.

Talented porteños who fled the country in search of better prospects abroad immediately after the crisis have since returned. Now, together with those who held court through the troubled times, these artists have managed to bring a cosmopolitan level of sophistication and a sense of innovation to BA's arts scene. This creative resurgence has been attracting an ever-increasing number of foreigners to the city, seen as totally happening and affordable thanks to favorable exchange rates.

MUSIC & DANCE

Music and dance are well entwined in Buenos Aires, especially when it comes to the city's most famous export, the tango, and a growing Argentine export, cumbia digital. Today's Buenos Aires music scene is a hybrid of overlapping sounds and styles. Traditional styles of folklore, tango and cumbia are melded with digital technology creating a global music that's gaining recognition in music festivals around the world.

The classics are also represented. The Buenos Aires opera traditionally performs in palatial Teatro Colón (p71). This incredible facility, one of the finest in the world, underwent three years of renovations before reopening in 2010 during Argentina's Bicentenary celebrations. Other venues, such as the Teatro Avenida (p172), frequently host classical music, modern dance and ballet. And balletophiles will already know that BA is home to Julio Bocca, a superstar in the field who retired in 2007.

For classes, *milongas* and tango show listings, see p164.

THE STARS OF TANGO

Gardel

In June 1935 a Cuban woman committed suicide in Havana, and a woman in New York and another in Puerto Rico tried to poison themselves, all over the same man – whom none of them had ever met. The man was tango singer Carlos Gardel, known as El Zorzal Criollo (the King of Tango) or the songbird of Buenos Aires, who had just died in a plane crash in Colombia.

Born in France, Gardel was the epitome of the immigrant porteño whose destitute single mother brought him to Buenos Aires at the age of three. In his youth he worked at a variety of menial jobs and entertained his neighbors with his rapturous singing. A performing career began after he befriended Uruguayan-born José Razzano, and the two of them sang together in a popular duo until Razzano lost his voice. From 1917 onward Gardel performed solo.

Carlos Gardel played an enormous role in creating the tango *canción* (song). Almost single-handedly, he took the style out of Buenos Aires' tenements and brought it to Paris and New York. His crooning voice, suaveness and overall charisma made him an immediate success in Latin American countries. The timing couldn't have been better, as he rose to fame in tango's golden years of the 1920s and 1930s. Gardel became a recording and film star, but his later career was tragically cut short by that fatal plane crash.

Every day a steady procession of pilgrims visits Carlos Gardel's sarcophagus in the Cementerio de la Chacarita in Buenos Aires, where a lit cigarette often smolders between the metal fingers of his life-size statue. The large, devoted community of his followers, known as *gardelianos,* cannot pass a day without listening to his songs or watching his films. Another measure of his ongoing influence is the common saying 'Gardel sings better every day.' Elvis should be so lucky.

Piazzolla

Gardel may have brought tango to the world, but it was El Gran Ástor (the Great Ástor), as Argentines like to call Ástor Piazzolla (1921-92), who pushed its limits. The great Argentine composer and *bandoneón* virtuoso, who played in the leading Aníbal Troilo orchestra in the late 1930s and early 1940s, was the greatest innovator of tango. He revolutionized traditional tango by infusing it with elements of jazz and classical music such as counterpoints, fugues and various harmonies.

This new style, known as nuevo tango, became an international hit in Europe (Piazzolla lived on and off in Italy and France) and North America (he spent his early years and a couple of later stints in New York). In his native land, however, it encountered considerable resistance; a saying even stated 'in Argentina everything may change – except the tango'. It took years for Piazzolla's controversial new style to be accepted, and he even received death threats for his break with tradition.

Piazzolla was an incredibly prolific composer; it's estimated that his opus includes some 1000 pieces. These include soundtracks for about 40 films; an opera that he wrote with poet Horacio Ferrer, María de Buenos Aires; and compositions based on texts and poems by Borges.

Piazzolla's legacy lives on. Some of the greatest contemporary musicians, such as Yo-Yo Ma, have recorded albums dedicated to El Gran Ástor (such as the 1999 *Soul of the Tango – The Music of Ástor Piazzolla*). The new wave of electronic tango often samples his music and the 2003 album *Astor Piazzolla Remixed* features his songs remixed with dance beats and added vocals, all done by an international cast of DJs and producers.

The Tango

In the words of its poet laureate Discépolo, the 'tango is a sad thought you can dance to.' Though the exact origins can't be pinpointed, the dance itself is thought to have started in Buenos Aires in the 1880s. Legions of European immigrants, mostly lower-class men, arrived in Buenos Aires to seek their fortune in the new country. They settled on the capital's fringes such as La Boca and Barracas, but missing their motherlands and the women they left behind, sought out cafés and bordellos to ease the loneliness. Here (so the myth goes), these immigrant men danced with each other while they waited for their paramours to become available – women were scarce back then!

The perceived vulgarity of the dance that mainly belonged to the poor southern barrios was deeply frowned upon by the reigning porteño elites of Buenos Aires' plush northern suburbs, but it did manage to influence some brash young members of the upper classes. These rebel jet setters, known as *niños bien,* took the novelty to Paris and created a craze – a dance that became an acceptable outlet for human desires, expressed on the dance floors of elegant cabarets. The trend spread around Europe and even to the USA, and 1913 was considered by some as 'the year of the tango.' When the evolved dance, now refined and famous, returned to Buenos Aires, it finally earned the respectability it deserved. And so the golden years of tango began.

In 1955, however, Argentina became a military state intolerant of artistic or 'nationalistic' activities – including the tango, which had been highly popular with the people. Some tango songs were banned, and dance was forced underground due to curfews and a limit on group meetings. The dance didn't resurface until 1983, when the junta fell – and once it was back in the open again, it bloomed and underwent a renaissance. After being constrained by the rigors of military rule, Argentines suddenly wanted to experience new life, be creative and *move*. The tango became popular once again – and remains so to this day.

Tango Music

Small musical ensembles that accompanied early tango dances were influenced by polka, habanera, Spanish and Italian melodies, plus African *candombe* drums. The *bandoneón,* a type of small accordion, was brought into these sessions and has since become tango's signature instrument. The tango song was permeated with nostalgia for a disappearing way of life; it summarized the new urban experience for the immigrants. Themes ranged from profound feelings about changing neighborhoods to the figure of the mother, male friendship and betrayal by women. The lyrics, sometimes raunchy and sometimes sad, were sung in the street argot known as *lunfardo*.

No other musician has influenced tango like Carlos Gardel, the legendary singer who epitomized the soul of the genre (see boxed text, p33). He achieved stardom during tango's golden age, then became a cultural icon when his life was cut short by a plane crash at the height of his popularity. Over the years, other figures like Osvaldo Pugliese, Susana Rinaldi and Eladia Blásquez have also given life to the tango song. It was Àstor Piazzolla, however, who completely revolutionized the music with his *nuevo tango,* which introduced jazz and classical music currents into traditional songs – and ruffled some feathers along the way (see boxed text, p33).

Today, a clutch of new arrivals is keeping tango music alive and well, and in the spotlight. The most popular is the 12-musician cooperative Orquesta Típica Fernández Fierro (www.fernandezfierro.com), with their charismatic singer Walter Chino Laborde and several fantastic albums boasting new arrangements of traditional tangos. A documentary was made about them by Argentine-born Brooklyn-based director Nicolas Entel (www.orquestatipica.com)

Two other young orchestras to watch out for are Orquesta Típica Imperial (www.orquestaimperial.com.ar) who regularly play at *milongas* around town, and El Afronte (www.elafronte.com.ar) who play on Mondays and Wednesdays at Maldita Milonga (Peru 571; Map p76) in San Telmo. El Afronte can also be seen playing at the San Telmo Antique Fair on Sundays in front of the Iglesia Nuestra Senora de Belen.

You'll also find tango played constantly on the radio (particularly on the 24-hour, all-tango station, FM Tango 92.7).

Neo Tango

Like the rest of the music scene in Buenos Aires, a newer tango has evolved that's a hybrid of sounds and styles – making tango cool again with a younger audience. Musicians have been sampling and remixing classic tango songs, adding dance beats, breaks, scratches and synth lines, and committing other delightful heresies. This edgy genre has been called by many names: Fusion tango, electrotango, tango electronica or neo-tango.

Paris-based Gotan Project (a Franco-Suizo-Argentine trio) were the first to popularize this style with their debut album *La Revancha del Tango,* which throws into the mix samples from speeches by Che Guevara and Eva Perón and remixes by the likes of Austrian beatmeister Peter Kruder. Their follow-up albums (especially Lunático and Tango 3.0) don't break the mold like the first but are still great if you like the Gotan sound.

The best of the genre's album output so far is likely *Bajofondo Tango Club,* by the Grammy-winning collective Bajofondo. It's spearheaded by Argentine producer Gustavo Santaolalla, who won two best original score Oscars for *Brokeback Mountain* and *Babel;* he also scored the films *Amores Perros* and *21 Grams,* and produced albums by such prominent artists as Café Tacuba and Kronos Quartet. Praised as more Argentine than Gotan Project (only one of their core trio is Argentine) and more tango, the eponymous first album's classic samples blend with subtle performances by current tango musicians (including a variety of *bandoneonistas* and some great vocals from Adriana Varela) within a hypnotic framework of lounge, house and trip-hop. Their second album, *Mar Dulce,* is a catchy creation that throws more folk and rock into the mix and has a strong international cast of singers such as Spanish hip-hop star Mala Rodŕiguez and the Canadian-Portuguese Nelly Furtado.

Another neo-tango collective to make an international name for themselves is Tanghetto, with two Latin Grammy nominations. This six-member group mixes elements of rock, jazz, flamenco and *candombe* (a drum-based musical style of Uruguay).

Rock & Pop

Argentine rock started in the late 1960s with a trio of groups – Almendra (great melodies and poetic lyrics), Manal (urban blues) and Los Gatos (pop) – leading the pack. Evolution was slow, however; the 1966 and 1976 military regimes didn't take a shine to the liberalism and freedom that rock represented. It didn't help that anarchy-loving, beat-music rocker Billy Bond induced destructive mayhem at a 1972 Luna Park concert, re-enforcing the theme of rock music as a social threat.

Underground groups and occasional concerts managed to keep the genre alive, and after the Falklands War in 1982 (when English lyrics were not actually allowed on the air) radio stations found *rock nacional* and helped the movement's momentum gain ground. Argentine rock produced national icons like Charly Garciá (formerly a member of the pioneering group Sui Generis) and Fito Páez (a socially conscious pop-hippie). Sensitive poet-songwriter Alberto Luis Spinetta of Almendra fame also had an early influence on the Argentine rock movement, later incorporating jazz into his LPs. Another mythical figure is Andrés Calamaro, frontman of the popular 1970s band Los Abuelos de la Nada who later emigrated to Spain where he formed the acclaimed Los Rodríguez; he's been performing solo since the late 1990s. Many of these rockeros are still recording today. In 2010, Charly Garciáa released his album *Kill Gill* and Andrés Calamaro's *On the Rock* was nominated for a Latin Grammy.

More recent popular Argentine groups playing *rock nacional* include the now defunct Soda Stereo (ex-member Gustavo Cerati's *Fuerza Natural* won the 2010 Latin Grammy for best rock album); hippyish Los Divididos (descendants of the famous group Sumo); Mendozan trio Los Enanitos Verdes; the wildly unconventional Babasónicos; cultlike Patricio Rey y sus Redonditos de Ricota (their legendary leader Indio Solari now has a solo career); and Los Ratones Paranóicos, who in 1995 opened for the Rolling Stones' spectacularly successful five-night stand in Buenos Aires.

Los Fabulosos Cadillacs (who were the winners of a Grammy award in 1998 for best alternative Latin rock group) have popularized ska and reggae, along with groups such as Los Auténticos Decadentes, Los Pericos and Los Cafres. Almafuerte, descended from the earlier Hermética, is Buenos Aires' leading heavy-metal band. The bands Dos Minutos and Expulsados seek to emulate punk-rock legends the Ramones, who are popular in Argentina. The band Les Luthiers satirizes the middle class or the military using irreverent songs played with unusual instruments, many of which have been built by the band themselves. Another quirky character is the late Sandro, who was known as the Argentine Elvis, whose death in January 2010 saw tens of thousands of porteños gather in the streets of Buenos Aires to mourn his demise.

Argentine women also rock. Singer Patricia Sosa has a captivating voice and performs a mix of rock, soul and blues; her closest counterpart in the English-speaking world would be Janis Joplin. The most recent singer-songwriter who has gained fame abroad is Juana Molina, whose ambient music with electronic flair has been compared to Bjork's. Juana Chang and the Wookies combined indie-rock, garage and punk (she now sings with the Kumbia Queers). Keep an eye out for two newcomers, Denise Murz, a Lady Gaga style electro-pop diva, and the multi-talented, folksy Sol Pereyra.

Today some of Argentina's most cutting-edge bands include versatile Los Piojos (mixing rock, blues, ska and the Uruguayan music styles *murga* and *candombe*), catchy Miranda! (electro-pop), wacky Bersuit Vergarabat (utilizing multigenre tunes with political, offensive and wave-making lyrics), free-willed La Renga (blue-collar, no-nonsense and political), La Portuaria who collaborated with David Byrne (rock fusion influenced by jazz and R&B), Gazpacho (new wave of pop-rock), and Valentin y Los Volcanos (indie-pop with great guitar music). And don't miss the multicultural, alternative and eclectic Kevin Johansen.

Jazz & Blues

Both these brands of music have substantial numbers of fans and performers among porteños, and you should have no trouble catching live shows at key venues (see p160).

A fair number of Argentina's jazz greats have emigrated (Lalo Schifrin and Gato Barbieri among them). Among those who've stayed is guitarist Luis Salinas, whose music is mellow and melodic (along George Benson lines but a bit less poppy). Be sure to check out his jazz takes on such traditional Argentine forms as the *chacarera, chamamé* and tango. Dino Saluzzi, a bandoneón player originally from Salta who began recording in the 70s, was one of the first Argentine musicians to mix folklore, tango, and jazz. Dino's son José is considered one of Argentina's most promising young guitarists.

Another young musician and son of an Argentine jazz legend is Javier Malosetti, son of pianist Walter Malosetti. Javier's new group Electro Hope blend jazz, blues, rock and swing with Latin rhythms and funk. A hot new jazz guitarist is Tomás Becú, whose debut album, *Bushwick* (2007), is stellar. For wildly experimental jazz check out the Gordöloco Trío, who fuse ambient, funk and jazz in their 20-minute-long songs.

Drummer Sebastián Peyceré who favors a funk-tinged fusion has toured the country with Salinas, jammed at the Blue Note and played with the likes of Paquito D'Rivera, BB King and Stanley Jordan. BA's own version of the Sultans of Swing is the Caoba Jazz Band, who for years have been playing 1920s and '30s New Orleans-style jazz for the love of it. Also watch out for Andrea Tessa, one of the best voices in the current jazz circuit.

The high degree of crossover between Buenos Aires' blues and rock scenes is illustrated by the path of guitar wizard Pappo. An elder statesman, Pappo was in the groundbreaking rock group Los Abuelos de la Nada and became involved with the seminal blues/rock band Pappo's Blues, as well as Los Gatos and others. Once he sets to wailing on his Gibson, you'll forget the fact that Pappo's voice and original lyrics aren't so hot. He plays hard-driving, full-tilt rockin' blues and is especially great when covering such American masters as Howlin' Wolf, BB King and Muddy Waters.

Guitarist/singer Miguel 'Botafogo' Vilanova is an alumnus of Pappo's Blues and an imposing figure in his own right. Memphis La Blusera have been around BA's blues scene a long time and still put on a good show; they've worked with North American legend Taj Mahal. Also worth checking out is La Mississippi, a seven-member group that has been performing rock-blues since the late 1980s.

Latin & Electronica

Buenos Aires' young clubbers have embraced the *música tropical* trend that's swept Latin America in recent years. Many a BA booty is shaken to the lively, Afro-Latin sounds of salsa, merengue and especially *cumbia*. Originating in Colombia, *cumbia* combines an infectious dance rhythm with lively melodies, often carried by brass. An offshoot is *cumbia experimental* or *cumbia villera*, an electronic version that's now the hottest ticket in the city's *villas* and clubs. Three of the biggest names in digital *cumbia* are Villa Diamante, El Remolón, and Frikstailers, DJs from the collective known as Zizek Urban Beats Club which has its own record label, ZZK Records, and organizes a monthly dance party called Super Zizek (whatsupbuenosaires.com/superzizek).

The digital cumbia movement is more than just mixed sets from talented DJs. A forerunner of the movement is Axel Krygier, the king of psychedelic Latin, whose latest album *Pesebre* (2010) is a brilliant fusion of jazz, rock, cumbia, electronica, Argentine folklore and experimental sounds. Kumbia Queers is a female band from Argentina and Mexico whose version of cumbia is known as tropipunk.

Dance music is big in BA, with DJs working the clubs well into the morning. A few major electronic names to look out for are Bad Boy Orange (big on drums and bass); Aldo Haydar (a true veteran of progressive house); local boy made international star, Hernán Cattaneo (you loved him at Burning Man, remember?); and Gustavo Lamas (a blend of ambient pop and electro house). The trance-house master John Digweed has been known to spin in BA on his way to laying down summer grooves in Punta del Este, the Uruguayan beach resort.

One of BA's most interesting music spectacles is La Bomba del Tiempo, a collective of drummers that features some of Argentina's leading percussionists. Their explosive performances are conducted by Santiago Vázquez, who communicates with the musicians through a language of mysterious signs – the result is an incredible improvisational union that simulates electronic dance music and sounds different every time. During the summer, they play open-air at Cuidad Cultural Konex (see p170) every Monday evening; they're also featured at various happenings and parties in BA's clubs.

Folk Music

The folk music of Argentina is inspired by generations of immigrants and spans a variety of styles, including *chacarera, chamamé* and *zamba*. The late Atahualpa Yupanqui was a giant of Argentine folk music, which takes much of its inspiration from the northwestern Andean region and countries to the north, especially Bolivia and Peru. Los Chalchaleros, a northern Argentine folk institution, have been around for more than 50 years. Probably the best-known Argentine folk artist outside of South America is the late Mercedes Sosa of Tucumán whose progressive, politicized lyrics earned her the title "the voice of the voiceless ones."

Other contemporary performers include El Chaqueño Palavecino of Salta; Suna Rocha (also an actress) of Córdoba; Eduardo Falú; Antonio Tarragó Ross; Víctor Heredia; León Gieco (modern enough to adopt and adapt a rap style at times); and the Conjunto Pro Música de Rosario. Singer-songwriter-guitarist Horacio Guarany, whose 2004 album *Cantor De Cantores* was nominated for a Latin Grammy in the Best Folk Album category, performs in BA regularly. Of the younger generation, the artists to watch out for are Chango Spasiuk (an accordion player who popularized *chamamé* music abroad and has been making rounds at world-music festivals), Mariana Baraj (a singer and percussionist who experiments with Latin America's traditional folk music as well as elements of jazz, classical music and improvisation), and Soledad Pastorutti (whose first two albums have been Sony's top-sellers in Argentina – ever!).

Every genre of Argentine music is experiencing the same hybrid phenomenon of blending in electronic music with more traditional sounds. Digital folklore, much like digital cumbia and neo-tango, is exploding. Tonolec, a duo (singer and synth player), combine traditional folk songs of the Toba indigenous community from Argentina's north (some of which have been passed down orally) with an electronic sound. The singer also uses traditional instruments in their live gigs, creating a warm, world-music-style fusion. Two other digital folklore groups to look for are Onda Vaga, an acoustic band with smooth harmonies that add a jazzy feel to traditional folklore sounds, and Tremor, the only band represented by ZZK Records, who mix Andean flutes, the Argentine bombo legüero (drum), electric guitars, and a synthesizer, a blend of ancient and digital sounds in one fantastic band. Also with ZZK is the digital folklore DJ Chancha via Circuito, whose 2010 album *Río Arriba* mixes melodic flutes and slow tempos, making it more meditative than dance oriented.

For folk venues, see p161.

Ballet & Modern Dance

How many cities can boast of packing stadiums with crowds for dance performances? We're not sure, but Buenos Aires is definitely one of them. The porteño love of all things cultural takes some of the credit, but a larger part goes to BA's bad boy of ballet, Julio Bocca. And it's not just because he posed nude with his dance partner in *Playboy*. Born in 1967, Bocca started dancing at age four and at 14 was soloing with the Teatro Colón's chamber ballet. In 1985, following stints with troupes in Caracas and Rio de Janeiro, he took the gold medal at Moscow's International Ballet Competition, and the next year was invited by Mikhail Baryshnikov to join the American Ballet Theatre as principal dancer. In 1990 he formed his own troupe, Ballet Argentino, which has been

BUENOS AIRES STREET ART BOOM

Buenos Aires is known internationally for its innovative and booming street art scene that has reached critical mass in recent years. The huge increase in graffiti was triggered by the political chaos that followed the 2001 economic crisis. At first much of the street art, mostly angry scrawls on targets of ire such as banks and government buildings, was just a voice of dissent. These days, as Banksy's work is being auctioned at Sotheby's for dizzying sums, Buenos Aires street art has taken off as a veritable art form to aspire to. BA graffiti have been featured in several photo books and displayed in international exhibitions in Argentina and abroad.

While Buenos Aires street art varies from tags to sticker art and posters, it's the stencils that are getting the most attention. These well-crafted, often humorous and visually stunning graffiti show up on BA sidewalks, garbage cans and walls. Many of them are takeoffs of advertising slogans and logos, and satirical commentaries on current social issues.

The city has a number of street art collectives, the most famous of which are Bs As Stencil (www.bsasstencil.org), Rundontwalk (www.rundontwalk.com.ar), Burzaco Stencil and Fase. Some artists, such as Pum Pum (whose work can be seen on the walls of Mundo Bizarro, p150) and Gualicho (www.gualicho.cc), have become celebrities on the underground street art circuit. To check out the captivating work by these and other local artists, head to Post Street Bar (www.poststreetbar.com; Thames 1885), a trendy Palermo drinking hole covered in stencils; its upstairs art gallery (www.hollywoodincambodia.com.ar) specializes in street art.

And how about a graffiti tour? Yes, it actually exists in BA – reserve your spot with Graffiti Mundo (www.graffitimundo.com) and you'll be taken around neighborhoods with plenty of the colorful art.

Some of the best books on BA's street art scene are two publications by an independent Buenos Aires press, La Marca Editora: the 2005 *¡Hasta la Victoria, Stencil!* and its 2007 follow-up, *1000 Stencils,* which captures works from all over Argentina. Also, check out Matt Fox-Tucker and Guilherme Zauith's excellent *Textura Dos: Buenos Aires Street Art* (2010).

wildly popular at home and very well received abroad. In 2006 Bocca gave his farewell performance at American Ballet Theater, toured for the last time in 2007 and has since retired from dancing.

Internationally acclaimed dance companies to watch out for are Tangokinesis (www.tangokinesis.com), a contemporary tango group that's been around since 1992, Ballet del Mercosur and Ballet Concierto; the latter two mix classical with contemporary productions. More experimental troupes that combine dance with theater include El Descueve, Grupo Krapp and Compañia Contenido Bruto.

You can catch dance performances ranging from classical ballet to flamenco, Middle Eastern and all varieties of modern dance at venues such as the venerable Colón, Teatro Avenida and Teatro San Martín (it has its own ballet company, Ballet Contemporáneo del Teatro San Martín).

LITERATURE

You can't talk about Argentine literature without mentioning the influential epic poem by José Hernández, *Martín Fierro* (1872). Not only did this story about a gaucho outlaw lay the foundations of Argentine gauchesco literary tradition, but it also inspired the name of the short-lived but important literary magazine of the 1920s that published avant-garde works based on the 'art for art's sake' principle.

Many of the greatest lights of Argentine literature called Buenos Aires home and all but one had been extinguished by the end of the 20th century. The light that burned brightest was without doubt Jorge Luis Borges (1899–1986), one of the foremost writers of the 20th century. A prolific author and an insatiable reader, Borges possessed an intellect that seized on difficult questions and squeezed answers out of them. Though super-erudite in his writing, he was also such a jokester that it's a challenge to tell when he's being serious and when he's pulling your leg (though often it's a case of both at once). From early on one of his favorite forms was the scholarly analysis of nonexistent texts, and more than once he found himself in trouble for perpetrating literary hoaxes and forgeries. A few of these are contained in his *Universal History of Iniquity* (1935), a book that some point to as the origin of magic realism in Latin American literature.

Borges' dry, ironic wit is paired (in his later work) with a succinct, precise style that is a delight to read. His paradoxical *Ficciones* (1944) – part parable, part fantasy – blurs the line between myth and truth, underscoring the concept that reality is only a matter of perception and the number of possible realities is infinite. Other themes that fascinated Borges were the nature of memory and dreams, labyrinths, and the relationship between the reader, the writer and the written piece. *Collected Fictions* (1999) is a complete set of his stories.

Though he received numerous honors in his lifetime – including the Cer
Legion of Honor and an OBE – Borges was never conferred the Nobel. He jok
typical fashion: 'Not granting me the Nobel Prize has become a Scandinavian traditi
I was born they have not been granting it to me.'

Julio Cortázar (1914–84) is, after Borges, probably the author best known to readers outsi
Argentina. He was born in Belgium to Argentine parents, moved to Buenos Aires at age four and died in self-imposed exile in Paris at the age of 70. His stories frequently plunge their characters out of everyday life into surreally fantastic situations. One such story was adapted into the film *Blow-Up* by Italian director Michelangelo Antonioni. Cortázar's novel *Hopscotch* takes place simultaneously in Buenos Aires and Paris and requires the reader to first read the book straight through, then read it a second time, 'hopscotching' through the chapters in a prescribed but nonlinear pattern for a completely different take on the story.

The last surviving member of Borges' literary generation is Ernesto Sábato (b 1911), whose complex and uncompromising novels have been extremely influential on later Argentine literature. *The Tunnel* (1948) is Sábato's engrossing existentialist novella of a porteño painter so obsessed with his art that it distorts his relationship to everything and everyone else.

Adolfo Bioy Casares (1914–99) and Borges were close friends and occasional collaborators. Bioy's sci-fi novella *The Invention of Morel* (1940) not only gave Alain Resnais the plot for his classic film *Last Year at Marienbad*, it also introduced the idea of the holodeck decades before *Star Trek* existed.

Manuel Puig's (1932–90) first love was cinema, and much of his writing consists solely of dialogue, used to marvelous effect. Being openly gay and critical of Perón did not help his job prospects in Argentina so Puig spent many years in exile. His novel *The Buenos Aires Affair* (1973) is a page-turner delving into the relationship between murderer and victim (and artist and critic), presented as a deconstructed crime thriller. His most famous work is *Kiss of the Spider Woman* (1976), a captivating story of a relationship that develops between two men inside an Argentine prison; it was made into the 1985 Oscar-winning film of the same name, starring William Hurt.

Federico Andahazi's first novel, *The Anatomist*, caused a stir when published in 1997. Its ticklish theme revolves around the 'discovery' of the clitoris by a 16th-century Venetian who is subsequently accused of heresy. Andahazi (b 1963) based his well-written book on historical fact, and manages to have some fun while still broaching serious subjects. His prize-wining *El Conquistador* (2006) is a historical novel about an Aztec youth who 'discovers' Europe before Columbus reaches America, while his latest book *Pecar como Dios manda* (2008), hypothesizes that to understand the essence of a society you have to understand the web of sexual relations it is built upon.

Award-winning Ricardo Piglia (b 1941) is one of Argentina's most well-known contemporary writers. He pens hard-boiled fiction and is best known for his socially minded crime novels with a noir touch, such *The Absent City* (1992), *Money to Burn* (1997) and *Nocturnal Target* (2010).

Another prolific writer is Tomás Eloy Martínez (1934–2010). His *The Perón Novel* (1988) – a fictionalized biography of the controversial populist leader – and its sequel *Santa Evita* (1996) – which traces the worldwide travels of Evita's embalmed corpse – were both huge hits.

Two American expats have made an imprint on the BA literature scene. Anna Kazumi Stahl wrote *Flores de un solo día* (2001) in *rioplatense* (a variety of Spanish spoken in the Río de la Plata region), a novel about an American girl who has lived in Buenos Aires from the age of eight with her mute Japanese mother. Marina Palmer's *Kiss and Tango* (2005) tells a largely autobiographical story about a woman who drops her high-powered advertising job in New York to immerse herself in the seductive world of tango and Buenos Aires *milongas* (wait for it to become a movie starring Sandra Bullock!).

Of the younger generation of Argentine writers, two names are the talk of the town – Washington Cucurto and Gabriela Bejerman. Cucurto runs Eloísa Cartonera, a small publishing house that releases books by young authors made of recycled cardboard collected by the city's *cartoneros* (buy these in La Boca at Artisóbulo del Valle 666). Bejerman, a multimedia artist who launched a music career as Gaby Bex, recently released an album which incorporates some of her poetry with electro music. Other names to watch out for are Andrés Newman, Oliverio Coelho and Pedro Mairal.

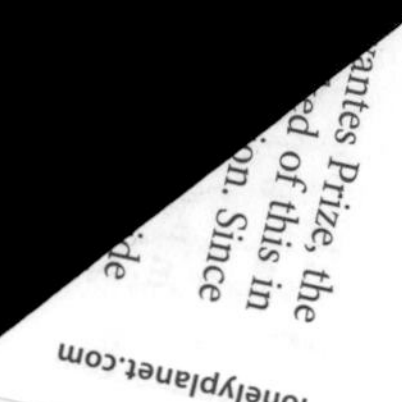

Buenos Aires is booming, too, with many young wordsmiths, and ery night of the week. Some of the spots that feature poetry events are a Drago 236; www.brandongayday.com.ar) in Villa Crespo and Asobi Bar (Araóz 2148) Thursdays poets and VJs (visual DJs) showcase their experiments with edia.

nts are listed on these two websites (in Spanish): www.poesiaurbana.com depoesia.com.ar.

THEATER

Theater is *huge* in Buenos Aires. The city's venues number more than 100, and annual attendance is in the hundreds of thousands. While productions range from classic plays to multimedia performances and lavish cabarets, the acting tends to be of a professional level across the board.

The city's vigorous theater community began a few years after BA became the capital in 1776, and continued blooming in the 19th century. The first form to become popular was *circo criollo,* colorful circus performance featuring trapeze artists, clowns and jugglers and playing with distinctly South American themes; the most famous work was *Juan Moreira,* about a gaucho persecuted by the law. Then came the *sainete,* informal grotesque drama focusing on immigrants and their dilemmas; its biggest proponent was Alberto Vacarezza. These days *sainete* is undergoing a revival, with theater groups like Teatro Escuela de Buenos Aires performing them around town. Formally, theater really took off in the late 19th century through the artistic and financial efforts of the Podestá family and playwrights such as Florencio Sánchez, Gregorio de Laferrere and Roberto Payró. It was in the 1980s that the theater community started breaking the traditional norms that spawned the avant-garde movement so prevalent in Argentina today. Two theaters instrumental in this break were Centro Cultural Ricardo Rojas (see p225) and the now-extinct Parakultural.

Argentina's most famous playwright is probably Juan Carlos Gené, a past director of the Teatro General San Martín who now runs Celcit (Centro Latinoamericano de Creación e Investigación Teatral; see the boxed text, p170). Some of the more established contemporary directors and playwrights in the off-Corrientes scene are Ricardo Bartis, Rafael Spregelburd, Federico León, Mauricio Kartun and Daniel Veronese. The rising stars of Argentine theater are Mariana Chaud, Matías Gandolfo, Mariano Pensotti, Santiago Gobernori, Matías Feldman and Lola Arias.

Unlike stage actors in some countries, those in Argentina seem to move seamlessly between stage, film and TV. Perhaps performers like Norma Leandro, Federico Luppi and Cecilia Roth feel less self-conscious about it since the Argentine public is smaller and work opportunities are fewer than in entertainment centers such as London, New York and Los Angeles.

Argentine theater is still having its love affair with European playwrights such as Beckett and Chekhov. The best of the classic theater can be seen at Teatro General San Martín and Teatro Nacional Cervantes (see p83).

Av Corrientes (between Avs 9 de Julio and Callao) is the traditional theater district of Buenos Aires – equivalent to New York's Broadway or London's West End – but theater companies and venues large and small are found throughout the city. Indeed, Av Corrientes has seen better days, and some theatergoers prefer to attend off-Corrientes (alternative/independent theater) shows; but don't be confused by the theater on Av Corrientes named Off Corrientes. The term has been around at least since 1982, the year Juan José Campanella (now a famous director) wrote and produced the play of the same name. The term 'off-off Corrientes' has entered the lexicon as well.

In recent years there has been an upswing of independent theater troupes who stage improvisational experimental works, some in their own theaters, mainly in Palermo, Abasto, Almagro and San Telmo, and some in one-off unconventional venues. For a list of the best of these independent theaters, see p170. Other offbeat troupes and shows to catch are El Teatro Sanitario de Operaciones (TSO), El Ojo del Panoptico, El Descuve and Grupo Ojcuro.

The 1980s also spawned a movement of *teatro callejero* (street theater) that is still popular today and can be seen in plazas, parks and sometimes even on the subway. The groups to watch out for are La Runfla, Grupo Boedo Antiguo, Brazo Largo and Las Chicas del Blanco. In the last ten years an increasing number of theater people have been going solo, which has given rise to a type of clandestine theater – writers and directors producing their own works in alternative spaces with minimal costs and without permits. Many are staged in private homes and mostly advertised by word-of-mouth. On occasion some of these performances will be listed on www.alternativateatral.com (in Spanish), the best source of information about independent theater.

Another popular movement in Argentina that got international fame through the Broadway performance of De la Guarda is circo moderno. This combination of traditional circus and contemporary dance and theater features a lot of aerial action, acrobatics and no words – great for those who don't speak Spanish. In 2005, Diqui James, one of the founding creators of De la Guardia, launched his solo act called Fuerzabruta. It's a mind-blowing show of lights, electronic music, aerial dancing, and water. You'll likely get wet. The troupe is often on tour, so be sure to check their website for show listings (www.fuerzabruta.net).

Watch out for shows by La Arena group (their last hit, Sanos y Salvos, was performed in various venues around BA); Mamushka production at Club de Trapecistas (www.clubdetrapecistas.com.ar); and performances by Brenda Angiel Aerial Dance Company (www.aerialdance.com).

Also worth checking out are community-oriented theater groups in Buenos Aires, who work with the people of the *barrios* in staging their plays. The most notable is the long-running Grupo de Teatro Catalinas Sur (www.catalinasur.com.ar) – who have their own venue in La Boca – and Circuito Cultural Barracas (www.ccbarracas.com.ar) – who have been throwing a theatrical wedding party for the last 10 years, with professional actors and theatergoers celebrating together.

The theater season is liveliest in winter, from June through August, but performances are on tap year-round. Many of the most popular shows move to the provincial beach resort of Mar del Plata for the summer.

FILM

Buenos Aires is at the center of the Argentine film industry, which despite the hardships caused by an acute lack of funding generated a wave of directors and films of the New Argentine Cinema. While this movement can't be pinned down as a school of cinema, as it includes a hodgepodge of themes and techniques, it is certainly a new movement of filmmaking that has been attracting international attention, earning awards and screenings at festivals in New York, Berlin, Rotterdam and Cannes. Sadly, much of the homegrown production is more acclaimed abroad than in Argentina, where people are generally more drawn to multiplexes that show Hollywood flicks and romantic comedies. Perhaps it's because these art-house films deal with themes that are too close to home – such as survival, alienation, search for identity and suppressed sexuality.

The film that's considered to have spearheaded the New Argentine Cinema is *Rapado* by Martín Rejtman, a minimalist 1992 feature that for the first time pushed the boundaries in a country where films were generally heavy with bad dialogue. In the late 1990s the government withdrew subsidies pledged to film schools and the movie

top picks

BUENOS AIRES FILMS

- Nueve reinas (Nine Queens, 2000) features great performances from Gastón Pauls and Ricardo Darín as two con men chasing the big score. Directed by Fabián Bielinsky.
- Valentín (2002) is a semi-autobiographical, poignant tale of an eight-year-old boy being raised by his grandmother in 1960s Buenos Aires. Directed by Alejandro Agresti.
- Sur (South, 1988) is about a man released from prison after the military dictatorship in 1983, haunted by encounters with people from his past; it's set to the beautiful score written by Piazzolla. Directed by Fernando Pino Solanas.
- Pizza, birra, faso (Pizza, Beer, Cigarettes, 1998) tells the story of four Buenos Aires gangster youths trying to survive on the city streets. Directed by Adrián Caetano and Bruno Stagnaro.
- La historia oficial (The Official Story, 1985) deals with the adoption of children of the 'disappeared' during the Dirty War, by those responsible for their parents' disappearance; it won an Oscar for best foreign-language film. Directed by Luis Puenzo.
- Un día de suerte (A Lucky Day, 2002) follows a young porteña fleeing dead-end Buenos Aires to Italy, reversing the route her grandfather took decades earlier. Directed by Sandra Gugliotta.
- El secreto de sus ojos (2009) is a dark thriller set in the mistrustful, pre-dictatorship 1970s; it won the 2010 Oscar for best foreign-language film. Directed by Pablo Trapero.
- Derecho de familia (Family Law, 2006) is the story of a young professor trying to break free from his father's influence as he becomes a father himself. Directed by Daniel Burman.

industry. Despite this, two films ignited 'the new wave' – the low-budget *Pizza, birra, faso* (Pizza, Beer, Cigarettes) by Adrián Caetano and Bruno Stagnaro (see p41), and Pablo Trapero's award-winning *Mundo grúa* (Crane World) in 1999, a black-and-white portrait of Argentina's working-class struggles. Trapero went on to become one of Argentina's foremost filmmakers, whose credits include *El bonaerense* (2000), the ensemble road movie *Familia rodante* (Rolling Family) in 2004, his 2006 film, *Nacido y criado* (Born and Bred), a stark story about a Patagonian man's fall from grace, and the 2010 noir film Carancho, a love story whose protagonist is a sleazy opportunist who frequents emergency rooms and accident scenes to find new clients for his legal firm.

One of its brightest stars of the New Argentine Cinema is Daniel Burman, Argentina's answer to Woody Allen, who deals with the theme of identity in the character of a young Jew in modern-day Buenos Aires. His films include *Esperando al mesíah* (Waiting for the Messiah, 2000), *El abrazo partido* (Lost Embrace, 2004) and *Derecho de familia* (Family Law; p41). Burman's other claim to fame is his co-production of Walter Salles' Che Guevara–inspired *The Motorcycle Diaries*. His most recent film, Dos hermanos (Brother and Sister, 2010), the story of aging siblings who've recently lost their mother, is based on the Argentine novel Villa Laura.

Another director to have made a mark on Argentina cinema is the late Fabián Bielinsky. He left behind a small but powerful body of work that includes his award-winning feature Nueve reinas (Nine Queens; p41), which even inspired a 2004 Hollywood remake, *Criminal*. His last film, the 2005 neo-noir flick *El Aura*, screened at Sundance and was the official Argentine entry for the 2006 Oscars.

Lucrecia Martel, who doesn't like to be labeled a New Argentine Cinema director, has left an indelible trace on Argentina's contemporary cinema. Her 2001 debut, *La ciénaga* (The Swamp), and the 2004 follow-up, *La niña santa* (The Holy Girl), both set in Martel's native Salta province, deal with the themes of social decay, Argentine bourgeois and sexuality in the face of Catholic guilt. Another acclaimed director, Carlos Sorin, takes us to the deep south of Argentina in two of his neorealist flicks, the 2002 *Historias mínimas* (Minimal Stories) and the 2004 *Bombón el perro* (Bombón the Dog).

Juan José Campanella's *El hijo de la novia* (Son of the Bride) received an Oscar nomination for best foreign-language film in 2001. His 2004 award-winning film *Luna de avellaneda* (Moon of Avellaneda) is a masterful story about a social club and those who try to save it. And in 2010 Campanella actually won the Oscar for best foreign-language film with his *El secreto de sus ojos* (p41).

Other noteworthy films include Luis Puenzo's Oscar-winning La historia oficial (The Official Story; p41); Sandra Gugliotta's bust-out directorial debut *Un día de suerte* (A Lucky Day; p41); *Un oso rojo* (A Red Bear, 2002) by Israel Adrián Caetano; *La libertad* (Freedom, 2001) and *Los muertos* (The Dead, 2004) by Lisandro Alonso; *Roma* (2004) by Adolfo Aristarain; *Iluminados por el fuego* (Enlightened by Fire, 2006) by Tristan Bauer; and *Mientras tanto* (Meanwhile, 2006) by Diego Leman. Two of the latest hit directors are Alexis Dos Santos with *Glue* (2006), a coming-of-age story about a sexually ambivalent adolescent, and Lucía Puenzo (daughter of Luis Puenzo) with *XXY*, a tale of a 15-year-old hermaphrodite that won multiple awards at Cannes in 2007. Recent movies to watch for are *El hombre de al lado* (The Man Next Door, 2009) by Mariano Cohn and Gastón Duprat, a black comedy about the uncomfortable intimacy of urban living spaces; and *Rompecabezas* (Puzzle, 2010), by writer/director Natalia Smirnoff, about a housewife who discovers a hidden talent for solving puzzles and, in so doing, finds herself.

VISUAL ARTS

Argentina's 2001 economic crisis was a mixed blessing for the visual artists of Buenos Aires. While the tough times made it even harder to earn a living from art, they also triggered a tidal wave of ideas and output that has largely swept aside the 'official arbiters' of public taste. Artists have been banding together for mutual support, increasingly engaging one another and the public in dialogues (often of a political nature) that generate further ideas and projects.

The sense that 'we've all been through this together' has drawn the public and the artists closer, and helped break the tyranny of the austere gallery and conservative critics dictating what's acceptable. The alternative art scene in BA was going strong before the crash but has really taken off since. You can now find galleries, exhibits and art events in the most unlikely places. The influx of foreign visitors, eager to pick up quality works at bargain prices, has helped things along. The day may indeed come when Buenos Aires' greatest innovators in visual arts no longer need to shop their works abroad to make it big.

As an example, porteño painter Guillermo Kuitca (b 1961), who lives and works in BA, did not exhibit in his home town from 1989 until 2003, when the city's modern art museum put on a retrospective. Kuitca is known for his imaginative techniques that include the use of digital technology to alter photographs, maps and other images and integrate them into larger-themed works. His work is on display at major international collections including the Met, MoMa and the Tate; he had solo and group shows at key art expos such as the Venice Biennale in 2007. A thirty-year retrospective of Kuitca's work opened at the Miami Art Museum in 2009 and has traveled to various galleries and museums in 2010.

Another artist who gained fame at home and abroad in his lifetime is Antonio Berni (1905-81). Berni would sometimes visit shantytowns and collect materials to use in his works. Various versions of his theme *Juanito Laguna Bañándose* (Juanito Laguna bathing) – a protest against social and economic inequality – have been commanding wallet-busting prices at auctions.

One of the more interesting contemporary artists is Roberto Jacoby, who has been active in diverse fields since the 1960s, from organizing socially flavored multimedia shows to setting up audiovisual installations. His most famous work, Darkroom, is a video performance piece with infrared technology meant for a single spectator. Other internationally recognized artists who experiment with various media are Buenos Aires-born, New York-based Liliana Porter, who imaginatively plays with video, paintings, 3D prints, photos and an eclectic collection of knickknacks; Graciela Sacco, whose politically and socially engaging installations often use public space as their setting; and the photographer Arturo Aguiar, known for playing with light and shadow in his mysterious works. Another artist to be aware of is Marcelo Bordese, whose paintings feature a medley of sexuality and religion in a disquieting yet captivating manner. Also watch out for young BA photographer Sebastián Friedman and his portrait photography that brings to light Argentina's social issues. And highly eclectic Argentine pop artist Marta Minujín is always worth a look out, adding fire to the Marshall McLuhan quote 'Art is anything you can get away with.'

In recent years Buenos Aires has experienced a growth of small galleries focused on showcasing local up-and-coming talent, in addition to more established Argentine and international artists. These include Daniel Abate (www.danielabategaleria.com.ar); **Appetite** (p113); Arte x Arte (p99); and Galería Alberto Sendrós (www.albertosendros.com).

Buenos Aires has also seen a rise in urban art interventions, a movement of diverse activist artists whose work calls attention to social and urban issues in the city's public spaces. The most prominent figure is Marino Santa María (www.marinosantamaria.com), whose award-winning Proyecto Calle Lanín is a must-see; it's a series of colorful murals along the narrow Calle Lanín (between Brandsen until Suarez) in the up-and-coming artist neighborhood of Barracas. Santa María is now a hot commodity, and his urban interventions are being commissioned in other places around BA and the rest of Argentina. A more controversial and politically engaging group is Mujeres Publicas (www.mujerespublicas.com.ar) who are fighting for women's rights through a variety of public art interventions, such as posting attention-grabbing posters; one of them said ¡Soy feliz, descubrí mi clitorís!'(I'm happy, I found my clitoris!).

Some works by late artists you might want to check out are the restored ceiling murals of Antonio Berni, Lino Spilimbergo and others in the Galerías Pacífico shopping center (p61) in the Microcentro. The late Benito Quinquela Martín, who put the working-class barrio of La Boca on the artistic map, painted brightly colored oils of life in the factories and on the waterfront. Xul Solar, a multitalented phenomenon who was a good friend of Jorge Luis Borges, painted busy, Klee-inspired dreamscapes. The former homes of both Quinquela (p79) and Solar (p96) are now museums showcasing their work.

To find out about current exhibits and openings, check out the following websites and blogs (all in Spanish): www.mapadelasartes.com/home, www.artistasdebuenosaires.blogspot.com, www.ramona.org.ar and www.arsomnibus.com.ar. The best times to be in BA if you want to discover the art world is during arteBA (p21) and the annual La Noche de los Museos (Night of the Museums; p22).

FILETEADO PORTEÑO

Walk around Buenos Aires enough and you can't help noticing the colorful painted swirls of *fileteado* (also knows as *filete*) decorating some public signs and buildings. This beautiful stylistic artwork originally appeared on early 20th-century horse carts, thought to have been inspired by intricate Italian metal designs. As time progressed, fileteado migrated to trucks and buses, softening these hulking vehicles with gaudy colors and symbols such as flowers, vines, birds, dragons and – of course – the Argentine flag.

Interestingly, this art form was once in danger of extinction. During the *Proceso,* or Dirty War (1976-1983), fileteado was banned from public transport systems. *Fileteadores* – or fileteado artists – had to think of other creative places for their works. They started decorating signs, posters, newsstands and buildings, eventually evolving their labors from simply decorative touches into works of art themselves. Fileteado has since become an integral part of Buenos Aires' artistic culture.

Today you can buy plaques at street fairs – or *ferias* – especially in San Telmo, where Carlos Gardel is a popular subject. Many plaques also serve to communicate proverbs and poetry. To see buildings covered in fileteado, keep your eyes peeled in San Telmo, La Boca and Abasto (especially near Museo Casa Carlos Gardel, p97). And consider taking the Fileteado Porteño tour (see p229); you'll also get the opportunity to create some of this lovely artwork yourself (or try www.fileteadoslucerom.com.ar).

SCULPTURE

Given its European origins, official public art in BA tends toward hero worship and the pompously monumental, expressed through equestrian statues of military figures like José de San Martín, Justo José de Urquiza and Julio Argentino Roca. Many have prominent positions in Buenos Aires' parks and plazas, especially in the neighborhood of Palermo. The median strips of Avenida 9 de Julio are another good – albeit busy – place to see some of the city's most prominent outdoor sculptures.

Among the most well-known contemporary sculptors is León Ferrari (b 1920), whose artwork deals with antireligious and anti-American political themes (he likes using cockroaches as symbols for the US). His most famous piece is *Western and Christian Civilization* (1964), which depicts Jesus Christ crucified on a fighter jet; his arms span the aircraft's wings as he holds a missile in each of his hands. The artist fled to Brazil during the military regime in 1976, but returned in 1991. His 2004 retrospective at the Centro Cultural Recoleta (p88) was briefly shut down due to a lawsuit by a Catholic priest, only to re-open to huge lines of people trying to see the controversial work. Despite his advanced age, Ferrari still occasionally exhibits in BA and abroad.

Another sculptor who has inspired political controversy is Alberto Heredia (1924-2000), whose pieces ridicule the solemnity of official public art and critique Argentine society and religion. Heredia's powerful *El Caballero de la Máscara* depicts a 19th-century caudillo (strongman) as a headless horseman. During the military dictatorship of 1976-83, this sculpture could not be exhibited under its original title *El Montonero,* which authorities thought implied associations with guerrilla forces. Also overtly political is Juan Carlos Distéfano (b 1933), who spent years of exile in Brazil while working on antigovernment themes. Distéfano used rich, textural surfaces of polyester, glass, fiber and resins to achieve colorful surfaces on his sometimes disturbing themes.

The late Rogelio Yrurtia's (1879-1950) works deal sympathetically with the struggles and achievements of working people; see his masterpiece *Canto al Trabajo* on the Plazoleta Olazábal (Av Paseo Colón) in San Telmo. Many of Yrurtia's smaller pieces are displayed at his own museum (p101) in Belgrano, along with other notable sculptors' artworks. The internationally renowned kinetic sculptures of Paris-based Julio le Parc (b 1928) mesmerize with their visual tricks achieved through the way light reflects on polished surfaces. For comic relief, the grotesque papier-mâché sculptures (made from trash and old books) of Yoël Novoa, who's been called 'the paper alchemist', appeal to audiences of almost any age or political persuasion.

Strong women sculptors include Norma D'Ippolito, who has won over 20 artistic awards and works mostly with Carrara marble, creating contemporary designs that often incorporate the human figure. Her *Homage to Raoul Wallenberg* honors the Swedish diplomat who helped Jews in WWII. Lucia Pacenza is another prize-winning artist who also specializes in marble sculptures, created mostly as outdoor urban pieces. She studied in Europe, Mexico and the US and has art installations in countries as far away as Australia. Another notable Argentine female sculptor is Claudia Aranovich, who converts diverse materials such as transparent resins, cast aluminum, glass and cement into organic shapes and natural portraits.

Note the prominent and beautiful sculpture *Floralis Genérica* (p86) in Recoleta's Plaza Naciones Unidas. Created by architect Eduardo Catalano, this 18-ton metal flower originally closed up its giant petals at night – until the mechanics stopped working.

ARCHITECTURE

Care for a colonial *cabildo* (town hall)? Fancy some fine French folderol, or do you prefer a pink palace? Perhaps a plethora of pastel-painted houses? Or just a simple block of flats? Buenos Aires still holds examples of many an architectural style in vogue at one time or another throughout the city's life. It has some amazing one-offs as well. You'll find old and new juxtaposed in sometimes jarring and often enchanting ways (occasionally in the same structure), though the new has been asserting itself more and more in recent years, and on a grander scale than ever before.

Little trace remains of the modest one-story adobe houses that sprang up along the mouth of the Riachuelo following the second founding of Buenos Aires in 1580. Many of them were occupied by traffickers of contraband, as the Spanish Crown forbade any direct export or import of goods from the settlement. The restrictions made the price of imported building materials prohibitively high, which kept things simple, architecturally speaking, since local materials left a lot to be desired. For an idea of how BA's first settlements used to be, visit El Zanjón de Granados (p105).

The houses stayed simple and the streets remained unpaved as BA grew slowly until 1776, when the Bourbon Crown decreed the creation of the new Viceroyalty of the Río de la Plata, with Buenos Aires as capital. Now things started moving faster, and at the hub of the activity lay what is today known as the Plaza de Mayo.

In the colonial scheme the street grid centered on the main plaza, which was surrounded by the town hall, cathedral and other important buildings. Arranged around the main plaza satellite-fashion were the various barrios, or neighborhoods, each with their own church, which usually shared its name with the barrio. Many towns in Latin America founded during the colonial period retain this layout at their centers.

Buenos Aires' Cabildo (old town hall; p63) is a fair example of colonial architecture, although its once plaza-spanning colonnades were severely clipped by the construction of Av de Mayo and the diagonals feeding into it. The last of the Cabildo's multiple remodels was a 1940s restoration to its original look, minus the colonnades. Most of the other survivors from the colonial era are churches. Sharing Plaza de Mayo with the Cabildo, the Catedral Metropolitana (p65) was begun in 1752 but not finished until 1852, by which time it had acquired its rather secular-looking neoclassicist facade.

Many examples of post-independence architecture (built after 1810) can be found in the barrios of San Telmo, one of the city's best walking areas, and Montserrat. San Telmo also holds a wide variety of vernacular architecture such as *casas chorizos* (sausage houses) – so called for their long, narrow shape (some have a 2m frontage on the street). The perfect example is Casa Mínima (p105).

In the latter half of the 19th century, as Argentina's agricultural exports soared, a lot of money accumulated in Buenos Aires, both in private and government hands. All parties were interested in showing off their wealth by constructing elaborate mansions, public buildings and wide Parisian-style boulevards. Buildings in the city in the first few decades of the boom were constructed mostly in Italianate style, but toward the end of the 19th century a French influence began to exert itself. Mansard roofs and other elements gave a Parisian look to parts of the city

top picks

QUIRKY BUILDINGS

- Obelisco (p71)
- Confitería del Molino (p103)
- Palacio de las Aguas Corrientes (p74)
- Iglesia Ortodoxa Rusa (p106)
- Facultad de Ingeniería (p106)
- Palacio Barolo (p74)

that remains to this day. The area of tree-lined Palermo Viejo still retains many of the 9th-century single-family homes which give the neighborhood its distinctive small-town charm.

By the beginning of the 20th century, art nouveau was all the rage, and many delightful examples of the style remain. Some of them, such as the former Confitería del Molino (p104) across from the Congreso, are not in such delightful condition, unfortunately.

Among the highlights of the building boom's first five decades is the presidential palace, known as the Casa Rosada (Pink House, officially Casa de Gobierno; p64), created in 1882 by joining a new wing to the existing post office. Others include the showpiece Teatro Colón (p71) and the imposing Palacio del Congreso (p74).

The 1920s saw the arrival of the skyscraper to BA, in the form of the 100m-high, 18-story Palacio Barolo (p74). This fabled, rocket-styled building was the tallest in Argentina (and one of the tallest in South America) from its opening in 1923 until the completion of the 30-story art deco Edificio Kavanagh (p82) in 1936. The Kavanagh in turn, when finished, was the largest concrete building in the world and remains an impressive piece of architecture.

In the 1930s, in Palermo and Recoleta, fancy apartment buildings started popping up. This trend would continue intermittently into the 1940s, by which time the city would also have a subway system with multiple lines.

Buenos Aires continued to grow upward and outward during Juan Perón's spell in power (1946-55). Though the economy flagged, anonymous apartment and office blocks rose in ever greater numbers. Bucking the trend were such oddball buildings as the Banco de Londres on Reconquista, designed in 1959 by Clorindo Testa, whose long architectural career in BA began in the late 1940s. The bank was finished by 1966, but Testa's Biblioteca Nacional (National Library; p96) – which must've looked pretty groovy to him on the drawing board in 1962 – was hideously dated by the time it opened (following many delays) in 1992. Its style is somewhere between late Offshore Oil Platform and early Death Star.

A heartening trend of 'architectural recycling' took off in Buenos Aires in the latter 20th century and continues today, helping to preserve the city's glorious old structures. Grand mansions have been remodeled (and sometimes augmented) to become luxury hotels, museums and cultural centers. Old markets have been restored to their original glory and then some, to live again as popular shopping malls, such as the Mercado de Abasto (p97) and Galerías Pacífico (p61).

At the same time, the first decade of the 21st century has seen an increasingly modern skyline develop in Buenos Aires. Soaring structures of glass and steel tower above earlier efforts, many innovative and quite striking, such as the Edificio Telefónica (originally named Edificio República) on Tucumán between Madero and Bouchard. It was designed by César Pelli, an Argentine native now living in the US, who also did Kuala Lumpur's Petronas Towers. The ultramodern building is super energy-efficient, and from some angles its shape evokes the hull of a ship. From other views its concave and convex planes give the structure the look of a false front.

One of the most ambitious architectural projects in BA today combines the repurposing of old structures and the construction of ultramodern ones. The ongoing renovation of Puerto Madero (p68) has turned dilapidated brick warehouses and mills into office buildings, upscale restaurants, luxury hotels and exclusive apartments. Contrasting with these charming low, long brick buildings is one of the city's tallest structures, the 558-ft high Torres El Faro, standing at the eastern section of Puerto Madero. It's a pair of joined towers that now house fancy apartments.

However, of all the architectural gems in this area, the most captivating are Calatrava's Puente de la Mujer (p68) and the four-story glass-domed Museo Fortabat (p68) by Uruguayan-born architect Rafael Viñoli.

ENVIRONMENT & PLANNING

Buenos Aires has its substantial share of problems faced by any major metropolis – noise and air pollution, urban sprawl, and tons of waste. Environmental and urban planning issues have finally been acknowledged in recent years and the city administration is slowly attempting to solve them.

THE LAND

At the continental edge of Argentina's fertile pampas heartland, Buenos Aires sits on an almost completely level plain of wind-borne loess and river-deposited sediments once covered by lush native grasses. The heart of the capital sprawls along the west bank of the Río de la Plata, which (despite every porteño's claim that it is the world's widest river) is more like a huge estuary. It ranges from 40km wide inland to over 200km at the mouth and discharges thick sediments along the coast and far out into the South Atlantic Ocean. Buenos Aires' highest elevation is only 25m and much of the city is barely above sea level.

top picks

NATURE BREAKS

- **Reserva Ecológica Costanera Sur** (p70) A bird-watcher's dream, just minutes from raging traffic.
- **Plaza San Martín** (p82) It's not huge but the grassy hills are perfect for picnics and smooching lovers.
- **Palermo's Parks** (p90) Acres and acres of grass and walking paths, with some thematic gardens adding interest.
- **Parque Lezama** (p105) It's more of an urban green burp but it's San Telmo's best stab at open space.
- **Tigre** (p200) Marshy tides and peaceful waterways; just an hour's drive north of the center.

GREEN BUENOS AIRES

You can jokingly refer to 'Buenos Aires' (literally, 'good airs') more accurately as 'Malos Aires' (bad airs). Indeed, air pollution can be astoundingly bad, and especially noticeable when you're walking down a street with a line of diesel buses roaring black clouds right into your path. The city's taxi fleet of over 40,000 vehicles doesn't help air quality either, nor do the hundreds of thousands of private vehicles clogging BA's streets every day. After all, this is not a city where emissions controls are taken seriously. Luckily enough for Buenos Aires, strong winds and rains frequently clear the air.

The center of Buenos Aires has hardly any rivers, which is fine since, if they existed, they'd probably be heavily polluted. La Boca's Riachuelo is the city's main waterway and so thick with pollutants that it looks and smells viscous. Noise pollution is another big problem, with constant construction, unmuffled vehicles and liberal use of the horn assaulting eardrums. BA has been named the 4th noisiest city in the world.

The city also creates millions of tons of garbage annually, and past feeble stabs at official recycling have only partially reduced this quantity. Most recycling is now done by *cartoneros* (see boxed text, p48), garbage-pickers who have virtually created a new vocation brought about by necessity after Argentina's most recent economic crisis.

From an ecological standpoint the biggest and brightest success story in the city is the Reserva Ecológica Costanera Sur (p70), located east of downtown. This little marshy paradise was originally created from landfill as the base for a city expansion, but during economic and political stalls over the past two decades it was taken over by indigenous marshy vegetation, migrating birds and aquatic rodents. Despite arson attempts, most likely by those with interests

CRITICAL MASS

Originally started in San Francisco in 1992, Critical Mass is an international bicycling event dedicated to improving bicycle awareness and reaffirming cyclists' rights. It's held in over 300 cities throughout the world, and though its goal is different in each city, it's not meant to be a race, protest, demonstration or means to cause trouble by maliciously blocking vehicular traffic.

In Buenos Aires, *Masa Crítica* has no set leaders or destinations. People just show up with their bikes at 4pm at the Obelisco, on the first Sunday of each month – and start riding somewhere. Expect several hundred people to participate – even up to a thousand on nice warm days. And you'll see all sorts of folks – activists, families, hipsters, foreigners – on tall bikes, low bikes and everything in between. There's even the odd costume, skateboarder and rollerblader. You'll be riding in the streets, but you're more protected than you think – think safety in numbers. Lots of yelling, cheering and horn-blowing required; expect to have a blast.

To find out more, check out www.masacriticabsas.com.ar (in Spanish) – and get in on the action soon, as the biking revolution is just beginning in Buenos Aires!

in developing the prime real estate, this green success story survives to give porteños an idea of what the Buenos Aires riverside used to be like hundreds of years ago.

BA's most recent and exciting ecologically-related project, however, is the development of protected bike lanes throughout the city – with a goal of 100km total – making pedaling a much less intimidating prospect. The most pleasant system is around Palermo's parks; from here you can ride nearly all the way to Reserva Ecológica Costanera Sur, which is best seen by bicycle anyway. For a map on these bike lanes, see www.mejorenbici.gob.ar/?id=2.

Also, an ambitious bike-share program (www.mejorenbici.gob.ar) was started in late 2010, giving city residents the opportunity to 'check out' a bicycle in one area – for free – and ride it to another, where they'd turn it in. This program is targeted to those who live in BA (and can prove it), rather than tourists. If you're just visiting and want more information on cycling around it, see p176, p219 and p229.

There's also an elevated bus rapid transit (BRT) system being constructed in the city, but won't really affect tourist transportation options, as it's focused on local needs.

Some hotels are trying to do their part by building with recycled materials and using energy-saving devices; these include Eco Pampa Hostel (p195), Mine Hotel (p193) and Casa Calma (p190). And keep an eye out for Own Hotel's new branch near Plaza de Mayo, which plans on opening in late 2011 and will supposedly be Argentina's first LEED-certified hotel.

Hopefully this green bug will continue to bite porteños, slowly changing their perception of what it means to take care of their environment – and beloved city.

URBAN PLANNING & DEVELOPMENT

Buenos Aires' urban planning and development is not an issue that concerns most Argentine politicians, unless it's an election year. More often than not, promises made during campaigning go flying out the window following victory. It almost seems a fortunate thing that much of the city was constructed and developed in the late 1800s, when times were good and money flowed like wine. This was a time when Argentina was one of the richest countries in the world

BUENOS AIRES' CARTONEROS

You'll see them mostly at night, hunched over at the curb, picking through the garbage and pushing loaded-down carts. These are not the homeless, or the crazy, or the drug-addicted, or even the city's petty thieves. These are regular people, but some of Buenos Aires' poorest citizens – they're *cartoneros,* or cardboard collectors. Many of them used to have regular jobs as skilled laborers or even businessmen, but were laid off with the 2001 crisis. With unemployment still substantial and no social security to cover them, collecting recyclables is one of the few ways they can make a living.

It's estimated that there are up to 20,000 *cartoneros* rummaging through Buenos Aires' trash heaps, though only a quarter of those are 'official' (accredited by the city and even wearing uniforms). About 70% are men. They sort through the city's 5,000 daily tons of waste, collecting cardboard, paper, metal, plastic, glass – anything they can sell by the kilo to the *depositos* (recycling companies) around town. They stake out their territory, perhaps about 15 city blocks, and are occasionally forced to pay police bribes. Many have been pricked by syringes or cut by broken glass. This isn't an easy job but it's decent work – once established, the daily take-home pay for a *cartonero* can be AR$100 or more.

While most *cartoneros* work independently, some work for neighborhood cooperatives that pay them a regular wage and organize vaccinations. Some cooperatives even provide child care for parents who go off on their nightly rounds. In the poorest families, however, even the young children have to work all night long. And some *cartoneros* are in their 50s and 60s.

In 2005 the City of Buenos Aires passed a 'Zero Garbage' law that sets quotas for the government to reduce the waste of recyclable materials – but the city's campaign was disorganized, and little has been accomplished. At least the *cartoneros* have played their part in helping BA's environment – an estimated 10% of the city's garbage is recycled by them.

It's not surprising that Argentina's economic crash has inflamed this side-business in recyclables, and that those less fortunate had to use their creativity and ingenuity to organize for themselves what their government could not. The *cartoneros* are a reminder to us that there is another side to the glittering richness of Buenos Aires' center, and that there is another part of this city where the poor people live.

Want to find out more? Visit Eloisa Cartonera (☎ 15-5502-1590; Aristóbulo del Valle 666; ⏰ Mon-Sat 2-6pm). This grass-roots non-profit buys clean cardboard from *cartoneros* and turns it into inexpensive books. You can ask *cartonero*-related questions here and someone might have the answers. It's located in an edge part of La Boca, so if you're uncomfortable visiting alone (or don't speak Spanish) go with Anda Responsible Travel's La Boca tour (p229).

and heavy immigration brought skilled labor and organized ideas from old Europe. Even into the early 1900s, large parks and plazas were put into place and wide avenues constructed, along with the subway and train lines.

In the past few decades economic times have become tougher, the population has risen and urban sprawl has seen the city's suburbs stretch for endless hundreds of kilometers; Buenos Aires has now become one of the most populated cities on the planet. Shantytowns or *villas miserias,* most of them located in barrios furthest from the center, hold the poorest of the city's inhabitants; some pop up even in the inner city, such as the sizeable shambles behind Retiro Bus Station. Puerto Madero, however, is one relatively new development that has worked out well for Buenos Aires and now looks great to boot. Its eastern section has been a very fast-developing urbanization area, with several tall towers with luxury apartments and offices completed.

Certain sections of the city that are often visited by tourists, such as San Telmo and Palermo Viejo, have also seen a gentrification process take place in the past few years. Quite a few high-rise buildings have sprung up in Palermo Viejo – with more going up – causing protests among the neighbors who prefer to retain the area's traditionally low-rise aspect.

For a few new green-based transportation projects going on in BA, see the section Green Buenos Aires.

GOVERNMENT & POLITICS

The politics of Buenos Aires is entangled with that of Argentina in general, because most national government institutions – not to mention the economic and financial sectors and a large percentage of the electorate – reside here.

The city of Buenos Aires (also known as the Capital Federal) was given the status of federal district (similar to that of Mexico City and Washington, DC) in 1880. Though at that point it began to function independently from the surrounding province of Buenos Aires (whose capital was moved to La Plata), the city's residents didn't have a lot of say in its administration; the president of the republic appointed the mayor.

Argentina's constitution was reformed in the 1990s, giving the federal district the freedom to elect its mayor, and in 1996 Fernando de la Rúa of the Radical Party became Buenos Aires' first mayor elected by majority vote. De la Rúa went on to serve as Argentina's president until the economic crash of late 2001 drove him from office. The current mayor is Mauricio Macri, owner of the Boca Juniors football club and right-wing businessman, who was elected in 2007 after winning 60% of the vote. Ever the rising star, Macri plans to make a presidential run in 2011.

The reforms also gave Buenos Aires a 60-member Poder Legislativo (legislature), elected by proportional representation to four-year terms, with the possibility of reelection for an additional term. Half the seats are up for election every two years. After completing two consecutive terms, neither the mayor nor any legislator may run for the same office again until four years have elapsed.

The largest political party is the Partido Justicialista (PJ), also known as the Peronist Party (since it was founded by Juan Perón); traditionally it has been supported by working class people. Other parties include the Frente para la Victoria (FPV), Unión Cívica Radical (UCR), Partido Socialista (PS), Propuesta Republicana (PRO) and Coalición Cívica (CC).

MEDIA

NEWSPAPERS & MAGAZINES

Argentina is South America's most literate country, supporting a wide spectrum of newspapers and magazines despite the continuing economic crisis. The capital is home to more than half a dozen nationwide dailies, several of them now online, and some with unambiguous political leanings. The centrist tabloidlike *Clarín* (www.clarin.com) has one of the largest circulations of any newspaper in the Spanish-speaking world, and publishes an excellent Sunday cultural section. *La Nación* (www.lanacion.com.ar), founded in 1870 by former president Bartolomé Mitre, is another very popular and moderate paper revered by a more conservative readership.

Página 12 (www.pagina12.com.ar) provides refreshing leftist perspectives, plenty of popular opinions and a good weekend pullout. *Ámbito Financiero* (www.ambitoweb.com), the morning voice of the capital's financial community, also has a stellar entertainment and cultural section. *El Cronista* (www.cronista.com) and *Buenos Aires Económico* are its rivals. All appear weekdays only.

The English-language daily *Buenos Aires Herald* (www.buenosairesherald.com) covers Argentina and the world from an international perspective, emphasizing commerce and finance. Another English-language paper also aimed at travelers and expatriates is the *Argentina Independent* (www.argentinaindependent.com), which provides in-depth articles about BA and Argentina. *Argentinisches Tageblatt* (www.tageblatt.com.ar) is a German-language weekly that appears on Saturdays.

North American and European newspapers such as *The New York Times, USA Today,* the *Guardian* and *Le Monde* are available at kiosks on Florida. Magazines such as *Time, Newsweek* and the *Economist* are also fairly easy to obtain.

RADIO

Dozens of FM stations specialize in music, news and information for everyone. La 2x4 FM 92.7 (www.la2x4.com.ar) has tango; FM 98.7 (www.radionacional.gov.ar) has Argentine folk; FM 97.4 has classical music; FM 95.9 has national/international rock and pop; FM 98.3 has Argentine rock nacional only; and FM 97.1 has BBC in English.

For those looking for something less mainstream, FM 88.7 La Tribu (www.fmlatribu.com) is one of Argentina's oldest community radios and has gained international acclaim for its alternative and independent stance on many issues – the likes of Manu Chao and Naomi Klein even hang out there when in BA. Radio 10 (AM 710) is something like the *National Enquirer* of radio stations, while La Colifata (www.lacolifata.org) – literally 'The Crazy One', on FM 100.1 – is operated by psychiatric patients from an asylum.

TELEVISION

Privatization and the cable revolution have brought a wider variety of programming to the small screen, though prime time still seems overrun with reality shows, bimbo-led dance parties and *telenovelas* (soap operas). Get used to seeing semi-naked girls behind every popular TV show host, dancing and pouting in the background. A fun show to watch is *Caiga Quien Caiga,* a weekly news roundup that uses hidden cameras, satire and sound effects to comment on current affairs.

In addition to 80 cable channels that include CNN, ESPN, BBC and a variety of European channels, Argentina has five regular channels:

Canal 2 Also known as América TV (www.america2.com.ar), this channel is heavy on the sports, news and entertainment, and also known for the daily lunch-time talk show by Mirta Legrand, who has been on the air for half a century, hosting a lunch and talking about current issues with guests.

Canal 7 The state-run channel is known for its general interest and cultural programming, offering the most serious TV news, and is also home to the satirical show 'Peter Capusotto y Sus Videos', a fantastic, yet cutting, look at Argentine life.

Canal 9 (www.canal9.com.ar, in Spanish) Smut at its best, Canal 9 expresses no shame in using sex to sell; it imports trashy shows such as *Top Model* and *Living with My Ex.*

Canal 11 (www.telefe.com.ar) Also known as Telefé, this channel is known for its popular, long-running weekly talk show hosted by Susana Gimenez.

Canal 13 (www.canal13.com.ar) Grupo Clarín's high-quality channel, offering *Caiga Quien Caiga* along with the popular news show *Telenoche.* Argentina's most famous host Marcelo Tinelli currently hosts the hugely popular 'Bailando por un Sueño' (Dancing for a Dream) on this channel.

LANGUAGE

Spanish, commonly referred to as *castellano,* is the official language of Argentina and is spoken throughout the country. Also known as *rioplatense* (from Río de la Plata), the brand spoken in Buenos Aires has a strong Italian flavor to it, from the sing-song of its intonation to the amount and variety of gesticulation employed. Quite a few porteños study English, especially those in tourism and business, and many understand English better than they can speak it.

NIP & TUCK – GOING UNDER THE KNIFE IN BUENOS AIRES *Kristie Robinson*

In a country where Gonzalo Otálora last year hit the headlines for his book *Feo* – about the plight of the ugly in Argentina and the discrimination they face in the 'land of the beautiful' – it is no wonder that nobody thinks twice about going under the knife.

In fact, the president herself – Christina Kirchner – is often dubbed 'the queen of botox' in the local media, and arguably has the smoothest face of any 54-year-old in the southern hemisphere. With such leadership, it comes as no surprise to learn that no other country in the world has a higher ratio of plastic surgery operations to population. Reports suggest that one in 30 Argentines have had some sort of procedure during their lifetime, something which is aided by medical insurance that offers one aesthetic surgery a year. So big is the phenomenon that a couple of years ago nightclubs would encourage people in on quieter nights by raffling an operation a night – something that was quickly banned in many provinces, but still exists in others.

According to the Society of Plastic Surgeons of Buenos Aires, demand for plastic surgery has risen 200% since 2002, and it is no coincidence that this all happened after the economic crisis hit. Argentina was suddenly cheaper, and tourism of all levels increased – but the boom in 'medical tourism' has been nothing short of revolutionary. Rather than paying US$15,000 for a facelift in the United States, many have elected to head to the 'Paris of the South' and combine the surgery with a bit of tango, beef and sightseeing for a third of the price.

Plastic surgery holidays have become the norm, and packages including airport pickup, hotels, the surgery itself and follow-up procedures are widely available. Men are particularly targeted in the campaign to reel in the foreign and aesthetically aware, and two in every 10 patients opting for surgery in Argentina now are male.

Wander around Recoleta, the ritzy neighborhood that is home to many of the clinics, and nobody bats an eyelid at someone walking down the street with plasters on their faces having obviously just had a nip and tuck. Many tourists have embraced how accepted they feel and say they can really enjoy a post-op break.

However, the dangers of any medical procedure, let alone one on foreign turf where you may not even speak the language, are quick to be pointed out. Many opportunists have jumped on the bandwagon, keen to exploit this wealthy overseas market.

For information on accredited clinics and surgeons, visit the Argentine Society of Plastic Surgeon's website, www.sacper.com.ar. One highly-regarded plastic surgeon is Dr Williams Bukret (www.drbukret.com), and a company that helps tourists with traveling and surgical details is Ren-u Medical Tourism Argentina (☎ 15-6649-2458; www.ren-u.com).

Kristie Robinson is a journalist who has been living in Argentina for five years, and is founder and editor of The Argentina Independent.

The practice is slipping these days, but some members of immigrant communities have retained their native language as a badge of identity. For example, literary giant Jorge Luis Borges, whose grandmother was English, learned to read in that language before Spanish. Though Argentina's largest historical immigrant group was Italian, the language is not as widely spoken (or even understood) as some visitors from the Old Country expect it to be. Speakers of German are numerous enough to support their own weekly newspaper, *Argentinisches Tageblatt.*

For useful phrases in Argentine Spanish, see the Language chapter p237.

RELIGION

Roman Catholicism remains the officially supported religion of Argentina, though the constitution was changed in 1994 to allow non-Catholics to serve as president. And while only a small percentage of Argentines attend mass regularly, you'll see many porteños exhibiting signs of faith, such as crossing themselves when passing a church. For a good show of serious Catholicism near Buenos Aires, head to Luján (p200); for not-so-serious Catholicism, check out Tierra Santa (p100).

Argentina's national census doesn't track religious affiliation, so accurate figures are tough to come by. One thing is known, however – Buenos Aires has the second largest Jewish population in the Americas (after New York). Jews have undergone successive waves of emigration to Argentina with the troughs under pro-Nazi Perón, during the Dirty War (when Jews were victimized in disproportionate numbers) and most recently with the economic troubles.

Protestants account for about 2% of Argentina's population, as do Muslims. The biggest mosque in South America resides in Palermo: Centro Islámico Rey Fahd (p90).

The country has its share of Jehovah's Witnesses and Mormons, as well as Hare Krishnas (see p178). And, as in many other parts of Latin America, evangelical Protestantism had been making inroads among traditionally Catholic Argentines – especially within the working class – but now seems to be slowing down.

Spiritualism and veneration of the dead have remarkable importance in Argentina. Visitors to Recoleta and Chacarita cemeteries in Buenos Aires – vital places for comprehending Argentine religious culture – will see steady processions of pilgrims going to the resting places of icons like Eva Perón, psychic Madre María and tango singer Carlos Gardel. Followers come to communicate and ask favors by laying their hands on the tombs and leaving arcane offerings (see p88).

NEIGHBORHOODS

top picks

- **Cementerio de la Recoleta** (p86) Get lost in a mazelike city of the dead.
- **Plaza de Mayo** (p63) Be part of BA's culture of protest at this historic plaza.
- **Teatro Colón** (p71) Join the audience at this imposing world-class arts venue.
- **El Zanjón de Granados** (p77) Glimpse this city's unique architectural history.
- **Reserva Ecológica Costanera Sur** (p70) Picnic, cycle and play happy family at this ecological reserve.
- **Museo Nacional de Bellas Artes** (p88) Wander past the works of Europe's and Argentina's great artists.
- **Palacio Paz** (p82) Immerse yourself in the opulence of this French-style palace.
- **Feria de San Telmo** (p118) Hunt for collectibles at this bustling street market.

NEIGHBORHOODS

Buenos Aires is a surprise to many travelers. Some come expecting a more 'South American' atmosphere, perhaps more ethnic-looking people or a less cosmopolitan feel. Or maybe they take BA's nickname – the 'Paris of South America' – a little too literally and think it's more European than it really is.

This is a unique city. It certainly has beautiful European-style architecture in many of its neighborhoods, but with rough edges that add an effortless casualness. There are impressive historical sights, cobbled colonial streets, shiny modern high-rises and unpretentious blue-collar neighborhoods. There are leafy parks, luxurious palaces, ethnic barrios and downtrodden shanty towns. Put simply, there's something for everyone.

This is a unique city. It certainly has beautiful European-style architecture in many of its neighborhoods, but with rough edges that add an effortless casualness.

BA is a huge city, but most key attractions are clustered in just a handful of barrios. For the most part you can walk from one to another without too much trouble, and this is truly the best way to get to know the metropolis. Sure, there's too much traffic, the air could be cleaner and most sidewalks have broken tiles, but there are few hills to puff up and a relaxing café, restaurant or ice-cream shop is always around the corner. And if you need to hop to the other side of town public transportation is cheap and plentiful.

The center is the bustling heart of Buenos Aires, buzzing frantically from dawn to dusk. This is where you'll notice many awesome old European buildings, along with some not-quite-so-charming modern constructions. Florida is a pedestrian shopping street that always heaves with activity, and to the east are the docklands of Puerto Madero – a relatively new barrio that claims the capital's most expensive real estate.

South of the center lies the charming neighborhood of San Telmo. The buildings here are less imposing and more colonial than in the city's center, and narrow cobblestone streets add to its quaintness.

Further south of San Telmo is scrappy La Boca, the city's most visually colorful neighborhood, whose painted corrugated metal houses are often used as a symbol for BA.

West of the center is Congreso and Tribunales, the city's legal quarters, which have plenty of impressive buildings along with an endearing, slightly run-down flavor.

Immediately to the north of the center is Retiro, with its fine plazas and gorgeous palaces. It's mostly an upper-class neighborhood, though the city's main train and bus stations are also located here, and they're definitely not upscale. Northwest of Retiro lies swanky Recoleta, boasting an extensive Gothic cemetery that's a must-see for any visitor. Recoleta is *the* place to eyeball BA's upper classes, and harbors opulent cafés, restaurants and expensive boutiques.

Beyond Recoleta is the huge neighborhood of Palermo. Filled with extensive parklands and monumental statues, it's a refuge for the middle class. Its sub-neighborhood Palermo Viejo is home to the trendiest eateries and most fashionable boutiques. Belgrano is even further north and mostly made up of residential streets that offer a haven for higher-class porteños.

Over to the west the more working-class barrios of Villa Crespo, Once, Caballito and Boedo are unpretentious, but sections of them are gentrifying fast. The capital's main Jewish, Peruvian and Korean populations live around the Once area.

Note that on holidays, opening hours for the sights listed in this chapter tend to be similar to weekend hours. Some sights are closed on Monday, and while many offer tours these will usually be given in Spanish. For companies that organize bus, bike and walking tours see p229.

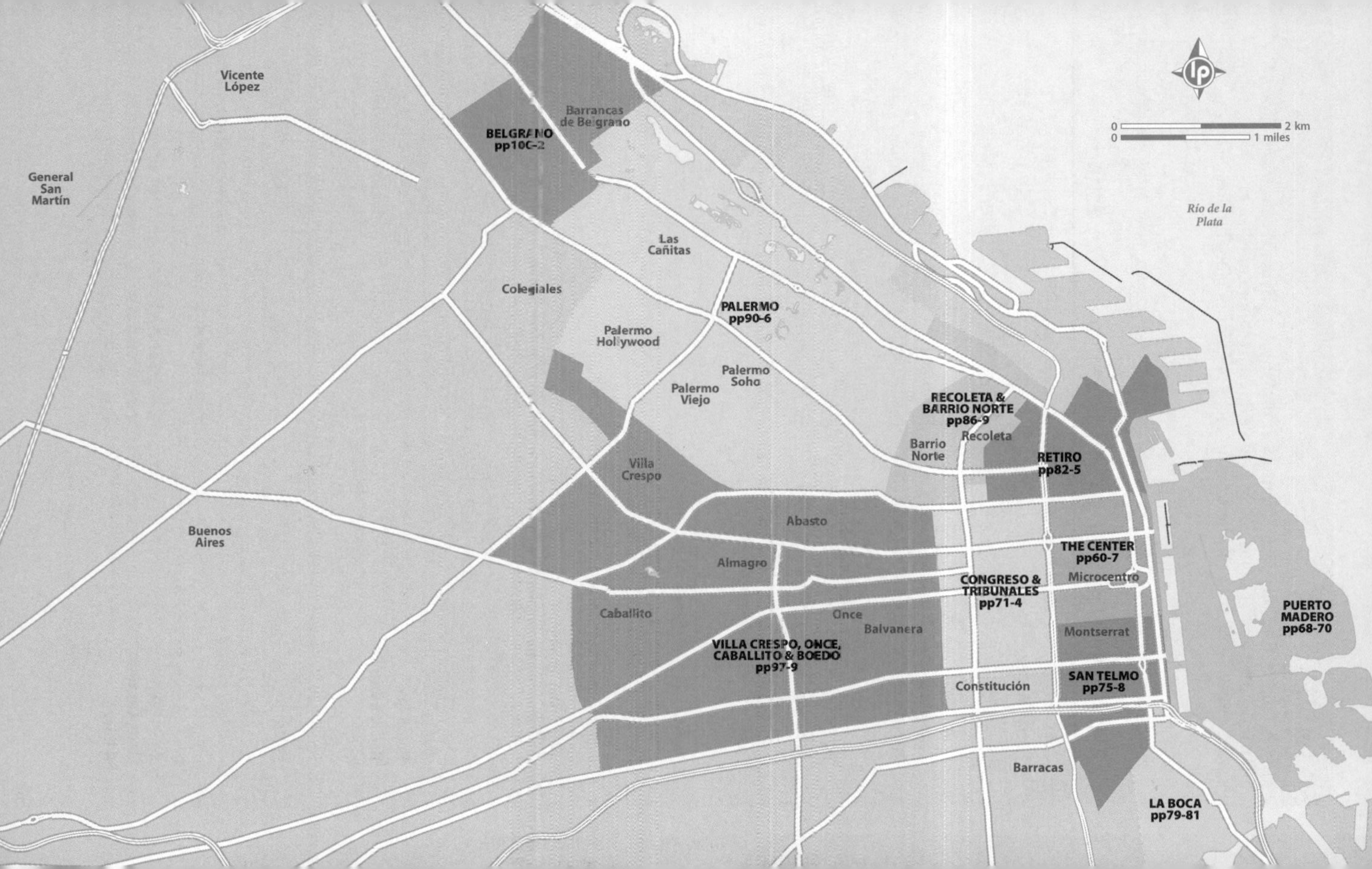

0 — 2 km
0 — 1 miles
Río de la Plata
Vicente López
General San Martín
Barrancas de Belgrano
BELGRANO pp100-2
Las Cañitas
Colegiales
PALERMO pp90-6
Palermo Hollywood
Palermo Soho
Palermo Viejo
RECOLETA & BARRIO NORTE pp86-9
Recoleta
Barrio Norte
RETIRO pp82-5
Villa Crespo
Abasto
Almagro
Buenos Aires
THE CENTER pp60-7
Microcentro
CONGRESO & TRIBUNALES pp71-4
Caballito
Once
Balvanera
VILLA CRESPO, ONCE, CABALLITO & BOEDO pp97-9
Montserrat
PUERTO MADERO pp68-70
SAN TELMO pp75-8
Constitución
Barracas
LA BOCA pp79-81

ITINERARY BUILDER

Mix and match for your own unique Buenos Aires experience. From tango shows to hip bars and historical sights, there is a wealth of recommended sights, shops, eateries and entertainment to choose from in eight popular neighborhoods.

AREA / ACTIVITIES	Sightseeing	Shopping	Eating
The Center & Puerto Madero	Plaza de Mayo (p63) Manzana de las Luces (p66) Reserva Ecológica Costanera Sur (p70)	Galerías Pacíficos (p61) El Ateneo (p111) Musimundo (p112)	Tomo I (p125) Brasserie Berry (p125) El Mercado (p126)
Congreso & Tribunales	Teatro Colón (p71) Plaza del Congreso (p74) Palacio de las Aguas Corrientes (p74)	Zival's (p112)	Chan Chan (p128) Pizzería Güerrín (p129) Plaza Asturias (p128)
San Telmo	El Zanjón de Granados (p77) Plaza Dorrego (p75) Museo Histórico Nacional (p77)	Gil Antigüedades (p112) Mercado de San Telmo (p113) Cualquier Verdura (p114)	La Vineria de Gualterio Bolívar (p129) Amici Miei (p129) Wafles Sur (p131)
La Boca	Fundación Proa (p79) Museo de Bellas Artes de la Boca Benito Quinquela Martín (p79) El Caminito (p79)		El Obrero (p131) Il Matterello (p131) Los Petersen (p131)
Retiro	Plaza San Martín (p82) Palacio Paz (p82) Museo de Arte Hispano-americano Isaac Fernández Blanco (p83)	Tierra Adentro (p114) Autoría (p114) Galería 5ta Avenida (p116)	Filo (p132) Gran Bar Danzón (p132) Sipan (p132)
Recoleta & Barrio Norte	Cementerio de la Recoleta (p86) Museo Nacional de Bellas Artes (p88) Floralis Genérica (p86)	Feria Plaza Francia (p118) Av Alvear (p111) Wussman Shop (p116)	L'Orangerie (p133) Cumaná (p134) 788 Food Bar (p134)
Palermo	Museo de Arte Latino-americano de Buenos Aires (Malba; p90)	Atípica (p119) Capital Diseño & Objetos (p120) Papelera Palermo (p120)	Little Rose (p137) Don Julio (p137) Il Ballo de Mattone (p136)
Villa Crespo, Once, Caballito & Boedo	Museo Casa Carlos Gardel (p97) Museo Argentino de Ciencias Naturales (p99) Mercado de Abasto (p97)	Mercado de Abasto (p97) Calle Murillo (p111) Calle Aguirre Outlets (p111)	Sarkis (p140) Pan y Arte (p140) Bi Won (p139)

HOW TO USE THIS TABLE

The table below allows you to plan a day's worth of activities in any area of the city. Simply select which area you wish to explore, and then mix and match from the corresponding listings to build your day. The first item in each cell represents a well-known highlight of the area, while the other items are more off-the-beaten-track gems.

Drinking	Nightlife & Arts	Tango Shows
Café Richmond (p151) **La Cigale** (p144) **Café Tortoni** (p151)	**Asia de Cuba** (p157) **Bahrein** (p157) **Confitería Ideal** (p168)	**Café Tortoni** (p167) **Tango Porteño** (p166) **El Querandí** (p165)
Cruzat Beer House (p145) **Los 36 Billares** (p145) **Café de Los Angelitos** (p152)	**Maluco Beleza** (p159) **Ávila Bar** (p169) **Teatro Colón** (p71)	**Los 36 Billares** (p145)
Gibraltar (p146) **La Puerta Roja** (p146) **Bar Plaza Dorrego** (p152)	**Mitos Argentinos** (p160) **Centro Cultural Torquato Tasso** (p165) **Museum** (p159)	**El Viejo Almacén** (p166) **La Ventana** (p166) **El Balcón** (p167)
	Teatro de la Ribera (p170)	
Florida Garden (p153) **Café Retiro** (p152) **Milión** (p147)	**Teatro Nacional Cervantes** (p83) **Teatro Coliseo** (p172) **El Living** (p158)	
La Biela (p153) **Casabar** (p148) **Clásica y Moderna** (p153)	**Notorious** (p161) **Basement Club** (p158)	
Casa Cruz (p149) **Congo Bar** (p149) **Mundo Bizarro** (p150)	**Crobar** (p158) **Pachá** (p160) **La Peña del Colorado** (p161)	
Las Violetas (p153) **Cervecería Cossab** (p151) **878** (p150)	**Cuidad Cultural Konex** (p170) **El Camarín de las Musas** (p170) **Amerika** (p156)	**Complejo Tango** (p165) **Esquina Carlos Gardel** (p166) **Esquina Homero Manzi** (p166)

GREATER BUENOS AIRES

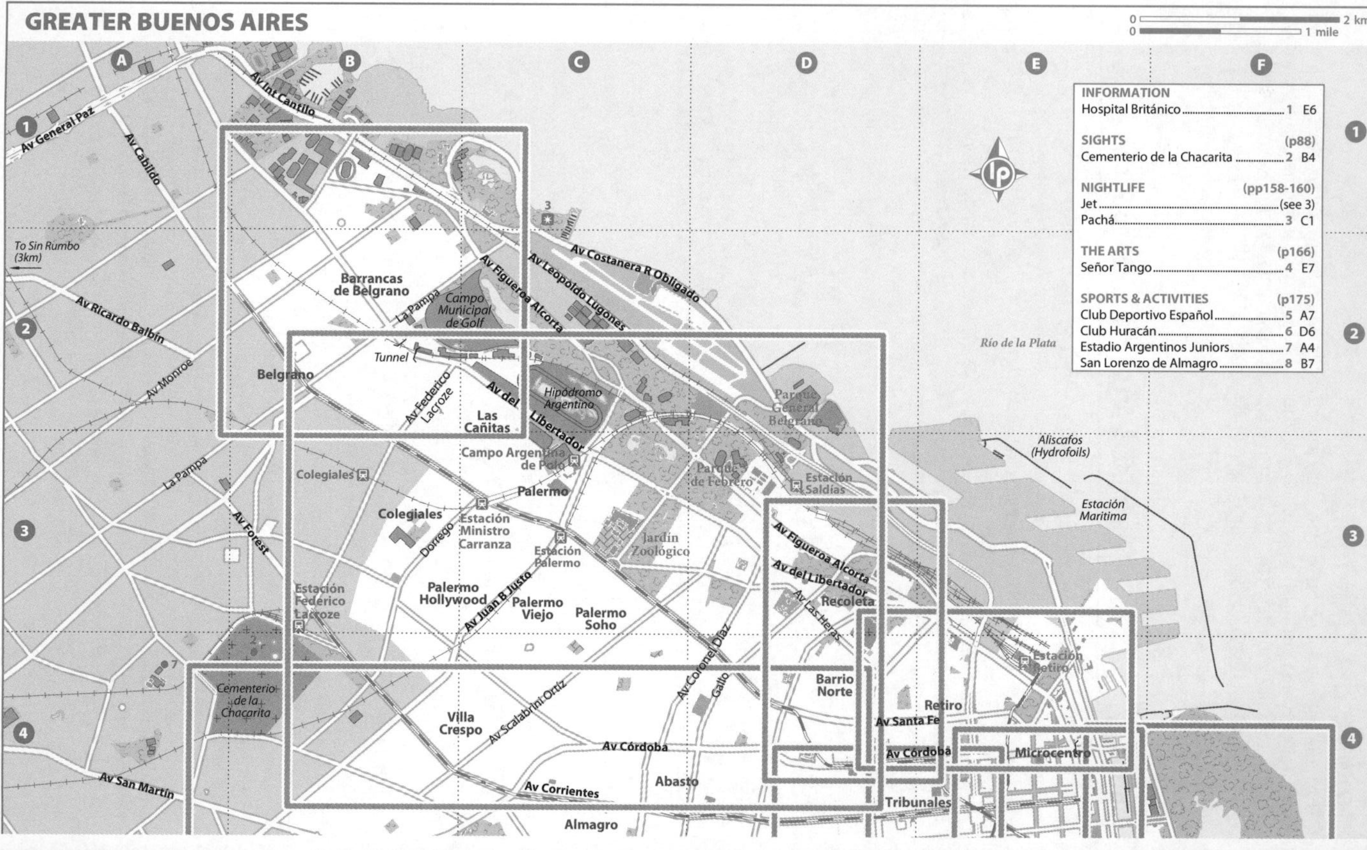

MAP INDEX
1 San Telmo p76
2 Retiro p84
3 La Boca p80
4 Puerto Madero p69
5 The Center p62
6 Congreso & Tribunales p72
7 Villa Crespo, Once, Caballito & Boedo p98
8 Recoleta & Barrio Norte p87
9 Palermo p92
10 Belgrano p101
Caballito
Once
Balvanera
Congreso
Monserrat
Constitución
San Telmo
Puerto Madero
Reserva Ecológica Costanera Sur
La Boca
Parque Lezama
Barracas
Estación Constitución
Estación Once
Boedo
Avellaneda
Parque de Centenario
Parque Rivadavia
Parque Avellaneda
Parque Almirante Guillermo Brown
Lago Lugano
Golf Club
Riachuelo
Canal Sur
Vuelta de Rocha
Av Díaz Vélez
Av Rivadavia
Av Belgrano
Av Callao
Av Independencia
Defensa
Av San Juan
Av Boedo
Av Juan de Garay
Av Entre Ríos
Av Jujuy
Av Patricios
Brandsen
Sargento Ponce
Av Montes de Oca
Av Caseros
Av Amancio Alcorta
Av Vélez Sarsfield
Av Sáenz
Av La Plata
Av Castañares
Av Juan Alberdi
Av Gaona
Av Nazca
Av Perito Moreno
Av Eva Perón
Av FF de la Cruz
Av 27 de Febrero
To Club Atlético Vélez Sársfield (4km)
To Feria de Mataderos (4km); Gaucho Musuem (4km)
To Autódromo Municipal (2km)

THE CENTER

Drinking p144 & p151; Eating p125; Shopping p111; Sleeping p182

Buenos Aires' center is where bustle meets hustle and endless lines of business suits and power skirts move hastily along the narrow streets in the shadow of skyscrapers and old European buildings. During the day it's a heaving mass of humanity and traffic jams, but after the work-day exodus it becomes a much more tranquil place. Stretching from Retiro to San Telmo (and flanked by Congreso and Puerto Madero) this downtown area is the heart and brain of the city, and made up of the sub-neighborhoods of the Microcentro, Plaza de Mayo and Montserrat.

Pedestrian Florida is the main artery of the Microcentro, filled with businesspeople, shoppers and tourists using this vehicle-free access from north to south of the city without bus fumes and honking taxis. Buskers, beggars and street vendors thrive here as well, adding color and noise. In recent years two other streets – Reconquista and Suipacha – have also been made pedestrian, easing the burden on crowded Florida. Perpendicular Lavalle is also vehicle-free, running east-west through the center. Adding elegance to the area are buildings such as the beautiful Galerías Pacíficos (p61), which might have you wondering exactly what continent you're on.

Further south is Buenos Aires' busy banking and financial district, which interestingly enough offers several quirky museums to investigate. After that comes Plaza de Mayo, often filled with people resting on benches or taking photos of surrounding buildings, such as the impressive Casa Rosada (Pink House, or presidential palace; p64). This plaza is also the preferred target of many civil protests (most of which are peaceful), so if anyone needs to voice their opinions in Buenos Aires, there's a good chance they'll do it here. Unfortunately, there are often unsightly barricades meant to discourage large numbers of *piqueteros* (picketers) from congregating; after all, many of the protests are about how the government should be thrown out.

Furthest south and closest to San Telmo is Montserrat, highlighted by the Manzana de las Luces (p66), a block of historic buildings that was the city's original center for high culture and learning. Close by are another couple of interesting museums worth a short visit.

For information on massive Av 9 the Julio and the landmark Obelisco, see under Congreso & Tribunales (p71). All north-south street names change at Av Rivadavia.

MICROCENTRO

As the heart of the city, the Microcentro is often a first stop for tourists. It's a busy place with tall buildings and people running around getting business done. Most streets and sidewalks are narrow, concentrating activity and making it difficult to find your own breathing space at times. Luckily, Plaza San Martín (p82) is just a short stroll away, and Puerto Madero (and its ecological reserve, p68) are also nearby, ready to offer a bit of traffic-free peace.

The Microcentro boasts some pretty impressive buildings. You can't miss the imposing Galerías Pacíficos (p61), located right on pedestrian Florida, while over to the east is the Ex-Correo Central (p61), the city's old post office. Closer to Plaza de Mayo are the Spanish Renaissance **Standard Bank** (Map p62; 1924; cnr Florida & Diagonal Roque Sáenz Peña) building, often sprayed with graffiti and the locus of noisy activities, and the **Edificio Menéndez-Behety** (Map p62; 1926; Diagonal Roque Sáenz Peña 543) – once headquarters of a Patagonian wool empire. Nearby is the French-style **Casa de la Cultura** (Map p62; 1896; Av de Mayo 575), the original *La Prensa* newspaper building; it's worth a peek inside.

top picks

FOR FREE

- BA's street markets (p118)
- Walking tours (p229)
- 'Donation' tango shows (p164)
- El Caminito (p79)
- Museo Nacional de Bellas Artes (p88)
- Parque 3 de Febrero (p90)
- Cementerio de la Recoleta (p86)
- Reserva Ecológica Costanera Sur (p70)

Several unusual museums also call the Microcentro home, from ex-president Mitre's home (he was Argentina's first president) to money, police and tango museums; there are also a few churches in the area to explore. Just wandering the Microcentro's streets and taking it all in is a great way to feel the vibe of the city.

GALERÍAS PACÍFICO Map p62

☎ 5555-5110; www.progaleriaspacifico.com.ar; cnr Florida & Av Córdoba; 10am-9pm Mon-Sat, noon-9pm Sun; Línea B Florida, Línea C Lavalle

Covering an entire city block, this beautiful French-style shopping center has fulfilled the commercial purpose that its designers envisioned when they constructed it in 1889. The worldwide economic crisis of the 1890s necessitated the sale of part of the building to the Ferrocarril del Pacífico for its administrative offices. The railroad subsequently acquired the rest of the building, which became state property after Juan Perón's nationalization of the railroads.

In 1945 the completion of vaulted ceilings and a central cupola made space for a dozen paintings by muralists Antonio Berni, Juan Carlos Castagnino, Manuel Colmeiro, Lino Spilimbergo and Demetrio Urruchúa. All were adherents of the *nuevo realismo* (new realism) school, heirs of an earlier social-activist tendency in Argentine art. For many years the building went semi-abandoned, but a joint Argentine-Mexican team repaired and restored the murals in 1992.

The beautiful structure, which is dotted with fairy lights at night, is now a central meeting place sporting upscale stores and a large food court. Occasional free (ie donation) tango shows take place in front on pedestrian Florida, and the excellent Centro Cultural Borges takes up the top floor. Tours in English and Spanish at 11:30am and 4:30pm, Monday to Friday.

IGLESIA SANTA CATALINA Map p62

☎ 4326-6190; Plaza San Martín 705; Línea B Florida, Línea C Lavalle

Santa Catalina was founded in 1745, when it became Buenos Aires' first convent. In 1806 British troops first invaded the city, and in July 1807 they took shelter in the convent. The soldiers holed up here for two days, and despite damaging the property did not hurt the nuns. Today Santa Catalina is a church, and a peek inside reveals beautiful gilded works and a baroque altarpiece created by Isidro Lorea, a Spanish carver.

TRANSPORTATION: THE CENTER

Bus Take bus 29 to San Telmo; 29, 64, and 152 to La Boca; 64 to Recoleta; 29, 59, 64 and 152 to Palermo's Plaza Italia.

Subte Nearly all Subte lines radiate from the center, going either north-south from Retiro to San Telmo, or towards Palermo and other points east.

EX-CORREO CENTRAL Map p62

Sarmiento 151; Línea B LN Alem

It took 20 years to complete the massive Correo Central (main post office; 1928), which fills an entire city block. This beaux arts structure was originally modeled on New York City's main post office; the mansard roof was a later addition. The building is now being turned into a cultural center with possible museum, but no one knows when it will open; check it out during your tenure and cross your fingers.

MUSEO MITRE Map p62

☎ 4394-8240; www.museomitre.gov.ar; Plaza San Martín 336; admission AR$5, Monday free; 1-5:30pm Mon-Fri; Línea B Florida

This museum is located in the colonial house where Bartolomé Mitre – Argentina's first legitimate president elected under the constitution of 1853 – resided with his family. Two courtyards, salons, an office, a billiards room and Mitre's old bedroom are part of the sprawling complex. Mitre's term ran from 1862 to 1868, and he spent much of it leading the country's armies against Paraguay. After leaving office he founded the influential daily *La Nación,* still a porteño institution. Since part of the museum is in open air, you may find it closed during heavy rain.

MUSEO HISTÓRICO DR ARTURO JÁURETCHE Map p62

☎ 4331-1775; Sarmiento 364; admission free; 10am-6pm Mon-Fri; Línea B Florida, Línea B LN Alem

Spread out on different mezzanines, this museum makes sense of Argentina's chaotic economic history. It includes good, well-lit displays on the country's early

THE CENTER

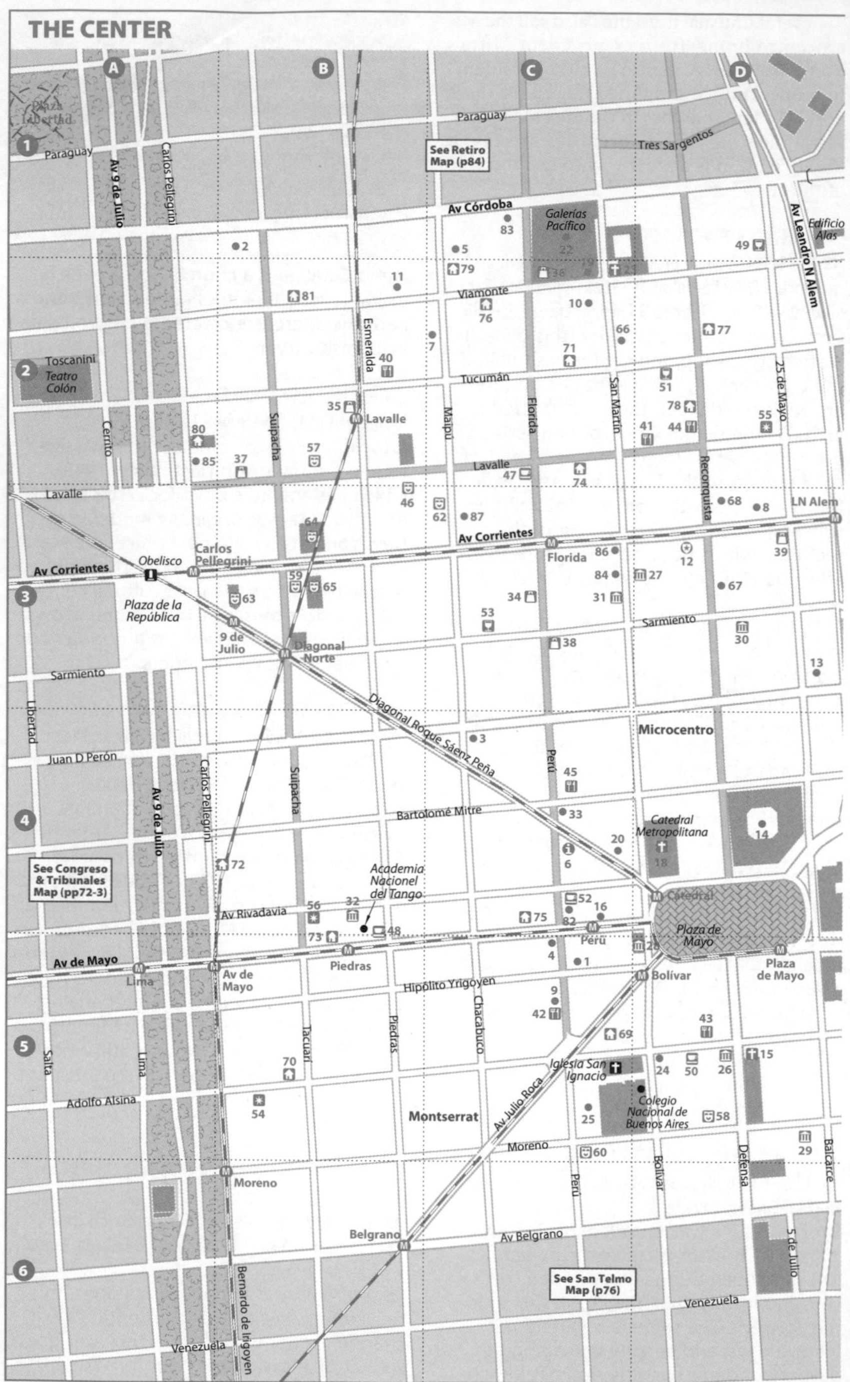
Plaza Libertad
Paraguay
Carlos Pellegrini
Av 9 de Julio
See Retiro Map (p84)
Tres Sargentos
Av Córdoba
Galerías Pacífico
Edificio Alas
Av Leandro N Alem
Viamonte
Esmeralda
Toscanini
Teatro Colón
Tucumán
Florida
San Martín
25 de Mayo
Cerrito
Suipacha
Maipú
Lavalle
Reconquista
LN Alem
Av Corrientes
Obelisco
Carlos Pellegrini
Plaza de la República
9 de Julio
Diagonal Norte
Sarmiento
Diagonal Roque Sáenz Peña
Libertad
Juan D Perón
Microcentro
Perú
Bartolomé Mitre
Catedral Metropolitana
See Congreso & Tribunales Map (pp72-3)
Academia Nacionel del Tango
Av Rivadavia
Catedral
Plaza de Mayo
Av de Mayo
Lima
Piedras
Hipólito Yrigoyen
Chacabuco
Bolívar
Salta
Tacuarí
Iglesia San Ignacio
Colegio Nacional de Buenos Aires
Adolfo Alsina
Montserrat
Av Julio Roca
Moreno
Defensa
Balcarce
Belgrano
Av Belgrano
See San Telmo Map (p76)
5 de Julio
Venezuela
Bernardo de Irigoyen

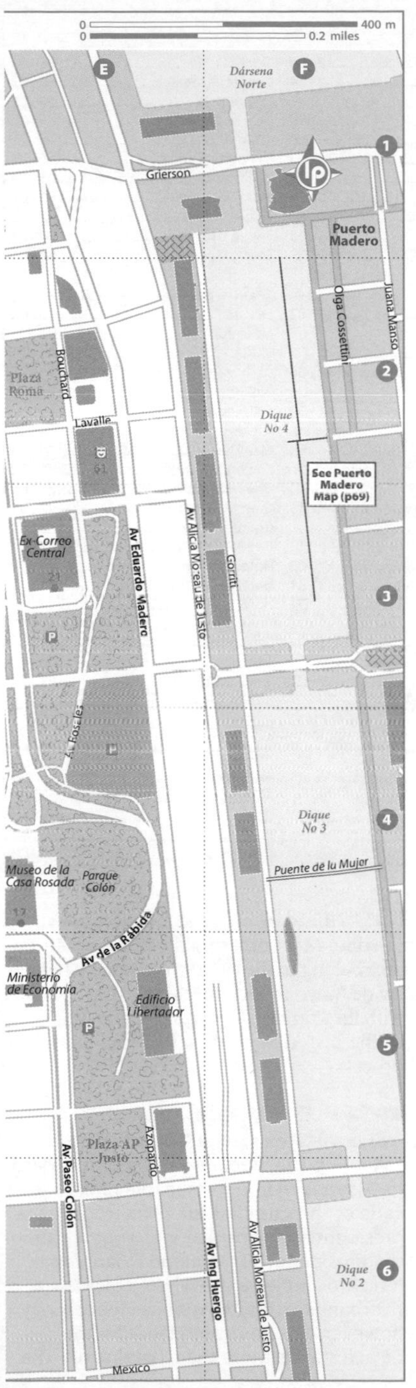

economic regions, the financing of political independence and the establishment of public credit. There are also interesting exhibits on paper money and counterfeiting, which have no doubt been scrupulously studied by BA's producers of phony banknotes. Examples of old currency, such as the million-peso bill from 1981, give an idea of the hyperinflation porteños have had to live with in the past. Handiest of all for the traveler: one display offers tips on distinguishing between real and fake paper money.

MUSEO DE LA POLICÍA FEDERAL

Map p62

☎ 4394-6857; Plaza San Martín 353, 7th fl; admission free; 🕑 2-6pm Mon-Thu; Ⓜ Línea B Florida

Located across from the Museo Mitre is this quirky police museum. On display are a whole slew of uniforms and medals, all proudly presented. There are also 'illegal activities' exhibits (cockfighting and gambling displays), drug paraphernalia (including a fake arm stuck with a needle!), plenty of guns and even a stuffed police dog. Avoid taking kids into the room way in back – grisly forensic photos, along with dummies of hacked up murder victims, are barf-bag specials. Note: you'll need to bring photo ID.

MUSEO MUNDIAL DEL TANGO Map p62

☎ 4345-6967; Av Rivadavia 830; admission AR$15; 🕑 2-8pm Mon-Fri; Ⓜ Línea D Piedras

Located below the Academia Nacional del Tango is this tango museum – for fans of the dance only. Just a couple of large rooms are filled with tango memorabilia, from old records and photos to historic literature and posters. Tango shoes are also featured, but the highlight has to be one of Carlos Gardel's famous fedora hats. Enter via Av Rivadavia.

PLAZA DE MAYO

Where Diagonal Roque Sáenz Peña meets Av Rivadavia you'll find the historic Plaza de Mayo, ground zero for many of the city's most vehement protests. When Juan de Garay refounded Buenos Aires in 1580, he laid out the large Plaza del Fuerte (Fortress Plaza) in accordance with Spanish law. Later called the Plaza del Mercado (Market Plaza), then the Plaza de la Victoria (after victories over British invaders in 1806 and 1807), the

THE CENTER

INFORMATION
Academia Buenos Aires 1 C5
Alianza Francesa 2 B1
Biblioteca Lincoln (see 7)
Centro Cultural Borges (see 19)
Expanish 3 C4
Farmacity 4 C5
Federal Express 5 C1
Florida Tourist Kiosk 6 C4
Instituto Cultural Argentino-Norteamericano 7 C2
Instituto Goethe 8 D3
MasterCard 9 C5
OCA 10 C2
Say Hueque 11 B2
Tourist Police 12 D3
University of Buenos Aires (UBA) 13 D3

SIGHTS (pp60-7)
Banco de la Nación 14 D4
Basílica de San Francisco 15 D5
Casa de la Cultura 16 C4
Casa Rosada 17 E4
Catedral Metropolitana 18 D4
Centro Cultural Borges 19 C2
Edificio Menéndez-Behety 20 C4
Ex-Correo Central 21 E3
Farmacia de la Estrella (see 26)
Galerías Pacífico 22 C1
Iglesia Santa Catalina 23 C2
Libreriá de Avila 24 D5
Manzana de las Luces 25 C5
Museo de la Ciudad 26 D5
Museo de la Policía Federal 27 D3
Museo del Cabildo 28 D5
Museo Etnográfico Juan B Ambrosetti 29 D5
Museo Histórico Dr Arturo Jáuretche 30 D3
Museo Mitre 31 C3
Museo Mundial del Tango 32 B4
Standard Bank 33 C4

SHOPPING (pp111-12)
Casa López (see 22)
El Ateneo 34 C3
El Coleccionista 35 B2
Montagne 36 C2
Musimundo 37 B2
Musimundo 38 C3
Winery 39 D3

EATING (pp125-6)
Brasserie Berry 40 B2
California Burrito Company (CBC) 41 D2
D'Oro 42 C5
Furai-Bo 43 D5
Pura Vida 44 D2
Tomo 1 (see 80)
Vía Flamina 45 C4

ENTERTAINMENT (p164)
Cartelera Espectáculos 46 B3

DRINKING (pp143-53)
Café Richmond 47 C2
Café Tortoni 48 B4
La Cigale 49 D1
La Puerto Rico 50 D5
Le Bar 51 D2
London City 52 C4
New Brighton 53 C3

NIGHTLIFE (pp155-61)
Alsina 54 B5
Bahrein 55 D2
Cocoliche 56 B4

THE ARTS (pp163-72)
Atlas Cinemas 57 B2
Café Tortoni (see 48)
Celcit 58 D5
Confitería Ideal 59 B3
El Querandí 60 C5
Escuela Argentina de Tango (see 19)
La Puerto Rico (see 50)
Luna Park 61 E2
Plaza Bohemia 62 C3
Teatro del Pueblo 63 B3
Teatro Gran Rex 64 B3
Teatro Opera 65 B3

SPORTS & ACTIVITIES (pp173-80)
Le Parc 66 C2
Megatlon 67 D3
YMCA 68 D3

SLEEPING (pp182-4)
562 Nogaró Buenos Aires 69 C5
Clan House 70 B5
Claridge Hotel 71 C2
Gran Hotel Argentino 72 B4
Gran Hotel Hispano 73 B5
Grand King Hotel 74 C2
Hotel Avenida 75 C4
Hotel Carsson 76 C2
Hotel Facón Grande 77 D2
Hotel Lafayette 78 D2
Hotel Maipú 79 C2
Panamericano Hotel & Resort 80 A2
V & S Hostel Club 81 B2

TRANSPORTATION (pp216-22)
Aerolíneas Argentinas 82 C4
Air Canada 83 C1
Air France (see 86)
Alitalia 84 C3
Continental 85 A2
KLM 86 C3
Omnilíneas 87 C3

plaza acquired its present and final name of Plaza de Mayo, after the date Buenos Aires declared independence from Spain, May 25, 1810.

Today, the grassy plaza attracts camera-toting tourists (as well as the occasional camera thief) along with activists. And, on Thursday at 3:30pm, the Madres de la Plaza de Mayo still march around the plaza in their unrelenting campaign for a full account of Dirty War atrocities during the military dictatorship between 1976 and 1983. For more history on the Dirty War in Argentina, see p27.

In the center of the plaza is the Pirámide de Mayo, a small obelisk built to mark the first anniversary of BA's independence from Spain. Looming on the north side of the plaza is the headquarters of Banco de la Nación (1939), the work of famed architect Alejandro Bustillo. Most other public buildings in this area belong to the late 19th century, when the Av de Mayo first connected the Casa Rosada with the Plaza del Congreso, obliterating most of the historic and dignified Cabildo in the process.

CASA ROSADA Map p62

Línea D Catedral, Línea A Plaza de Mayo

Taking up the whole east side of the Plaza de Mayo is the unmistakeable pink facade of the Casa Rosada (Pink House), the presidential palace that was begun during the presidency of Domingo F Sarmiento. It now occupies a site where colonial riverbank fortifications once stood; today, however, after repeated landfills, the palace stands more than 1km inland. The

KEEPING YOUR MAYOS & PEÑAS STRAIGHT

Some first-time (or maybe second-time) visitors may get confused with certain similar-sounding street and attraction names. Keep them straight:

25 de Mayo Street that goes north-south from Retiro to Plaza de Mayo (Mayo is Spanish for the month of May).

Av de Mayo Large avenue that goes east-west from Plaza del Congreso to Plaza de Mayo.

Diagonal Roque Sáenz Peña Diagonal street that stretches from Plaza de Mayo to the Obelisco.

Luis Sáenz Peña Street that goes from Plaza del Congreso through Constitución.

Plaza de Mayo BA's most important plaza.

Rodriguez Peña Street that goes from Recoleta to Plaza del Congreso.

offices of 'La Presidenta' Cristina Kirchner are here, but the presidential residence is in the calm suburbs of Olivos, north of the center.

The side of the palace that faces Plaza de Mayo is actually the back of the building. It's from these balconies that Juan and Eva Perón, General Leopoldo Galtieri, Raúl Alfonsín and other politicians have preached to throngs of impassioned Argentines when they felt it necessary to demonstrate public support. Madonna also crooned from here for her movie *Evita*.

The salmon-pink color of the Casa Rosada palace, which positively glows at sunset, could have come from President Sarmiento's attempt at making peace during his 1868–74 term (by blending the red of the Federalists with the white of the Unitarists). Another theory, however, is that the color comes from painting the palace with bovine blood, which was a common practice back in the late 19th century.

Off-limits during the military dictatorship of 1976–83, the Casa Rosada is now reasonably accessible to the public. Free half-hour tours (☎ 4344-3600; Saturday and Sunday only, continuously from 10am-6pm) are given; bring photo ID.

Underneath the Casa Rosada, excavations have unearthed remains of the Fuerte Viejo, a ruin dating from the 18th century. These were previously accessible via entry to the Museo de la Casa Rosada, which has been closed for several years but may be open sometime in the future.

In 1955 naval aircraft strafed the Casa Rosada and other nearby buildings during the Revolución Libertadora, which toppled Juan Perón's regime. On the north side of the appropriately bureaucratic Ministerio de Economía, an inconspicuous plaque commemorates the attacks (look for the bullet holes to the left of the doors). The inscription translates as, 'The scars on this marble were the harvest of confrontation and intolerance. Their imprint on our memory will help the nation achieve a future of greatness.'

Towering above the Casa Rosada, just south of Parque Colón on Av Colón, is the army headquarters at the Edificio Libertador, the real locus of Argentine political power for many decades. It was built by military engineers inspired by the beaux arts Correo Central. A twin building planned for the navy never got off the ground.

CATEDRAL METROPOLITANA Map p62

☎ 4331 2845; www.catedralbuenosaires.org.ar; San Martín 27; 8am-7pm Mon-Fri, 9am-7:30pm Sat & Sun; Línea D Catedral, Línea E Bolívar, Línea A Plaza de Mayo

This solemn cathedral was built on the site of the original colonial church and not finished until 1827. It's a significant religious and architectural landmark, and carved above its triangular facade and neoclassical columns are bas-reliefs of Jacob and Joseph. The spacious interior is equally impressive, with baroque details and an elegant rococo altar.

More importantly, however, the cathedral is a national historical site that contains the tomb of General José de San Martín, Argentina's most revered hero. In the chaos following independence, San Martín chose exile in France, never returning alive to Argentina (although in 1829 a boat on which he traveled sighted Buenos Aires on its way to Montevideo). Outside the cathedral you'll see a flame keeping his spirit alive.

Tours of the church and crypt are given at 3:30pm Monday to Saturday; tours of just the crypt are at 11:45am Monday to Friday. All tours are conducted in Spanish. Occasional free choir concerts are also on the docket.

MUSEO DEL CABILDO Map p62

☎ 4342-5729; Bolívar 65; admission AR$4; 10:30am-5pm Wed-Fri, 11:30am-6pm Sat & Sun; Línea D Catedral, Línea E Bolívar, Línea A Plaza de Mayo

Modern construction – including the building of Av de Mayo – has twice truncated the mid-18th-century Cabildo (town council; 1765), but still standing is a representative sample of the colonnade that once spanned Plaza de Mayo. The two-storey building – which was a jail from 1821 to 1878 – features among its collection a few mementos of the early 19th-century British invasions, some modern paintings in colonial and early independence-era styles and temporary exhibits. The interior patio is home to a small crafts fair on Thursdays and Fridays, and the café is a great place to relax.

MONTSERRAT

Full of history and notable old buildings, Montserrat is BA's oldest neighborhood, and its most interesting sections are squeezed between the Plaza de Mayo area and San Telmo. Once home to BA's most distinguished families, Montserrat was also the political, economic and cultural center of the city, symbolized by the landmark Manzana de las Lucas (p66). Here you'll find a whole block's worth of city history; take a tour to peek at the tunnels underneath.

Unsurprisingly, Montserrat also claims the city's oldest churches, including the Iglesia San Ignacio (in the Manzana de las Luces) and the Basílica de San Francisco, established by the Franciscan order in 1754. Booklovers should check out the Librería de Avila (Map p62; cnr Alsina & Bolívar). Established in 1785, it's BA's oldest bookstore.

Interesting museums in the area include the Museo de la Cuidad, which harbors a collection of some of the city's oldest relics, and the Museo Etnográfico Juan B Ambrosetti, an anthropological museum that's worth a look through.

MANZANA DE LAS LUCES Map p62

☎ 4342-3964; www.manzanadelasluces.org; Perú 272; Línea E Bolívar

In colonial times, the Manzana de las Luces (Block of Enlightenment) was Buenos Aires' most important center of culture and learning. Even today the site still symbolizes high culture in the capital – the Universidad de Buenos Aires currently administers a prestigious college preparatory school here.

The first people to occupy the Manzana de las Luces were the Jesuits, who built several structures including the Procuraduría (1730; administrative headquarters) – part of which still survives today. (Unfortunately for the Jesuits, they were eventually expelled from the premises – and Argentina – in 1767 by the Spanish, who felt politically threatened by them.) Along with housing offices, these buildings hosted converted indigenous people from the provinces. Later, during the 19th century they were also home to various museums, legislative offices, schools and universities.

On the north side of the block are two of the five original buildings that still remain. Within these buildings are Jesuit defensive tunnels discovered in 1912, connecting the block to strategic spots around the city; today these tunnels can be visited on guided tours.

The city's oldest church, the Iglesia San Ignacio (1734), is also located here, originally built in adobe in 1661 and rebuilt or remodelled several times after. Today there remains only a single original cloister; it shares a wall with the Colegio Nacional de Buenos Aires (1863), a prep school where generations of the Argentine elite still send their children to receive secondary schooling.

Tours (AR$7; 3pm Mon-Fri; 4:30pm & 6pm Sat & Sun) in Spanish are available. Classes, workshops, theater and the Mercado de las Luces (a gift market) also take place on the premises.

MUSEO DE LA CIUDAD Map p62

☎ 4343-2123; Defensa 219; admission AR$1, Mon & Wed free; 11am-7pm Mon-Fri, 10am-8pm Sat & Sun; Línea E Bolívar, Línea A Plaza de Mayo

Wander among the permanent and temporary exhibitions on porteño life and history, including historical photographs, old furniture and toys, and a research library. Salvaged doors and ancient hardware are also on display next door at the museum's annex. Nearby, at the corner of Alsina and Defensa, is the Farmacia de la Estrella (1835), a functioning homeopathic pharmacy with gorgeous woodwork and elaborate late-19th-century ceiling murals depicting health-oriented themes.

MUSEO ETNOGRÁFICO JUAN B AMBROSETTI Map p62

☎ 4331-7788; www.museoetnografico.filo.uba.ar; Moreno 350; donation AR$3; 🕒 1-7pm Tue-Fri, 3-7pm Sat & Sun; Ⓢ Línea A Plaza de Mayo

This small but attractive anthropological museum was created by Juan B Ambrosetti not only as an institute for research and university training, but as an educational center for the public. On display are archaeological and anthropological collections from the Andean Northwest and Patagonia. Beautiful indigenous artifacts are also featured, while an African and Asian room showcases some priceless pieces.

PUERTO MADERO

Eating p126; Sleeping p184

Amble around Buenos Aires' youngest and least conventional barrio, Puerto Madero, located just east of the center and San Telmo. Here you'll find a long line of old brick warehouses that have been converted into some of the city's trendiest lofts, offices, hotels and restaurants. Four prominent *diques* (dikes) make this area reminiscent of London's docklands – indeed Puerto Madero's original blueprints drew on London's Millwall and Royal Albert Docks for inspiration. The neighborhood is still a work in progress, with millions of US dollars still being poured into high-rise construction projects that dominate the skyline. But most of the work has been done already; cobbled promenades make walking a pleasure for pedestrians, and there are plenty of upscale restaurants and cafés in which to rest. Puerto Madero is worth some exploration, and most of the time there won't be a vehicle in sight.

Things haven't always been neat and trendy here, however. The city's waterfront was an object of controversy in the mid-19th century, when competing commercial interests began to fight over the location of a modernized port for Argentina's burgeoning international commerce. Two ideas came to light. One was to widen and deepen the channel of the Riachuelo to port facilities at La Boca, which indeed happened as planned. The other was proposed by Eduardo Madero, a wealthy exporter with strong political ties and solid financial backing. Madero proposed transforming the city's mudflats into a series of modern basins and harbors consistent with the aspirations and ambitions of a cosmopolitan elite. This also occurred, but not quite as he had planned.

By the time of its final completion in 1898 (four years after Madero's death), Puerto Madero had exceeded its budget and Madero himself had come under scrutiny. Suspicions arose from Madero's attempts to buy up all the landfill in the area and from his links to politicians who had acquired nearby lands likely to increase in value. And the practical side of the scheme didn't go so well either. By 1910 the amount of cargo was already too great for the new port, and poor access to the rail terminus at Plaza Once made things even worse. New facilities in a rejuvenated La Boca partly assuaged these problems, but congressional actions failed to solve the major issues until the 1926 completion of Retiro's Puerto Nuevo.

Today, Puerto Madero has finally found its feet. On the east side of the dikes, five-star hotels such as the Hilton and the Philippe Starck–designed Faena Hotel + Universe (p184) have planted roots and invested millions. High-rise condos and apartment buildings are everywhere, and the cutting-edge Colección de Arte Amalia Lacroze de Fortabat (aka Museo Fortabat) – a museum designed by Rafael Viñoly and housing the collection of rich Argentine socialite Amalia Fortabat – is a shiny landmark.

Other unique sights in Puerto Madero include the distinctive Puente de la Mujer, which spans Dique 3 and is a beautifully modern bridge resembling a sharp fishhook or even a harp – but is supposed to represent a couple dancing the tango. Designed by Spaniard Santiago Calatrava and mostly built in Spain, this 160m-long pedestrian span cost AR$6 million and rotates 90° to allow water traffic to pass (when it's functioning, that is). There's also an unusual museum in the form of the Museo Fragata Sarmiento (p70), a former naval ship that mostly served as a training ground for Argentina's navy.

On the easternmost edge of Puerto Madero – with the muddy waters of the Río de la Plata lapping at its sides – is the Reserva Ecológica Costanera Sur (p70), a large marshy space full of reedy lagoons, wildlife and peaceful dirt paths. Come here when the air, noise and concrete of downtown Buenos Aires become too much to bear. The reserve is a sharp contrast to the upscale lofts, restaurants and hotels nearby, and thankfully it's available to everyone for no cost at all.

COLECCIÓN DE ARTE AMALIA LACROZE DE FORTABAT Map p69

☎ 4310-6600; www.coleccionfortabat.org.ar; Olga Cossettini 141; admission AR$15; noon-9pm Tue-Sun; bus 4

Rivaling Palermo's Malba for cutting-edge looks is this stunning art museum, prominently located at the northern end of Puerto Madero. It shows off the collection of billionairess and philanthropist Amalia Lacroze de Fortabat, Argentina's wealthiest woman. She is the major stockholder of Argentina's largest cement company.

The building was designed by renowned Uruguayan architect Rafael Viñoly, and is a creation of steel, glass and concrete – the last

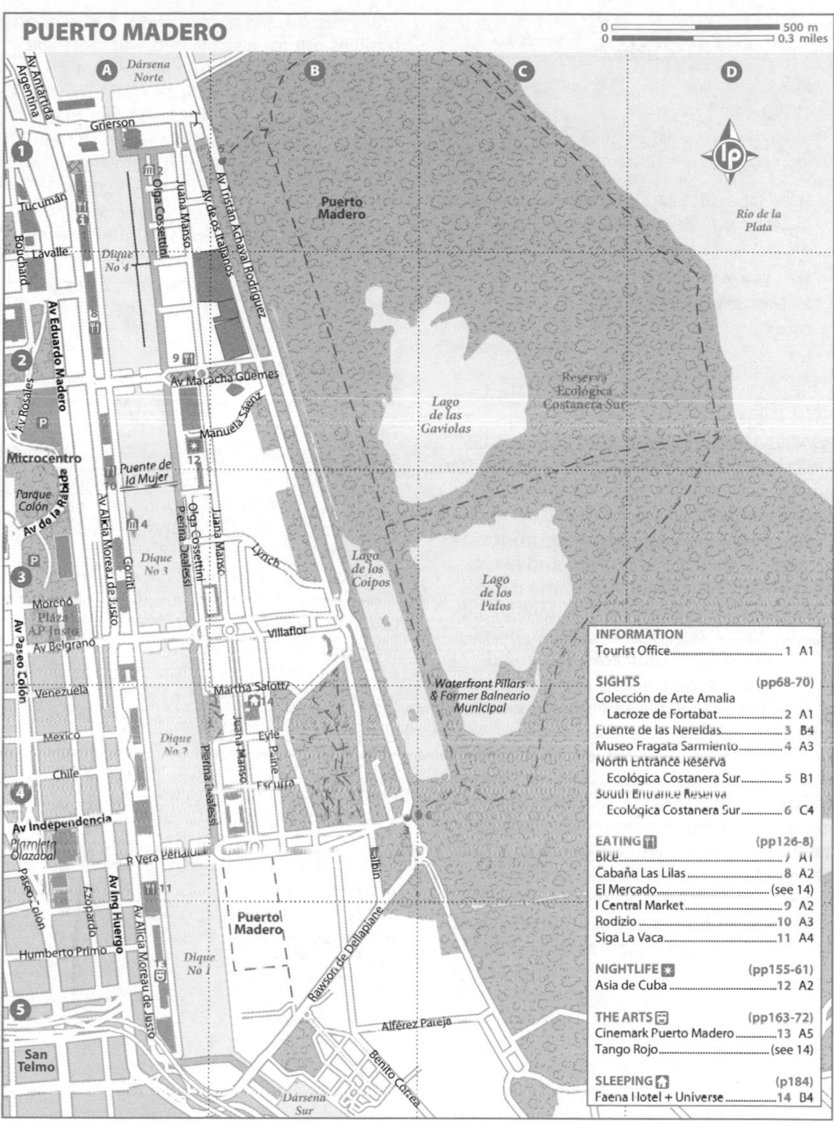

a most appropriate material considering its patroness. Finished in 2008, it encompasses over 6000 square meters, with several airy floors showcasing works by famous Argentine and international artists. There are galleries devoted to Antonio Berni and Raúl Soldi (both famous Argentine painters) and works by international stars like Dali, Klimt, Rodin and Chagall; look for Warhol's colorful take on Fortabat herself in the family portrait gallery. The most interesting thing about the museum itself, however, might be the movable aluminum panels above the glassy ceiling. They tilt open and close, keeping sun off the delicate artworks. Lacroze requested this feature so that she could see her collection and the stars at the same time.

Spanish tours given Tuesday to Sunday at 3pm and 5pm; call ahead for group tours in English.

TRANSPORTATION: PUERTO MADERO

Bus The buses 64, 126, 152 run along LN Alem/ Paseo Colón, which get you within three blocks of Puerto Madero.

Subte The closest Subte stops are LN Alem (Línea B) and the end lines of Líneas A, D and E, which terminate at Plaza de Mayo.

Tram BA's short light-rail system parallels Puerto Madero's docks, and may someday extend to La Boca.

RESERVA ECOLÓGICA COSTANERA SUR Map p69

☎ 4893-1588; Av Tristán Achával Rodríguez 1550; 8am-7pm Tue-Sun Nov-Mar, 8am-6pm Tue-Sun Apr-Oct; 4

During the military Proceso of 1976–83, access to the Buenos Aires waterfront was limited, as the area was diked and filled with sediments dredged from the Río de la Plata. While plans for a new satellite city across from the port stalled, trees, grasses, birds and rodents took advantage and colonized this low-lying, 350-hectare area that mimics the ecology of the Delta del Paraná.

In 1986 the area was declared an ecological reserve. Mysterious arson fires, thought to have been started by those with financial interests in the prime real estate, have occasionally been set. But permanent scars haven't remained – this beautifully lush marshy land survives hardily, and the reserve has become a popular site for outings and hikes. On sunny weekends you'll generally see dozens of picnickers, cyclists and families out for a stroll. Bird-watchers will adore the 250-plus bird species that pause to rest here, and a few lucky folks might spot a river turtle or nutria (semi-aquatic rodent). Further in at the eastern shoreline of the reserve you can get a close-up view of the Río de la Plata's muddy waters.

Tours are available on weekends at 10.30am or 3.30pm; Friday night full moon tours are also available (call). On the weekends and holidays you can rent bikes just outside either the northern or southern entrance.

MUSEO FRAGATA SARMIENTO Map p69

☎ 4334-9386; Dique 3; admission AR$2; 10am-7pm; 64, 152

Over 23,000 Argentine naval cadets and officers have trained aboard this 85m sailing vessel, which traveled around the world 37 times between 1899 and 1938. Built in Birkenhead, England, in 1897 at a cost of £125,000, this impeccably maintained ship never participated in combat. On board are detailed records of its lengthy voyages, a gallery of its commanding officers, plenty of nautical items including old uniforms, and even the stuffed remains of Lampazo (the ship's pet dog), serenely posed. Peek into the ship's holds, galley and engine room and note the hooks where sleeping hammocks were strung up.

US president Theodore Roosevelt (look for his photo) was a distinguished guest on board, but perhaps the greatest test of the ship's seaworthiness was the visit of Roosevelt's successor, William Howard Taft, who weighed more than 140kg and, no doubt, came to dine on board.

CONGRESO & TRIBUNALES

Drinking p152; Eating p128; Shopping p112; Sleeping p184

Congreso is an interesting neighborhood mix of old-time cinemas, theaters and bustling commerce tinged with a hard-core political flavor. The buildings still hold a European aura, but there's more grittiness here than in the center. It's more local-city feel and faded-glory atmosphere, and lacks the business-suit crowds. However, this doesn't prevent Congreso from being a great place to wander around and explore.

Separating Congreso from the center is Av 9 de Julio, 'the widest street in the world!' as proud porteños love to boast. This may be true, as it's 16 lanes at its widest; nearby side streets Cerrito and Pellegrini make it look even broader. Fortunately, traffic islands provide raised breaks for the thousands of pedestrians who cross this monstrosity every day, but it's still an intimidating walk (and can't be done in one green light without breaking into a run – trust us). At Av 9 de Julio and Corrientes lies the city's famous Obelisco, which soars 67m above the oval Plaza de la República. Dedicated in 1936, on the 400th anniversary of the first Spanish settlement on the Río de la Plata, the stately Obelisco symbolizes Buenos Aires much as the Eiffel Tower represents Paris or the Washington Monument does Washington, DC. Following major soccer victories, boisterous fans circle this landmark in jubilant, honking celebration; it's also often used as the zero point for measuring distances from the city center.

Just a couple of blocks to the northwest of the Obelisco is Plaza Lavalle and the austere neoclassical Escuela Presidente Roca (1902). Across the way lies the French-style Palacio de Justicia (1904) and its Tribunales (federal courts). The landmark Teatro Colón also stands nearby and adds its own elegance to the area. At the northeast end of Plaza Lavalle, Jewish symbols adorn the facade of the Templo de la Congregación Israelita, Argentina's largest synagogue. Concrete sidewalk planters, constructed after recent attacks against Jewish targets, discourage potential car bombs. The Museo Judío Dr Salvador Kibrick (Map p72; ☎ 4123-0832; Libertad 769; admission AR$30, bring photo ID; 3-5:30pm Tue & Thu) is in the synagogue and contains items and exhibits related to Argentine Jewish history.

Six blocks west of Plaza Lavalle is the Palacio de las Aguas Corrientes, a wonderful Scandinavian-designed building covered in English bricks and enameled tiles. If you like unusual buildings it's worth a look; plan your visit in time to see the bizarre little museum inside (p74). Finally, head around seven blocks south of Plaza Lavalle to the Palacio del Congreso, with its plaza and obligatory monument. This site is another locus for the nation's *piqueteros* (picketers) and their grievances.

Congreso lies west of Av 9 de Julio and is a short walk from Plaza de Mayo, in the center. Av Corrientes is a major thoroughfare and the city's old theater district. Av de Mayo is also a major street, and connects two significant places – Plaza del Congreso and Plaza de Mayo. All north-south street names change at Av Rivadavia.

TEATRO COLÓN Map p72

☎ 4378-7100; www.teatrocolon.org.ar; Libertad 621; Línea D Tribunales

One of Buenos Aires' biggest landmarks and major sources of pride is the gorgeous and imposing seven-story Teatro Colón, a world-class facility for opera, ballet and classical music. The Colón is the city's main performing-arts venue and the only facility of its kind in the country. It was the southern hemisphere's largest theater until the Sydney Opera House was built in 1973. It occupies an entire city block, seats 2500 spectators and provides standing room for another 500. Opening night was in 1908 with a presentation of Verdi's *Aïda,* and visitors have been wowed ever since. Teatro Colón has hosted some very prominent figures, such as Enrico Caruso, Plácido Domingo, Luciano Pavarotti and Arturo Toscanini. There are ballet and opera productions, and occasional free concerts are given. Presidential command performances sometimes occur on the winter patriotic holidays of May 25 and July 9.

Renovations on the Colón halted worthwhile behind-the-scenes workshop tours (offered in several languages), but hopefully they'll start up again in 2011. Held daily, these behind-the-scenes workshop tours are offered every 15 minutes from 9am-3.45pm and last an hour (US$15). They're given in English or Spanish. If you want a tour in Portuguese or French, call ☎ 4378-7128 two days in advance to

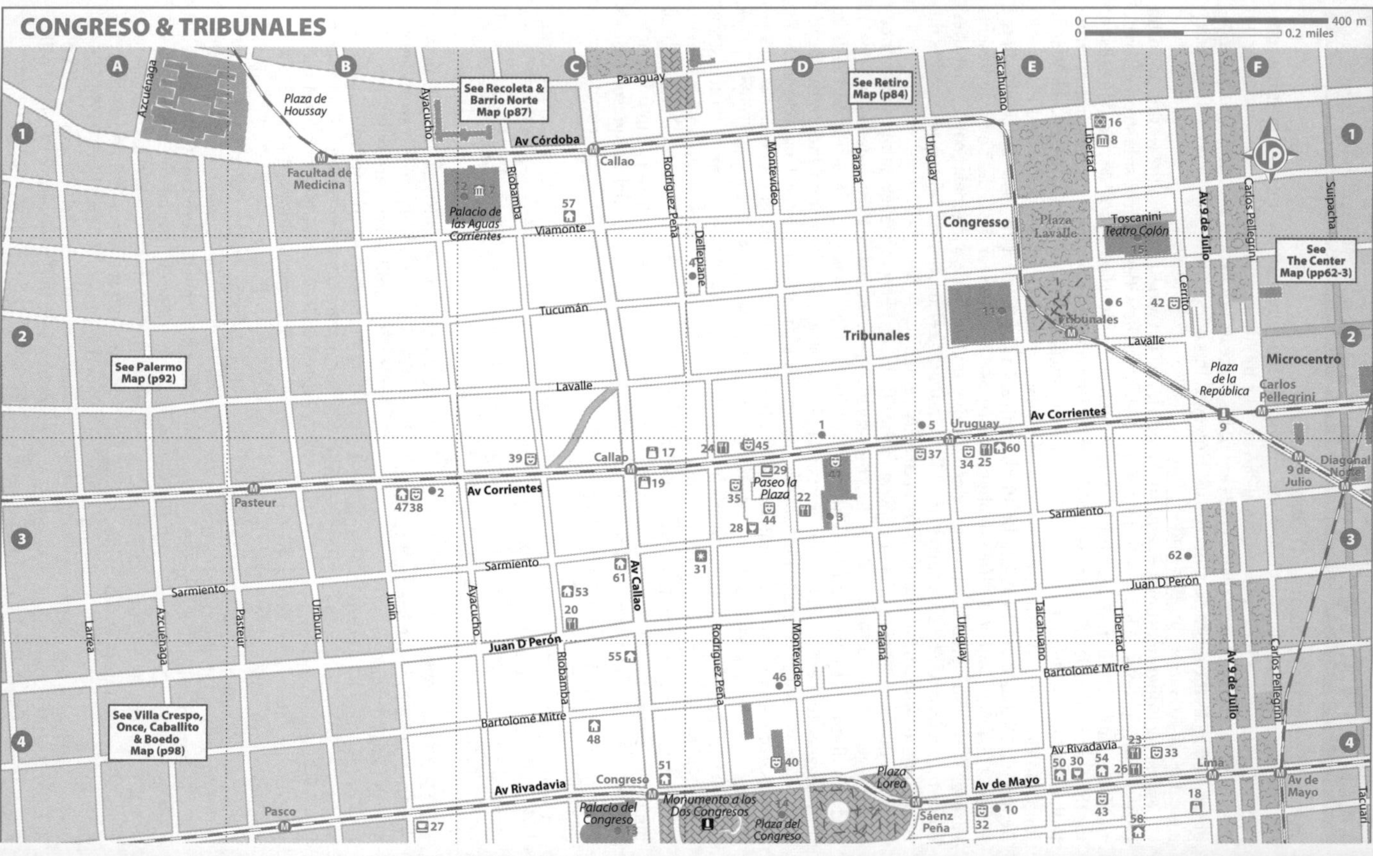
CONGRESO & TRIBUNALES
0 400 m
0 0.2 miles
See Recoleta & Barrio Norte Map (p87)
See Retiro Map (p84)
See The Center Map (pp62-3)
See Palermo Map (p92)
See Villa Crespo, Once, Caballito & Boedo Map (p98)
Plaza de Houssay
Facultad de Medicina
Palacio de las Aguas Corrientes
Congresso
Tribunales
Microcentro
Plaza Lavalle
Teatro Colón
Plaza de la República
Paseo la Plaza
Plaza Lorea
Monumento a los Dos Congresos
Plaza del Congreso
Palacio del Congreso
Av Córdoba
Av Corrientes
Av Callao
Av 9 de Julio
Av Rivadavia
Av de Mayo
Juan D Perón
Azcuénaga
Ayacucho
Paraguay
Talcahuano
Callao
Rodríguez Peña
Montevideo
Paraná
Uruguay
Libertad
Carlos Pellegrini
Suipacha
Riobamba
Viamonte
Dellepiane
Toscanini
Cerrito
Tucumán
Lavalle
Sarmiento
Bartolomé Mitre
Larrea
Pasteur
Uriburu
Junín
Pasco
Congreso
Sáenz Peña
Lima
Tacuarí
Diagonal Norte
9 de Julio

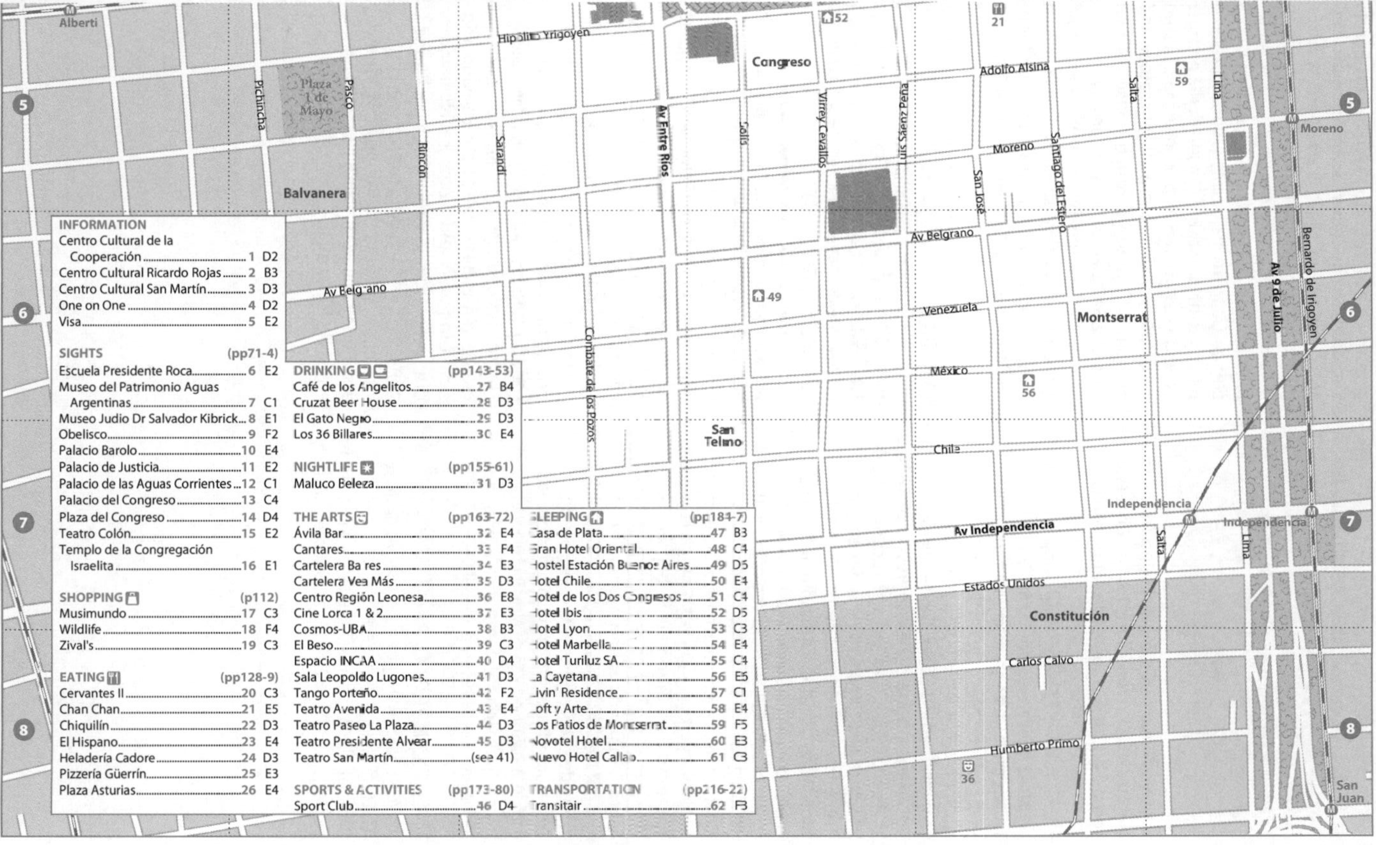
INFORMATION
Centro Cultural de la Cooperación 1 D2
Centro Cultural Ricardo Rojas 2 B3
Centro Cultural San Martín 3 D3
One on One 4 D2
Visa 5 E2
SIGHTS (pp71-4)
Escuela Presidente Roca 6 E2
Museo del Patrimonio Aguas Argentinas 7 C1
Museo Judio Dr Salvador Kibrick 8 E1
Obelisco 9 F2
Palacio Barolo 10 E4
Palacio de Justicia 11 E2
Palacio de las Aguas Corrientes 12 C1
Palacio del Congreso 13 C4
Plaza del Congreso 14 D4
Teatro Colón 15 E2
Templo de la Congregación Israelita 16 E1
SHOPPING (p112)
Musimundo 17 C3
Wildlife 18 F4
Zival's 19 C3
EATING (pp128-9)
Cervantes II 20 C3
Chan Chan 21 E5
Chiquilín 22 D3
El Hispano 23 E4
Heladería Cadore 24 D3
Pizzería Güerrín 25 E3
Plaza Asturias 26 E4
DRINKING (pp143-53)
Café de los Angelitos 27 B4
Cruzat Beer House 28 D3
El Gato Negro 29 D3
Los 36 Billares 30 E4
NIGHTLIFE (pp155-61)
Maluco Beleza 31 D3
THE ARTS (pp163-72)
Ávila Bar 32 E4
Cantares 33 F4
Cartelera Baires 34 E3
Cartelera Vea Más 35 D3
Centro Región Leonesa 36 E8
Cine Lorca 1 & 2 37 E3
Cosmos-UBA 38 B3
El Beso 39 C3
Espacio INCAA 40 D4
Sala Leopoldo Lugones 41 D3
Tango Porteño 42 F2
Teatro Avenida 43 E4
Teatro Paseo La Plaza 44 D3
Teatro Presidente Alvear 45 D3
Teatro San Martín (see 41)
SPORTS & ACTIVITIES (pp173-80)
Sport Club 46 D4
SLEEPING (pp184-7)
Casa de Plata 47 B3
Gran Hotel Oriental 48 C4
Hostel Estación Buenos Aires 49 D5
Hotel Chile 50 E4
Hotel de los Dos Congresos 51 C4
Hotel Ibis 52 D5
Hotel Lyon 53 C3
Hotel Marbella 54 E4
Hotel Turiluz SA 55 C4
La Cayetana 56 E5
Livin' Residence 57 C1
Loft y Arte 58 E4
Los Patios de Monserrat 59 F5
Novotel Hotel 60 E3
Nuevo Hotel Callao 61 C3
TRANSPORTATION (pp216-22)
Transitair 62 F3
Alberti
Hipólito Yrigoyen
Congreso
Adolfo Alsina
Salta
Lima
Moreno
Plaza 1 de Mayo
Pichincha
Pasco
Rincón
Sarandí
Av Entre Ríos
Solís
Virrey Cevallos
Luis Sáenz Peña
San José
Santiago del Estero
Balvanera
Av Belgrano
Av 9 de Julio
Bernardo de Irigoyen
Venezuela
Montserrat
Combate de los Pozos
México
San Telmo
Chile
Independencia
Av Independencia
Estados Unidos
Constitución
Carlos Calvo
Humberto Primo
San Juan

TRANSPORTATION: CONGRESO & TRIBUNALES

Bus Take bus 6 from Retiro, bus 64 from the Microcentro.

Subte Líneas A and B from the Microcentro.

reserve. Expect to see everything from the basement workshops to the rehearsal rooms, and the stage and seating areas.

PLAZA DEL CONGRESO Map p72

Línea A Congreso, Sáenz Peña

Down in the Congreso area, at the west end of Av de Mayo, is the Plaza del Congreso, often full of cooing pigeons and the families feeding them. The Monumento a los Dos Congresos honors the congresses of 1810 in Buenos Aires and 1816 in Tucumán, both of which led to Argentine independence. The enormous granite steps symbolize the high Andes, and the fountain at its base represents the Atlantic Ocean.

Across Av Callao from the plaza is the colossal green-domed Palacio del Congreso. Costing more than twice its projected budget, the Congreso set a precedent for contemporary Argentine public works projects. Modeled on the Capitol in Washington, DC, and topped by an 85m dome, the palace was completed in 1906.

Inside the Congreso, the Senado offers free guided tours in English and Spanish (☎ 4010-3000, ext 2410; Mon, Tue, Thu & Fri at 11am & 4pm). Go to the entrance at Hipólito Yrigoyen 1849; bring photo ID.

PALACIO BAROLO Map p72

☎ 4381-1885; www.pbarolo.com.ar; Av de Mayo 1370; Línea A Sáenz Peña

One of the Congreso area's most striking buildings is this 22-story concrete edifice, commissioned by cotton tycoon Luis Barolo and designed by Italian architect Mario Palanti. Finished in 1923, it was Buenos Aires' highest skyscraper (until construction of Edificio Kavanagh, in Retiro; see p82). The building's unique design was inspired by Dante's *Divine Comedy;* its height (100 meters) is a reference to each *canto* (or song), the number of its floors to verses per song (ie 22) and its divided structure to hell, purgatory and heaven. At the top is a lighthouse with an amazing 360-degree view of the city.

You can see this building via 45-minute guided tours in English and Spanish, which are given on the hour from 4pm to 7pm Monday to Thursday (AR$40). Special tours, in which the lighthouse is turned on, take place Thursdays at 8pm and include a glass of wine (AR$70).

PALACIO DE LAS AGUAS CORRIENTES Map p72

cnr Avs Córdoba & Riobamba; Línea D Facultad de Medicina, Callao

Swedish engineer Karl Nyströmer and Norwegian architect Olaf Boye helped create this gorgeous and eclectic waterworks building. Popularly known as Obras Sanitarias, it dates from 1894 and occupies an entire city block. Topped by French-style mansard roofs, the building's facade consists of 170,000 glazed tiles and 130,000 enameled bricks from England.

On the building's 2nd floor is the small but quirky Museo del Patrimonio Aguas Argentinas (☎ 6319-1104; admission free; 9am-1pm Mon-Fri). The collection of pretty tiles, faucets, handles, ceramic pipe joints from England and even old toilets and bidets is well lit and displayed. Guided visits offer a backstage glimpse of the building's inner workings and huge water tanks (Monday, Wednesday and Friday at 11am). Bring photo ID and enter via Riobamba.

SAN TELMO

Drinking p146; Eating p129; Shopping p112; Sleeping p187

San Telmo is a lovely neighborhood full of cobbled streets, colonial mansions and rich history. Only a quick walk south of Plaza de Mayo, it's like stepping a hundred years into the past. As a hugely popular tourist destination, however, it's been gentrifying fast. Dozens of guesthouses have opened their doors, fancy boutiques continue to spring up and foreigner-fueled demand has skyrocketed real-estate prices. San Telmo locals are shuddering to think their beloved barrio might become the next Palermo Viejo (p90).

Historically, San Telmo is famous for the violent street fighting that took place when British troops, at war with Spain, invaded the city in 1806. They occupied it until the following year, when covert porteño resistance became open counterattack. British forces advanced up narrow Defensa, but the impromptu militia drove the British back to their ships. Victory gave porteños confidence in their ability to stand apart from Spain, even though the city's independence had to wait another three years.

After this San Telmo became a fashionable, classy neighborhood, but in the late 19th century a yellow-fever epidemic hit and drove the rich into higher ground, west and north of the present-day Microcentro. As European immigrants began to pour into the city, many older mansions in San Telmo became *conventillos* (tenements) to house poor families. One such *conventillo* was the Pasaje de la Defensa (Map p76; Defensa 1179). Originally built for the Ezeiza family in 1880, it later housed 32 families. These days, it's a charmingly worn building with antique shops clustered around atmospheric leafy patios. For another walk into the past visit impressive El Zanjón de Granados (p77).

The heart of San Telmo is Plaza Dorrego (cnr of Defensa & Humberto Primo), which hosts its extremely popular Sunday antiques market, the Feria de San Pedro Telmo (p118). Streets are closed to traffic, and the plaza itself is filled with dozens of booths selling antiques and old collectibles. Street performers from metallic human statues to drumming bands to professional tango dancers entertain the crowds. Calle Defensa is closed to traffic from Av Belgrano all the way to Parque Lezama, which has its own weekend crafts fair/flea market – though it's much less crowded than Plaza Dorrego's. It's the supposed location of the first founding of Buenos Aires, way back in 1536. Across Av Brasil from the park is the striking late-19th-century Russian Orthodox church Iglesia Ortodoxa Rusa, the work of architect Alejandro Christopherson and built from materials shipped over from St Petersburg. Also nearby is the Museo Histórico Nacional (p77), the city's National History Museum.

To the north, on the more industrial Av Paseo Colón, the oval Plazoleta Olazábal features Rogelio Yrurtia's masterful sculpture *Canto al Trabajo* (moved here from its original site on Plaza Dorrego). Across the *plazoleta*, the neoclassical and seriously ugly Facultad de Ingeniería of the Universidad de Buenos Aires (originally built for the Fundación Eva Perón) is an oddball landmark once described by Gerald Durrell as 'a cross between the Parthenon and the Reichstag.' One block southwest, a different sort of architectural oddity is the brick Iglesia Dinamarquesa (Map p76; Carlos Calvo 257), a neo-Gothic Lutheran church dating from 1930 and designed using blueprints from Danish architects Rönnow and Bisgaard. Two blocks to the west, the Mercado San Telmo (Map p76; 8am-8pm) is an antique market also harboring a mishmash of clothes, housewares and cheap eateries; it's been running since 1897. The main section is still a meat and vegetable market, and the whole thing takes up the interior of a city block, though you wouldn't be able to tell just by looking at the modest sidewalk entrances. Note the amazing original ceiling.

The neocolonial and baroque Iglesia Nuestra Señora de Belén (Map p76; Humberto Primo 340) was a Jesuit school until 1767, when the Bethlemite order took it over. Jorge Luis Borges fans should stroll past the Centro Nacional de la Música (Map p76; México 564), which used to be the Biblioteca Nacional – where Borges worked as director for many years.

San Telmo is south of the center – enough to make it officially blue-collar in Buenos Aires. The two main veins in this barrio are Balcarce and Defensa; they're where you'll find most things of interest to tourists. To the east of Balcarce the streets become industrial and deserted at night, and, along with the more southern edges toward La Boca, should probably be avoided. During the day they're fine, however, and way over to the east is one end of Puerto Madero – an upscale area that's easily walkable from San Telmo.

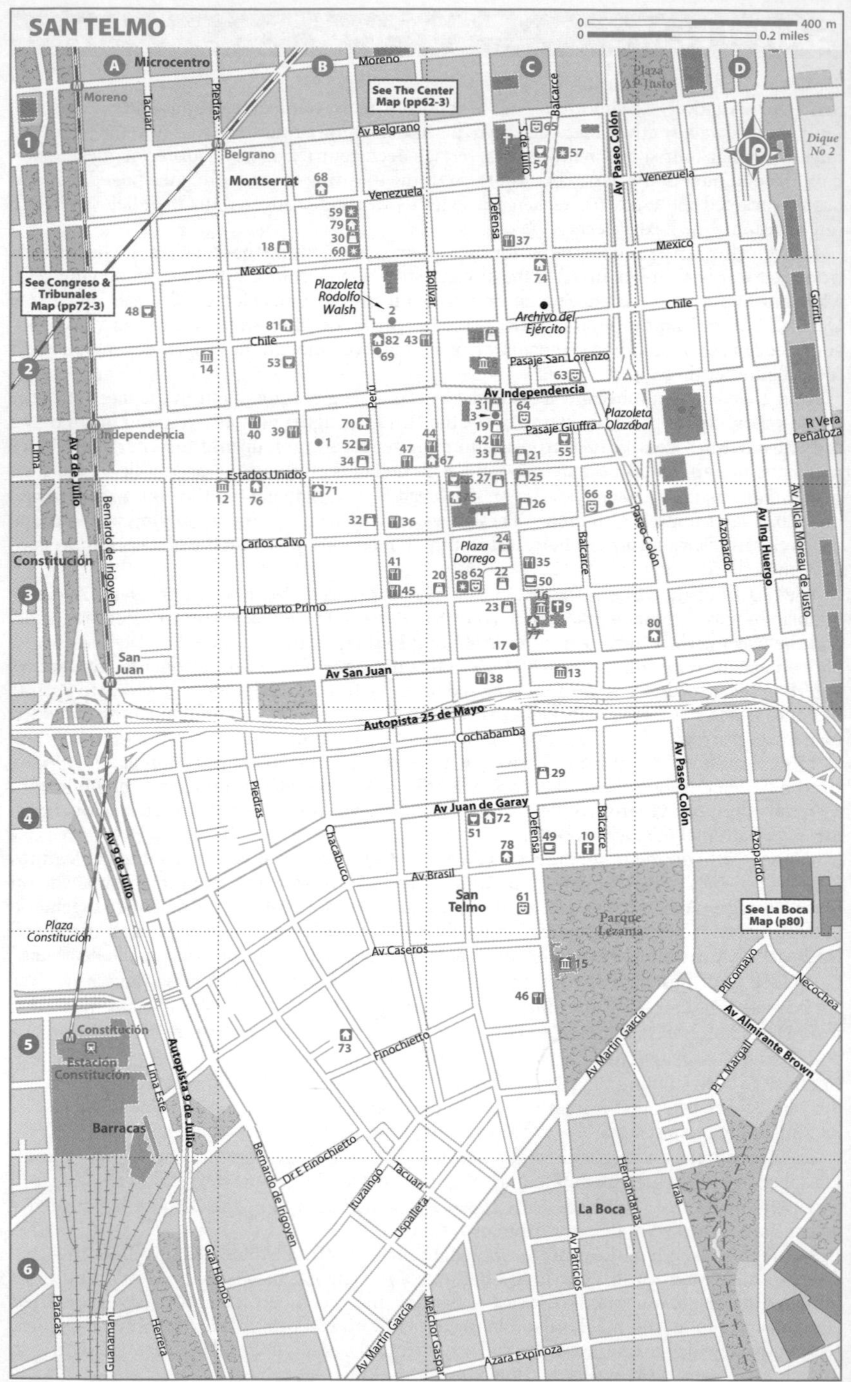
SAN TELMO
0 400 m
0 0.2 miles
Microcentro
Moreno
Tacuarí
Piedras
See The Center Map (pp62-3)
Plaza AP Justo
Balcarce
Av Belgrano
Belgrano
5 de Julio
Av Paseo Colón
Dique No 2
Montserrat
Venezuela
Defensa
Mexico
Bolívar
Plazoleta Rodolfo Walsh
See Congreso & Tribunales Map (pp72-3)
Chile
Archivo del Ejército
Gorriti
Perú
Pasaje San Lorenzo
Av Independencia
Plazoleta Olazábal
Pasaje Giuffra
Independencia
Lima
Av 9 de Julio
R Vera Peñaloza
Estados Unidos
Bernardo de Irigoyen
Av Alicia Moreau de Justo
Carlos Calvo
Paseo Colón
Azopardo
Av Ing Huergo
Constitución
Plaza Dorrego
Humberto Primo
San Juan
Av San Juan
Autopista 25 de Mayo
Cochabamba
Av Juan de Garay
Chacabuco
Av Brasil
San Telmo
Parque Lezama
See La Boca Map (p80)
Plaza Constitución
Av Caseros
Pilcomayo
Necochea
Av Almirante Brown
Av Martín García
Pi Y Margall
Finochietto
Estación Constitución
Lima Este
Autopista 9 de Julio
Barracas
Dr E Finochietto
Tacuarí
Ituzaingó
Uspallata
Hernandarias
Irala
La Boca
Gral Hornos
Av Patricios
Paracas
Guanumuni
Herrera
Av Martín García
Melchor Gaspar
Azara Expinoza

SAN TELMO

INFORMATION
Rayuela 1 B2
Say Hueque 2 B2
Tangol 3 C2

SIGHTS (pp75-9)
Centro Nacional de la Música 4 B2
Convento de Santo Domingo 5 C1
El Zanjón de Granados 6 C2
Facultad de Ingeniería 7 D2
Iglesia Dinamarquesa 8 C3
Iglesia Nuestra Señora de Belén 9 C3
Iglesia Ortodoxa Rusa 10 C4
Mercado San Telmo 11 C3
Museo Argentino del Títere 12 B3
Museo de Arte Moderno de Buenos Aires 13 C3
Museo del Traje 14 A2
Museo Histórico Nacional 15 C5
Museo Penitenciario Nacional 16 C3
Pasaje de la Defensa 17 C3

SHOPPING (pp112-14)
Appetite 18 B1
Bokura 19 C2
Cualquier Verdura 20 C3
El Buen Orden 21 C2
Feria de San Pedro Telmo 22 C3
Gil Antigüedades 23 C3
Hernani 24 C3
Imhotep 25 C2
L'Ago 26 C3
L'Ago 27 C2
Materia Urbana 28 C2
Mercado San Telmo (see 11)
Moebius 29 C4
Pablo Ramírez 30 B1
Puntos en el Espacio 31 C2
Puntos en el Espacio 32 B3
Un Lugar en el Mundo 33 C2
Walrus Books 34 B2

EATING (pp129-31)
Amici Miei 35 C3
Bar El Federal 36 B3
Brasserie Petanque 37 C1
Café San Juan 38 C3
Casal de Catalunya 39 B2
Comedor Nikkai 40 B2
Dylan 41 B3
El Desnivel 42 C2
La Poesia 43 B2
La Vineria de Gualterio Bolívar 44 C2
Origen 45 B3
Parrilla 1880 46 C5
Wafles Sur 47 B2

DRINKING (pp143-53)
647 Dinner Club 48 A2
Bar Británico 49 C4
Bar Plaza Dorrego 50 C3
Doppelganger 51 C4
Gibraltar 52 B2
La Puerta Roja 53 B2
M Buenos Aires 54 C1
Pride Café 55 C2
Territorio 56 C2

NIGHTLIFE (pp155-61)
La Trastienda 57 C1
Mitos Argentinos 58 C3
Museum 59 B1
Tango Queer 60 B1

THE ARTS (pp163-72)
Centro Cultural Torquato Tasso 61 C4
El Balcón 62 C3
El Viejo Almacén 63 C2
La Scala de San Telmo 64 C2
La Ventana 65 C1
Teatro La Carbonera 66 C3

SLEEPING (pp187-9)
Arka Hostel 67 C2
Axel Hotel 68 B1
Ayres Porteños Hostel 69 B2
Bohemia Buenos Aires 70 B2
Circus Hostel 71 B3
Cocker B&B 72 C4
Garden B&B 73 B5
La Casa de Marina 74 C2
La Gurda Hostel 75 C3
Lina's Tango Guesthouse 76 B3
Lugar Gay 77 C3
Noster Bayres 78 C4
Posada de la Luna 79 B1
Ribera Sur Hotel 80 D3
Telmo Tango Hostel 81 B2

TRANSPORT (pp216-22)
Líneas Aéreas del Estado (LADE) 82 B2

EL ZANJÓN DE GRANADOS Map p76

☎ 4361-3002; www.elzanjon.com.ar; Defensa 755; tours 11am, noon, 1pm & 2pm Mon-Fri, every 30 mins from 1 6pm Sun; 29

One of the more unique places in Buenos Aires is this amazing urban architectural site. It's become the realized dream of Jorge Eckstein, who found these ruins after purchasing land for a business project and then spent years renovating them into what you see today. The Zanjón (ravine) now offers a fascinating glimpse into the city's architectural history.

A series of old tunnels, sewers and cisterns (built from 1730 onwards) were constructed above a river tributary and provided the base for one of BA's oldest settlements, which later became a family mansion and then tenement housing and some shops. Meticulously reconstructed brick by brick, and very attractively lit, this 'museum' also contains several courtyards and even a watchtower. There are a few relics on display in the various halls and rooms, but the highlights are the spaces themselves.

You can choose between hour-long tours Monday through Friday (AR$50) or half-hour tours on Sunday (AR$30). It's best to call and reserve ahead of time, especially if you need English-speaking guides.

MUSEO HISTÓRICO NACIONAL Map p76

☎ 4307-1182; Defensa 1600; admission free; 11am-6pm Wed-Sun; 29

Located in Parque Lezama, considered to be the very spot where Buenos Aires was founded, is the city's national historical museum. It's dedicated to exhibiting items related to Argentina's revolution on May 25, 1810.

TRANSPORTATION: SAN TELMO

Bus Take bus 59 to Recoleta and Palermo, bus 29 to La Boca, Plaza de Mayo and Palermo.
Subte Línea C connects the western edge of San Telmo with Retiro.

top picks

ARTSY MUSEUMS

- Museo Nacional de Bellas Artes (p88)
- Museo de Arte Latinoamericano de Buenos Aires (Malba; p90)
- Museo Nacional de Arte Decorativo (p91)
- Colección de Arte Amalia Lacroze de Fortabat (Museo Fortabat; p68)
- Museo de Arte Moderno de Buenos Aires (MAMBA; p78)

Inside, exhibits are a bit sparse, but at least they're neatly displayed. There are several portraits of presidents and other major figures of the time, and you can peek into a recreated version of José de San Martín's bedroom – he was a military hero and liberator of Argentina (along with other South American countries). Old documents are also on display, and there's a video room as well.

Perhaps the most interesting exhibit, however, is of a few paintings depicting Africans in Argentina celebrating Carnaval and playing *candombe* (a drum-based musical genre invented in the early 18th-century by slaves brought to the Rio de la Plata region). Argentina's black history is limited and mysterious – the country did have a slave trade, but today there are very few people of African descent here.

Argentine hero Manuel Belgrano's watch was stolen from this museum in 2007, and things have never been the same since. Expect tight security during your visit – bags and backpacks have to be checked in, and guards are everywhere.

MUSEO DE ARTE MODERNO DE BUENOS AIRES Map p76

☎ 4342-2938; www.museodeartemoderno.buenosaires.gov.ar; Av San Juan 350; admission AR$1, free Tue; noon-9pm Mon-Fri, 11am-8pm Sat & Sun; 29

Housed in a recycled tobacco warehouse, this museum (abbreviated MAMBA) opened in December 2010 after being closed for five years due to a 85 million peso remodel (which will continue through 2012). It was still closed during our research period, but you can expect five floors of slick new exhibition halls showing off multi-media presentations of contemporary Argentine artists, along with classic international works. There's also a library, 240-seat auditorium, gift shop and café.

MUSEO PENITENCIARIO Map p76

☎ 4361-0917; Humberto Primo 378; admission free; 2-6pm Thu-Sun; 29

Dating from 1760, this building was a convent and later a women's prison before it became a penal museum in 1980; reconstructed old jail cells give an idea of the prisoners' conditions. Don't miss the tear gas canisters for controlling riots, the tennis balls used to hide drugs and the effeminate mannequins showing off past prison fashions.

MUSEO DEL TRAJE Map p76

☎ 4343-8427; Chile 832; admission by donation; 3-7pm Tue-Sun; Línea C Independencia

Near the Montserrat border, this small clothing museum is always changing its wardrobe. You can hit upon wedding outfits from the late 1800s, popular fashions from the early 1900s or even clothing worn by travelers on the Silk Road. If you're lucky, accessories such as hair combs, top hats, antique eyeglasses and elegant canes might be on display. Tours (in Spanish) are given Sunday at 5pm; information in English is available.

CONVENTO DE SANTO DOMINGO Map p76

☎ 4331-1668; cnr Defensa & Belgrano; Línea E Bolívar, Línea A Plaza de Mayo

Marking the approach into San Telmo, this 18th-century Dominican building has a long and colorful history. On its left tower you'll see the replicated scars of shrapnel launched against British troops who holed up here during the invasion of 1806. The basílica (tours by appointment only) displays the flags that were captured from the British. Secularized during the presidency of Bernardino Rivadavia (1826–27), the building became a natural history museum, its original single tower serving as an astronomical observatory, until Governor Juan Manuel de Rosas restored it to the Dominican order.

LA BOCA

Eating p131 Sleeping p188

Blue-collar and raffish to the core, La Boca is very much a locals' neighborhood, and is often portrayed as a symbol of Buenos Aires. In the mid-19th century, La Boca became home to poor Spanish and Italian immigrants who settled along the Riachuelo – the sinuous river that divides the city from the surrounding province of Buenos Aires. Many of them came during the booming 1880s and ended up working in the numerous meat-packing plants and warehouses here, processing and shipping out much of Argentina's vital beef. After sprucing up the barges the port dwellers splashed leftover paint on the corrugated-metal siding of their own houses, unwittingly giving La Boca what would become one of its main claims to fame. However, this has created its own problems and the color that made it famous has also found its way into the river; industrial wastes and petroleum have taken their toll over the years, and today the abandoned port's waters are trapped under a thick layer of rainbow sludge. Rusting hulks of sunken ships can also be seen offshore, keeping La Boca's history very much in the present.

El Caminito is the barrio's most famous street and the target tourist destination here. Named after a tango song, this short alleyway offers a colorful panorama that has inspired a million photographs. Busloads of camera-laden tourists often crowd the lively surrounding streets, especially on weekends when a small crafts fair sets up near the river. Buskers, street musicians and tango dancers perform for spare change, and you can get your photo taken with them or behind fun cardboard cut-outs. Nearby, a couple of art museums are worth a wander through, and next to the river a pedestrian walkway gives you a close-up sniff of the Riachuelo.

The symbol of the community's solidarity is the Boca Juniors soccer team, the former club of disgraced superstar Diego Maradona. The team plays at La Bombonera stadium, which is just four blocks inland and contains a museum detailing the team's successes, among other things.

On the way into La Boca, note the Casa Amarilla, which is found in the 400s block along Av Almirante Brown. This is a replica of the country house belonging to Almirante Brown, the Irish founder of the Argentine navy. Three blocks further on (look to your left at the kink in the road), you'll notice the curious Gothic structure called Torre Fantasma (Ghost Tower). As you reach the Riachuelo, you can alight from the bus and walk the last few hundred meters. Get a good look at the Puente Nicolás Avellaneda, which spans the Riachuelo, linking La Boca to the industrial suburb of Avellaneda; before the bridge's completion in 1940, floods had washed away several others. From here follow the riverside walkway all the way to El Caminito.

La Boca sits at the southern end of downtown, just south of San Telmo. The main avenue, Av Almirante Brown, runs down the middle of the neighborhood and to the river, where it turns west onto Av Don Pedro de Mendoza and passes by El Caminito. All buses stop here and then head back. La Bombonera stadium is four blocks north of the river, up Del Valle Iberlucea.

FUNDACIÓN PROA Map p80

☎ 4104-1000; www.proa.org; Av Don Pedro de Mendoza 1929; admission AR$10; 11am-7pm Tue-Sun; 29, 64, 152

High ceilings, white walls and large halls display all the changing exhibits that pass through this elegant art foundation. Only the most cutting-edge national and international artists are invited to show here, helping to stimulate the BA art scene with stunning contemporary installations in a wide variety of media and themes. Video rooms and an auditorium have modern offerings as well, and there's an impressive library. The rooftop terrace is *the* stylish place in La Boca for relaxing with a drink or snack, boasting a view of the Riachuelo. Plenty of cultural offerings throughout the year include talks, lectures, workshops, music concerts and cinema screenings, and there's even free wi-fi.

MUSEO DE BELLAS ARTES DE LA BOCA BENITO QUINQUELA MARTÍN

Map p80

☎ 4301-1080; www.museoquinquela.gov.ar; Av Don Pedro de Mendoza 1835; suggested donation AR$5; 10am-6pm Tue-Fri, 11am-6pm Sat & Sun; 29, 64, 152

Once the home and studio of Benito Quinquela Martín (1890–1977), this fine-arts

TRANSPORTATION: LA BOCA

Bus Take buses 29, 64 and 152 from the center; they all end up at El Caminito.

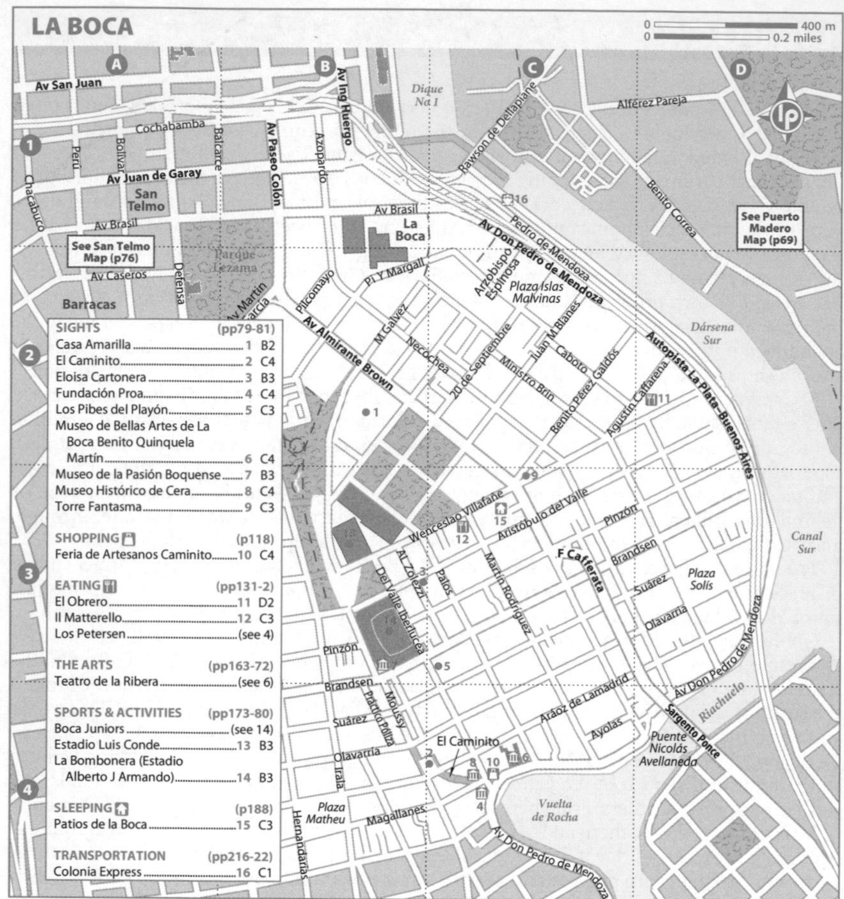

museum exhibits his works and those of more contemporary Argentine artists. Some exhibits are temporary, but the museum always offers good and well-displayed collections in spacious halls.

In keeping with the museum's maritime theme is the small but excellent permanent collection of painted wooden bowsprits, which are the carved statues projecting forward at the front of ships. There are also outdoor sculptures on the rooftop terraces, and the top tier has awesome views of the port. The top floor displays Martín's surrealist paintings, whose broad, rough brush-strokes and dark colors use the port, silhouettes of laboring men, smokestacks and water reflections as recurring themes.

MUSEO DE LA PASIÓN BOQUENSE

Map p80

☎ 4362-1100; www.museoboquense.com; Brandsen 805; admission AR$28; 10am-6pm; 29, 64, 152

High tech and spiffy, this *fútbol* (soccer) museum chronicles the rough-and-tumble neighborhood, La Bombonera stadium, soccer idols' histories, video highlights, the championships, the trophies and, of course, the gooooals. There's a 360° theater in a giant soccer-ball auditorium, an old jersey collection and a gift shop. The museum is right under the stadium, a couple of blocks from the tourist part of El Caminito; peek at the pitch for a few extra pesos.

LA BOCA WARNING

La Boca is not the kind of neighborhood for casual strolls – it can be downright rough in spots. Don't stray far from the riverside walk, El Caminito (and its nearby tourist streets) or the Bombonera stadium, especially while toting expensive cameras. And certainly don't cross the bridge over the Riachuelo; there's nothing to see there anyway. To safely see La Boca with a walking tour, check the walking tours section on p229; Anda Responsible Travel has an especially good option.

LOS PIBES DEL PLAYÓN Map p80

☎ 4303-4010; www.pibesdelplayon.blogspot.com; Del Valle Iberlucea 938; 9am-6pm; 29, 64, 152

This small bakery is a locally-owned cooperative run by an energetic woman, Cristina Mangravide, who wanted to improve the lives of La Boca's poorest children. Home made baked goods, including *alfajores* – those delicious sweet cookie sandwiches Argentina is famous for – are created by troubled local teenagers and sold here to anyone who stops by. It's a great cause – the kids are kept busy being taught skills that will hopefully aid them in the future, and you can help them while satisfying your sweet tooth.

MUSEO HISTÓRICO DE CERA Map p80

☎ 4301-1497; www.museodecera.com.ar; Del Valle Iberlucea 1261; admission AR$10; 11am-8pm; 29, 64, 152

Wax reconstructions of historical figureheads (literally) and dioramas of scenes in Argentine history are the specialty of this small and very tacky private institution. Among the historical Argentine personages depicted are no less than Juan de Solís, Guillermo Brown, Mendoza, Garay and Rosas. In addition, there are also stuffed snakes and creepy wax limbs depicting bite wounds – all barely worth the price of admission.

RETIRO

Drinking p147 & p152; Eating p132; Shopping p114; Sleeping p189

Well located and exclusive, Retiro is one of the ritziest neighborhoods in Buenos Aires – but it hasn't always been this way. The area was the site of a monastery during the 17th century, and later became the country *retiro* (retreat) of Agustín de Robles, a Spanish governor. Since then, Retiro's current Plaza San Martín – which sits on a bluff – has played host to a slave market, a military fort and even a bullring. Things are much quieter and more exclusive these days.

French landscape architect Carlos Thays designed the forestlike Plaza San Martín, whose prominent monument is the obligatory equestrian statue of José de San Martín. Important visiting dignitaries often come to honor the country's liberator by leaving wreaths at its base. On the downhill side of the park you'll see the Monumento a los Caídos de Malvinas, a memorial to the young men who died in the Falklands War.

Surrounding the plaza are several landmark public buildings, such as the Palacio San Martín (p82). An art nouveau mansion originally built for the elite Anchorena family, it later became the headquarters of the Foreign Ministry; today it's used mostly for official purposes. Additionally, there's the impressive Palacio Paz (aka Círculo Militar; p82), built in 1909 for *La Prensa* founder Jose C Paz; it was the largest private residence in Argentina at 12,000 sq meters, and is definitely worth a tour for its amazingly decorated rooms and halls. Within the same large building is the Museo de Armas (p83), a not-to-be-missed stop for weapons buffs.

On an odd triangular block at the corner of Florida and Santa Fe, the neo-Gothic Palacio Haedo (Map p84; Av Santa Fe 690) was the mansion of the Haedo family at the turn of the 19th century; it now houses the country's national park service. Nearby is a private apartment building that was author Jorge Luis Borges' last residence in Argentina (Map p84; Maipú 994); look for a plaque on the wall. One landmark you can't miss is the 120m Edificio Kavanagh (Map p84; Florida 1035), an art deco monstrosity that at the time of its construction (1935) was the tallest concrete structure in the world. Close by is the Basílica de Santísimo Sacramento (Map p84; Plaza San Martín 1039), a French-style church consecrated by the Anchorena family in 1916.

The 76m Torre de los Ingleses (p83) is a landmark across from Estación Retiro (Retiro train station), which was built in 1915 when the British controlled the country's railroads. While much of Retiro is a chic, upper-class area, the part beyond the Retiro bus station has long been a shantytown and not a place in which to go exploring.

Toward Retiro's north is the luxurious Museo de Arte Hispanoamericano Isaac Fernández Blanco (p83), whose leafy garden makes a welcome break from the bustle of Retiro. And on the other side of Av 9 de Julio is the remarkable Teatro Nacional Cervantes (p83), which boasts Spanish architecture and a small theatrical museum. Across the street is Plaza Lavalle and other sights; see the Congreso neighborhood (p71) for details.

Retiro is just north of the Microcentro and east of Recoleta; most of the area is compact and easily seen on foot. Major transport hubs include the train and bus stations, and important thoroughfares are Avs del Libertador, Santa Fe and Córdoba.

PALACIO SAN MARTÍN Map p84

☎ 4819-8092, ext 8150; Arenales 761; Ⓢ Línea C San Martín

Built in 1912 for the powerful Anchorena family, this impressive mansion is actually three independent buildings around a stone courtyard. It was designed by architect Alejandro Christophersen and sports marble staircases, grandiose dining rooms and a garden containing a chunk of the Berlin Wall. A small but good museum displays pre-Columbian artifacts from the northwest, along with some paintings by Latin American artists. Tours are available but can be suspended at any time.

PALACIO PAZ Map p84

☎ 4311-1071, ext 147; www.palaciopaz.com.ar; Santa Fe 750; admission by tour only AR$20; 🕑 tours 11am & 3pm Tue-Fri, 11am Sat; Ⓢ Línea C San Martín

Once the private residence of José C Paz – founder of the still-running newspaper *La Prensa* – this opulent, French-style palace is the grandest in BA. Inside its 12,000 sq meters are ornate rooms with marble walls, salons gilded in real gold and halls boasting beautiful wood-tiled floors. The pièce de résistance is the circular grand hall with mosaic floors, marble details and stained-glass cupola. Nearly all materials came from

Europe and were then assembled here; there's also a modest garden out back. Tours in English (AR$35) are available on Wednesday and Thursday at 4pm.

MUSEO DE ARMAS Map p84

☎ 4311-1071; Av Santa Fe 702; admission AR$10; 1-7pm Mon-Fri; Línea C San Martín

Even if you've spent time in the armed forces, you probably have never seen so many weapons of destruction. This maze-like museum exhibits a frighteningly large but excellent collection of over 2000 bazookas, grenade launchers, cannons, machine guns, muskets, pistols, armor, lances and swords; even the gas mask for a combat horse is on display. The evolution of rifles and handguns is especially thoroughly documented, and there's a small but impressive Japanese weapons room. The whole collection is very extensive, impressive, clean and well labeled, and may make you feel like blowing something up.

TORRE DE LOS INGLESES Map p84

Plaza Fuerza Aérea Argentina; Línea C Retiro

Standing prominently across from Plaza San Martín, this 76m-high miniversion of London's Big Ben was a donation from the city's British community in 1916. During the Falklands War of 1982, the tower was the target of bombs, and the government officially renamed it Torre Monumental – but the name never really stuck. The plaza in which it stands used to be called Plaza Británica, but is now the Plaza Fuerza Aérea Argentina (Argentine Air Force Plaza).

MUSEO DE ARTE HISPANOAMERICANO ISAAC FERNÁNDEZ BLANCO Map p84

☎ 4327-0228; www.museofernandezblanco.buenosaires.gov.ar; Suipacha 1422; admission AR$1; 2-7pm Tue-Fri, 11am-7pm Sat & Sun; Línea D San Martín

Dating from 1921, this museum is in an old mansion of the neocolonial Peruvian style that developed as a reaction against French influences in turn-of-the-19th-century Argentine architecture. Its exceptional collection of colonial art includes silverwork from Alto Perú (present-day Bolivia), oils with religious themes, Jesuit statuary, costumes, furniture, colonial silverware and antiques. There's little effort to place items in any historical context, but everything is in great condition and well lit, and the curved ceiling on the 1st floor is beautifully painted. The museum also has an interior garden that offers a green sanctuary from the bustling city.

Also known as the Palacio Noel, after the designing architect, the museum building and its collections suffered damage (since repaired) from the 1992 bombing of the Israeli embassy, which at the time was located at Arroyo and Suipacha. The space where the embassy was located has since become a small park; you can still see the outline of the building on a neighboring wall.

TRANSPORTATION: RETIRO

Bus Take bus 59 to Recoleta and Palermo, buses 22, 45 & 126 to San Telmo, bus 150 to Congreso.

Subte Línea C connects Retiro with the western edge of San Telmo.

top picks

QUIRKY MUSEUMS

- Museo del Patrimonio Aguas Argentinas (p74)
- Museo Histórico de Cera (p81)
- Museo de la Pasión Boquense (p80)
- Museo de la Policía Federal (p63)
- Museo del Traje (p78)
- Museo de Armas (p83)

TEATRO NACIONAL CERVANTES Map p84

☎ 4815-8883; www.teatrocervantes.gov.ar; Av Córdoba 1155; Línea D Tribunales

Six blocks southwest of Plaza San Martín, you can't help but notice the lavishly ornamented Cervantes theater. This landmark building dates from 1921 and was built with private funds but was acquired by the state after it went broke in 1926. Its facade was designed as a replica of Spain's Universidad de Alcalá de Henares. The building underwent remodeling after a fire in 1961. From the grand tiled lobby to the main theater, with its plush red-velvet chairs, you'll smell the long history of this place (somewhat musty). The Cervantes is definitely showing its age, with worn carpeting and rough edges, but improvement

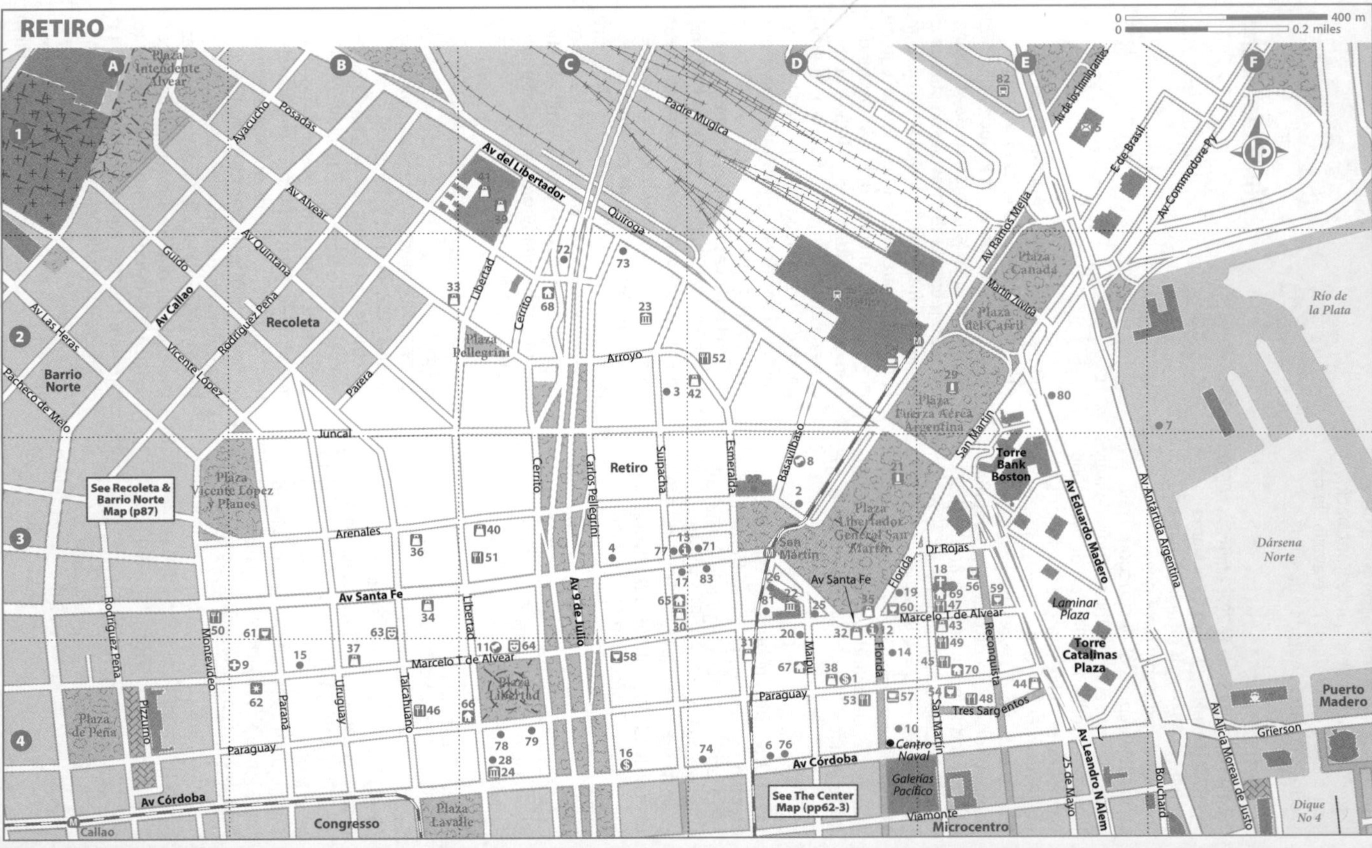
RETIRO
0 400 m
0 0.2 miles
Plaza Intendente Alvear
Ayacucho
Posadas
Av Alvear
Av Quintana
Guido
Av Callao
Rodríguez Peña
Recoleta
Av Las Heras
Pacheco de Melo
Barrio Norte
Vicente López
Parera
Av del Libertador
Libertad
Cerrito
Plaza Pellegrini
Quiroga
Padre Mugica
Arroyo
Juncal
See Recoleta & Barrio Norte Map (p87)
Plaza Vicente López y Planes
Arenales
Carlos Pellegrini
Retiro
Suipacha
Esmeralda
Basavilbaso
Av 9 de Julio
Av Santa Fe
Marcelo T de Alvear
Montevideo
Paraná
Uruguay
Talcahuano
Plaza Libertad
Plaza de Peña
Pizzurno
Paraguay
Av Córdoba
Callao
Congresso
Plaza Lavalle
See The Center Map (pp62-3)
Viamonte
Microcentro
Galerías Pacífico
Centro Naval
Maipú
Florida
San Martín
Reconquista
Tres Sargentos
Dr Rojas
Plaza Libertador General San Martín
Plaza Fuerza Aérea Argentina
Av Ramos Mejía
Martín Zuviría
Plaza Canadá
Plaza del Carril
Av de los Inmigrantes
E de Brasil
Av Commodore Py
Torre Bank Boston
Av Eduardo Madero
Laminar Plaza
Torre Catalinas Plaza
Av Leandro N Alem
25 de Mayo
Bouchard
Av Antártida Argentina
Av Alicia Moreau de Justo
Grierson
Río de la Plata
Dársena Norte
Puerto Madero
Dique No 4

RETIRO

INFORMATION

- Alhec 1 D4
- American Express 2 D3
- British Arts Centre 3 C2
- Casa de Misiones Tourist Office 4 C3
- Correo Internacional 5 E1
- DHL Internacional 6 D4
- Dirección Nacional de Migraciones 7 F2
- French Consulate 8 D3
- Hospital Británico Clinic 9 B4
- Hostelling International 10 D4
- Italian Consulate 11 C4
- Plaza San Martín Tourist Kiosk 12 D3
- Secretaría de Turismo de la Nación 13 C3
- Tangol 14 D4
- Tourist Kiosk (see 82)
- VOS 15 B4
- Western Union 16 C4
- Wow Argentina 17 C3

SIGHTS (pp82-5)

- Basílica de Santísimo Sacramento 18 E3
- Edificio Kavanagh 19 D3
- Jorge Luis Borges' Last Residence 20 D3
- Monumento a los Caidos de Malvinas 21 D3
- Museo de Armas 22 D3
- Museo de Arte Hispanoamericano Isaac Fernández Blanco 23 C2
- Museo Nacional del Teatro 24 C4
- Palacio Haedo (Parques Nacionales) 25 D3
- Palacio Paz 26 D3
- Palacio San Martín 27 D3
- Teatro Nacional Cervantes 28 C4
- Torre de los Ingleses 29 E2

SHOPPING (pp114-16)

- Autoría 30 C3
- Camping Center 31 D4
- Casa López 32 D3
- Gabriella Capucci 33 B2
- Galería 5ta Avenida 34 B3
- Galería Ruth Benzacar 35 D3
- Josefina Ferroni 36 B3
- Kel Ediciones 37 B4
- La Martina 38 D4
- María Vázquez 39 C1
- Papelera Palermo 40 C3
- Patio Bullrich 41 C1
- Tierra Adentro 42 D2
- Welcome Marroquinería 43 E3
- Winery 44 E4

EATING (pp132-3)

- Dadá 45 E4
- El Cuartito 46 B4
- El Federal 47 E3
- Empire Thai 48 E4
- Filo 49 E4
- Freddo 50 A3
- Gran Bar Danzón 51 C3
- Le Sud 52 D2
- Sipan 53 D4

DRINKING (pp143-53)

- Buller Brewing Company 54 E4
- Café Retiro 55 D2
- Druid In 56 E3
- Florida Garden 57 D4
- Flux Bar 58 C4
- Kilkenny 59 E3
- Marriott Plaza Bar 60 D3
- Milión 61 B3

NIGHTLIFE (pp155-61)

- El Living 62 B4

THE ARTS (pp163-72)

- Atlas Cines Patio Bullrich (see 41)
- Escuela Argentina de Tango 63 B3
- Teatro Coliseo 64 C4

SLEEPING (pp189-90)

- Casa Calma 65 C3
- Dazzler Hotel 66 C4
- Elevage Hotel 67 D4
- Four Seasons Buenos Aires 68 C2
- Hotel Central Córdoba 69 E3
- Hotel Principado 70 E4

TRANSPORT (pp216-22)

- American Airlines 71 D3
- Avis 72 C2
- British Airways 73 C2
- Buquebus Office 74 D4
- Buquebus Terminal 75 F4
- Colonia Express office 76 D4
- Delta 77 C3
- Hertz 78 C4
- Lan 79 C4
- Manuel Tienda León (MTL) 80 E2
- New Way 81 D3
- Retiro Bus Terminal 82 E1
- Swissair 83 D3

projects are planned. Until then, enjoy the elegance – however faded – with a tour (call for current schedules). It presents theater, comedy, musicals and dance at affordable prices.

MUSEO NACIONAL DEL TEATRO

Map p84

☎ 4815-8883, ext 156; Av Córdoba 1199; admission free; 10am-6pm Mon-Fri; Línea D Tribunales

Inside the Teatro Cervantes (enter via the corner door) is the tiny Museo Nacional del Teatro (National Theater Museum). Exhibits trace Argentine theater from its colonial beginnings, stressing the 19th-century contributions of the Podestá family – Italian immigrants who popularized the *gauchesca* drama *Juan Moreira*. Items include a gaucho suit worn by Gardel in his Hollywood film *El Día Que Me Quieras* and the *bandoneón* belonging to Paquita Bernardo, the first Argentine woman to play the accordion-like instrument (she died of tuberculosis in 1925 at the age of 25). There is also a photo gallery of famous Argentine stage actors.

RECOLETA & BARRIO NORTE

Drinking p147 & p153; Eating p133; Shopping p116; Sleeping p190

Recoleta is the Rolls Royce of Buenos Aires. It's where the rich live in luxury apartments and mansions while spending their free time shopping in expensive boutiques such as Cartier and Armani. It's where the privileged proudly walk their pampered poodles and have their hair dyed an even richer hue. It's where the elite sip at elegant cafés in their best Sunday threads – even on Thursdays. And it's also where they're all finally put to rest, in their famous cemetery (read on).

This fashionable barrio was, interestingly enough, first constructed as a result of sickness. Many upper-class porteños in the 1870s originally lived in southerly San Telmo, but during the yellow-fever epidemic they relocated as far away as they could, which meant clear across town to Recoleta and Barrio Norte. Today you can best see much of the wealth of this sumptuous quarter on Av Alvear, where many of the old mansions (and newer boutiques) are located.

Full of lush parks, grand monuments, French architecture and wide avenues, Recoleta is best known for its Cementerio de la Recoleta. This must-see attraction is an astonishing necropolis where, in death as in life, generations of the Argentine elite repose in ornate splendor (see the boxed text, p88).

Alongside the cemetery, the Iglesia de Nuestra Señora del Pilar (1732) is a baroque colonial church and national historical monument; there's a small museum upstairs (AR$5). Next door is the Centro Cultural Recoleta (p88), one of the city's best cultural centers. Just in front, the Plaza Intendente Alvear holds the very popular weekend crafts fair, Feria Plaza Francia (p118). And across the way in RM Ortiz is 'Restaurant Row', Recoleta's culinary tourist trap – although a few places are worth a sit-down (p133).

Notable buildings in this barrio are the beautiful French-styled Palais de Glace and the decrepit neo-Gothic Facultad de Ingeniería (Map p87; Engineering School; cnr General Las Heras & Azcuénaga), which was designed by Uruguayan architect Arturo Prins and never quite completed.

A beautiful and interesting sculptural piece to the north is Floralis Genérica, located smack in the center of Plaza Naciones Unidas (just behind the Museo Nacional de Bellas Artes). It was designed and funded entirely by architect Eduardo Catalano, and finished in 2002. The giant aluminum and steel petals are 20m high and used to close like a real flower, from dusk until dawn – until the gears broke, that is.

Barrio Norte is not an official neighborhood as such but rather a largely residential southern extension of Recoleta. Some people consider it as a sub-neighborhood of Recoleta (and parts of it are sometimes lumped in with Retiro or Palermo, too) – it all really depends on who you talk to. However, Barrio Norte does have a more accessible feel than its ritzier sibling, especially around busy Av Santa Fe. Here you'll find hundreds of shops, all vying for shoppers' attention, and all conveniently located on bus and Subte lines (not things you'll see much of in Recoleta).

The University of Buenos Aires' medical school, along with a few hospitals and many medical supply stores, lie further south close to functional Av Córdoba. Here the vibe is full of youthful student energy, and a casual crafts market often operates at Plaza de Houssay.

Recoleta sits elegantly between Retiro and Palermo, while Barrio Norte is just to the south and closer to Once. Recoleta's main attractions are concentrated around the cemetery, and you can easily walk here from the center. Main thoroughfares include Avs Las Heras, Santa Fe, Córdoba, Callao and del Libertador.

CEMENTERIO DE LA RECOLETA Map p87

☎ 4803-1594; cnr Junín & Guido; admission free; 7am-6pm; 59

This cemetery is arguably Buenos Aires' number-one attraction, and a must on every tourist's list. You can wander for hours in this amazing city of the dead, where countless 'streets' are lined with impressive statues and marble sarcophagi. Peek into the crypts and check out the dusty coffins – most of which hold the remains of the city's most elite sector of society – and try to decipher the history of its inhabitants. Past presidents, military heroes, influential politicians and the just plain rich and famous have made it past

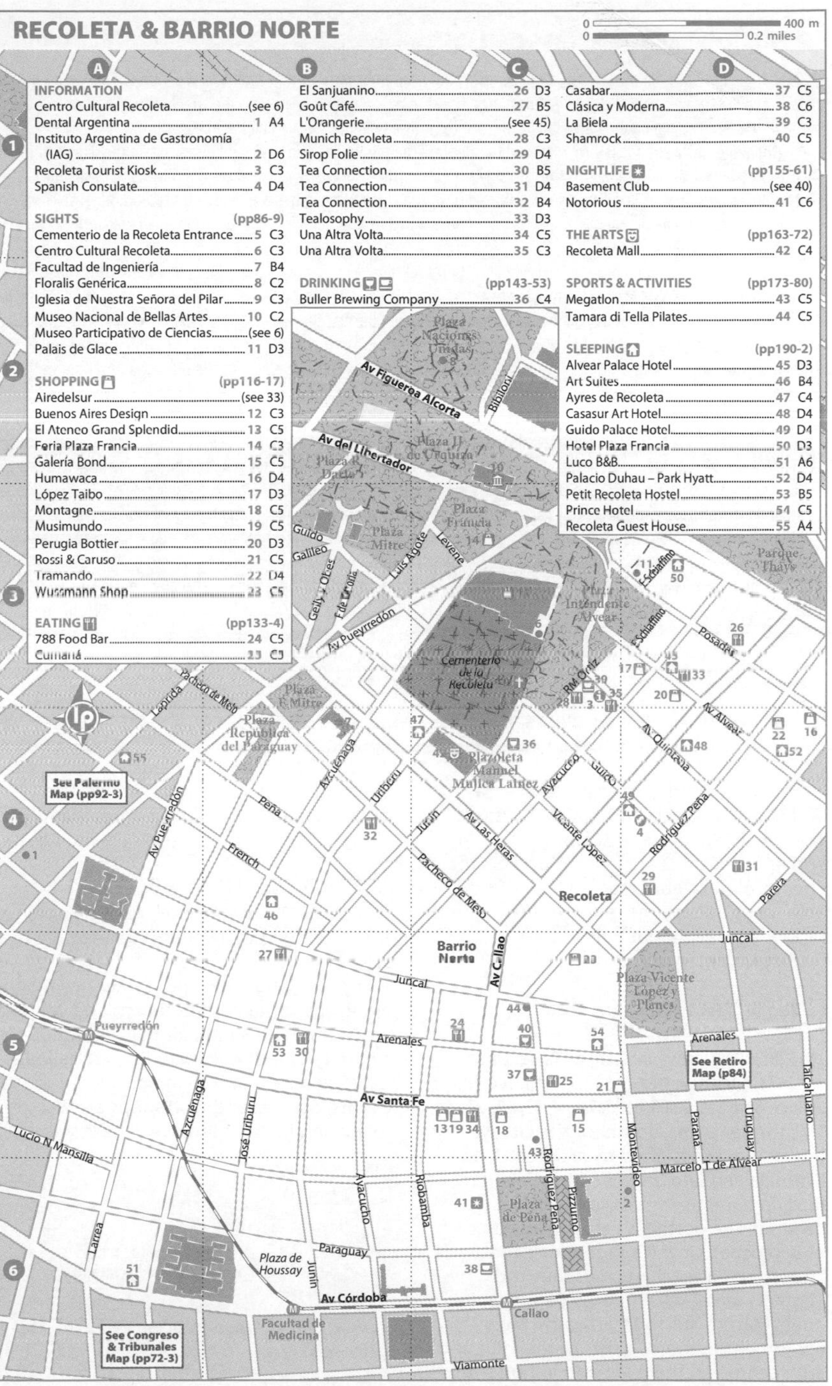
RECOLETA & BARRIO NORTE
0 400 m
0 0.2 miles
A
B
C
D
1
2
3
4
5
6
INFORMATION
Centro Cultural Recoleta .... (see 6)
Dental Argentina 1 A4
Instituto Argentina de Gastronomía (IAG) 2 D6
Recoleta Tourist Kiosk 3 C3
Spanish Consulate 4 D4
SIGHTS (pp86-9)
Cementerio de la Recoleta Entrance 5 C3
Centro Cultural Recoleta 6 C3
Facultad de Ingeniería 7 B4
Floralis Genérica 8 C2
Iglesia de Nuestra Señora del Pilar 9 C3
Museo Nacional de Bellas Artes 10 C2
Museo Participativo de Ciencias .... (see 6)
Palais de Glace 11 D3
SHOPPING (pp116-17)
Airedelsur .... (see 33)
Buenos Aires Design 12 C3
El Ateneo Grand Splendid 13 C5
Feria Plaza Francia 14 C3
Galería Bond 15 C5
Humawaca 16 D4
López Taibo 17 D3
Montagne 18 C5
Musimundo 19 C5
Perugia Bottier 20 D3
Rossi & Caruso 21 C5
Tramando 22 D4
Wussmann Shop 23 C5
EATING (pp133-4)
788 Food Bar 24 C5
Cumaná 25 C3
El Sanjuanino 26 D3
Goût Café 27 B5
L'Orangerie .... (see 45)
Munich Recoleta 28 C3
Sirop Folie 29 D4
Tea Connection 30 B5
Tea Connection 31 D4
Tea Connection 32 B4
Tealosophy 33 D3
Una Altra Volta 34 C5
Una Altra Volta 35 C3
DRINKING (pp143-53)
Buller Brewing Company 36 C4
Casabar 37 C5
Clásica y Moderna 38 C6
La Biela 39 C3
Shamrock 40 C5
NIGHTLIFE (pp155-61)
Basement Club .... (see 40)
Notorious 41 C6
THE ARTS (pp163-72)
Recoleta Mall 42 C4
SPORTS & ACTIVITIES (pp173-80)
Megatlon 43 C5
Tamara di Tella Pilates 44 C5
SLEEPING (pp190-2)
Alvear Palace Hotel 45 D3
Art Suites 46 B4
Ayres de Recoleta 47 C4
Casasur Art Hotel 48 D4
Guido Palace Hotel 49 D4
Hotel Plaza Francia 50 D3
Luco B&B 51 A6
Palacio Duhau – Park Hyatt 52 D4
Petit Recoleta Hostel 53 B5
Prince Hotel 54 C5
Recoleta Guest House 55 A4
Plaza Naciones Unidas
Av Figueroa Alcorta
Bibiloni
Av del Libertador
Plaza J J de Urquiza
Plaza R Darío
Plaza Francia
Plaza Mitre
Guido
Galileo
Gelly y Obes
F de Oro
Luis Agote
Levene
Av Pueyrredón
Cementerio de la Recoleta
Plaza Intendente Alvear
Parque Thays
Posadas
R M Ortiz
Av Alvear
Av Quintana
Pacheco de Melo
Laprida
Plaza E Mitre
Plaza República del Paraguay
Plazoleta Manuel Mujica Lainez
Azcuénaga
Uriburu
Peña
Ayacucho
Guido
Vicente López
Rodríguez Peña
Junín
Av Las Heras
French
Recoleta
Parera
See Palermo Map (pp92-3)
Barrio Norte
Av Callao
Juncal
Plaza Vicente López y Planes
Pueyrredón
Arenales
See Retiro Map (p84)
Av Santa Fe
Talcahuano
Paraná
Uruguay
Montevideo
Lucio N Mansilla
José Uriburu
Marcelo T de Alvear
Riobamba
Plaza de Peña
Pizzurno
Larrea
Paraguay
Plaza de Houssay
Av Córdoba
Callao
Facultad de Medicina
See Congreso & Tribunales Map (pp72-3)
Viamonte

GLORIOUS DEATH IN BUENOS AIRES

Only in Buenos Aires can the wealthy and powerful elite keep their status after death. When decades of dining on rich food and drink have taken their toll, Buenos Aires' finest move ceremoniously across the street to the Cementerio de la Recoleta (p86), joining their ancestors in a place they have religiously visited all their lives.

Argentines are a strange bunch who tend to celebrate their most honored national figures not on the date of their birth, but on the date of their death (after all, they're nobody when they're born). Nowhere is this obsession with mortality more evident than at Recoleta, where generations of the elite repose in the grandeur of ostentatious mausoleums. Real estate here is among Buenos Aires' priciest: there's a saying that goes 'It is cheaper to live extravagantly all your life than to be buried in Recoleta.'

It's not just being rich that gets you a prime resting spot here: your name matters. Those lucky few with surnames like Alvear, Anchorena, Mitre or Sarmiento are pretty much guaranteed to be laid down. Evita's remains are here (in the Familia Duarte sarcophagus), but her lack of aristocracy and the fact that she dedicated her life not to BA's rich but rather to its poor infuriated the bigwigs. To find her, go up to the first major intersection from the entrance, where there's a statue. Turn left, continue until a mausoleum blocks your way, go around it to the right and turn right at the wide 'street.' After three blocks look to the left and you'll likely see people at her site, along with bunches of flowers.

A larger and much less touristy graveyard is Cementerio de la Chacarita (p58; ☎ 4553-9338; 680 Guzman; 🕑 7am-6pm), located in the neighborhood of Chacarita. The cemetery opened in the 1870s to accommodate the yellow-fever victims of San Telmo and La Boca. Although much more democratic and modest, Chacarita's most elaborate tombs match Recoleta's finest. One of the most visited belongs to Carlos Gardel, the famous tango singer. Plaques from around the world cover the base of his life-size statue, many thanking him for favors granted. Like Evita, Juan Perón and others, Gardel is a quasi saint toward whom countless Argentines feel an almost religious devotion. The anniversaries of Gardel's birth and death days see thousands of pilgrims jamming the cemetery's streets.

Another spiritual personality in Chacarita is Madre María Salomé, a disciple of the famous healer Pancho Sierra. Every day, but especially on the second day of each month (she died on October 2, 1928), adherents of her cult cover her tomb with white carnations. Other crypts to look for are that of Juan Perón and aviator Jorge Newbery. To visit Chacarita, take Línea B of the Subte to the end of the line at Federico Lacroze and cross the street.

the gates here. Hunt down Evita's grave, as all visitors try to do; find directions within the boxed text.

Tours in English are available Monday and Thursday at 11am; Spanish tours run Tuesday to Sunday at 9:30am, 11am, 2pm and 4pm. All tours are free. Volunteers for Friends of Recoleta Cemetery sell affordable maps outside the gates, or buy Robert Wright's excellent pdf guide at www.recoletacemetery.com.

MUSEO NACIONAL DE BELLAS ARTES Map p87

☎ 5288-9900; www.mnba.org.ar; Av del Libertador 1473; admission free; 🕑 12:30-8pm Tue-Fri, 9:30am-8pm Sat, Sun & holidays; 🚌 17, 62, 67

This former pump house for the city waterworks was designed by architect Julio Dormala and later modified by Alejandro Bustillo (famous for his alpine-style civic center in the northern Patagonian city of Bariloche). Now it's Argentina's most important national arts museum and contains many key works by Benito Quinquela Martín, Xul Solar, Edwardo Sívori and other Argentine artists of the 19th and 20th centuries. There are also impressive international works on the ground floor by European masters such as Cézanne, Degas, Picasso, Rembrandt, Toulouse-Lautrec and Van Gogh. Other offerings include temporary exhibits, a cinema, concerts and classes. Call in advance for tours in English.

CENTRO CULTURAL RECOLETA Map p87

☎ 4803-1040; www.centroculturalrecoleta.org; Junín 1930; 🕑 2-9pm Mon-Fri, 10am-9pm Sat & Sun; 🚌 59

Part of the original Franciscan convent and alongside its namesake church and cemetery, this renovated cultural center houses a variety of facilities, including art galleries, exhibition halls and a cinema. Plenty of events, courses and workshops are also offered, and its Museo Participativo de Ciencias (p91)

TRANSPORTATION: RECOLETA & BARRIO NORTE

Bus Buses 59 and 64 go from the Microcentro up Av Las Heras.

Subte Línea D covers the southern section of Recoleta.

is a children's hands-on science museum. There are occasional free outdoor films in summer too.

PALAIS DE GLACE Map p87

☎ **4804-1163; www.palaisdeglace.gov.ar; Posadas 1725; 2-8pm Tue-Fri, 8am-8pm Sat & Sun; 17, 62, 67**

Housed in an unusual circular building that was once an ice-skating rink and a tango hall (happily not necessarily at once, though!), the spacious Palais de Glace now offers a variety of rotating cultural, artistic and historical exhibitions. Be sure to check out the 2nd floor, worth a peep for its interesting ceiling and other architectural details. Art exhibitions are often hosted here; tours in Spanish are offered at 4.30pm and 5:30pm on Saturday and Sunday.

PALERMO

Drinking p148; Eating p134; Shopping p117; Sleeping p193

Palermo is heaven on earth for Buenos Aires' middle class. Its large, grassy parks – regally punctuated with grand monuments – are popular destinations on weekends when families fill the shady lanes, cycle the bike paths and paddle on the peaceful lakes. Palermo's green spaces, however, haven't always been for the masses. The area around Parque 3 de Febrero was originally the private retreat of 19th-century dictator Juan Manuel de Rosas and became public parkland only after his fall from power – on February 3, 1852. Ironically for Rosas, the man who overthrew him – former ally Justo José de Urquiza – sits on his mount in a mammoth equestrian monument at the corner of Avs Sarmiento and Presidente Figueroa Alcorta. The park's more interesting destinations, however, include the Jardín Japonés (p95); the Jardín Zoológico (p95); the Jardín Botánico Carlos Thays; the Planetario Galileo Galilei (planetarium; see p91); the Campo Argentino de Polo (polo grounds); and the Hipódromo Argentino (racetrack). Just south of the zoo, and a major landmark in Palermo, is Plaza Italia, a half-moon shaped traffic island and important transport hub. Close by is La Rural (aka Predio Ferial), a large venue hosting anything from fashion shows to agriculture and farming expositions.

For the tourist, Palermo's best feature is the sub-neighborhood of Palermo Viejo. Roughly bounded by Santa Fe, Scalabrini Ortiz, Córdoba and Dorrego, this is one of the capital's most trendsetting areas. It's further divided into Palermo Hollywood (north of the train tracks) and Palermo Soho (south of the tracks), all full of beautiful old buildings, leafy sidewalks and cobbled streets. Dozens of ethnic, ultramodern restaurants cater to anyone yearning for Japanese, Vietnamese, Brazilian, Greek or even Norwegian food, though modern international cuisine tops the list (see p134). There are also many bars and nightclubs in the area; hanging out around Plaza Serrano on any weekend night is a blast. Buenos Aires' most cutting-edge designers have also opened up dozens of boutiques here, and there are many fancy housewares stores and other fun themed shops. Finally, there's plenty of places to lay your head – countless boutique hotels, guesthouses and hostels also call this area home.

Another popular (but much smaller and more laid-back) neighborhood in Palermo is further north in Las Cañitas; it occupies a wedge of blocks close to the polo grounds. It's mostly a residential area on the border with Belgrano and named after the fields of sugar cane that used to grow here. The only sweet things here now, however, are the luscious desserts at the dozens of restaurants on Av Báez, the main business street. Just a few blocks long, it's densely packed with eateries, bars, cafés and even a club or two, and it positively buzzes at night. Southeast of Las Cañitas is the landmark **Centro Islámico Rey Fahd** (Map p92; ☎ 4899-0201; www.ccislamicoreyfahd.org.ar; Av Bullrich 55), built with Saudi money on land donated by ex-president and current outlaw Carlos Menem. Tours in Spanish run on Tuesday, Thursday and Saturday at noon (bring photo ID and enter via Av Int Bullrich).

Many important museums and elegant embassies are also located in Palermo, mostly in the sub-neighborhood of Palermo Chico (also called Barrio Parque), an elite area bordering Recoleta that is home to many of the city's rich and famous.

Palermo is one of Buenos Aires' largest barrios and is situated northwest of Recoleta. Main thoroughfares include Av Santa Fe, Av del Libertador and, at Palermo's southern edge, Av Córdoba.

MUSEO DE ARTE LATINOAMERICANO DE BUENOS AIRES (MALBA) Map p92

☎ 4808-6541; www.malba.org.ar; Av Figueroa Alcorta 3415; admission AR$20, Wed AR$8; noon-8pm Thu-Mon, to 9pm Wed; 67, 102

Sparkling inside its glass and cement walls is this airy modern-art museum, one of BA's newest and finest. Created by art patron Eduardo F Costantini, it contains some of the best works of classic and contemporary Latin American artists, such as Argentines Xul Solar and Antonio Berni, plus some pieces by Mexican duo Diego Rivera and Frida Kahlo. Excellent temporary exhibits are shown in several different halls, and there are occasional kids' programs and a cinema that screens art-house films. A small bookstore, gift shop and fancy café-restaurant complete the picture. Call for tours in English.

BUENOS AIRES FOR KIDS

Travelers with children have a good range of choices when it comes to activities in Buenos Aires. On weekends Palermo's parks bustle with families taking walks, picnicking or playing sports. The shopping malls fill with strollers, while family-friendly places like zoos, museums and theme parks also make for popular destinations. Porteños just adore children – and it shows.

Green spots in the city include Palermo's Parque 3 de Febrero, where on weekends traffic isn't allowed on the ring road around the rose garden (here you can rent bikes, boats and in-line skates). Other good stops for kids here include the Planetario Galileo Galilei (Map p92; ☎ 4771-9393; www.planetario.gov.ar; Av Sarmiento & Roldán), zoo (p95) and Japanese garden (p95). If you're downtown and need a nature break, try the Reserva Ecológica Costanera Sur (p70), a large nature preserve with good bird-watching, pleasant dirt paths and no vehicular traffic; bike rentals are available here, too.

Most large modern shopping malls come with playground, video arcade, multiplex and toy shops. Paseo Alcorta (p121) has plenty of mechanical rides next to the large food court, while Mercado de Abasto (p97) boasts a full-blown Museo de los Niños (Children's Museum; Map p98; ☎ 4861-2325; www.museoabasto.org.ar; Av Corrientes 3247; admission adult/2-18 yrs AR$12/24 Mon-Fri, AR$15/30 Sat & Sun; 🕑 1-8pm Tue-Sun, daily Jan-Feb) where kids enter a miniature city complete with post office, hospital and even TV station. Abasto also has a mini-amusement park.

In San Telmo the Museo Argentino del Títere (Puppet Museum; Map p76; ☎ 4307-6917; www.museoargdeltitere.com.ar; Piedras 905; admission free; 🕑 museum 9:30am-12:30pm, 3-6pm Tue, Wed & Fri, 3-6pm Thu, Sat & Sun; family puppet shows 4pm & 5:30pm Sat & Sun Feb-Sept, 5:30pm Oct-Dec, adult puppet shows 9pm Sat May-Nov) has a fascinating collection of international and Argentine puppets, but it's the inexpensive shows (AR$25) that will amuse the little 'uns. Make sure to visit the Museo Participativo de Ciencias (Map p87; ☎ 4806-3456; www.mpc.org.ar; Junín 1930; admission AR$16; 🕑 10am-5pm Mon-Fri, 3:30-7:30pm Sat & Sun, hours can vary per season) in the Centro Cultural Recoleta. This science museum has interactive displays that focus on fun learning – signs say *'prohibido no tocar,'* (not touching is forbidden). Christian parents might want to take the kids to Tierra Santa (p100), a religious theme park unlike anywhere you've ever been.

Outside the center in Caballito is Museo Argentino de Ciencias Naturales (Natural Science Museum; p99), with myriad rooms containing giant dinosaur bones, dainty seashells, scary insects, and amusing stuffed animals and birds.

Heading to Tigre (p200) just north of the center makes a great day excursion. Take the fun Tren de la Costa there; it ends at Parque de la Costa (p202), a typical amusement park with rides and activities. Boat trips and a craft & housewares market are nearby.

About a 45-minute drive outside the city is the exceptional zoo Parque Temaikén (☎ 034-8843 6900; www.temaiken.org.ar; Ruta Provincial 25km 1, Escobar; adult/child 3-10 yr AR$65/50, parking AR$12; 🕑 10am-7pm Tue-Sun Dec-Feb, till 6pm Mar-Nov). Only the most charming animal species (like meerkats and tigers) are on display here, roaming freely around spacious natural enclosures. The beautiful grounds are tidy and park-like, and exceptional exhibits include a butterfly house, fine aquarium and a large aviary (parrots and toucans galore). Interactive areas provide mental stimulation, and services include stroller rentals, gift stores and restaurants. Just outside Temaikén is a large playground run by Heladería Munchi. Tuesdays admission is half-off (unless it's a holiday).

Most restaurants welcome kids, but if a place looks 'very fine' you can ask if they take children your age. The same is true for accommodations (except perhaps for small boutique hotels or guesthouses) – again, one question is all it takes to find out.

For more particulars on traveling with children in BA, see p223.

MUSEO NACIONAL DE ARTE DECORATIVO Map p92

☎ 4801-8248; www.mnad.org; Av del Libertador 1902; admission AR$5, Tuesday free; 🕑 2-7pm Tue-Sun Mar-Dec, 2-7pm Tue-Sat Jan & Feb; 🚌 59, 60

This museum is housed in the stunning beaux arts mansion called Residencia Errázuriz Alvear (1917), which features such beautiful elements as Corinthian columns and a gorgeous marble staircase inspired by the palace of Versailles. There's also an amazing hall which has a carved wooden ceiling, stained-glass panels and a huge stone fireplace.

The mansion was once the residence of Chilean aristocrat Matías Errázuriz and his wife, Josefina de Alvear, and now displays many of their very posh belongings. Everything from renaissance religious paintings and porcelain dishes to Italian sculptures and period furniture was owned by Errázuriz, and some artwork by El Greco, Manet

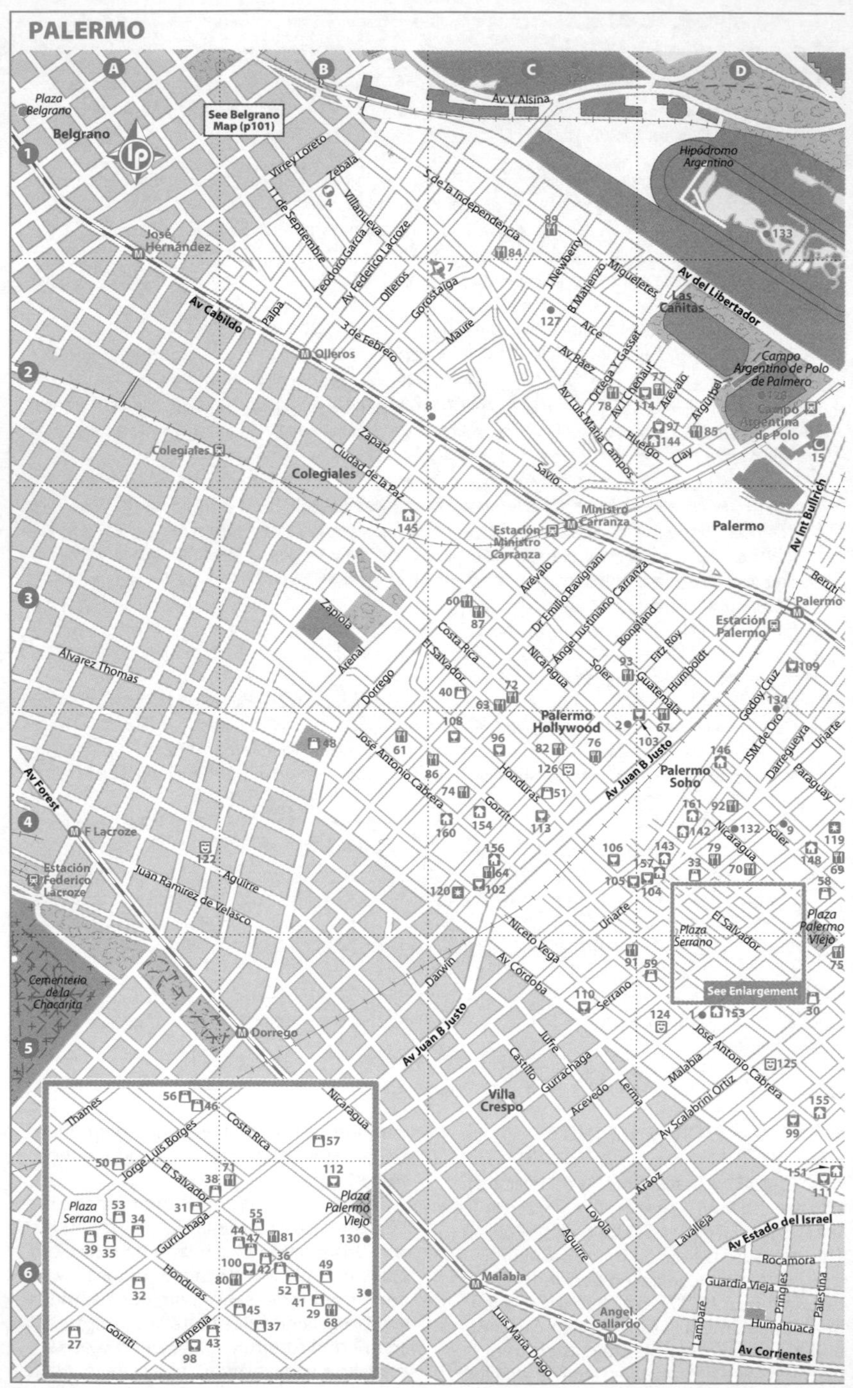
PALERMO
See Belgrano Map (p101)
Plaza Belgrano
Belgrano
José Hernández
Av Cabildo
Olleros
Colegiales
Colegiales
Av V Alsina
Hipódromo Argentino
Av del Libertador
Las Cañitas
Campo Argentino de Polo de Palmero
Campo Argentino de Polo
Ministro Carranza
Estación Ministro Carranza
Palermo
Av Int Bullrich
Estación Palermo
Palermo Hollywood
Palermo Soho
Av Juan B Justo
Alvarez Thomas
Av Forest
F Lacroze
Estación Federico Lacroze
Juan Ramirez de Velasco
Aguirre
Cementerio de la Chacarita
Dorrego
Villa Crespo
Av Córdoba
Av Scalabrini Ortiz
Av Estado del Israel
Malabia
Angel Gallardo
Av Corrientes
Luis María Drago
Plaza Serrano
Plaza Palermo Viejo
See Enlargement
Thames
Jorge Luis Borges
El Salvador
Costa Rica
Nicaragua
Gurruchaga
Honduras
Gorriti
Armenia

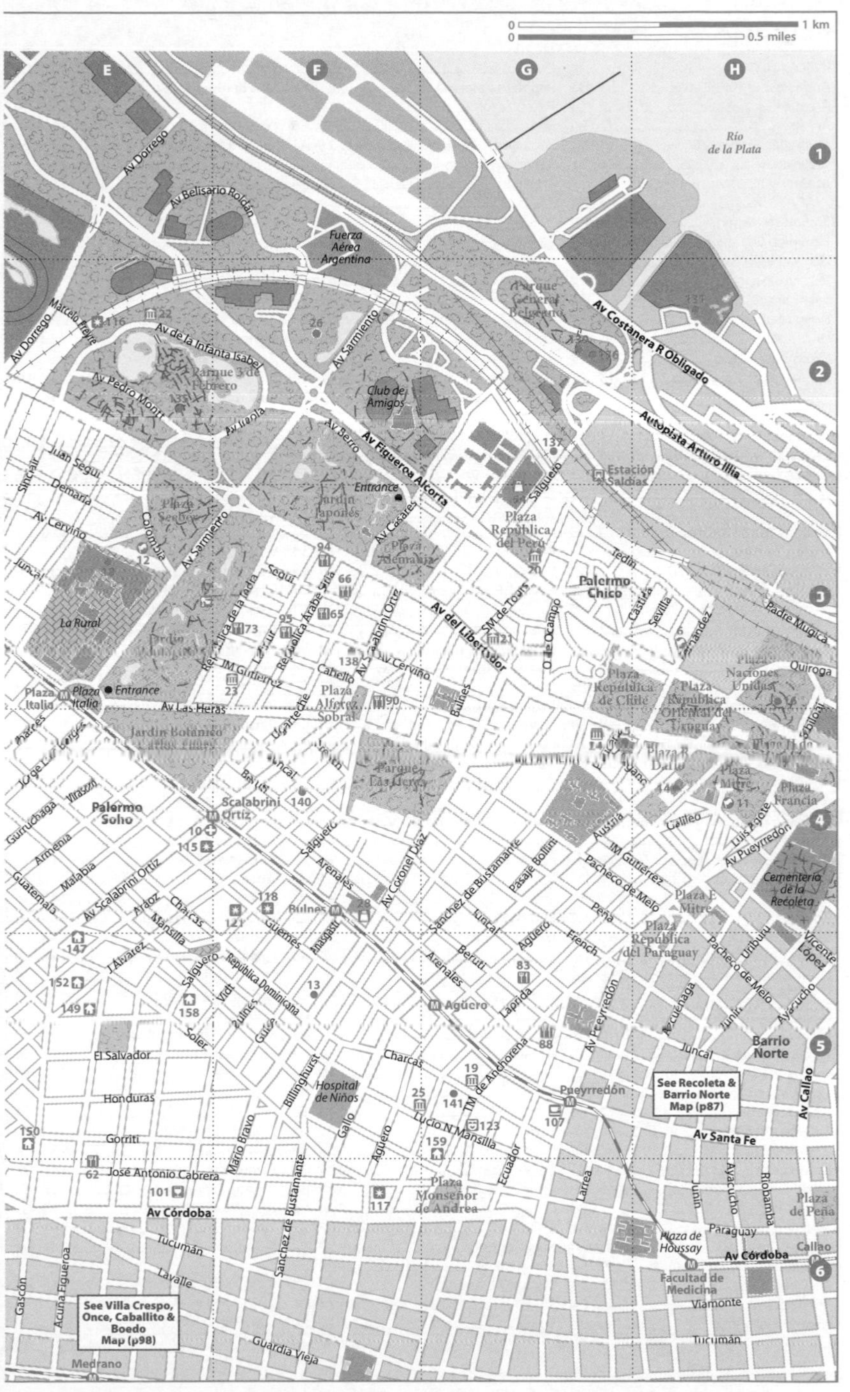

Río de la Plata
Av Costanera R Obligado
Autopista Arturo Illia
Av Figueroa Alcorta
Av del Libertador
Av Sarmiento
Av Dorrego
Av Belisario Roldán
Fuerza Aérea Argentina
Parque General Belgrano
Parque 3 de Febrero
Club de Amigos
Jardín Japonés
Plaza República del Perú
Palermo Chico
La Rural
Plaza Italia
Jardín Botánico Carlos Thays
Palermo Soho
Scalabrini Ortiz
Bulnes
Agüero
Pueyrredón
Plaza Alférez Sobral
Parque Las Heras
Cementerio de la Recoleta
Barrio Norte
Plaza República del Paraguay
Hospital de Niños
Plaza Monseñor de Andrea
Plaza de Houssay
Facultad de Medicina
Av Santa Fe
Av Córdoba
Av Callao
Av Scalabrini Ortiz
Av Las Heras
Av Coronel Díaz
Av Pueyrredón
See Recoleta & Barrio Norte Map (p87)
See Villa Crespo, Once, Caballito & Boedo Map (p98)

PALERMO

INFORMATION

Anda Responsible Travel 1 D5
Areatres 2 C4
Areatres 3 B6
Australian Embassy & Consulate 4 B1
Automóvil Club Argentino (ACA) 5 G4
Biblioteca Nacional (see 14)
Canadian Embassy 6 H3
German Embassy 7 C2
Instituto Geográfico Militar 8 C2
Say Hueque 9 D4
Swiss Medical 10 E4
UK Embassy 11 H4
US Embassy 12 E3
Vamos 13 F5

SIGHTS (pp90-6)

Biblioteca Nacional 14 H4
Centro Islàmico Rey Fahd 15 D2
Floralis Genérica 16 H3
Jardín Zoológico 17 E3
La Rural 18 E3
Museo Casa de Ricardo Rojas 19 G5
Museo de Arte Latinoamericano de Buenos Aires (Malba) 20 G3
Museo de Arte Popular José Hernández 21 G3
Museo de Artes Plásticas Eduardo Sívori 22 E2
Museo Evita 23 F3
Museo Nacional de Arte Decorativo 24 G4
Museo Xul Solar 25 F5
Planetario Galileo Galilei 26 F2

SHOPPING (pp117-21)

28 Sport 27 A6
Alto Palermo 28 F4
Arte Étnico Argentino 29 B6
Atípica 30 D5
Bokura 31 A6
Bolivia 32 A6
Boutique del Libro 33 D4
Calma Chicha 34 A6
Capital Diseño and Objetos 35 A6
Cora Groppo 36 B6
DAM 37 B6
El Cid 38 A6
Feria Plaza Serrano 39 A6
Hermanos Estebecorena 40 C3
Humawaca 41 B6
Jazmín Chebar 42 B6
Josefina Ferroni 43 A6
Juana de Arco 44 B6
La Mercería 45 B6
Lo de Joaquin Alberdi 46 A5
Maria Cher 47 B6
Mercado de las Pulgas 48 B4
Mishka (see 54)
Mishka 49 B6
Mission 50 A6
Mission 51 C4
Nadine Zlotogora (see 29)
Owoko 52 B6
Papelera Palermo 53 A6
Paseo Alcorta 54 G3
Rapsodia 55 B6
Recursos Infantiles 56 A5
Sabater Hermanos 57 B5
Trosman 58 D4
Zivals 59 D5

EATING (pp134-9)

Almacén Oui Oui 60 C3
Artemisia 61 B4
Artemisia 62 E6
Azema Exotica Bistró 63 C3
Bangalore 64 C4
Bella Italia 65 F3
Bella Italia Grill & Bar 66 F3
Bio 67 D4
Cluny 68 B6
Don Julio 69 D4
El Último Beso 70 D4
Freud & Fahler 71 B6
Green Bamboo 72 C3
Guido's Bar 73 F3
Il Ballo de Mattone 74 C4
Krishna 75 D5
La Dorita 76 C4
Las Cholas 77 D2
Las Cortaderas 78 C2
Lelé de Troya 79 D4
Little Rose 80 B6
Mark's Deli & Coffeehouse 81 B6
Miranda 82 C4
Museo Evita Restaurante (see 23)
Natural Deli 83 G5
Natural Deli 84 C1
Novecento 85 D2
Olsen 86 C4
Oui Oui 87 C3
Oviedo 88 G5
Persicco 89 C1
Persicco 90 F3
Rave 91 C5
Social La Lechuza 92 D4
Sudestada 93 C3
Un Altra Volta 94 F3
Voulezbar 95 F3

DRINKING (pp143-53)

Acabar 96 C4
Antares 97 D2
Antares 98 A6
Bach Bar 99 D5
Bar 6 100 B6
Bulnes Class 101 E6
Carnal 102 C4
Casa Coupage 103 D4
Casa Cruz 104 D4
Chueca 105 C4
Congo Bar 106 C4
El Olmo 107 G5
Home Hotel 108 C4
Kim y Novak 109 D3
Mundo Bizarro 110 C5
Sitges 111 D6
Sugar 112 B6
Unico 113 C4
Van Koning 114 D2

NIGHTLIFE (pp155-61)

Club Aráoz 115 E4
Crobar 116 E2
Glam 117 F6
La Peña del Colorado 118 F4
Los Cardones 119 D4
Niceto Club 120 C4
Thelonious Bar 121 F4

THE ARTS (pp163-72)

Caserón Porteño (see 145)
Dance & Move 122 A4
Escuela Brasileña de Danzas 123 G5
La Viruta 124 D5
Salon Canning 125 D5
Tiempo de Gitanos 126 C4

SPORTS & ACTIVITIES (pp173-80)

Boulder 127 C2
Campo Argentino de Polo 128 D2
Campo Municipal de Golf 129 C1
Centro Valletierra 130 B6
Costa Salguero Driving Range 131 H2
Espacio Oxivital 132 D4
Hipódromo Argentino 133 D1
Home Hotel (see 108)
Kurata Dojo 134 D3
Parque 3 de Febrero 135 E2
Parque General Belgrano 136 G2
Salguero Tenis 137 G2
Ser Spa 138 F3
Sprint Haupt 139 G2
Tamara di Tella Pilates 140 F4
Vida Natural 141 G5

SLEEPING (pp193-6)

Abode 142 D4
Bait Hostel 143 D4
Casa Las Cañitas 144 D2
Caserón Porteño 145 B3
Che Lulu Guesthouse 146 D4
Duque Hotel 147 E5
Eco Pampa Hotel 148 D4
Hotel Costa Rica 149 E5
Ke Viva el Mundo 150 E5
Livian Guesthouse 151 D6
Magnolia Hotel 152 E5
Mine Hotel 153 D5
Noa Noa Lofts 154 C4
Old Friends Hotel 155 D5
Own Hotel 156 C4
Palermitano 157 D4
Posada Palermo 158 E5
Reina Madre Hostel 159 G5
Rendezvous Hotel 160 C4
Rugantino Hotel 161 D4

TRANSPORTATION (pp216-22)

Automóvil Club Argentino (ACA) (see 5)

TRANSPORTATION: PALERMO

Bus Take buses 29, 59, 64 and 152 from the Microcentro to Plaza Italia; bus 39 from Congreso to Palermo Viejo; bus 111 from the Microcentro to Palermo Viejo.

Subte Línea D is the fastest way to Palermo's Plaza Italia area.

and Rodin can also be seen. There are guided tours in English Tuesday to Saturday at 2:30pm (AR$15). There's also a lovely café outside, which provides a relaxing break on a sunny day.

JARDÍN ZOOLÓGICO Map p92

☎ 4011-9900; www.zoobuenosaires.com.ar; cnr Avs Las Heras & Sarmiento; admission AR$15-22, under 12 yr free; 🕑 10am-6pm Tue-Sun, till 5pm Apr-Sep; Ⓢ Línea D Plaza Italia

Set on 18 hectares in the middle of Palermo, Buenos Aires' Jardín Zoológico is a decent zoo, with many 'natural' and good-sized animal enclosures and over 350 species represented. On sunny weekends it's packed with families enjoying the large green spaces, artificial lakes and, of course, the creatures themselves. Some of the buildings housing the animals are impressive; be sure to check out the elephant house. An aquarium, a monkey island, reptile house and large aviary are other highlights; a few special exhibits (like the sea lion show or carousel) cost extra.

The zoo is noted for having successfully bred condors and white tigers, and for having an educational farm with a petting zoo for the kids. Waterfowl, Patagonian hares, nutria (semi-aquatic rodent) and feral house cats roam wild.

JARDÍN JAPONÉS Map p92

☎ 4804-4922; www.jardinjapones.org.ar; cnr Avs Alcorta & Casares; admission AR$8; 🕑 10am-6pm; 🚌 67, 102

First opened in 1967 and then donated to the city of Buenos Aires in 1979 (on the centenary of the arrival of Argentina's first Japanese immigrants), Jardín Japonés is one of the capital's best-kept gardens – and makes a wonderfully peaceful rest stop. Inside you can enjoy a Japanese restaurant (which serves great sushi) along with lovely ponds filled with koi and spanned by pretty bridges. The teahouse makes a good break, and bonsai trees are available for purchase. Japanese culture can be experienced through occasional exhibitions and workshops on ikebana, haiku, origami, *taiko* (Japanese drumming) and many other things; check the website for schedules. Tours in Spanish at 3pm daily.

MUSEO DE ARTES PLÁSTICAS EDUARDO SÍVORI Map p92

☎ 4774-9452; www.museosivori.org.ar; Av de la Infanta Isabel 555; admission AR$1, free Wed & Sat; 🕑 noon-8pm Mon-Fri, 10am-8pm Sat & Sun; 🚌 10, 34

Named for an Italo-Argentine painter who studied in Europe, this modern museum of Argentine art (located in Palermo's Parque 3 de Febrero) has open spaces allowing frequent and diverse exhibitions. Sívori's Parisian works reflect European themes, but later works returned to Argentine motifs, mainly associated with rural life on the Pampas. However most works on display are by other well-known Argentine artists, such as Benito Quinquela Martín, Antonio Berni and Fernando Fader. There's a sculpture garden and slick café on the premises, and occasional theater, concerts, courses and workshops are offered.

MUSEO EVITA Map p92

☎ 4807-0306; www.museoevita.org; Lafinur 2988; locals/foreigners AR$5/15; 🕑 11-7pm Tue-Sun; Ⓢ Línea D Plaza Italia

Practically everybody who's anybody in Argentina has their own museum, and Eva Perón (1919–52) is no exception. The Museo Evita immortalizes the Argentine heroine with plenty of videos, historical photos, books, old posters, newspaper headlines – even her fingerprints are recorded. However, the prize memorabilia has to be her wardrobe: dresses, shoes, handbags, hats and blouses lie proudly behind glass, forever pressed and pristine. Even Evita's old wallets and perfumes are exposed for everyone to see. Our personal favorite is a picture of her kicking a soccer ball – in heels. Upscale café-restaurant on premises.

MUSEO DE ARTE POPULAR JOSÉ HERNÀNDEZ Map p92

☎ 4803-2384; www.museohernandez.org.ar; Av del Libertador 2373; admission AR$1, Sun free; 🕑 1-7pm Wed-Fri, 10am-8pm Sat & Sun; 🚌 67, 102

The first building of this modest-sized museum has modern craft and folkloric

WALKING THE DOG

Buenos Aires supports a legion of *paseaperros* (professional dog walkers), who can be seen with up to 20 canines on leashes. They'll stroll through areas like Recoleta, Palermo's parks and even downtown with a variety of dogs ranging from scruffy mongrels to expensive purebreds, each of their tails happily a-waggin'.

Paseaperros are employed by busy apartment dwellers who either can't or won't take the time to exercise their animals properly – and are willing to pay up to AR$300 per month for this unique walking service. Since most *paseaperros* don't pay taxes, they can really 'clean up' in the city – figuratively speaking.

Every day thousands of canines deposit tons (almost literally) of excrement in the streets and parks of the capital. You'll be aware of this fact soon after stepping into the streets of Buenos Aires. Cleaning up after one's pooch is already a city requirement, but enforcement is nil, so be very careful where you tread – you'll see dog piles of all textures and sizes lining almost every sidewalk. One to especially step clear of is the author-named *dulce de leche* variety.

Still, the capital's leashed packs are a remarkably orderly and always entertaining sight, and make great snapshots to bring back home.

items in great condition, plus a basement for diverse temporary exhibitions that range from gaucho accoutrements to modern toys to chess sets. In the back are permanent exhibitions on Mapuche crafts, such as exquisitely detailed ponchos, plus a strangely incongruent collection of fabulous and gaudy Carnaval costumes.

MUSEO XUL SOLAR Map p92

☎ 4824-3302; www.xulsolar.org.ar; Laprida 1212; admission AR$10; noon-8pm Tue-Fri, noon-6:30pm Sat, closed Feb; Línea D Aguero, Pueyrredón

Xul Solar was a painter, inventor, poet and friend of Jorge Luis Borges. This museum (located in his old mansion) showcases over 80 of his unique and colorful yet subdued paintings. Solar's Klee-esque style includes fantastically themed, almost cartoonish figures placed in surreal cubist landscapes. It's great stuff, and bizarre enough to put him in a class of his own. Tours in Spanish are available Tuesday and Thursday at 4pm and Saturday at 3:30pm.

MUSEO CASA DE RICARDO ROJAS Map p92

☎ 4824-4039; Charcas 2837; Línea D Aguero, Pueyrredón

Walk under the facade, modeled after the Casa de Independencia in Tucumán, and behold a quaint courtyard surrounded by European and Incan architectural motifs. Famous Argentine educator and writer Ricardo Rojas lived here from 1929 to 1957, and in his office wrote his renowned work *El Santo de la Espada* (1933). Note the glass case displaying his original books; the library contains 20,000 volumes. An old dining room with period furniture also gives an idea of the past. Give a ring for opening hours, as the museum was closed for remodeling at research time.

BIBLIOTECA NACIONAL Map p92

☎ 4808-6000; www.bn.gov.ar; Agüero 2502; 9am-9pm Mon-Fri, noon-7pm Sat & Sun, tours in Spanish 3pm Mon-Fri; 59, 60

After two decades of construction problems and delays, the national library finally moved into this rather ugly, mushroom-shaped behemoth in 1992. Prominent Argentine and Latin American literary figures, such as Ernesto Sábato, have lectured here, and other events include workshops, concerts and cultural activities. Tours in English are offered on Monday, Tuesday and Thursday at 3pm. Bring photo ID and be ready to fill out a form to enter. There's no internet access and it may be closed in January.

VILLA CRESPO, ONCE, CABALLITO & BOEDO

Drinking p153; **Eating** p150; **Sleeping** p196

Buenos Aires' easterly regions – south of Palermo and east of Congreso – are refreshingly local, with just a few interesting sights dotting the map. They're blue-collar neighborhoods with an occasional surprise for the tourist, such as some artsy galleries, a few renovated cafés and a couple of shopping outlets.

Becoming trendier every day, Villa Crespo's rising popularity is mainly due to its proximity to Palermo Viejo – it's just south of Av Córdoba, which divides the two neighborhoods. Skyrocketing real estate prices in Palermo Viejo mean that restaurants, bars and renters are heading south for more options, and Villa Crespo's peaceful, no-nonsense streets has them. It's also easily accessible via Subte, which doesn't hurt one bit.

You'd have a hard time finding more of a melting pot in Buenos Aires than the ethnically colorful neighborhood of Once (pronounced 'ohn-seh'), which holds sizable populations of Jews, Peruvians and Koreans. Its busy commercial heart is at Estación Once (Once train station), where an astounding concentration of inexpensive garment shops are located. Lively trade keeps the area bustling both day and night with the energy of immigrant commerce. There's a colorful, almost third-world feel to this neighborhood – which can be a welcome change in Buenos Aires.

Near the Once neighborhood is Mercado de Abasto (p97), one of the city's most attractive shopping malls – both inside and out. It also has great entertainment for kids, from a mini-amusement park to a 'children's museum' (see the boxed text, p91). Outside the eastern side of the mall is a small statue of Carlos Gardel, the famous tango singer who first crooned in this neighborhood; four blocks northeast on Jean Jaurés is the Museo Casa Carlos Gardel, a museum honoring him. Many alternative theaters can also be found in this area.

West of Once is Caballito, a calm and pleasant neighborhood where locals go about their daily routines and tourists are nowhere to be seen. The large and circular Parque del Centenario holds the Museo Argentino de Ciencias Naturales (p99), a good natural-science museum that's definitely worth a peek for its musty taxidermy and cool skeleton room.

The bohemian neighborhood of Boedo hasn't seen too many tourists – yet. It holds a few interesting bars and especially atmospheric cafés, such as the gorgeous Las Violetas (p153) and Esquina Homero Manzi (p166), which also puts on pricey tango shows. The intersection of Av San Juan and Boedo is especially historic and right on the Subte line.

All these neighborhoods are east of the center and easily accessible via the Subte. Villa Crespo is just south of Palermo Viejo and north of Caballito, while Once is just west of Congreso (Plaza Miserere stop on the Subte). Boedo lies south, and most sights here are reached via the Boedo Subte stop.

MERCADO DE ABASTO Map p98

☎ 4959-3400; www.abasto-shopping.com.ar; Av Corrientes 3247; 🕐 10am-10pm; Ⓢ Línea B Carlos Gardel

Further west, in the Abasto district, the historic Mercado de Abasto (1895) has been recycled by US-Hungarian financier George Soros into one of the most beautiful shopping centers in the city. The building, once a large vegetable market, received an architectural prize in 1937 for its Av Corrientes facade; at night the spotlighted and lofty arches are visible all the way from Av Pueyrredón. It holds more than 200 stores, a large cinema, a large food court and a kosher McDonald's. It's great for families, with a good children's museum, video/arcade games and even a small amusement park. The small Abasto neighborhood was once home to tango legend Carlos Gardel, and on the gentrified pedestrian street off Av Anchorena is a statue of the singer.

MUSEO CASA CARLOS GARDEL Map p98

☎ 4964-2071; Jean Jaurés 735; admission AR$1, free Wed; 🕐 11am-6pm Mon, Wed-Fri, 10am-7pm Sat & Sun; Ⓢ Línea B Carlos Gardel

Small but noteworthy is this tribute to tango's most famous voice. Located in Gardel's old house, the museum traces his partnership with José Razzano and displays old memorabilia. There isn't a whole lot to see, so only true fans or the curious should hike it over to this section of town; look for the cluster of colorfully painted buildings.

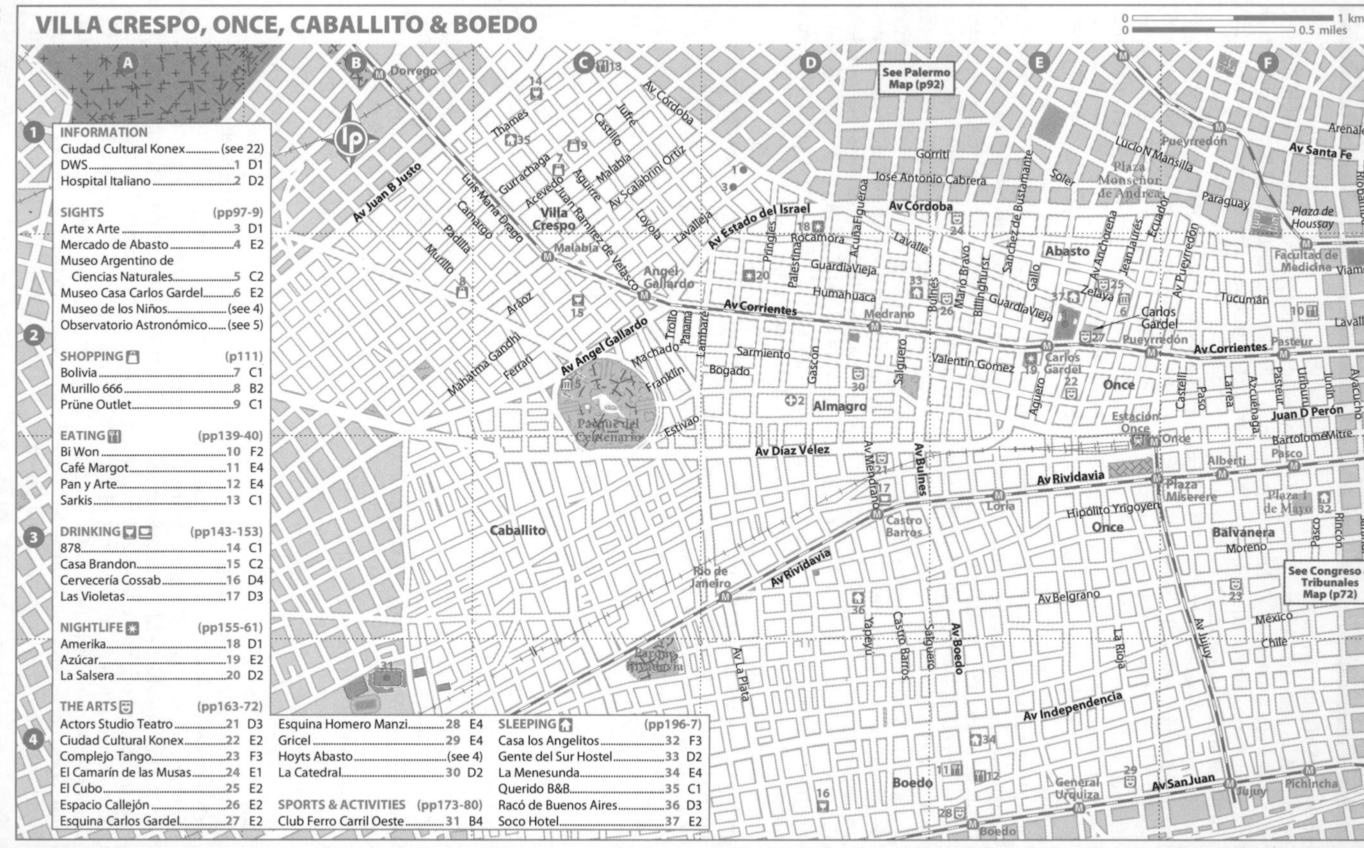
VILLA CRESPO, ONCE, CABALLITO & BOEDO
0 — 1 km
0 — 0.5 miles
INFORMATION
Ciudad Cultural Konex (see 22)
DWS 1 D1
Hospital Italiano 2 D2
SIGHTS (pp97-9)
Arte x Arte 3 D1
Mercado de Abasto 4 E2
Museo Argentino de Ciencias Naturales 5 C2
Museo Casa Carlos Gardel 6 E2
Museo de los Niños (see 4)
Observatorio Astronómico (see 5)
SHOPPING (p111)
Bolivia 7 C1
Murillo 666 8 B2
Prüne Outlet 9 C1
EATING (pp139-40)
Bi Won 10 F2
Café Margot 11 E4
Pan y Arte 12 E4
Sarkis 13 C1
DRINKING (pp143-153)
878 14 C1
Casa Brandon 15 C2
Cervecería Cossab 16 D4
Las Violetas 17 D3
NIGHTLIFE (pp155-61)
Amerika 18 D1
Azúcar 19 E2
La Salsera 20 D2
THE ARTS (pp163-72)
Actors Studio Teatro 21 D3
Ciudad Cultural Konex 22 E2
Complejo Tango 23 F3
El Camarín de las Musas 24 E1
El Cubo 25 E2
Espacio Callejón 26 E2
Esquina Carlos Gardel 27 E2
Esquina Homero Manzi 28 E4
Gricel 29 E4
Hoyts Abasto (see 4)
La Catedral 30 D2
SPORTS & ACTIVITIES (pp173-80)
Club Ferro Carril Oeste 31 B4
SLEEPING (pp196-7)
Casa los Angelitos 32 F3
Gente del Sur Hostel 33 D2
La Menesunda 34 E4
Querido B&B 35 C1
Racó de Buenos Aires 36 D3
Soco Hotel 37 E2
See Palermo Map (p92)
See Congreso & Tribunales Map (p72)
Dorrego
Av Juan B Justo
Thames
Gurruchaga
Acevedo
Luis María Drago
Camargo
Padilla
Murillo
Villa Crespo
Malabia
Aguirre
Juan Ramírez de Velasco
Castillo
Jufré
Av Córdoba
Av Scalabrini Ortiz
Loyola
Lavalleja
Angel Gallardo
Av Estado del Israel
Araoz
Mahatma Gandhi
Ferrari
Av Angel Gallardo
Machado
Franklin
Trolio
Panamá
Lambaré
Estivao
Parque del Centenario
Caballito
Río de Janeiro
Av Rivadavia
Parque Rivadavia
Av La Plata
Pringles
Rocamora
Palestina
Acuña Figueroa
Guardia Vieja
Humahuaca
Av Corrientes
Medrano
Sarmiento
Bogado
Gascón
Almagro
Salguero
Av Díaz Vélez
Av Mendrano
Av Bulnes
Castro Barros
Yapeyú
Av Boedo
Boedo
Gorriti
José Antonio Cabrera
Av Córdoba
Lavalle
Bulnes
Mario Bravo
Billinghurst
Sánchez de Bustamante
Gallo
Abasto
Av Anchorena
Jean Jaurés
Zelaya
Carlos Gardel
Valentín Gomez
Agüero
Once
Estación Once
Av Rivadavia
Loria
Hipólito Yrigoyen
Av Belgrano
La Rioja
Av Independencia
General Urquiza
Av San Juan
Jujuy
Soler
Lucio N Mansilla
Plaza Monseñor de Andrea
Pueyrredón
Ecuador
Av Pueyrredón
Paraguay
Arenales
Av Santa Fe
Riobamba
Plaza de Houssay
Facultad de Medicina
Viamonte
Tucumán
Lavalle
Pasteur
Castelli
Paso
Larrea
Azcuénaga
Uriburu
Junín
Ayacucho
Juan D Perón
Bartolomé Mitre
Alberti
Pasco
Plaza Miserere
Plaza 1 de Mayo
Balvanera
Moreno
Rincón
Sarandí
México
Chile
Av Jujuy
Pichincha

TRANSPORTATION: VILLA CRESPO, ONCE, CABALLITO & BOEDO

Bus Take bus 140 from the Microcentro to Villa Crespo, bus 26 to Once, bus 105 to Caballito, bus 126 to Boedo.

Subte Líneas A, B and E are the fastest way to these neighborhoods.

MUSEO ARGENTINO DE CIENCIAS NATURALES Map p98

☎ 4982-6595; www.macn.secyt.gov.ar; Ángel Gallardo 470; admission AR$3; 2-7pm; Línea B Angel Gallardo

Way over to the west, the oval Parque del Centenario is a large open space containing this excellent natural-science museum. On display are collections of meteorites, rocks and minerals, seashells, insects and dinosaur replicas. Life-size models of a basking shark and ocean sunfish are impressive, and the taxidermy and skeleton rooms are especially amusing. Bring the kids; they can mingle with the hundreds of children who visit on school excursions.

Nearby is the Observatorio Astronómico (☎ 4863-3366; www.asaramas.com.ar; Patricias Argentinas 550). Call or check the website, as observation hours change depending on the season.

ARTE X ARTE Map p98

☎ 4772-6754; Lavalleja 1062; 1-8pm Mon-Fri; Línea B Angel Gallardo

Art-gallery lovers shouldn't miss this large exhibition space, which takes up 1800 sq meters (not bad for an alternative gallery). Anyone can just enter and see what's on display, which can range from photography to digital art to video installations. It's all contemporary, and there's a library and auditorium as well. Closed December through March; might be open on Saturdays in 2011.

BELGRANO

Eating p140

Bustling Av Cabildo, the racing heartbeat of Belgrano, is an overwhelming jumble of noise and neon. It's a two-way street of clothing, shoe and housewares shops that does its part in supporting porteños' mass consumerism. For a bit more peace and quiet, head to the blocks on either side of the avenue, where Belgrano becomes a leafy barrio of museums, plazas, parks and good local eateries.

A block east of Av Cabildo, the barrio's plaza is the site of the modest but fun Feria Plaza Belgrano (p118). On a sunny weekend it's full of shoppers and families with strollers. Near the plaza stands the Italianate Iglesia de la Inmaculada Concepción, a church popularly known as La Redonda (The Round One) because of its impressive dome.

Just a few steps from the plaza is the Museo Histórico Sarmiento (p100), which honors one of the most forward-thinking Argentines in history. Also close by is the Museo de Arte Español Enrique Larreta (p100), a mansion with gorgeous art pieces and gardens. About five blocks north is yet another museum, the Museo Casa de Yrurtia (p101), honoring the well-known Argentine sculptor.

Four blocks northeast of Plaza Belgrano, French landscape architect Carlos Thays took advantage of the contours of Barrancas de Belgrano to create an attractive, green public space on one of the few natural hillocks in the city. Retirees spend the afternoon at the chess tables beneath its *ombú* tree, and on Saturday and Sunday evenings the band shell hosts a popular outdoor *milonga* (tango event; see p167)

Across Juramento from Barrancas, Belgrano's growing Chinatown fills three blocks on Arribeños, with more Chinese businesses spilling over into the side streets. Don't come on Monday, however, as many places shut down then; do come on Chinese New Year (p21), when festivities abound.

You'll probably head into Belgrano via Av Cabildo, either by bus or Subte (the Subte runs right under Cabildo). Plaza Belgrano is one block east of Cabildo at Juramento; most sights are around the plaza. Barrancas de Belgrano is the location of Belgrano's bus and train stations and is located about four blocks from the plaza.

PRAYING FOR KITSCH

Tired of the same old Sunday sermons? Tierra Santa (Map p101; ☎ 4784-9551; www.tierrasanta-bsas.com.ar; Av Costanera R Obligado 5790; adult/child 3-11yr AR$30/12; 9am-9pm Fri, noon-10pm Sat, Sun & holidays Apr-Nov, 4pm-midnight Fri-Sun & holidays Dec-Mar) might be exactly what you need.

Enter this religious and wonderfully tacky theme park, roughly based on Jerusalem, and head straight to the manger scene. Here, colorful lights and minimally animatronic figures swoon over baby Jesus. Better yet is the creation of the world, which features real rushing waters and life-size fake animals. From here it's a 30-second walk to witness the 40ft-tall animatronic Jesus rise from the Calvary mound, open his eyes and finally turn his palms toward the emotional devoted below. Miss the show? Don't fret: another resurrection is just around the corner.

The park isn't just for Christians – there are reproductions of the Wailing Wall, along with a synagogue and a mosque. So regardless of religious affiliation, enjoy nibbling on a shawarma or take in an Arabic dancing show. It's a spectacle you won't find anyplace else on earth – especially not in Jerusalem.

MUSEO DE ARTE ESPAÑOL ENRIQUE LARRETA Map p101

☎ 4784-2640; www.museolarreta.buenosaires.gov.ar; Juramento 2291; admission AR$1, Thu free; 1-7pm Mon-Fri, 10am-8pm Sat & Sun; Línea D Juramento

Hispanophile novelist Enrique Larreta (1875–1961) resided in this elegant colonial-style house across from Plaza Belgrano, which now displays his private art collection to the public. It's a grand and spacious old building, and contains classic Spanish art, period furniture, wood-carved religious items and shields and armor. The wood and tiled floors are beautiful, and everything is richly lit. Tours in Spanish are given at 5pm Monday to Friday, plus 4pm and 6pm on Saturday and Sunday. Be sure to stroll through the lovely gardens out the back.

MUSEO HISTÓRICO SARMIENTO Map p101

☎ 4782-2354; www.museosarmiento.gov.ar; Juramento 2180; admission AR$5, Thu free; 1-6pm Mon-Fri, 3-7pm Sat & Sun; Línea D Juramento

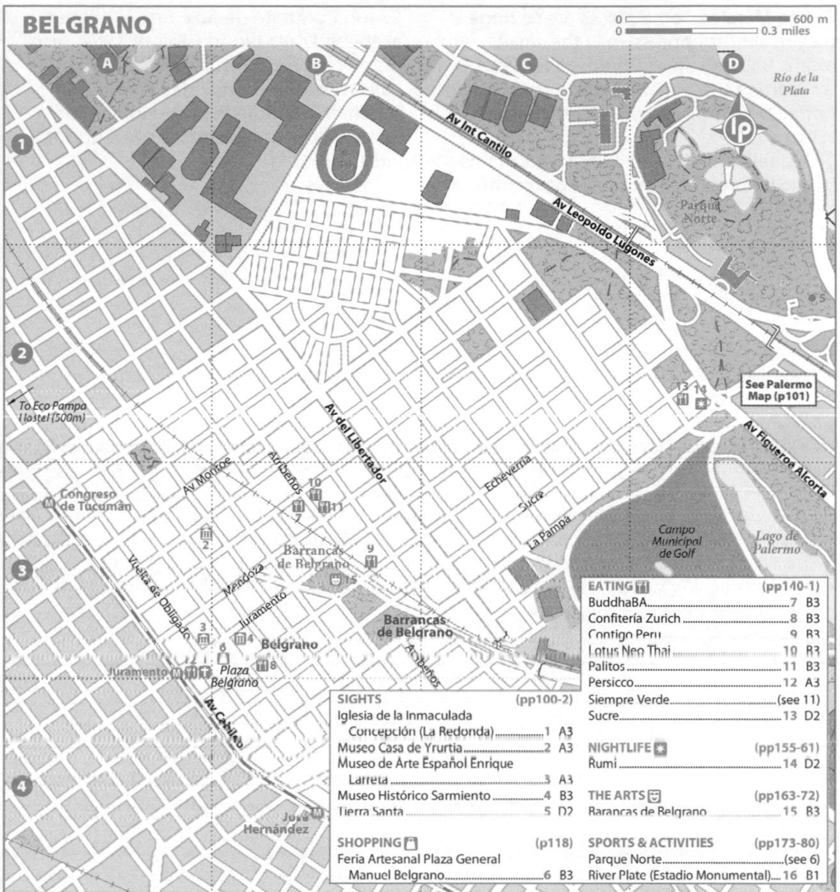

Opposite Plaza Belgrano, this museum contains memorabilia of Domingo F Sarmiento, one of Argentina's most famous presidents, diplomats and educators. Despite his provincial origins, the classically educated Sarmiento was an eloquent writer. He analyzed 19th-century Argentina from a cosmopolitan, clearly Eurocentric point of view, most notably in his masterful polemic *Facundo* (subtitled *Civilization and Barbarism*).

The building itself was briefly the site of the Congreso Nacional during the presidency of Nicolás Avellaneda (1874–80), when both chambers voted to federalize the city of Buenos Aires. The house holds Sarmiento's desk, bed and other furnishings, along with old photos, antique knickknacks and the ex-president's own ear horn. It's for history fanatics only.

MUSEO CASA DE YRURTIA Map p101

☎ 4781-0385; O'Higgins 2390; admission AR$5, Tue free; 1-7pm Tue-Fri, 3-7pm Sat & Sun; Línea D Juramento

Reclusive Rogelio Yrurtia (1879–1950), best known for his sculpture *Canto al Trabajo* on Plazoleta Olazábal in San Telmo, designed this neocolonial residence. The home is full of Yrurtia's work – which focuses on human torsos – and works by his wife, painter Lía

TRANSPORTATION: BELGRANO

Bus Buses 29, 59, 64 and 152 all connect Belgrano to downtown.

Subte Línea D is the fastest way to Belgrano; the Juramento stop leaves you a block from the plaza.

Correrea Morales. Some pieces are so huge they're almost oppressive in the small rooms housing them. There are also pieces by Yrurtia's teacher and father-in-law, Lucio Correa Morales, and by other sculptors and artists.

A small and attractive garden contains a larger-than-life-size statue of boxers titled Grupo Combate de Box, first exhibited at the St Louis World's Fair of 1904. Also noteworthy is Yrurtia's eclectic furniture collection, which includes pieces from Japan, the Middle East and India. And keep a lookout for Picasso's *Rue Cortot, Paris*.

WALKING TOURS

THROUGH THE HEART OF BUENOS AIRES

1 Plaza San Martín Start at this leafy plaza (p82), the green heart of Retiro and a haven for loungers on a sunny day. It was designed by French landscape architect Carlos Thays; notice the statue of a proud José de San Martín astride his horse at the western tip of the plaza.

2 Palacio Paz Cross Av Santa Fe to the Círculo Militar (1909), a striking building that houses this incredible mansion (p82). Time it right so you can catch an English-speaking tour (otherwise they're in Spanish), and take in the grandeur of a long-ago era.

3 Museo de Armas Located at the other end of the Círculo Militar is this weapons museum (p83). Inside is room after room of guns, swords and cannons, all well displayed and lit. Weapons buffs will definitely want to linger.

4 Galerías Pacífico Find your way down to pedestrian Florida and walk south to this elegant shopping mall (p61), one of the capital's most beautiful. Even if you don't like to shop, you should take a peek inside at the ceiling murals; there's often free (donation) tango just outside.

5 Café Richmond Buenos Aires is famous for its cafés, and the Richmond (p151) is a classic. Stop by if you need a quick break; the old-time atmosphere will make it easy to think back on the days when Jorge Luis Borges used to sip his coffee here.

6 Teatro Colón Now head west a few blocks on pedestrian Lavalle and cross Av 9 de Julio, considered by many the world's widest street. Your destination is the impressive Teatro Colón (p71), BA's opera house and a major source of pride for porteños.

7 Obelisco The city's premiere landmark is this 67m monument (p71). Not only is the obelisco used as ground zero for measuring distances from the city center, it's *the* place to honk your car's horn when your soccer team wins a major victory.

8 Av Corrientes Back in the day this major avenue was the main theater district in BA, and even today some of the city's largest theaters still live here. Av Corrientes is also known for its many bookstores (though the books sold here are practically all in Spanish).

9 Plaza de Mayo Hit Florida again and make your way south to Diagonal Roque Sáenz Peña. You'll end up at historic Plaza de Mayo (p63), where the presidential palace, main cathedral and other important buildings are located. If you have extra energy continue south on the Historical Saunter walk (p105), or head west on the Plaza de Mayo to Congreso walk (p103).

WALK FACTS

Start Plaza San Martín
End Plaza de Mayo
Distance 3km
Duration 2½ hours

THROUGH THE HEART OF BUENOS AIRES

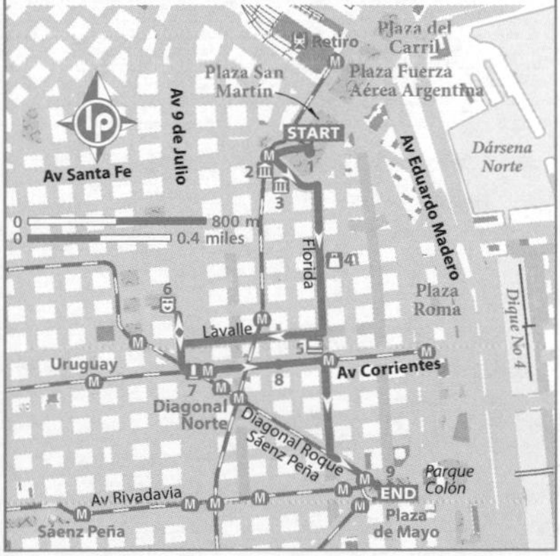

PLAZA DE MAYO TO CONGRESO

1 Plaza de Mayo Full of history, this is Buenos Aires' most important plaza (p60) and the main location where throngs of citizens gather on occasion to air their many grievances. Couples stroll while tourists come to take photos of the plaza's numerous attractions, and vendors sell flapping flags and patriotic pins.

2 Casa Rosada The plaza's main attraction, the Pink House (p64) holds presidential offices. You can take tours inside, and a modest museum (currently closed for remodelling) lies off to the south side and holds ruins of a fort in its basement.

WALK FACTS

Start Plaza de Mayo
End Obelisco
Distance 4km
Duration Three hours

PLAZA DE MAYO TO CONGRESO

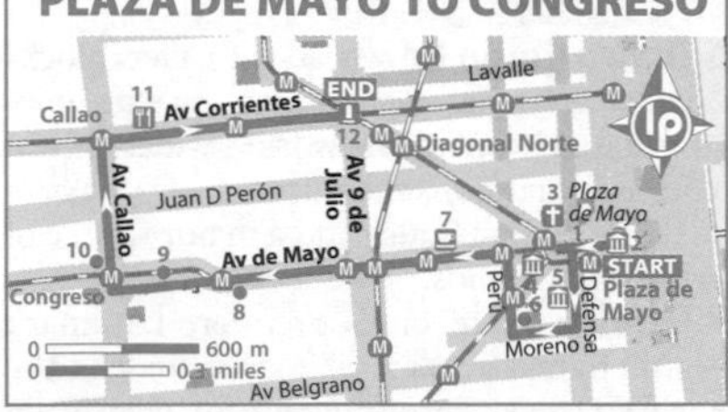

3 Catedral Metropolitana Also on the plaza is BA's most important cathedral (p65). Pop inside for a look around. The tomb of General José de San Martín (you've noticed his name here and there?) is located here, and a flame burns outside to keep his spirit alive.

4 Museo del Cabildo Right near the cathedral is this small museum; it's BA's old town council (p66), but don't expect overly impressive exhibits. Walk around to the back patio, where a café provides refreshments and a small crafts market sets up on Thursday and Friday.

5 Museo de la Ciudad From Plaza de Mayo, head south via Defensa to this city museum (p66), which traces part of the city's history. Across the way is the baroque Basílica de San Francisco, opened by the Franciscan order in 1754; inside, a large tapestry by Horacio Butler has replaced a fire-damaged altarpiece.

6 Manzana de las Luces Once Buenos Aires' center of learning, this 'Block of Enlightenment' (p66) was built in 1730 and is one of the city's oldest building clusters. Now it's a cultural center of sorts, offering classes and workshops.

7 Café Tortoni If you need a break, scoot over to this historic café (p151), arguably the city's most famous. The Tortoni has become so popular with tourists it's almost a caricature of itself, but still offers a classic café experience and affordable tango shows at night.

8 Palacio Barolo Keep going on Av de Mayo, and see if you can cross super-wide Av 9 de Julio in one go (hint: You'll have to run!). Stop in at this amazing, neo-gothic historical building (p74) and, if you time things right, hop on a tour. You'll get a grand vista of Buenos Aires from the cupola on the 22nd floor.

9 Plaza del Congreso After a few blocks you'll come to the green-topped Palacio del Congreso (p74), located in this important plaza.

10 Confitería del Molino One of BA's most amazing buildings is this decrepit, windmill-topped rococo structure that presently molders in BA's air. It was designed by Italian architect Francisco Gianotti and originally opened its doors in 1916 as a bakery, café and salon where artists and politicians would meet, but closed in 1997 for financial reasons.

11 Heladería Cadore If you haven't tried Argentina's top-notch ice cream, then here's your chance. Head north a few blocks to this small *heladería artesanal* (p140) for a tasty treat – it's some of the best ice cream in the city.

12 Obelisco Head back to the center via bustling Av Corrientes, home to BA's traditional theater district. The Teatro General San Martín (p172) often has good (and free) art exhibitions. Your destination is the city's phallic landmark, the Obelisco (p71).

DOCKSIDE STROLL

1 Tourist Office It's not an exotic start, but you can pick up practical information at this tourist office (p232). It's interestingly located under an old cargo crane at Dique 4.

WALK FACTS

Start Tourist kiosk at Dique 4
End Reserva Ecológica Costanera Sur
Distance 3km, not including the reserve
Duration 1½ hours, not including the reserve

DOCKSIDE STROLL

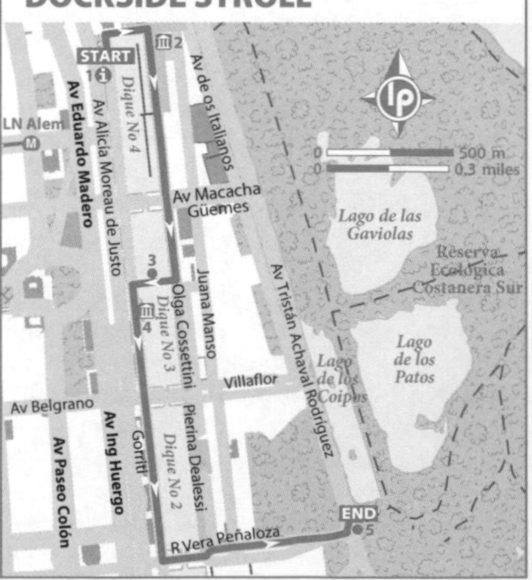

2 Colección de Arte Amalia Lacroze de Fortabat Puerto Madero's shiny jewel of a museum (p68) is ensconced within the glassy walls of this cutting-edge building. Also called Museo Fortabat, classic and contemporary art fans shouldn't miss it.
3 Puente de la Mujer Walk down along Dique No 4 and glance across the way to the old brick warehouses, now turned into expensive lofts and restaurants. Soon you'll come to this attention-grabbing suspension bridge (p68), designed by Spaniard Santiago Calatrava and mostly built in Spain.
4 Museo Fragata Sarmiento Stop at this interesting museum (p70) – you can't miss it, as it's aboard the only ship you'll see. Walk the plank, pay your ticket and explore all the fascinating holds of this vessel.
5 Reserva Ecológica Costanera Sur Stroll down the pebbled pedestrian walk for several blocks, then cut east on R Vera Peñaloza and look for the elegant fountain called La Fuente de las Nereidas. Just beyond is the southern entrance to this marshy reserve (p70), which offers the only real nature walk (or bike ride) in central BA.

HISTORICAL SAUNTER

1 El Zanjón de Granados Time your walk to tour this amazing series of tunnels and brick archways, which formed the foundations of BA's oldest homes. Discovered in 1985 – filled with rubble and ancient trash – they have since been renovated into slick, mysteriously lit passageways that are well worth the effort to visite them. (For more info see p77).
2 Casa Mínima Near El Zanjón, this decaying white-stucco-and-brick building at San Lorenzo 380 is a good example of the narrow-lot style known as *casa chorizo* (sausage house). Barely 2m wide, the lot was reportedly an emancipation gift from slave owners to their former bondsmen.
3 Desnivel If you're hungry for a *parrilla* (barbecue) stop at this lively restaurant (p131), which has become a bit overrun with tourists in the past years. There's good reason for this – the steaks are cheap and luscious, and the gruff service can be entertaining.
4 Mercado San Telmo Don't miss strolling through this old covered market (p75), which has been running since 1897. Locals come to buy their fruits and vegetables here, but there are also plenty of souvenir stands and antiques sellers for the tourists.

WALK FACTS

Start El Zanjón de Granados
End Bar Británico
Distance 1.5km
Duration 2½ hours

HISTORICAL SAUNTER

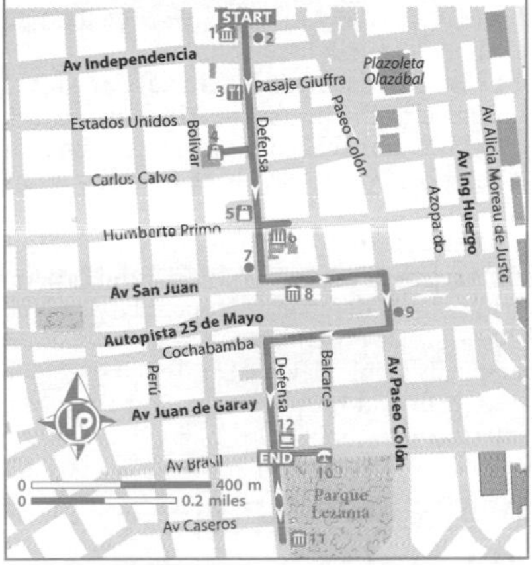

5 Plaza Dorrego Back on Defensa you'll soon reach the heart of the barrio, Plaza Dorrego. From Monday to Saturday it's a busy yet relatively peaceful place, but come Sunday BA's most well-known market – the Feria de San Telmo (p118), sets up in the plaza and surrounding streets. It's quite a scene, and even if you don't like to shop you shouldn't miss it. Even on Saturday there are some vendors on the plaza.
6 Museo Penitenciario For funky prison paraphernalia, check out this penal museum (p78), then go next door to the Iglesia Nuestra Señora de Belén, an old Jesuit school.
7 Pasaje de la Defensa Drop into this old mansion (p75), a *conventillo* (tenement) once owned by the Ezeiza family (of airport fame). Inside are a gaggle of souvenir shops, but you'll get an idea of how the well-to-do – and the poor who came after them – once used to live.
8 Museo de Arte Moderno de Buenos Aires Recently opened after years of renovations is this modern art museum (p78). Expect contemporary, cutting-edge exhibitions, along with works by classic Argentine artists.
9 Club Atlético Memorial With unending heavy traffic, the freeway location of this memorial is simply awful – but so is its history.

This is one of the secret detention centers where thousands of people were tortured and killed during Argentina's Dirty War (1976–84). There isn't much left beyond an excavated basement where a 3-story building used to be, but the scene is somber nonetheless.

10 Parque Lezama Families stroll through this large park, and on sunny weekends a crafts market pops up. Note the old men playing chess, and glance up at the blue spires of the Iglesia Ortodoxa Rusa – an attractive Russian Orthodox church.

11 Museo Histórico Nacional For a bit of insight into the history of Argentina, check out this national history museum (p77). Buenos Aires is believed to have been founded at this very location.

12 Bar Británico Rest your tired feet at this atmospheric corner bar-café (p152) and order a drink – you deserve it. Hopefully you'll be able to snag a prized window seat – they boast especially scenic views of San Telmo street life passing by and Parque Lezama just across the intersection.

DEATH, ART, SHOPPING... AND SEX!

1 Cementerio de la Recoleta Start with a bang and visit BA's top tourist destination – Recoleta's cemetery (p86). You can easily spend hours in here carefully examining the hundreds of elaborate sarcophagi. Just remember to bring your camera; the feral cats make great subjects with monuments in the background.

2 Recoleta Mall Swing past this upscale, newly renovated shopping mall. It was being renovated at research time, promising nearly 100 shops, a 10-screen multiplex cinema and rooftop garden.

3 Facultad de Ingeniería Turn right out of the cemetery, then zigzag your way to this amazing neo-Gothic engineering school, designed by Uruguayan architect Arturo Prins and never quite completed. It could use a bit more upkeep, but despite its ragged appearance it's still one of BA's most stand-out buildings.

4 Acapulco Albergue Transitorio Porteños are a loving bunch, so to speak, and 'love hotels' – which rent rooms by the hour – are fairly commonplace. If you and your partner need some time alone, think about stopping by Azcuénaga No 2008 for a quickie – it takes American Express.

5 Buenos Aires Design Need to shop for your home? Then stop in at this large mall (p117); it's worth a look for the most cutting-edge furniture and lifestyle products.

6 Museo Nacional de Bellas Artes Now cut across Plaza Francia and head to this excellent museum (p88), which contains both national and international classical art from all over the world. Everything is well displayed and lit, and best of all – it's free.

7 Floralis Genérica After you've had an eyeful of impressionist masters, walk around the museum and cross Av Alcorta to reach this giant metal flower sculpture, designed and funded by architect Eduardo Catalano. At night the giant aluminum petals used to close like a real flower, but the mechanisms broke.

8 Feria Plaza Francia Head back down Alcorta – passing the mammoth Facultad de Derecho building along the way. Cross the footbridge and make your way up Plaza Intendente Alvear (look for the 'Paseo Recoleta' sign). If it's a weekend, browse through the stalls of this fun crafts market.

9 Centro Cultural Recoleta After you tire of the hippies and mimes at the market, stop by this cultural center (p88) and see what they have showing in their art galleries. If you have kids, the Museo Participativo de Ciencias (see the boxed text, p91) might just grab their attention.

WALK FACTS

Start Cementerio de la Recoleta
End La Biela cafe
Distance 2-3km
Duration Three hours

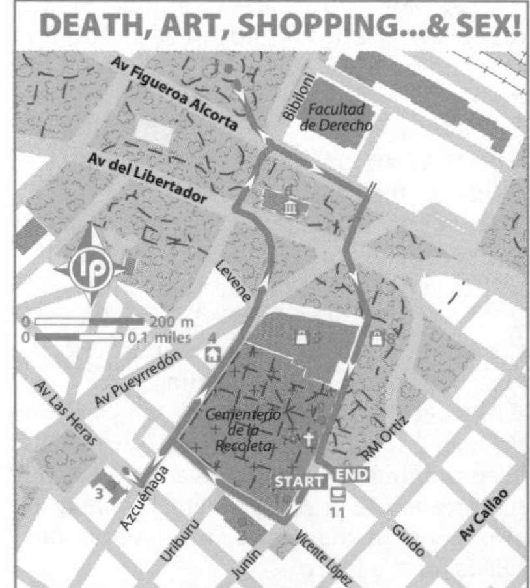

10 Iglesia de Nuestra Señora del Pilar Right next to the cultural center is this pretty church. If you time it right, check out the small museum upstairs, home to religious vestments, paintings, writings and interesting artifacts. You can also snap a photo of the Recoleta cemetery through window grills.
11 La Biela Now that you're tired, amble down to restaurant-filled RM Ortiz and end your walk at this fine café (p153), where you can sit amongst rich porteños high on caffeine. If it's sunny grab a table outside on the front patio – it's worth the extra pesos.

WALKING THE GREEN

1 Parque 3 de Febrero Palermo's huge expanses of grassy lawns are the city's lungs – peaceful green spaces that were once the aristocracy's stomping ground. It's best on weekends when families bring picnics, and *fútbol* (soccer) games pop up. The road around the rose garden is cut off to vehicular traffic, but cruisers can rent bicycles (or rollerblades) on weekends.
2 Museo de Artes Plásticas Eduardo Sívori Just a bit further, those interested in modern art can peek into this contemporary museum (p95), which showcases Argentine art. There's a relaxing cafe as well.
3 Rosedal If you like flowers, head across the road and cross the bridge to this rose garden, where you can stop to sniff the pretty blooms. Continue across the garden until you come to Av Iraola, turn left onto it for about a block, then veer to the right to reach Av Sarmiento.
4 Jardín Japonés Cross Av Sarmiento (carefully!), and head along Av Berro for about 500m to BA's Japanese garden (p95). This little paradise is meticulously maintained with koi ponds, pretty bridges and a tea shop, making a welcome break from roads and traffic.
5 Museo de Arte Latinoamericano de Buenos Aires (Malba) Now skim around Plaza Alemania and jog around a few residential streets to reach Malba, an airy museum (p90) that's almost more style than substance – though there are some excellent artworks here.
6 Museo de Arte Popular José Hernàndez For more culture, go two blocks south to this much more modest museum (p95), which exhibits handicrafts and folkloric items.
7 Un Altra Volta Back on Av del Libertador, stop in at this luscious ice cream shop (p140) for a peaked cone of *dulce de leche granizado* (milk caramel with chocolate flakes). Pastries, snacks and drinks are also on offer, and there are sidewalk tables for sunny days.
8 Museo Evita After satisfying your sweet tooth, head down the street (alongside the sometimes odiferous zoo) to this interesting museum (p95), where you can check out the collected memorabilia on Argentina's most famous female personality. It's modern and well presented, and there's a fine cafe-restaurant on the premises.
9 Jardín Zoológico If you feel like visiting some exotic animals, buy a ticket and head into this zoo (p95). As far as Latin American zoos go, it's pretty humane for most animals – and has some impressive buildings, too. Enter via Plaza Italia.

WALK FACTS

Start Parque 3 de Febrero
End Jardín Zoológico
Distance 5km
Duration 3-4 hours

WALKING THE GREEN

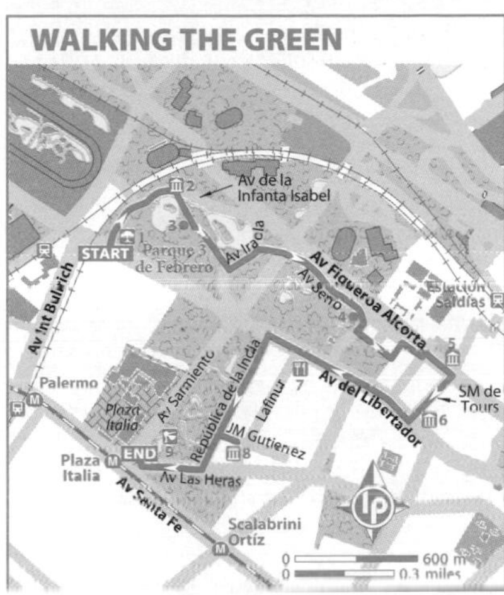

SHOPPING

top picks

- **Mercado de San Telmo** (p113)
- **Gil Antigüedades** (p112)
- **Materia Urbana** (p114)
- **Boutique del Libro** (p117)
- **Airedelsur** (p116)
- **Josefina Ferroni** (p115)
- **El Ateneo Grand Splendid** (p111)
- **Papelera Palermo** (p120)
- **Juana de Arco** (p119)

WHAT'S YOUR RECOMMENDATION? www.lonelyplanet.com/Buenos Aires

SHOPPING

Despite a global recession and a major drop in the purchasing power of the Argentine peso in the last few years, Buenos Aires' citizens continue to shop as if there's no tomorrow. Just a peek into the nearest mall on a weekend will make you wonder how people who seem to be making so little can spend so much. And it's not just an act of hedonistic consumerism; it's seen as a social pursuit that allows you to look good while you're doing it – after all, you never know who you're going to run into.

Shopping is often a family event, with many malls catering to children by offering special play areas and video arcades. Paseo Alcorta (p121) in Palermo has an especially large kids' playground on the 3rd floor, while Mercado de Abasto (p97) in Once sports an excellent children's museum and small amusement park complete with rides. Almost all modern malls also have multiplex cinemas and large food courts complete with fast-food outlets and ice-cream parlors. Some even offer health clubs, beauty shops and internet cafes.

If the thought of entering a shopping mall makes you want to run screaming in the other direction, stuff your pockets with pesos and head over to one of the city's wonderful outdoor street markets (p118). On sunny weekend afternoons, these promenades come alive with craft and antique stalls, tango dancers, street performances and vendors selling treats from fresh-squeezed orange juice to homemade empanadas.

Interested in design? Make a beeline for Palermo Soho, where avant-garde fashion designers' boutiques line the pretty tree-shaded streets. You'll find housewares emporiums and hip lingerie shops, young designer showcases, and impossibly cool cafes where beautiful women (often laden down with shopping bags) take a coffee break.

You'll pass through various other shopping districts, many centrally located in the city, without even trying. Downtown, Calle Florida is a must for any tourist, even if you're not looking to buy; it's a multipurpose pedestrian strip that buzzes with shoppers, tourists, performers and commuters. As a large avenue, Av Santa Fe is a bit less pedestrian-friendly, but equally prominent as the city's main service and shopping artery. San Telmo is *the* place for antiques, while Av Pueyrredón near Once train station is the place for cheap clothing. The largest concentration of jewelry shops is on Libertad south of Av Corrientes. For more on popular shopping strips, see p111.

A note before you hit the dressing room: clothing sizes correspond to the European system. Buenos Aires is an incredibly body-conscious city, and porteños also have lucky genes, so Argentine women are often slimmer than their counterparts in other Latin American countries (and visitors from the US, the UK, Europe and Australia). Clothing produced here reflects this fact, though larger sizes can be found in some of the bigger stores.

OPENING HOURS

Store hours generally run from 9am or 10am to 8pm or 9pm weekdays, with many open for at least a few hours on Saturday. Most stores close on Sunday, unless they're located close to one of the street markets – shop owners can't pass up the kind of earning potential that comes with heavy pedestrian traffic.

TAXES & REFUNDS

Taxes are included in quoted or marked prices: what you see is what you pay. Some places, however, might add a surcharge (or *recargo*) to credit card purchases – ask before you buy.

If you buy more than AR$70 in merchandise from a store that displays a 'Tax Free Shopping' sticker, you're entitled to a tax refund. Just ask the merchant to make out an invoice for you (you'll need ID); upon leaving the country show the paperwork to a customs official, who'll stamp it and tell you where to obtain your refund. Give yourself some extra time at the airport for this transaction.

BARGAINING

As in other Western countries, bargaining is not acceptable in stores. High-price items like jewelry and leather jackets can be exceptions at some places, especially if you buy more than one item. Ask politely if there's a *'descuento'* (discount) – many shops and vendors will knock 10% off if you pay in cash. At street markets you can try negotiating for better prices, but usually only if you're purchasing multiple items from the seller; keep in mind you may be talking to the artists themselves, who are trying to make a basic living. Even if a price seems inflated for tourists, consider whether it's worthwhile (or culturally respectful) to haggle over a few dollars. Generally speaking, if you're not willing to pay the marked price, it's best to move on.

When asking about a price, be clear about whether the vendor is quoting in pesos or dollars. Most sellers quote in pesos, but a few unscrupulous ones switch to dollars after striking a deal. If you have any doubts about the trustworthiness of the seller, it's also wise to check your change carefully before walking away with your purchase.

THE CENTER

The main shopping street in the center is Florida. Most travelers to Buenos Aires take the obligatory stroll down this heaving pedestrian street, lined on either side (and in the evenings, down the middle) with shops and vendors selling clothes, shoes, jewelry, housewares and cheesy souvenirs. Touts zero in on tourists, offering good deals on leather jackets and *cambio* (currency change). We'll tell you now: you won't find the cheapest prices on leather jackets here (try Calle Murillo or Calle Aguirre instead, see p111) and you should definitely avoid changing money on the streets – fake bills and other scams are an occasional problem here.

EL ATENEO Map p62 Books & Music

☎ 4325-6801; Florida 340 & 629; 9am-8pm Mon-Fri, till 5pm Sat; hr vary slightly by store

Buenos Aires' landmark bookseller stocks a limited number of books in English (including some Lonely Planet guidebooks) and also has a decent selection of music CDs. There are several branches within the city, including a gorgeous branch called the Grand Splendid (Map p87; Av Santa Fe 1860), an old renovated cinema where Carlos Gardel got his career started. It's often counted among the most beautiful bookstores in the world; you can soak up the glamour by sitting down for espresso at the bookstore café, located on the old stage.

SHOPPING STRIPS

- Av Santa Fe between Scalabrini Ortiz and Av 9 de Julio (Map p92) – Almost 30 blocks of shops selling everything – especially clothes. Continues in Belgrano as Av Cabildo, with an even higher concentration of stores, movie theaters and fast-food outlets. Put on your walking shoes.
- Florida (Map p62) – A pedestrian shopper's paradise, with souvenir stores, leather shops, clothing boutiques and plenty of services for both locals and tourists. Along with its little sister, Lavalle (also pedestrian), it's the walking lifeblood of Buenos Aires' downtown. Street vendors lay down their goods on blankets in the evening.
- Av Alvear (Map p87) – The Cadillac of shopping streets, ritzy Alvear has loads of upscale boutiques for your already overcharged credit card. International designers such as Louis Vuitton, Giorgio Armani, Nina Ricci, Bang & Olufsen, Hermès and Cartier share real estate with fancy art galleries and opulent mansions.
- Calle Defensa (Map p76) – San Telmo's antiques row is a magnet for tourists, especially on Sunday when the antique market is in full swing. Don't expect rock-bottom bargains; international demand and an adjustment to devaluation have kept prices high, especially for the best pieces. Recently, clothing and other boutiques have mushroomed here.
- Av Pueyrredón between Avs Corrientes and Rivadavia (Map p98) – In the barrio of Once, Pueyrredón is packed solid with stores selling clothes, shoes, accessories, appliances, luggage and household bargains, while street merchants hawk watches and electronic gizmos. Goods are the cheapest in town, but quality is low.
- Calle Murillo 600 block (Map p98) – Located in Villa Crespo, Calle Murillo is the best place in town to snag a relatively cheap but high-quality leather jacket. This block is stuffed with leather factory shops selling jackets and accessories. Bargain like mad, especially if you're paying in cash. One of the nicer (and pricier) shops is Murillo 666 (Map p98; 4855-2024; Murillo 666).
- Calle Aguirre outlets (Map p98) – The 800 block of this street is outlet row, with deals on shoes and clothes mostly. Ladies, check out the Prüne outlet (Map p98; 4776-8500; Gurruchaga 867) for stylish leather bags. There are also lots of other outlets on nearby Av Córdoba.

MONTAGNE

Map p62 Camping & Outdoor Equipment

☎ 4312-9041; www.montagneoutdoors.com.ar; Florida 719; ⏰ 10am-8:30pm Mon-Sat, 10am-8pm Sun

This shop sells popular outdoor clothing and gear that is stylish, good quality and made in Argentina. Upstairs, there's a small but high-quality selection of tents, backpacks and camping gear – perfect if you need some last-minute items on your way to Patagonia. There are several other Montagne branches, including one in Barrio Norte (Map p87; Av Santa Fe 1780).

EL COLECCIONISTA Map p62 Music

☎ 4322-0359; www.elcoleccionistacd.com.ar; Esmeralda 562; ⏰ 10:30am-7:30pm Mon-Fri

This small place has an eclectic selection of jazz, blues, salsa, Celtic and symphonic rock CDs. It will buy used musical instruments, so trade in that guitar or drum you're tired of lugging around and trade it in for a cool *bandoneón* (the accordion-esque instrument you'll hear in every tango band). Staff are knowledgeable and you can pick up the business cards of teachers offering lessons.

MUSIMUNDO Map p62 Music

☎ 4322-9298; Florida 267; ⏰ 10am-9pm

With over 50 branches throughout the city, this is Argentina's largest music retailer, offering both national and international selections. Listening stations make selecting the hippest CDs a snap. There are branches in the Microcentro (Map p62; Lavalle 925), Barrio Norte (Map p87; Av Santa Fe 1844), Congreso (Map p72; Av Corrientes 1753) and most shopping centers.

CONGRESO & TRIBUNALES

Congreso is where the city's politicos hang out, and is not really known as a shopping destination. That said, Av Corrientes has many of the city's discount bookstores among other things, and despite most books being in Spanish, it's fun to wander through them.

WILDLIFE

Map p72 Camping & Outdoor Equipment

☎ 4381-1040; www.wildlifesports.com.ar; Hipólito Yrigoyen 1133; ⏰ 10am-8pm Mon-Fri, 10am-1pm Sat

If you're looking to buy (or sell) all manner of outdoor and camping equipment before traveling on from Buenos Aires, this is the place. Crampons, knives, tents, backpacks, climbing ropes, foul-weather clothing and military gear can be found at this somewhat offbeat shop.

ZIVAL'S Map p72 Music

☎ 5128-7500; www.tangostore.com; Av Callao 395; ⏰ 9:30am-10pm Mon-Sat

This is one of the better music stores in town, especially when it comes to tango, jazz and classical music. Listening stations and a big sale rack are pluses, and it'll ship CDs, DVDs and sheet music abroad, too (check the website). There's also a branch in Palermo Viejo (Map p72; at Serrano 1445). The store ships worldwide; take a look at the online catalogue, then download a few sample tracks on iTunes to get an idea of what you like before buying.

SAN TELMO

San Telmo has traditionally been Buenos Aires' antiques neighborhood. In recent years, however, San Telmo's popularity with tourists has attracted other kinds of stores. Fashion boutiques and housewares shops are moving in, changing the general feel on the streets. Locals fear that their beloved neighborhood might become another Palermo, but even with rising real-estate prices, San Telmo is not likely to lose its gritty authenticity or charm.

EL BUEN ORDEN Map p76 Antiques

☎ 4307-8608; www.elbuenorden.com.ar; Defensa 894; ⏰ 11am-7pm

If you fancy an old-fashioned little shop where you can sort through shelves full of knickknacks, old jewelry, Jackie O-style sunglasses, old lace, musty shoes, opera gloves, pillbox hats and antique figurines, then this place is for you. There's no real order to the place – the name is clearly something of a joke.

GIL ANTIGÜEDADES

Map p76 Antiques & Fashion

☎ 4361-5019; www.gilantiguedades.com.ar; Humberto Primo 412; ⏰ 11am-1pm & 3-7pm Tue-Sun

A window display of Great Gatsby–style flapper dresses and vintage nightgowns pulls the passerby into San Telmo's finest antiques emporium. Decorative objects like china teapots and leather hatboxes are overshadowed by the stunning array of silk slips and lacy Victorian gowns – John Galliano, Catherine Deneuve and Salvatore Ferragamo are among the famous people who've stopped by for inspiration on visits to Buenos Aires.

HERNANI Map p76 Antiques

☎ 4362-4437; Defensa 1047; 🕓 11:30am-6:30pm

An old family business for generations, this very upscale antique store sells only top-drawer pieces. Grand old furniture, huge mirrors, giant urns, shiny chandeliers, rich tapestries and reproductions of famous statuary give this place a museum-like feel. Prices are in the thousands of (US) dollars.

IMHOTEP Map p76 Antiques

☎ 4862-9298; Defensa 916; 🕓 11am-6pm Sun-Fri

Come find the funkiest old knickknacks at this eccentric shop. Small oddities such as Indian statuettes, ceramic skulls, Chinese snuff boxes, precious stone figurines and gargoyles make up some of the bizarre trinkets here. Larger prize finds may include a boar's head or a slot machine.

MERCADO DE SAN TELMO

Map p76 Antiques

Defensa, Bolívar, Carlos Calvo & Estados Unidos Streets; 🕓 10am-7pm

Occupying an entire city block, this market was built in 1897 by Juan Antonio Buschiazzo, the same Italian-born Argentine architect who designed the Recoleta Cemetery. The wrought-iron interior and glass skylights make it one of BA's most atmospheric markets; it's also where locals shop for fresh produce, cheese, and meat. Look for secondhand leather luggage, delicate wine decanters, and retro sunglasses at the peripheral antique stalls. More stalls open on weekends than weekdays.

APPETITE Map p76 Art

☎ 4331-5405; Chacabuco 551; 🕓 2-7pm Mon-Sat

To see what's happening in the contemporary erotic art world, take a peek into this grungy, rough-and-tumble space – appropriately, an old meatpacking warehouse. It's certainly not fine art, and you wouldn't want it to be – instead, expect fantasy, sexual and sometimes violent themes. At the time of writing, Appetite was temporarily closed while the gallery undergoes a transition – just walk by to see what's going on.

WALRUS BOOKS Map p76 Books

☎ 4300-7135; www.walrus-books.com.ar; Estados Unidos 617; 🕓 noon-8pm Tue-Sun

Run by an American photographer, this tiny shop is probably the best English-language bookstore in Buenos Aires. New and used literature and nonfiction books – more than 4000 titles – line the shelves at this well-organized place, and there's a selection of Latin American classics translated into English.

MOEBIUS Map p76 Fashion & Accessories

☎ 4361-2893; Defensa 1356; 🕓 10am-1pm & 3-8:30pm Tue-Sat, 11am-8:30pm Sun

This funky little shop feels like the walk-in closet of the fashionable artist sister you never had: the racks are crowded with owner-designer Lilliana Zauberman's kaleidoscopic 1970s-style jersey dresses, whimsical ruffled bikinis, skirts printed with koi fish and frog patterns, cherry-red trench coats, and handbags made from recycled materials. Around 15 designers sell their work here – keep an eye out for unusual recycled-material items.

PUNTOS EN EL ESPACIO

Map p76 Fashion

☎ 4307-1742; www.puntosenelespacio.com.ar; Perú 979; 🕓 11am-8pm

With over 40 designers represented, this large store is a good place to check out original edgy unisex collections by rising stars in the local fashion world. Each designer shows his work on a separate rack; look for funky raingear and the playful Hacer Pie footwear line. A second location, focused on accessories and home decor, has opened more recently on the corner of Defensa and Independencia, a few blocks away.

UN LUGAR EN EL MUNDO

Map p76 Fashion

☎ 4362-3836; Defensa 891; 🕓 10:30am-8pm

Lots of fun, young and creative designs (all from Argentine artists) line the racks at this clothing boutique. They're mostly women's cutting-edge styles, utilizing thin fabrics and colorful patterns in clingy tops that draw attention. Accessories such as patent-leather zipper shoes and vinyl retro bags are also available.

CUALQUIER VERDURA

Map p76 Housewares

☎ **4300-2474; www.cualquierverdura.com.ar; Humberto Primo 517; ⌚ noon-8pm Thu-Sun**

Located in a lovely, refurbished old house, this fun store sells eclectic items from vintage clothing to funny soaps (look for these in the 'bathroom') to recycled floppy-disc lamps to contemporary knickknacks and novelty toys. Wander through the outdoor patio and note the stained-glass windows on the wall and *mate*-drinking Buddha above the fountain.

L'AGO Map p76 Housewares & Accessories

☎ **4362-3641/4702; www.lagosantelmo.com; Defensa 919 & 970; ⌚ 10am-7:30pm**

Kitschy-cool home decor – from fluorescent-hued *mate* sets to Frida Kahlo kitchen magnets, eclectic lighting, plastic kewpie dolls, recycled Elvis wallets and Marilyn Monroe handbags – attracts hipsters and travelers to cute-as-a-button L'Ago. A second location has opened across the street; don't miss buttery handmade soaps scented like chocolate, coffee, and passion fruit.

MATERIA URBANA

Map p76 Housewares & Art

☎ **4361-5265; www.materiaurbana.com; cnr Defensa & Chile; ⌚ 11am-7pm**

This innovative design shop shows the work of over 100 local artists; one-of-a-kind finds include offbeat line drawings, abstract photography, carved wood statuettes, leather animal organizers, clothes, and jewelry made from silver, wood, and coral. There's nearly constant foot traffic at Materia Urbana, especially during the street fair on Sunday.

RETIRO

Retiro is a classy, expensive neighborhood, home to a fair share of the city's upscale leather shops and art galleries. But it also serves the downtown business and tourism sector, with a mix of bookstores, outdoor clothing stores, and souvenir and wine shops.

AUTORÍA Map p84 Art & Accessories

☎ **5252-2474; www.autoriabsas.com.ar; Suipacha 1025; ⌚ 9:30am-8pm Mon-Fri, 10am-2pm & 4:30-8pm Sat**

This cool designer's showcase – stocked with make-a-statement silver jewelry, edgy art books, sculptural fashion, and funky objects from painted dolls to whimsical leather desk sculptures – brings a welcome taste of the avant-garde to this suit-and-tie neighborhood.

GALERÍA RUTH BENZACAR

Map p84 Art

☎ **4313-8480; www.ruthbenzacar.com; Florida 1000; ⌚ 11:30am-8pm Mon-Fri**

The first contemporary art gallery in BA, this underground space (access downstairs) is supremely well-located right at the head of pedestrian Florida. Internationally known Argentine artists whose work has graced the walls here include Leandro Erlich, Jorge Macchi, Flavia Darin and Nicola Costantino. Just show up and have a look around.

TIERRA ADENTRO

Map p84 Art & Accessories

☎ **4393-8552; Arroyo 882; ⌚ 10am-8pm Mon-Fri, 10am-6pm Sat**

Shop with a conscience at one of the city's few fair-trade stores. Tierra Adentro works with nonprofit organizations to help preserve indigenous communities in northern Argentina. Fair trade practices brought this fine range of hand-woven cushion covers, colorful wall hangings, and striking Mapuche silver necklaces to the capital city.

KEL EDICIONES Map p84 Books

☎ **4814-3788; www.kel-ediciones.com; MT de Alvear 1369; ⌚ 9am-7pm Mon-Fri, 9:30am-1:30pm Sat**

This shop's slogan is 'Books in English for Everyone'. Subjects include literature, travel, cooking, philosophy, art, history and religion, along with novels, dictionaries, even some Lonely Planet titles. If you're looking for something specific, do a search first on the website.

CAMPING CENTER

Map p84 Camping & Outdoor Equipment

☎ **4314-0305; Esmeralda 945; ⌚ 10am-8pm Mon-Fri, 10am-5pm Sat**

You won't find any bargains here, but if you're taking off on a backpacking trip through Patagonia or Chile, you'll appreciate the selection of high-quality camping and mountaineering equipment at this modern store. There's rock-climbing gear and plenty of expensive, outdoor brand-name clothing from the USA.

FASHION-FORWARD

Say the words 'Argentina' and 'fashion' in the same sentence; the image that springs to most minds is the chiseled physique and blue-blooded aura of Nacho Figueras, the porteño polo player and model who jumped to international fame when Ralph Lauren chose him as the face of his Polo fashion and fragrance line. Of course, it's not exactly breaking news that Argentina produced yet another pretty face (let's face it, he's one of many in his home country). Perhaps more impressive, though much lesser-known on the international stage, are Argentina's über-innovative high-fashion designers.

After the 2001 economic crash, hundreds of talented young designers emerged from the woodwork in an attempt to scrape out a living. Several of the more ambitious stylemakers have since matured into full-fledged designers with luxury sportswear lines and outposts in the US, Europe and Asia; household names in Buenos Aires include Maria Cher (Map p92; www.maria-cher.com.ar; El Salvador 4714), known for deconstructed garments with an urban twist, Pablo Ramírez (Map p76; www.pabloramirez.com.ar; Perú 587), and Jazmín Chebar (Map p92; www.jazminchebar.com.ar; El Salvador 4702, Palermo), whose playful, feminine work was chosen for display at the Louvre during Paris Fashion Week in 1999. Known for recycling fabrics, Martín Churba is the mastermind behind the Tramando collective (Map p87; www.tramando.com; Rodriguez Peña 1973), with stores in Recoleta, New York and Tokyo. Sophisticated and understated, Cora Groppo (Map p92; www.coragroppo.com; cnr El Salvador & Armenia) reworks volume and texture in everyday garments from striking cropped jackets to multi-layered wrap tops. Jessica Trosman (Map p92; www.trosman.com; Armenia 1998), who approaches fashion with an architectural eye, sells her designs all over the world and has been featured in several noteworthy international fashion publications from Phaidon's *Sample* (2005) to the more recent *100 New Fashion Designers* (Laurence King, 2008).

Though these forward-thinking designers have already started branching out to other parts of the world, their flagship stores remain in Buenos Aires. Take a stroll through Palermo Soho, or upscale shopping malls like Patio Bullrich and Paseo Alcorta, to see their fashions on the rack – and on the beautiful women who shop there regularly. Don't be surprised if you see a few Nacho lookalikes hanging around in mirrored sunglasses.

GABRIELLA CAPUCCI Map p84 — Fashion

☎ 4815-3636; www.gabriellacapucci.com; Av Alvear 1477; 🕑 10am-8pm Mon-Sat

While this place is certainly not for everyone, this girly boutique is undeniably unlike other stuffy ones on this upscale avenue. All-original sequined T-shirts, creative handbags, wispy scarves, vintage tops, velvet pillows and eclectic accessories fill this small space. Crocheted flowers, huge beads and fake pink orchids decorate or camouflage, satin and animal prints. Colors are bright and the costume jewelry is wild.

MARÍA VÁZQUEZ Map p84 — Fashion

☎ 4815-6333; www.mvzmariavazquez.com.ar; Libertad 1632; 🕑 11am-9pm Mon-Fri, 10am-6pm Sat

One of the better-known Argentine designers, María Vázquez creates lingerie-like cocktail dresses in thin silks, lacy cotton and smooth satin. Details such as beads, sequins and glitter add a catchy sheen to her sexy productions, which also include signature jeans. Celebrities such as Shakira, Xuxa and Naomi Campbell have snapped up her designs. There are other branches located in shopping malls around town.

CASA LÓPEZ Map p84 — Leather Goods

☎ 4311-3044; www.casalopez.com.ar; MT de Alvear 640/658; 🕑 9am-8pm Mon-Fri, 10am-6:30pm Sat & Sun

Start up the limousine and make sure there's enough room for some of BA's finest selection of quality leather jackets, luggage, bags and accessories. The look is conservative, not hip; service is almost too attentive, so be prepared to chat. Other branches are located in Galerías Pacífico (p61) and Patio Bullrich (p116).

WELCOME MARROQUINERÍA Map p84 — Leather Goods

☎ 4312-8911; MT de Alvear 500; 🕑 10am-2pm & 3-5:30pm Mon-Fri, 10am-2pm Sat

Going strong since 1930, this upscale shop claims to be the oldest leather goods company in Argentina. Handmade, exclusively designed luggage, briefcases, handbags, accessories and a small selection of both men's and women's shoes are available. Quality is high, with prices to match.

JOSEFINA FERRONI Map p82 — Shoes

☎ 5811-1951; www.josefinaferroni.com.ar; Arenales 1278; 🕑 2-8pm Mon, 11am-8pm Tue-Sat

Argentina's answer to Jimmy Choo. The old-school glamour and coquettish colors of these gorgeously crafted boots, platform heels, and open-toed flats have earned Josefina Ferroni countless porteña fans and growing international exposure. There's a second location in Palermo (Map p92; Armenia 1687).

GALERÍA 5TA AVENIDA

Map p84 Shopping Mall

Av Santa Fe 1270; 11am-8pm Mon-Sat

Looking for vintage or secondhand clothing? This old shopping gallery is an obligatory stop. Used funky wearables are sold here at several shops, and prices are relatively fair for even the grungiest backpacker. Find the bargain racks for the best deals, though some selections are for the desperate only.

PATIO BULLRICH Map p84 Shopping Mall

4814-7500; www.shoppingbullrich.com.ar; Av del Libertador 750; 10am-9pm

Buenos Aires' most exclusive shopping center once hosted livestock auctions, but these days it tends toward sales of Persian rugs, double-breasted tweed suits and Dior's latest designs. Three floors hold fine boutiques such as Lacoste, Lacroix and Versace, along with fancy coffee shops, a cinema complex and a food court.

LA MARTINA Map p84 Sporting Equipment

4576-7999; www.lamartina.com; Paraguay 661; 10am-8pm Mon-Fri, 10am-2pm Sat

Polo is a high-class sport in Buenos Aires, an unmistakable symbol of wealth and refinement – but even if you've never mounted a horse, it's interesting to look around at the gorgeous leather riding boots, helmets and saddles at Argentina's premiere polo shop. You'll likely see some handsome and impeccably dressed polo players striding through the aisles. Other locations can be found around the city.

WINERY Map p84 Wine

4311-6607; www.winery.com.ar; Av Leandro N Alem 880; 9am-8:30pm Mon-Sat

One of several slick chain stores that offer a great selection of Argentine wines. At this location, you can sip before you buy: at the modern lounge downstairs, there are more than 20 different wines by the glass available, plus a five-wine tasting option (AR$50). There's another branch with just a café in the Microcentro (Map p62; Av Corrientes 300).

RECOLETA & BARRIO NORTE

Exclusivity is the key word here. If you have the bucks and are willing to pay top dollar for the best quality goods, then you'll want to shop in these neighborhoods. The city's best leather shops are based here, along with a few top fashion boutiques and a handful of international names such as Armani, Cartier, Hermés and Versace.

AIREDELSUR Map p87 Housewares

4803-6100; www.airedelsur.com; Av Alvear 1883 (1129); 10:30am-7:30pm Mon-Fri, to 4:30pm Sat

The Airedelsur label was beloved by *porteños* long before it was featured in *Vogue*. Designer Marcelo Lucini collaborates with Argentine craftsmen to create stunningly original home decor made with alpaca silver, wood, onyx and other all-natural materials. Queen Rania of Jordan reportedly picked up more than 200 pieces for her palaces.

LÓPEZ TAIBO Map p87 Leather Goods

4804-8585; www.lopeztaibo.net; Av Alvear 1902; 10am-8pm Mon-Fri, 10am-6pm Sat

Absolutely the best leather goods can be found at this Recoleta boutique which has been offering excellence and tradition since 1897. The black-clad staff offer attentive service to the well-dressed businessman or traveler searching for shoes, belts, jackets, briefcases and – for those who fly in the face of PETA – fur. You'll see a few other branches around the city.

ROSSI & CARUSO Map p87 Leather Goods

4814-4774; www.rossicaruso.com; Av Santa Fe 1377; 9:30am-8pm Mon-Fri, 10am-7pm Sat

Should you be in the market for a fine leather saddle or a serious gaucho knife, you've come to the right place. The leather goods here, from riding boots and belts to messenger bags, saddles, and the occasional silver *mate* vessel, are beautifully made from Argentine materials. Expect professional service and sky-high prices. Other BA branches include one in Galerías Pacífico (p61).

WUSSMANN SHOP

Map p87 Paper & Stationery

4811-2444; www.wussmannshop.com.ar; Rodriguez Peña; 10:30am-8pm Mon-Fri, 11am-2pm Sat

Writers and artists delight in the gorgeous handmade paper at this chic stationery shop. Leatherbound journals, monogrammed stationery, and oversized sketchbooks are made with recycled paper; come here for one-of-a-kind invitations and notecards or hand-painted wrapping paper to spruce up a special gift.

PERUGIA BOTTIER Map p87 Shoes

☎ 4804-6340; Av Alvear 1866; 10am-8pm Mon-Fri, 10am-2pm Sat

In business for over 50 years, this may be Buenos Aires' finest women's shoe store. The European-inspired designs are made from both Argentine and Italian leathers, and change seasonally. Shoes are handmade and take 10 days to finish; prices are expensive, of course, and vary according to style and material.

GALERÍA BOND Map p87 Shopping Mall

Av Santa Fe 1670; 10am-9pm Mon-Sat

For the edgiest tattoos and piercings in town, you can't beat this grungy shopping center. Buenos Aires' skateboarder-wannabes, along with their punk rock counterparts, also come here to shop for the latest styles and sounds. Expect everything from Hello Kitty to heavy metal.

BUENOS AIRES DESIGN

Map p87 Shopping Mall

☎ 5777-6000; Av Pueyrredón 2501; 10am-9pm Mon-Sat, noon-9pm Sun

The trendiest and finest home furnishings are all under one roof here. This is the ideal place to look for that snazzy light fixture, streamlined toilet or reproduction Asian chair. Also good for everyday appliances and housewares, along with cute decor and art objects.

PALERMO

Palermo Viejo, a large sub-neighborhood of Palermo, is a fashionista's shopping paradise. A few years ago, most of the storefronts were showcases for cutting-edge clothes; these days, the barrio hosts a wider range of designers selling high-end wares from home accessories and books to fancy stationery, soaps, candles, souvenirs, kids' toys and gourmet chocolate. It's easy to spend hours or even days shopping in Palermo; many design-minded travelers consider an afternoon here part of the sightseeing circuit.

MERCADO DE LAS PULGAS

Map p92 Antiques

cnr Álvarez Thomas & Dorrego; 10am-7pm Tue-Sun

This dusty and dim covered flea market sells antiques – precious things such as old furniture, glass soda bottles, ceramic vases, paintings, bird cages, elegant mirrors and metal garden furniture.

BOUTIQUE DEL LIBRO Map p92 Books

☎ 4483-6637; www.boutiquedellibro.com.ar; Thames 1762; 10am-10pm Mon-Thu, till 11pm Fri, 11am-11pm Sat, 2-10pm Sun

Take a break from shopping at this cool literary sanctuary. Beautiful art and design books bring in a fashionable local crowd; if you don't read Spanish there are a couple of shelves with quality English titles, and the café in back (with cute outside patio) is a perfect excuse to stop for a cup of coffee.

OWOKO Map p92 Children's

☎ 4502-9905; www.owoko.com.ar; El Salvador 4694; 11am-8pm Mon-Sat, 3-7pm Sun

This popular kids' clothing store has a sense of humor: the philosophy is that children should be able to enjoy their T-shirts and accessories as they would toys or games. These high-quality garments tell the story of Planet Owoko and its colorful characters; stop in and you'll see local moms browsing the latest collection (or the sale rack). With many locations across the city.

RECURSOS INFANTILES

Map p92 Children's

☎ 4834-6177; Jorge Luis Borges 1766; 3-8pm Mon, 8am-8pm Tue-Sun

Small but fun, this kids' store offers some pretty amazing toys – and all are made in Argentina. There are your typical stuffed animals, wood toys and puzzles, plus other cool stuff such as miniature puppet theatres and unique handmade instruments. Look for books in Spanish and racks of cute clothes, plus a tiny café that caters to hungry little bellies (and tired parents).

ARTE ÉTNICO ARGENTINO

Map p92 Crafts & Textiles

☎ 4832-0516; www.arteetnicoargentino.com; El Salvador 4656; 11am-7pm Mon-Sat

Bright and beautiful woven *mantas* (blankets) are the main attraction at this upscale

STREET MARKETS

Whether or not you have pesos to burn, wandering through a weekend street fair is a quintessential Buenos Aires experience. You'll pass local artisans selling their creative wares (which make great souvenirs and gifts), along with casual pass-the-hat entertainers like buskers, mimes and tango dancers. Nearby restaurants and cafes offer highly sought-after sidewalk tables where you can take a break and order coffee, sandwiches, or a bottle of wine – and there's hardly a better vantage point from which to watch the parade of well-off locals, giddy tourists, and dreadlocked artists carrying display cases of handmade jewelry.

Prices are generally fair as quoted, but if you have doubts just do some comparison shopping. You can try to ask for a deal if you're buying several items, but remember that most vendors are artists that don't make much money – if you really like something and it's reasonably priced, it's best to just pay the stated price. If you think you're being overcharged, you can always just say *'no, gracias,'* and continue on your way.

While walking through any street fair, it's essential that you remain aware of your surroundings and any valuables on your person – pickpockets notoriously prey on distracted shoppers.

Feria Plaza Francia (Map p87; www.feriaplazafrancia.com; cnr Avs Pueyrredon y del Libertador; 11am-8pm Sat, Sun & holidays) Located in Recoleta, this lovely street fair features hundreds of booths selling high-quality leather accessories, bronze jewelry, woven hats, handmade crafts, sandals, kitschy souvenirs and dozens of different creative types of goods. Hippies gather, bakers circulate their pastries and mimes perform (or just stand very still). The website gives a great overview of what's available.

Feria de Artesanos Caminito (Map p80; cnr Caminito & Mendoza; from noon-6pm Thu-Sun & holidays) Tango themes dominate the goods at this small and lively crafts fair, giving La Boca even more color than usual. Tango dancers and buskers compete for your attention, and along Caminito itself are many drawings, paintings and pictures to buy.

Feria de Anticuarios (4743-8371; www.delanticuario.com; Estación Las Barrancas; 9:30am-8pm Sat, Sun & holidays) This cute antiques market, in the northern suburb of Acassuso, has goods cheaper than the San Telmo fair and it's also smaller and less crowded. Dig through old silverwork, records, books, small collectibles, lighting fixtures and antique hardware. The best way here is on the Tren de la Costa, which begins in Olivos at Estación Maipú; get to this train station from downtown via buses 59, 60 and 152 (or take the regular Mitre train line to Tren de la Costa).

Feria de Mataderos (Off Map p58; 4323-9532; www.feriademataderos.com.ar; cnr Avs Lisandro de la Torre & de los Corrales; 11am-8pm Sun Mar-Dec, 6pm-midnight Sat Jan-Feb) In the working-class barrio of Mataderos is this excellent folk market. Merchants offer handmade crafts and regional cuisine like *locro* (a corn and meat stew) and *humita* (a savory corn and cheese mixture wrapped in husks). Folk singers, dancers and gauchos on horseback entertain, and there's a nearby **gaucho museum** (Off Map p58; 4687-1949; Av de los Corrales 6436; admission AR$2; 12-6:30pm Sun Mar-Dec). From downtown, take bus 155 (also marked 180) or 126; the market is about an hour's ride away, but worth it – you can also take a taxi to and from Mataderos if you're pinched for time. Call ahead in between seasons to make sure it's open.

Feria de San Pedro Telmo (Map p76; Plaza Dorrego; www.feriadesantelmo.com; 10am-5pm Sun) Tourists and locals alike flock to this fun *feria* (fair) – here you are sure to find jewelry, artwork, vintage clothing, collectibles and much, much more. Tango shows, buskers and mimes entertain, while sidewalk cafés provide welcome breaks. Because of these crowds, Calle Defensa is cut off to traffic from Av Belgrano to Parque Lezama, where there's a simple weekend crafts market. There are also occasional live tango bands and Brazilian-style drumming parades.

Feria Artesanal Plaza General Manuel Belgrano (Map p101; www.belgrarte.com.ar; Plaza Belgrano, cnr Juramento & Cuba; 10am-8pm Sat, Sun & holidays) That's a mouthful. Belgrano hosts this pleasant neighborhood market, great on a sunny weekend, featuring high-quality imaginative crafts, as well as some kitschy stuff. The performers and tarot readers draw a crowd, too.

Feria Plaza Serrano (Map p92; Plaza Serrano; 11am-7pm Sat & Sun) Costume jewelry, hand-knit tops, funky clothes, hippie bags, glass jewelry and leather accessories fill the crafts booths at this popular fair on fashionable Plaza Serrano in Palermo Viejo. It's not large, but the plaza is surrounded with trendy bars, restaurants, and market-style shops where indie designers sell their work. In warmer weather, the feria often opens on Wed-Fri afternoons, as well.

shop, located in an old house. The most detailed ones are, unsurprisingly, the most beautiful and expensive. All are made from wool and natural dyes, and can also be used as light rugs. Expect to pay from AR$2000 up.

ATÍPICA Map p92 Crafts & Textiles

☎ 4833-3344; www.atipicaobjetos.com.ar; El Salvador 4510; 2-8pm Mon-Fri, 11am-8pm Sat

Run by a mother-and-daughter team, this tiny shop stocks crafts from local and northern Argentine artists who use indigenous techniques for their works. All of the items are handmade and unique, and include picture frames, wall hangings, mask replicas, gourd bowls, small boxes, textiles and jewelry. Quality is high and prices fair.

MISSION Map p62 Crafts & Textiles

☎ 4832-3285; www.centralmission.com.ar; Pasaje Russel 5009; 10am-10pm

Tucked into a side street near Plaza Serrano is this small shop with Argentine-made crafts and souvenirs. It's a good place to pick up some gaucho knives, cowhide pillow covers, a leather belt, a *mate* set or some flattened wine bottles for dad. Check out the excellent website for shopping inspiration. Also in Palermo Hollywood at Honduras 5567.

BOKURA Map p92 Fashion

☎ 4833-3975; www.bokura.com.ar; El Salvador 4677; 11am-8pm

Look no further for the latest hipster threads. Catering to young men, this funky store carries stylish denim jeans with trendy patches and that 'used' look, along with retro-designed T-shirts and classic-line sweaters. The store itself is worth a peek, as it features Asian decor and amazing tile accents. There's also a branch in San Telmo (Map p76; Defensa 891).

BOLIVIA Map p98 Fashion

☎ 4832-6284; www.boliviaonline.com.ar; Gurruchaga 1581; 11am-8pm Mon-Sat, 3-8pm Sun

There's almost nothing here that your young, hip and possibly gay brother wouldn't love, from the striped cut-off cowboy shirts to the floral Puma sneakers to the Mexican-bag-fabric plastic belts. Metrosexual to the hilt, and paradise for the man who isn't afraid of patterns, plaid or pastels. A few other locations have opened more recently in this part of the city; the one at Acevedo 638 is particularly spacious.

DAM Map p92 Fashion

☎ 4833-3935; www.damboutique.com.ar; Honduras 4775; 11:30am-8:30pm Mon-Sat

Spice up a boring black wardrobe with a brightly flowered sixties-style dress or a one-piece jumpsuit patterned with little green apples from DAM. Playful, vibrant, occasionally outrageous, designer Carola Besasso's casual line is a hit with artistic young porteñas.

EL CID Map p92 Fashion

☎ 4832-3339; www.elcid.us; Gurruchaga 1732; 11am-8pm Mon-Sat

Some of the finest men's threads can be found at this Palermo Viejo boutique, which highlights Nestor Goldberg's designer shirts, pants, jackets, accessories and jeans. Materials are of the highest quality, and tailoring is classy, hip and casual.

HERMANOS ESTEBECORENA Map p92 Fashion

☎ 4772-2145; www.hermanosestebecorena.com; El Salvador 5960; 11am-1pm & 1:30-9pm Mon-Fri, 11am-9pm Sat

The Estebecorena brothers apply their highly creative skills toward smartly designed tops, jackets that fold into bags, polo-collar work shirts and even supremely comfortable, nearly seamless underwear. The focus is on original, highly stylish, very functional men's clothing that makes the artsy types swoon. Selection is limited, but what's there really counts.

JUANA DE ARCO Map p92 Fashion & Accessories

☎ 4833-1621; www.juanadearco.net; El Salvador 4762; 11am-8pm Mon-Sat, 2-8pm Sun

Mariana Cortes has designed adorable bits of fabrics sewn into girly sets that would be best showcased during a pillow fight. Brightly colored T-shirts, button belts and boxer shorts are other choices, and G-strings can be bought creatively packaged in egg cartons. Descend the staircase to discover crocheted swimsuits, woven accessories that will start conversations, and animal-stamped pillow cases.

LA MERCERÍA Map p92 Fashion & Accessories

☎ 4831-8558; Armenia 1609; 🕑 11am-8pm Mon-Fri, 10am-9pm Sat, 1-8pm Sun

Attracting crowds of giggling ladies on a busy weekend, this boutique is stuffed full of bright and colorful accessories like costume jewelry, pillows, scarves, belts, perfumes and lots of handbags. Huge hats, over-the-top and perfect for race-track parties, are undoubtedly a highlight. Frilly, glitzy and designed for self-assured women.

NADINE ZLOTOGORA Map p92 Fashion

☎ 4831-4203; www.nadinez.com; El Salvador 4683; 🕑 11am-8pm Mon-Sat

Nadine Z's gorgeous dresses and tops combine feminine styles with nearly dreamy fabrics, creating fantastically romantic wearables. Thick and billowy base textiles, often in natural colors and floral prints, are layered with lacy tulle and silky edging – a feast for the eyes as well as the skin.

RAPSODIA Map p92 Fashion

☎ 4832-5363; www.rapsodia.com.ar; El Salvador 4757; 🕑 10am-8pm Mon-Sat, noon-9pm Sun

With fabrics from linen to leather, street casual to sequins, this larger boutique shop is a must for fashion mavens. Old and new are blended with exotic twists into creative styles with hipster, gypsy and even military accents. There are also cutting-edge jeans, wild bikinis and a small kids' section, plus sofas to rest your weary feet. Thanks to its runaway popularity, there are now more than a dozen Rapsodia locations in the city.

CALMA CHICHA
Map p92 Housewares & Leather Goods

☎ 4831-1818; www.calmachicha.com; Honduras 4909; 🕑 10am-8pm Mon-Sat, noon-8pm Sun

Always fun and accessible, Calma Chicha specializes in creative housewares and accessories that are locally produced from leather, faux leather, sheepskin, cowhide, and brightly hued fabric. The tongue-in-cheek collection includes butterfly chairs (hint: they'll fold easily into a suitcase), throw rugs, leather placemats, messenger bags and the ever-popular penguin pitchers – yes, exactly the kind they use to serve house wine at neighborhood *parrillas*.

CAPITAL DISEÑO & OBJETOS
Map p92 Housewares & Accessories

☎ 4834-6555; www.capitalpalermo.com.ar; Honduras 4958; 🕑 10am-8pm Mon-Sat

There's nothing you – or anyone – really needs at this whimsical knickknacks store – unless it's that very creative recycled purse (made from soda can pop tops) or that stringy but hip rug that resembles a shaggy dog. Sexy female anarchists should stock up on the Che Guevara bikini. Needless to say, this spot is a great wander through with friends.

SABATER HERMANOS
Map p92 Housewares

☎ 4833-3004; www.shnos.com.ar; Gurruchaga 1821; 🕑 11am-8pm Mon-Sat, 1-7pm Sun

Step into this little store and let both your eyes and nose be entertained by rows and rows of deliciously scented soaps, products of one Spanish family's proud soap-making tradition. Bars of various shapes and sizes come in flavors like chocolate, green tea, rose, lavender, strawberry and lime (our favorite).

HUMAWACA Map p92 Leather Goods

☎ 4832-2662; www.humawaca.com; El Salvador 4692; 🕑 11am-8pm Mon-Sat, 2-7pm Sun

Award-winning designer Ingrid Gutman brings both form and functionality to Argentine leather, producing handbags, backpacks and wallets with clean modernist lines. You'll also see her distinctive collection for sale at Malba. Look for a second location in Recoleta (Map p87; Posadas 1380).

PAPELERA PALERMO
Map p92 Paper & Stationery

☎ 4833-3081; www.papelerapalermo.com.ar; Honduras 4945; 🕑 10am-8pm Mon-Sat, 2-8pm Sun

Sure, everyone e-mails these days – but step into this wonderful stationery store and you'll be tempted to start penning letters again. A large selection of gorgeous wrapping papers, handmade spiral notebooks (look for the Jesus and Evita motifs) and leather or rabbit-skin booklets all inspire.

28 SPORT Map p92 Shoes

☎ 4833-4287; www.28sport.com; Gurruchaga 1481; 🕑 11am-1:30pm, 2:30-8pm Mon-Sat

For the retro-sports fanatic, there's nothing better than this unique shop with a sense of humor and a vintage twist. Focusing on only one product and one style – men's '50s sport-style shoes – the cobblers here can concentrate on quality and craftsmanship. Inspiration comes from football, boxing and bowling shoes, and only 12 pairs of each design are produced.

MISHKA Map p92 Shoes

☎ 4833-6566; El Salvador 4673; 🕑 11am-8pm Mon-Sat

Well-regarded designer Chelo Cantón was once an architect but now creates wonderfully unique footwear with a retro-hip, feminine and slightly conservative vibe. Try on a pair of high-heeled granny boots for size, or, if you're not that adventurous, go for more traditional ballet flats in velvet and brocade. Also located in Palermo's Paseo Alcorta (p121) shopping mall.

ALTO PALERMO Map p92 Shopping Mall

☎ 5777-8000; www.altopalermo.com.ar; Av Coronel Díaz 2098; 🕑 10am-10pm

Smack on bustling Av Santa Fe, this popular, shiny mall offers dozens of clothing shops, bookstores, jewelry boutiques, and electronics and houseware stores. Look for Timberland, Lacoste, Hilfiger and Levi's (plus many Argentine brands, too). Services include a food court, a cinema complex and a good kids' area on the 3rd floor.

PASEO ALCORTA Map p92 Shopping Mall

☎ 5777-6500; www.paseoalcorta.com.ar; Salguero 3172; 🕑 10am-10pm

One of the largest and most upscale malls in the city. All the popular Argentine women's clothing shops are represented, as are international boutiques such as YSL, Lacroix and Dior. Other stores sell leather goods, kids' clothes, men's designs, sportswear and accessories. There's a large food court, a cinema complex and a children's play area.

LO DE JOAQUIN ALBERDI Map p92 Wine

☎ 4832-5329; www.lodejoaquinalberdi.com.ar; Borges 1772; 🕑 noon-9:30pm

Nationally produced wines for every taste and budget line the racks and cellar of this attractive wine shop. Pop across the street to the sister wine-bar, Cabernet, for a glass of Malbec on the patio.

EATING

top picks

- **Amici Miei** (p129)
- **Don Julio** (p137)
- **Green Bamboo** (p134)
- **La Vineria de Gualterio Bolívar** (p129)
- **Sipan** (p132)
- **Oviedo** (p134)
- **Cumaná** (p134)
- **Oui Oui** (p138)
- **Il Ballo del Mattone** (p136)

WHAT'S YOUR RECOMMENDATION? www.lonelyplanet.com/Buenos Aires

EATING

It's official: one of the best reasons to visit Buenos Aires is the food. Thanks to a high concentration of Spanish and Italian immigrants settling here a few generations ago, traditional pizzerias and old-school Galician restaurants proliferate alongside an ever-growing number of cutting-edge eateries where famed chefs fuse seemingly disparate cuisines (Japanese-Peruvian food, anyone?) or try their hands at classic French dishes. But the real star of the local food scene is the beef raised on the grassy pampas outside the city. The quality of produce in richly agricultural Argentina is excellent; on your plate beside one of the finest steaks in the world, you might enjoy grilled pumpkin from Neuquén and a glass of Malbec produced in Mendoza, followed by a dessert of strawberries, grown in Tucumán and topped with cream provided by the province's famous dairy cows. You'll eat so well in Buenos Aires that you'll need to power-walk between lunch and dinner to work off the excess calories.

Buenos Aires is packed with *parrillas* (steakhouses) in every neighborhood, serving perfect slabs of meat at reasonable prices. In fact, you can order a *bife de chorizo* (sirloin) at many cafés, bars or restaurants, but for the best cuts and selection, be sure to visit a *parrilla*. In every neighborhood, you'll find great steak sandwiches, fresh salads, deep-dish pizzas and traditional Italian pasta. Most bars and cafes feature surprisingly large menus and stay open into the wee morning hours, making them great places for late-night snacks. See the Drinking chapter (p144) for our bar and cafe listings.

But those who enjoy more exotic tastes are in luck: Palermo has become Buenos Aires' food mecca, offering a range of Armenian, Brazilian, Mexican, French, Indian, Japanese, Southeast Asian and Middle Eastern cuisines, plus various 'international' eateries that specialize in fusion cuisine. Don't be taken in by appearances alone: many restaurants are slick and contemporary but only offer so-so food. If you're not willing to trade good cooking for flashy ambience, do your homework ahead of time: quite a few of the shining stars on the food scene don't compromise on either score. When in doubt, a crowded reservation list (and dining room) is always a good sign.

The most thorough online guide to BA restaurants is www.guiaoleo.com (in Spanish); for listings in English, try www.saltshaker.net.

If you're looking for a cooking class, see p224.

PRACTICALITIES

Opening Hours

Restaurants are generally open daily from noon to 3:30pm for lunch and 8pm to midnight or 1am for dinner. We note specific hours in reviews only if a restaurant's opening times are widely different from these. It's also a good idea to call ahead to confirm hours, since these can change.

Few places open early in the morning since Argentines don't eat much breakfast, but you can find the occasional breakfast/brunch spot. A sure bet for that morning *medialuna* (croissant) and *cortado* (coffee with milk) are the city's many cafes, which often stay open from morning to late at night without a break.

How Much?

Thanks to climbing inflation, dinner in Buenos Aires has become less of a traveler's bargain than it once was. Still, relatively speaking – especially when you factor in the incredibly high quality of steak and wine, plus the fact that you're not expected to tip exorbitantly – there are foodie deals to be found. At finer restaurants, most dinner mains run from AR$30 to AR$45. Lunches are more affordable, especially if you take advantage of a *menu ejecutivo* (set lunch menu) at fancier restaurants. You won't have a wide selection of entreés, but the price almost always includes dessert, coffee and a glass of wine or sparkling water.

Be aware that not all restaurants accept credit cards – always ask first if you want to use one. Don't be surprised to see a per-

PRICE GUIDE

$$$	mains over AR$38
$$	mains AR$20-38
$	mains under AR$20

MISCELLANEOUS FOOD DEFINITIONS

agua de canilla – tap water (drinkable in BA)
alfajor – Argentina's candy bar; a round cookie sandwich
chopp – draft beer
cortado – coffee with milk
cubierto – cover charge
la cuenta – the bill
dulce de leche – Argentina's version of caramel
entrada – appetizer
jugo (exprimido) – juice (freshly squeezed)
licuado – fruit shake
medialuna – croissant
milanesa – breaded cutlet
postre – dessert
propina – tip
submarino – chocolate bar in milk
sandwiches de miga – thin, crustless sandwiches
tenedor libre – all-you-can-eat restaurant

person *cubierto* (cover charge) tacked on to the bill, usually ranging from AR$3 to AR$8. This covers the use of utensils and bread – it does *not* relate in any way to the tip.

Tipping

You should tip about 10% to 15% of the total bill; keep in mind that tips cannot be added to credit-card purchases. The word for tip in Spanish is *propina*.

Booking Tables

If you're headed to a popular restaurant, especially on weekends, reservations are recommended. Even at more casual eateries, it never hurts to reserve a table ahead of time to be sure – if you don't speak much Spanish, ask a staff member at your hotel to make the call for you. Porteños (BA inhabitants) are notoriously late diners, and most eat no earlier than 9pm (later on weekends). If you arrive when the restaurant first opens you're likely to get a table anywhere – but you might miss out on the people-watching and the liveliness of a local dinnertime crowd.

THE CENTER

You won't find Buenos Aires' best cuisine in the center, as most restaurants here cater to business power-lunches or quick takeout. Some eateries don't even open for dinner since the working masses beeline home after the day is done. Even bars tend to open and close relatively early here. All this doesn't mean you won't find a decent bite to eat, however, and vegetarians especially will find some good choices. Also, five-star hotels often house top-notch restaurants that are worth a visit – and are definitely open for dinner (with reservations). These include Tomo 1 in the Panamericano (p125), Le Sud in the Sofitel (p132) and El Mercado and El Bistró in the Faena (p184).

TOMO 1 Map p62 Modern Argentine $$$

☎ 4326-6695; Carlos Pellegrini 521; mains AR$110-250; ⏰ lunch & dinner Mon-Fri, dinner Sat

Though some might find the sky-high prices and formal decor off putting, Tomo 1 has long been a big deal in the foodie sphere. Chef sisters Ada and Ebe Concaro proudly promote the 'porteño gourmet' tradition – a blend of Italian and Spanish cooking methods – in a series of menus featuring seasonal produce, homemade pasta and fresh fish. Sample their famed cuisine with a three-course *prix fixe* menu. It'll set you back AR$235 per person for lunch, or AR$250 for dinner; luckily, it comes with amuse-bouches, a great glass of wine, mineral water, coffee and petits fours.

BRASSERIE BERRY Map p62 French $$$

☎ 4394-5255; www.brasserieberry.com.ar; Tucumán 775; mains AR$32-65; ⏰ lunch Mon-Thu, lunch & dinner Fri & Sat

With its leather banquettes, classic French bistro chairs, blackboard wine lists, and rich cuisine, this brasserie has an authentic Lyonnaise feel. Drawn in by a *prix fixe* lunch and consistently efficient service, bankers and executives take over the place on weekday afternoons; when the downtown crowd heads home for dinner, the brasserie is a quieter, more romantic venue for sampling quiche and Bordeaux.

FURAI-BO Map p62 Japanese $$

☎ 4334-3440; Adolfo Alsina 429; mains AR$30-48; ⏰ lunch Mon-Fri, dinner Wed-Sat

This traditional Japanese teahouse – unlike the myriad flashy and fashion-conscious sushi restaurants that are slowly overtaking Palermo – is the real deal. Walk up the staircase of the antique building into a calm space meant to resemble a Buddhist temple; on weekend evenings, live instrumentalists set the mood with ambient ceremonial music. The house specialty is homemade ramen noodles with pork. The menu also includes excellent sushi and katsu, plus unusual sweet treats like wasabi ice cream.

D'ORO Map p62 Italian $$

☎ 4342-6959; Perú 159; mains AR$25-45; ⌚ lunch & dinner Mon-Sat

You might expect average spaghetti from a downtown eatery that caters primarily to the in-and-out lunch crowd, but D'Oro is a serious Italian wine bar and restaurant to rival many others in the city. Come for thin, crispy oven-baked pizzas, mushroom risotto, cappellini tossed with fresh basil and tomatoes, fettucine with shellfish, and garlic-topped focaccia. There's a short but well-chosen selection of wines by the glass and a friendly sommelier on hand to recommend one. Like many other downtown institutions, D'Oro is far more mellow after the chaotic lunch rush has finished.

PURA VIDA Map p62 Vegetarian $$

☎ 4393-0093; Reconquista 516; mains AR$25-36; ⌚ 9am-5:30pm Mon-Fri

Wheatgrass shots, anyone? This sleek and uberhealthy eatery helps counteract the effects of the high-cholesterol porteño diet. Kick off the morning with a fresh fruit and granola bowl or a tall glass of 'Green Monster' (a juice made with cucumber, apple, lemon and fresh parsley.) At lunch, sink your teeth into a hummus and avocado sandwich or a portabella and sun-dried tomato salad – you'll feel less guilty when you're indulging in a huge steak and a half-liter of Malbec later on.

CALIFORNIA BURRITO COMPANY (CBC) Map p62 Mexican $$

☎ 4328-3057; Lavalle 441; mains AR$18-30; ⌚ 8am-11pm Mon-Fri

This modern burrito joint – claimed by its American owners to be the first in South America – is hugely popular with travelers, expats and the business crowd. Flour tortillas are loaded up with your choice of meat, rice, beans and salsa, and rolled into large, San Francisco–style burritos the likes of which BA has never seen. A tip: get the *fuego* sauce if you like it mildly spicy. The vegetarian burritos and house margaritas are welcome extras.

PUERTO MADERO

One of the city's best walking areas is Puerto Madero, where pedestrian paths border old brick warehouses that have been tastefully converted into expensive offices, lofts and – most importantly for the traveler – fine restaurants. Nearly all of these upscale eateries boast views of the nearby *diques* and many sport covered outdoor terraces. You won't get the best bang for your buck in this elegant strip, and the cuisine isn't the most inspired, but it's the location that counts.

Cabaña Las Lilas (Map p69) is the most famous *parrilla* restaurant here, but many consider it a tourist trap – a bit overrated and way overpriced. We don't review it here, but if you have money to burn, by all means try it.

EL MERCADO Map p69 Mediterranean $$$

☎ 4010-9200; Hotel Faena + Universe; Martha Salotti 445, Dique 2; mains AR$90-120; ⌚ 7am-2am

Don't despair if you're not staying at the otherworldly Philippe Starck–designed Faena Hotel + Universe. You can still get a feel for the place at the antique-strewn, shabby-chic (emphasis on *chic*) El Mercado, where the stylish set digs into *ceviche* (raw fish), rack of lamb and empanadas baked in an adobe mud oven. The award-winning chef Mariano Cid de la Paz presides over the place and El Bistro, its more flamboyant (and expensive) sister across the hall – walk by to catch a glimpse of the blindingly white space punctuated with blood-red accents and whimsical plaster unicorns.

RODIZIO Map p69 Brazilian $$$

☎ 4334-3638; Av Alicia Moreau de Justo 838; mains AR$60-70; ⌚ lunch & dinner

If you love meat and don't want a headache trying to figure out which cut to order, take a seat at upscale Rodizio, a Brazilian-style *churrasquería* (all-you-can-eat restaurant). You don't even have to queue up – just sit pretty at your table and knife-wielding waiters come by to slice chunks of meat off of long spits and right onto your plate. The cuts are all different, so you can be choosy and pace yourself. A cold appetizer buffet, one dessert and a coffee are included in the price.

BICE Map p69 Mediterranean $$$

☎ 4315-6216; Av Alicia Moreau de Justo 192; mains AR$38-95; ⌚ lunch & dinner

With branches all over the world, Bice is best known for its high-quality Italian cui-

THE WORLD'S BEST STEAKS

You walk into a traditional *parrilla,* breeze past the stuffed bull and sizzling grill at the entrance, and sit down hungry, knife and fork in hand. You don't know a word of Spanish and you've never had to choose between more than three cuts of steak in your life, but the menu has at least 10 choices. What do you do?

Don't fret. We'll give you a better idea of what will show up on your plate. There will always be variations from place to place on the items listed below, but no matter what you end up ordering it's unlikely to be unpalatable.

But first, a quick history lesson. The first Spaniards who arrived in the country brought cows, later abandoned when colonization efforts were thwarted by the native population. In Argentina's rich pampas the herds found a bovine equivalent of heaven: plenty of lush, fertile grasses on which to feed, with few natural predators to limit their numbers. Things were great until the Europeans decided to recolonize the pampas.

Today, intermixing with other European bovine breeds has produced a pretty tasty introduction to the epitome of Argentina's cuisine. Why is it so good? Any Argentine worth his or her salt will say it's because free-range Argentine cows eat nutritious pampas grass, thus lacking the massive quantities of corn, antibiotics and growth hormones that American or European stocks are given in feedlots (though this situation is changing quickly). This makes for a leaner, more natural-tasting meat that's actually more nutritious than grain-fed cattle.

Because of their country's ability to produce enormous quantities of beef, Argentines tend to eat a lot of it – and have perfected the art of grilling beef on the *asado* (barbecue). This involves cooking with coals and using only salt to prepare the meat. On the grill itself, slanted runners funnel the excess fat to the sides, and an adjustable height system directs the perfect amount of cook to the meat. The *asado* is a family institution, often taking place on Sunday in the backyards of houses all over the country. If you are lucky enough to be invited to one, do not turn it down. Here's what to expect:

A traditional *parrillada,* or mixed grill, is the most common preparation, and offers a little bit of everything. Expect *choripán* (a sausage-sandwich appetizer), *pollo* (chicken), *costillas* (ribs) and *carne* (beef). It can also come with more exotic items such as *chinchulines* (small intestines), *mojellas* (sweetbreads) and *morcilla* (blood sausage). Try them all, though certain pieces take some getting used to.

You may also get offered some of the following beef cuts, which are available at most *parrillas* (steakhouses):

Bife de chorizo	Sirloin; most popular cut and very tasty.
Bife de lomo	Tenderloin; the name says it all.
Bife de costilla	T-bone; also called *chuleta.*
Tira de asado	Short ribs.
Vacío	Flank steak; chewy but tasty.
Cuadril	Rump steak; often a thin cut.
Ojo de bife	Eye of round; a choice smaller morsel.

If you don't specify how you want your steak cooked, it will normally come *a punto* (medium-rare). To get it redder on the inside ask for *jugoso* (rare), and if you want it well-done – well, you're on your own (no, just kidding – say *bien hecho*). Be sure not to miss *chimichurri,* a tasty marinade often made of olive oil, garlic and parsley that adds a flavorful spiciness and will tantalize your taste buds. Occasionally you can also get *salsa criolla,* a condiment made of diced tomato, onion and parsley.

After your delicious Argentine steak, pass by the *asadores* (barbecuers) to thank them for the tasty meal. At the larger, more touristy *parrillas,* you may even be able to get them to pose for a snapshot right next to the impressively large circular barbecue pits, surrounded by staked hunks of meat.

sine. The homemade pastas (both fresh and dry) are exceptional: try the black fettuccini with shrimp or the spinach-and-ricotta ravioli with four-cheese sauce. There's also a luscious risotto with artichoke and asparagus as well as several meat and fish choices. End it all with gelato, a crepe, mousse with pears or white chocolate semifreddo. Service is good; test it by calling ahead and asking for a table near the water.

SIGA LA VACA Map p69 Parrilla $$$

☎ 4315-6801; Av Alicia Moreau de Justo 1714; lunch AR$38-52, dinner AR$46-52; lunch & dinner

Only the truly hungry should set foot in this excellent *tenedor libre* (all-you-can-eat) steakhouse, where mountains of food are available for consumption. It's unabashedly touristy, yes, but fun for carnivores who'd like to try various cuts of beef – and for traveling families with picky eaters to satisfy. After chowing down here, you'll probably want to work it off with a long walk towards the Costanera and the ecological reserve.

I CENTRAL MARKET

Map p69 Modern Argentine $$

☎ 5775-0330; cnr Pierina Dealessi & Macacha Güemes; mains AR$28-65; ⌚ 8am-midnight

This cool waterfront space, reminiscent of an upscale New York cafe, wears many hats: in the morning, there's a coffee counter where you can have espresso and scones while reading the paper, in the afternoon, there's a light lunch menu, outdoor seating, and a gourmet deli and kitchenwares shop to poke around, and by night, the glamorous dining room opens, serving contemporary Argentinian dishes with wine pairings.

CONGRESO & TRIBUNALES

Hardly inspiring in terms of contemporary cuisine, the Congreso area caters mostly for business with cheap *parrillas* and quick takeout. Walk around the side streets, though, and you're bound to stumble across some Chinese, Korean and Peruvian gems. The biggest cultural footprint in this area, however, is Buenos Aires' Little Spain neighborhood (in the blocks around Avs de Mayo and Salta); here you'll find a few good Spanish and Basque eateries serving traditional food. In the mood for sushi? Several casual but excellent Japanese eateries are tucked away on side streets west of Plaza del Congreso between Av Independencia and Av Rivadavia.

PLAZA ASTURIAS Map p72

Spanish $$

☎ 4382-7334; cnr Av de Mayo & Salta; mains AR$25-40; ⌚ lunch & dinner

Occupying a prime corner spot on grand Av de Mayo, this old-fashioned Spanish restaurant draws in a regular lunchtime crowd of locals nostalgic for their Galician grandmothers. The menu features expected staples like chorizo, ham, potato casserole, and pasta, as well as more adventurous dishes like *cazuela de mariscos,* a powerful seafood stew rich with mussels, garlic and herbs. Try the set lunch, which allows you to choose from a few dishes and includes coffee, dessert and a glass of wine.

EL HISPANO Map p72

Spanish $$

☎ 4382-7534; Salta 20; mains AR$22-65; ⌚ lunch & dinner

Tired of the same old steak? Head to this classy and atmospheric 50-year-old Spanish restaurant offering choices from octopus *cazuela* (stew) to frogs Provençal to snails à la Andaluza…or even just paella. Unsurprisingly, the place is really into seafood, including grilled trout, mussels, oysters and fried calamari. Don't forget desserts like *natilla* (custard) and *arroz con leche* (rice pudding) to round off your special non-steak meal (though it's got them on the menu as well).

CHIQUILÍN Map p72

Argentine $$

☎ 4373-5163; Sarmiento 1599; mains AR$20-38; ⌚ lunch & dinner

A local mainstay for 80 years, Chiquilín is an excellent place to safely take, say, your parents. It's a large, comfortable restaurant with a cozy and classic atmosphere (including hanging hams) that adds a bit of personality. Dressed-up staff are efficient, which is great because this place can bustle – even at 1am on a Saturday night. The best choices here are steak and pasta, though specials like paella on Monday and *puchero* (a meat-and-vegetable stew) on Wednesday offer welcome detours from the regular menu.

CHAN CHAN Map p72

Peruvian $

☎ 4382-8492; Hipólito Yrigoyen 1390; mains AR$18-35; ⌚ lunch & dinner Tue-Sun

This petite and colorful Peruvian eatery lies in the shadow of the towering Palacio Barolo. Thanks to fair prices and relatively quick service, the place is jam-packed at lunchtime with office workers sharing plates of *ceviche* and *papas a la huancaina* (potatoes with spicy cheese sauce). Having trouble deciphering the menu? Ask one of the cheerful waiters to explain the daily specials or just play it safe with an order of *arroz chaufa* (Peruvian-style fried rice) and a perfectly tangy pisco sour.

CERVANTES II Map p72

Argentine $

☎ 4372-5227; Juan D Perón 1883; mains AR$15-27; ⌚ lunch & dinner

A great, affordable choice in this area is Cervantes II, a popular, modern and unpretentious spot with a touch of old-world atmosphere. It's filled mostly with locals ordering an *agua de sifón* (soda water) to go along with their *bife de chorizo* or *ravioles con tuco* (ravioli with sauce). Short orders like *milanesas* (breaded steaks), omelets and fish dishes are also available. Portions are large and the service is usually efficient.

PIZZERÍA GÜERRÍN Map p72 Pizza $

☎ 4371-8141; Av Corrientes 1368; slices AR$3.50; ⏲ lunch & dinner

A quick pit-stop for those drawn to the theaters and cinemas on Av Corrientes is this cheap but classic old pizza joint. Just point at a pre-baked slice behind the glass counter and eat standing up with the rest of the crowd. To be more civilized, sit down and order one freshly baked – this way you can also choose from a greater variety of toppings for your pizza. *Empanadas* and plenty of desserts are also available.

SAN TELMO

The heart of San Telmo, Plaza Dorrego is surrounded by several cafe-restaurants that pop open their umbrellas from Monday to Saturday. On Sunday, however, the plaza (and a few surrounding streets) is taken over by vendors and tourists jamming the ever-popular antiques market. San Telmo has traditionally supported a large cluster of *parrillas*, but as the neighborhood inexorably gentrifies, more innovative, upscale and pricier restaurants and bars are moving in.

LA VINERIA DE GUALTERIO BOLÍVAR Map p76 Mediterranean $$$

☎ 4361-4709; www.lavineriadegualteriobolivar.com; Bolívar 865; tasting menu AR$230; ⏲ lunch from 1pm, dinner from 9pm Tue-Sun

Singlehandedly elevating San Telmo's gastronomic scene is this tiny gourmet restaurant overseen by chef Alejandro Digilio, formerly on the kitchen staff at Spain's El Bulli (considered by some to be the world's best restaurant). He's known for his experimentation with texture and temperature; sample his inventive contemporary cuisine with an elaborate tasting menu featuring small plates like quinoa curry and garlic salmon with bacon. Dishes are paired with fine Argentine wines, punctuated with palate-cleansing cocktails like a red-fruit blend with vodka and mint, and capped off, of course, with impossibly rich desserts.

AMICI MIEI Map p76 Italian $$$

☎ 4362-5562; www.amicimiei.com.ar; Defensa 1072; mains AR$35-55; ⏲ lunch & dinner Tue-Sun

There aren't many places in town where you can dine on gourmet black-truffle carpaccio while an impeccably dressed Italian tenor strides through the room crooning *'O Sole Mio'*. This lovely Italian eatery is known for refined service and Chef Sebastian Rivas' splurge-worthy homemade bread, pizza and pasta – check out the behind-the-scenes action in the glass-encased bakery on the side of the dining room. In warmer weather, feast on tagliatelle with shrimp on the rear terrace or at a charming table for two overlooking Plaza Dorrego.

CAFÉ SAN JUAN Map p76 International $$$

☎ 4300-1112; Av San Juan 450; mains AR$35-48; ⏲ lunch & dinner Tue-Sun

Having studied in Milan, Paris and Barcelona, chef Leandro Cristóbal now runs the kitchen at this renowned San Telmo bistro. Start with fabulous tapas – accented with cheese from an 85-year-old family business – then delve into the divine crushed-

TEA FOR TWO

Following in the grand tradition of Londoners and society ladies, porteños have taken to the ritual of afternoon tea. Which isn't to say that *mate* is on its way out, mind you – taking a break for chamomile and crumpets is just another excuse for these highly social souls to get together and dish on Cristina Kirchner's latest (alleged) plastic surgery.

At these grand tea institutions, you won't just be sipping Earl Grey – with an array of crustless sandwiches, sweets and pastries, the experience is more like a full meal. The grandmother of the tea scene is the lavish L'Orangerie (p133) at the Alvear Palace Hotel, where white-gloved service and impossibly elegant little cakes await guests fond of old-fashioned pleasantries. For a more contemporary, super-stylish tea service, head straight for Sirop Folie (Map p87; ☎ 4813-5900; http://siroprestaurant.com; Vicente Lopez 1661, Local 12; ⏲ from 10am Tue-Sun).

If you're short on time, pick up the trendiest tea leaves in town at the charming Tealosophy (Map p87; ☎ 4804-7020; www.tealosophy.com; Av Alvear 1883 £37; ⏲ 10:30am-8pm Mon-Sat) or soak up some old-world atmosphere among the wooden tea cabinets at El Gato Negro (p152).

almond-breaded shrimp, mushrooms from northern Argentina and an amazing pork *bandiola* (deliciously tender after nine hours' roasting). Most of the seafood is flown in daily from Patagonia, and the service is commendable. Reserve for dinner.

CASAL DE CATALUNYA

Map p76 Spanish $$

☎ **4361-0191; Chacabuco 863; mains AR$28-55; lunch & dinner Tue-Sun, dinner Mon**

Located in BA's Catalan cultural center – a beautiful 1886 building that was once a glamorous theater – is this excellent Catalan restaurant. Unsurprisingly big on seafood, its specialties run from a delicious garlic shrimp to fresh mussels and clams in tomato sauce to fish of the day with *aioli* (a garlic and olive oil sauce). Other typical Spanish dishes include *jamón serrano* (prosciutto-like ham), seafood paella and suckling pig. If you know what's good for you, don't miss the luscious *crema Catalana* for dessert.

BRASSERIE PETANQUE

Map p76 French $$

☎ **4342-7930; www.brasseriepetanque.com; cnr Defensa & Mexico; mains AR$28-45; lunch & dinner Tue-Sun**

This bright Parisian-style brasserie is a lively spot for Sunday brunch or a leisurely evening meal. Charismatic waiters pour complimentary aperitifs as you ponder steak tartare versus roasted chicken, *boeuf Bourguignon,* duck confit or grilled trout with almonds. There's a short but wise list of wines by the glass; the *prix fixe* lunch menu (AR$42) is a steal.

COMEDOR NIKKAI Map p76 Asian $$

☎ **4300-5848; Av Independencia 732; mains AR$20-60; lunch & dinner Mon-Sat**

Housed in the Asociación Japonesa building, this restaurant has some of BA's most authentic Japanese food, and the locals know it – come early if you don't want to wait. All your favorites are here, including tempura, teriyaki, ramen or udon noodles and – of course – lots of sushi and sashimi choices. Imported sake and Asahi beer are available too.

ORIGEN Map p76 International $$

☎ **4362-7979; Humberto Primo 599; mains AR$22-28; breakfast & lunch Mon & Tue, all day Wed-Sun**

Modern but unpretentious, this stylish corner bistro spills out onto the wide sidewalks; you'll have to fight for an outdoor table on a sunny afternoon. The creative menu features health-conscious dishes from stir-fry and whole-wheat pizza to homemade soups and green salads. There's also afternoon tea service, two-for-one glasses of wine at happy hour, and cappuccino served in delightfully oversized mugs.

MATE & ITS RITUAL

If there were an official national beverage in Argentina, then *mate* (mah-teh) would be it. More than a simple drink like tea or coffee, *mate* is an elaborate ritual shared among family, friends and coworkers. In fact, sharing is often the whole point.

Argentina is the world's largest producer and consumer of *yerba mate,* but it's also popular in parts of Chile, southern Brazil, Paraguay and especially Uruguay, which consumes twice as much of the stuff per capita as Argentina. (In fact, many *mate*-drinking Uruguayans will not go anywhere without a thermos under their arm and a *mate* gourd clasped in their hand. Perhaps *mateine,* a caffeine-like stimulant, has something to do with this 'addiction.')

Preparing *mate* is a ritual in itself, and there is an informal etiquette for drinking it. The *cebador* (server) fills the gourd almost to the top with *yerba,* then pours very hot water into the vessel, then passes it clockwise around a group. Each participant drinks the gourd dry each time, then hands the gourd back to the *cebador,* who refills it and gives it to the next person. A *bombilla* (a silvery straw with built-in filter), used to sip the *mate,* is shared by everyone. If you caught a cold on the plane over, do your companions a favor and ask for your own *bombilla* instead of sharing a straw with everyone.

An invitation to drink *mate* is a cultural treat you shouldn't turn down, though it's definitely an acquired taste. At first you'll probably find it grassy, bitter and too hot, but on the second or third round you kind of get used to it. Adding sugar helps with the taste and bitterness. Don't say 'gracias' until you've had enough, as this is a sign you want to stop drinking. Finally, remember not to hold the *mate* too long before passing it on, as somebody else is always waiting in line!

Perhaps because it is such a personal ritual of sorts, not many restaurants offer *mate* on the menu. A few places that do have it are Cumaná (p134) and La Peña del Colorado (p161).

EL DESNIVEL Map p76 Parrilla $

☎ 4300-9081; Defensa 855; mains AR$16-26; ⏲ lunch & dinner Tue-Sun, dinner Mon

This famous *parrilla* joint usually packs in both locals and tourists, serving them treats like chorizo sandwiches and *bife de lomo* (tenderloin steak). Add salad and a double espresso, and you can walk away happy and buzzing for around AR$10 to $AR30. The sizzling grill out front is torturous while you wait for a table – get here early, especially on weekends. Expect waiters to be either surly or charming.

PARRILLA 1880 Map p76 Parrilla $

☎ 4307-2746; Defensa 1665; mains AR$13-28; ⏲ lunch & dinner

For a good, solid *parrilla* experience away from the more touristy sections of San Telmo, make your way south to this popular joint; it's right across from Parque Lezama. The atmosphere is thick with history and locals enjoying all the juicy cuts of meat coming off of the open grill in front – try the *ojo de bife* (rib eye) or *pechito de cerdo* (pork ribs). The half portion of *bife de chorizo* is more than enough for one person. Just be careful walking out, as the area is a little dodgy after dark.

BAR EL FEDERAL Map p76 Argentine $

☎ 4300-4313; cnr Perú & Carlos Calvo; mains AR$12-30; ⏲ 8am-2am

Dating from 1864, this historic bar has a classic, somewhat rustic atmosphere accented with original wood, tile, and an eye-catching antique bar. The specialties here are sandwiches and *picadas* (shared appetizer plates), but there are also lots of pastas, salads, desserts and tall mugs of icy beer. While in the neighborhood, check out El Federal's equally historic sister, La Poesia, more recently opened in a converted pharmacy on the corner of Bolivar and Chile.

WAFLES SUR Map p76 Cafe $

☎ 15-5581-4540; www.waflessur.com; Estados Unidos 509; mains AR$12-30; ⏲ breakfast, lunch & dinner

Boasting a fresh, simple and budget-friendly menu of sweet and savory waffles, smoothies, coffee, and bottled craft beer, this cheery little shop is a happy addition to San Telmo. Doors open at 8am daily; patrons are free to dine in or just grab a takeaway iced cappuccino. Rushing isn't recommended, though, as a piping hot waffle slathered with *dulce de leche* is one of life's true pleasures.

LA BOCA

Though limited to just a handful of streets, the tourist area of La Boca does contain a number of traditional Argentine eateries – mostly offering classic steaks and pastas. As long as you don't expect fine cuisine you shouldn't be disappointed. Just remember not to wander off on an *aprés*-lunch stroll down unbeaten tourist paths, looking rich and lost, or you run the risk of meeting local bullies who want your lunch money.

LOS PETERSEN Map p80 Argentine $$

☎ 4104-1003; Fundación Proa, Av Pedro de Mendoza 1929; mains AR$22-45; ⏲ 10am-7pm Tue-Sun

Whether or not you're here to see the art exhibit at Fundación Proa, this sophisticated cafe-restaurant on the gallery's 2nd floor is an inviting venue for coffee, elegant sandwiches and salads, and *empanadas tucumánas* (empanadas stuffed with juicy hand-cut beef). The terrace offers sweeping views over the colorfully broken-down Riachuelo and the old port.

IL MATTERELLO Map p80 Italian $$

☎ 4307-0529; Martín Rodríguez 517; mains AR$22-40; ⏲ lunch & dinner Tue-Sat, lunch Sun

The plain atmosphere at this Genovese trattoria is nothing to write home about, but the food more than makes up for it. You can't go wrong with the *lasagne bolognese,* the *tagliatelle alla rucola* (tagliatelle with arugula) or the *strascinati* (tiny 'ear'-like pasta domes) with *amatriciana* (bacon and red pepper) sauce. For a special treat, however, try the *tortelli verde* (small pasta pillows stuffed with cheese and garlic). For dessert there's a great tiramisu and seasonal *crostate* (cream-filled pastry).

EL OBRERO Map p80 Parrilla $$

☎ 4362-9912; www.bodegonelobrero.com.ar; Agustín R Caffarena 64; mains AR$16-30; ⏲ lunch & dinner Mon-Sat

This is a restaurant you go to for ambience, history and a hearty meal washed down with house wine. The same family here has been running El Obrero since 1954;

throughout the years, a number of famous people have passed through for steak – including Bono and Robert Duvall – a fact that's proudly displayed in photos hanging on the walls. You'll also see old Boca Juniors jerseys, antique furniture, old tile floors and chalkboards showing the day's specials and standard *parrilla* fare. Take a taxi.

RETIRO

Just north of the Microcentro, posh Retiro is not generally known for its fine dining. Restaurants here also tend to cater to the business crowds, offering good-value midday specials and food to go – so all you have to do is find yourself a nice, grassy spot or shady bench in nearby Plaza San Martín where you can enjoy your impromptu picnic. Don't ignore the area's bars and cafes, which also serve meals and are sometimes more casual and interesting than traditional restaurants, and of course also offer a wider range of drinking options.

LE SUD Map p84 French $$$

☎ 4131-0131; Hotel Sofitel, Arroyo 841; mains AR$48-80; ⌚ breakfast, lunch & dinner

For a taste of Europe, dress up in your best threads and head on over to Le Sud, one of the city's finest French restaurants, elegantly ensconced in the posh hotel. Chef Olivier Falchi whips out simple yet authentic French fusion cuisine sprinkled with fresh herbs, spices and oils straight from the Mediterranean. Order the stewed rabbit or lemon ravioli and you'll be in Provence before it's time for dessert.

GRAN BAR DANZÓN Map p84 International $$$

☎ 4811-1108; www.granbardanzon.com.ar; Libertad 1161; mains AR$46-77; ⌚ dinner

It's hard to be hipper than this popular lounge-bar-restaurant. A cool-looking wine-conservation system makes it possible to order several wines by the glass instead of committing to a single Malbec; then again, with such an extensive and exciting list of wines by the bottle, you might be tempted to uncork a few and pair them with your duck confit, sushi, rabbit ravioli or risotto with king crab. The food is fine, if not fabulous, but make no mistake – you're here for the scene, the beautiful people, and of course, the Bonarda and Torrontés.

SIPAN Map p84 Peruvian-Japanese $$$

☎ 4315-0763; www.sipan.com.ar; Paraguay 624; mains AR$35-60; ⌚ lunch & dinner Mon-Sat

Japanese-Peruvian food is all the rage in Buenos Aires. Skip the pretentious Palermo eateries peddling overpriced sushi and taste-test the fresh, flavorful cuisine at Sipan. Tucked away in an unsuspecting shopping gallery, this sleek, low-lit pisco bar turns out imaginative sushi, classic dishes like miso soup and fried rice, seafood appetizers heaped high on ceramic spoons, and tangy cocktails made with pisco (grape brandy) the owners carried over from Peru.

FILO Map p84 Italian $$

☎ 4311-0312; www.filo-ristorante.com; San Martín 975; mains AR$28-45; ⌚ lunch & dinner

Popular with the 45-minutes-and-gone business lunch crowd and, by night, couples out on their third dinner date, this large, pop art–style Italian pizzeria tosses thin-crust pies with fresh toppings. Other tasty choices include *panini* (Italian-style sandwiches), pasta and a whirlwind of desserts. Try a pie piled high with prosciutto and arugula, then throw back some limoncello before checking out the downstairs art gallery.

EMPIRE THAI Map p84 Asian $$

☎ 4312-5706; www.empirethai.net; Tres Sargentos 427; mains AR$25-45; ⌚ lunch & dinner Mon-Fri, dinner Sat

The sultry lighting and sumptuous decor are your first clue that the place isn't a traditional Thai diner; the second is when you're still hungry after finishing your noodles. Nevermind – the scrumptious peanut satay and the moody New York–style ambience draw a cool crowd, and the place boasts one of the city's best selections of vodka. Give your palate a rest from all the steak and potatoes with crispy wrapped prawns, *paneng* pork in red curry and *tom ka gai* (chicken and coconut-milk soup).

EL FEDERAL Map p84 Argentine $$

☎ 4313-1324; San Martin 1015; mains AR$22-35; ⌚ 10am-midnight Mon-Fri, to 6pm Sat

This traditional corner eatery is something of a neighborhood institution. You'll find Argentinian comfort food – simple pastas, steaks and empanadas – as well as higher-end specialties like Patagonian lamb and elaborate desserts like a rich brownie cake with white-chocolate frosting. The old-school waiters and rustic wooden bar add to the charm. If you're looking for a classic Buenos Aires lunchtime experience without luxury or pretensions, you can't do much better than this.

DADÁ Map p84 International $$

☎ 4814-4787; San Martín 941; mains AR$22-35; ⏲ lunch & dinner Mon-Sat

The tiny bohemian Dada, with walls painted red and a bar cluttered with wine bottles, feels like an unassuming neighborhood bar in Paris. Get cozy in a corner seat and order something savory off the bistro menu – the fresh guacamole and homemade potato chips are perfect for sharing. At night the room clamors with locals reading the paper while dining on grilled salmon and groups of friends laughing over martinis – it's a fact worth noting that the bartenders at Dadá really know how to mix a drink.

EL CUARTITO Map p84 Pizza $

☎ 4816-1758; Talcahuano 937; slices AR$4-7; ⏲ lunch & dinner

In a hurry? Think fast, order and pay for your piece of pie, then eat at the counters standing up. Not only is it cheaper and faster this way, but you can chat up the chap next to you and enjoy the old sports posters without turning around. You can't get more local or traditional, and while it's mostly full of businessmen and male waiters, the gals are equally welcome. Sit down for more menu choices.

RECOLETA & BARRIO NORTE

Recoleta is the playground for the wealthy elite, full of beautiful apartment buildings, upscale boutiques and the occasional Baroque mansion. As you can imagine, the restaurants here aren't cheap, but if you want to rub shoulders with the upper classes, this is the place to be.

Practically everyone visits Recoleta's cemetery, so the two-block strip of touristy restaurants, bars and cafes lining nearby RM Ortiz is very convenient. Food here tends toward the overpriced and unexceptional, but many restaurants have outdoor terraces that are choice hangout spots on warm days. And the people-watching here is excellent, especially on weekends when the nearby craft market is in full swing.

L'ORANGERIE Map p87 French $$$

☎ 4808-2100; www.alvearpalace.com; Alvear Palace Hotel, Av Alvear 1891; full tea AR$160; ⏲ breakfast & lunch

The grand tearoom at the Alvear Palace Hotel is fit for a special occasion. At breakfast and lunchtime, chefs in tall white hats attend lavish buffet spreads; the Sunday brunch, featuring a fresh seafood station and a mouthwatering dessert display, is particularly elaborate. But most out-of-towners come for the formal afternoon tea, served from 4:30pm (from 5pm on Sunday). Call ahead to reserve a table in the sunny garden room, then show up with an appetite for tea, champagne and an endless array of exquisite cakes, sandwiches and pastries. Note that two people can share one tea service.

MUNICH RECOLETA Map p87 Argentine $$

☎ 4804-3981; RM Ortiz 1871; mains AR$28-45; ⏲ lunch & dinner

Except for the ever-rising prices, this traditional old place hasn't changed much since Jorge Luis Borges was a regular; try the *brochettes*, grilled salmon or homemade ravioli. Service is exceptional and the white window curtains make this a semi-private affair – two reasons you might find more porteños than tourists eating here, unlike at the flashier, more open restaurants nearby. Just make sure you can stomach the trophy animal heads looking down at you from the wall.

TEA CONNECTION Map p87 Cafe $$

☎ 4805-0616; www.teaconnection.com.ar; Uriburu 1595; mains AR$28-38; ⏲ breakfast, lunch & dinner

Tea lovers visiting Buenos Aires, look no further. At this sleek corner cafe, choose from over 30 types of black, red and green teas and health-conscious sandwiches, salads, vegetable tarts and pastries. Thirsty for something cold? Try a bottle of the fantastic fruit-infused water – the *maracuyá* blend evokes a Brazilian beach. Other locations have popped up around the city, including two in the neighborhood at Arenales 2102 and Montevideo 1655.

788 FOOD BAR
Map p87 Modern Argentine $$

☎ 4814-4788; www.788food-bar.com.ar; Arenales 1877; mains AR$25-35; ⌚ lunch & dinner Mon-Fri, dinner Sat

788 Food Bar is known for insulated bread boxes, delivered to your table on arrival, plus strong cocktails and simple but gourmet fusion cuisine. The atmosphere is unique – the restaurant is located inside an antique house – and the location, just a block off busy Av Santa Fe, is convenient. Try the set lunch menu or take advantage of a generous 'happy hour' that runs from 6pm to midnight on weekday evenings.

CUMANÁ Map p87
Argentine $

☎ 4813-9207; Rodríguez Peña 1149; mains AR$12-22; ⌚ lunch & dinner

If you've had your fill of steak and have an appetite for Argentina's regional cuisine, make a beeline for this colorful, budget-friendly eatery with huge picture windows and an old-fashioned adobe oven. Cumaná specializes in delicious *cazuela,* stick-to-your-ribs stews filled with squash, corn, eggplant, potatoes and meat. Also popular are the *empanadas, locro* (corn and meat stew) and *humita* (a corn, cheese and onion mixture wrapped in corn husks). Come early to guarantee a table – empty seats are scarce after 9pm.

EL SANJUANINO Map p87
Argentine $

☎ 4804-2909; Posadas 1515; mains AR$12-15; ⌚ lunch & dinner Tue-Sun

This friendly little place probably has the cheapest food in Recoleta, attracting both penny-pinching locals and thrifty tourists. Sit at one of the 10 tables and order spicy *empanadas,* tamales or *locro* (corn and meat stew). The curved brick ceiling adds to the atmosphere, but many take their food to go – Recoleta's lovely parks are just a couple of blocks away.

PALERMO

Palermo, particularly Palermo Viejo, is at the heart of innovative cuisine in Buenos Aires. Dozens of upmarket restaurants serve creative cuisine in a contemporary setting, but it's important to be discerning – in recent years, it seems like a new eatery opens every week, and while quality is generally high, only a few places are truly special.

Apart from the high-end *parrillas* where fine steaks and expensive wines rule, Palermo chefs often take inspiration from different ethnic cuisines. You'll find elements of Japanese, Indian, Vietnamese, Brazilian, Mexican, Middle Eastern, Greek and even Norwegian food throughout the neighborhood's dining scene. Just remember that most restaurants offer an Argentine approach to these international styles of cooking: don't expect spicy flavors, for example, because the locals can't stomach it.

Another sub-neighborhood of Palermo with exceptional eating is Las Cañitas, not far from Palermo Viejo. Traffic jams up here on the weekends, when hordes of diners descend on the few blocks of Av Báez where most of the area's restaurants and bars are concentrated.

OVIEDO Map p92
Spanish $$$

☎ 4821-3741; www.oviedoresto.com.ar; Beruti 2602; mains AR$55-85; ⌚ lunch & dinner Mon-Sat

The sole and sea bass at Oviedo are so fresh they're practically still flopping around. Famed chef Martin Rebaudino brings a contemporary Spanish flair to seafood – the fish is shipped directly from Mar del Plata each day – and serves up melt-in-your-mouth pork dishes that are also worth writing home about. A fantastic wine list and cordial service make Oviedo a fine dining experience you won't mind shelling out for.

GREEN BAMBOO Map p92
Vietnamese $$$

☎ 4775-7050; www.green-bamboo.com.ar; Costa Rica 5802; mains AR$45-62; ⌚ dinner

Take a welcome break from steak and step into this sultry Vietnamese eatery. There's just a short selection of dishes, all of which are well prepared and flavorful – though it's arguable whether they're worth the recently elevated prices. Find out for yourself with grilled shrimp, spicy chicken curry or duck with ginger. There are a few vegetarian options and the chef will add extra spice on request, a rarity in Buenos Aires. The tropical cocktails go down easily – appropriate for a low-lit place with a moody, romantic atmosphere – but reserve ahead, or you'll never move on from the bar.

OLSEN Map p92
Scandinavian $$$

☎ 4776-7677; Gorriti 5870; mains AR$40-65; ⌚ lunch & dinner Tue-Sun, brunch from 10:30am Sun

With its hip, relaxed vibe, too-cool crowd, and dramatic central fireplace, Olsen could indeed be located in the frosty climes of Scandinavia. Chef Germán Martitegui's

BEHIND CLOSED DOORS

A Buenos Aires culinary offshoot that has been getting a lot of press lately is the so-called 'closed-door restaurant' scene, or *puertas cerradas*. These restaurants are open only a few days per week, have timed seatings and are pricey *prix fixe*. They're not marked with signs and you have to ring a bell to enter. They won't even tell you the address until you make reservations (mandatory, of course). But if you want that spine-tingling feeling brought on by discovering something off the beaten path – or just like being part of an exclusive group – these places are for you.

We'll let you in on the secret with a few starting points. At Casa Saltshaker (www.casasaltshaker.com) you'll be dining in the chef's actual apartment, dinner party–style, with all of the guests seated around a communal table or two. Treintasillas (www.treintasillas.com), as the name suggests, has 30 seats and a fabulous gourmet tasting menu. For the finest Asian food in Buenos Aires, book a table at Cocina Sunae (www.cocinasunae.com), where chef Christina Sunae Wiseman adds a contemporary twist to traditional Korean, Vietnamese and Thai recipes handed down from her grandmother.

Vegetarians shouldn't miss Casa Felix (www.diegofelix.com), which also serves fish. When the weather's warm, you'll enjoy a dinner with a wine pairing in the chef's romantic old-fashioned courtyard. The prize for the most memorable dinnertime atmosphere in town, however, goes to the new-on-the-scene Cocina Garden (http://cocinagarden.blogspot.com). After cocktails around an outdoor fountain, you'll dine on American-inspired cuisine on the candlelit patio of this hacienda-style urban mansion.

cuisine (think venison ravioli with cherry compote or grilled tuna in yogurt dressing) can be hit or miss, and service is spotty, but the vodka selection is superlative. Luxuriate with a frozen red berry cocktail in the garden – it looks straight out of a magazine – or come for the popular Sunday brunch. Reserve ahead.

GUIDO'S BAR Map p92 — Italian $$$

☎ 4802-2391; República de la India 2843; set lunch AR$90; ⏲ lunch & dinner Mon-Fri, lunch Sat

Looking very much out of place amongst the tall, fancy apartment buildings of Palermo Chico, this traditional Italian joint – complete with checkered tablecloths and old movie posters – adds a splash of history and color to the neighborhood. Don't come craving a specific pasta dish or expecting refined service; in fact, don't come at all unless you're up for a unique dining experience. At Guido's, you don't order one dish, you pay a set price to try a variety of antipasti, pasta, pizza and risotto. Some claim the price is too high, considering you're not allowed much choice, others love the lively atmosphere and spontaneity.

CLUNY Map p92 — French $$$

☎ 4831-7176; El Salvador 4618; mains AR$36-57; ⏲ lunch & dinner Mon-Sat

Still one of Palermo Viejo's finest restaurants is the elegant Cluny, which features a lovely front patio, cozy white sofas and contemporary decor. Try the squash *sorrentinos* (large, round raviolis), Patagonian lamb or *magret de pato* (not for the weak: it's the breast of foie gras–producing ducks). Attentive service and a short but well-chosen wine list add to the experience.

SUDESTADA Map p92 — Asian $$$

☎ 4776-3777; www.sudestadabuenosaires.com; Guatemala 5602; mains AR$36-50; ⏲ lunch & dinner Mon-Sat

Sudestada's well-earned reputation comes from its spicy and well-prepared curries, tender stir-fries and delicious vegetarian and noodle dishes, all inspired by the cuisines of Thailand, Vietnam, Malaysia and Singapore. The grilled rabbit is fantastic, and the exotic Asian-inspired cocktails are delicious – as is the lychee *licuado* (milkshake). Note that if you order something spicy, *it's really spicy*. The set-lunch special is a great way to sample the house's signature dumplings and noodles.

AZEMA EXOTIC BISTRÓ Map p92 — International $$$

☎ 4774-4191; Angel Carranza 1875; mains AR$35-48; ⏲ dinner Mon-Sat

With exotic spices, foreign ingredients, and a penchant for crisp white wine, Paul Jean Azema bravely goes where few local chefs have gone before. His eclectic eatery takes inspiration from his diverse travels – tandoori salmon, Vietnamese noodles, and tangy *ceviche* all have their place on the menu – and the simple French-style space is inviting, especially when Azema himself is making the rounds to talk to dinner guests.

VOULEZBAR Map p92 International $$$

☎ **4802-4817; www.voulezbar.com.ar; Cerviño 3802; mains AR$35-44; ⌚ breakfast, lunch & dinner Mon-Sat**

This postcard-pretty corner cafe boasts fresh, creative cuisine, like salmon with mango salsa, shrimp risotto, gourmet tarts and grilled-squash salad. Service is notoriously slow and sometimes downright unfriendly, so don't come here if you're in a hurry – then again, in a setting as lovely as this, it's not a chore to have a more leisurely lunch.

FREUD Y FAHLER

Map p92 Mediterranean $$$

☎ **4833-2153; Gurruchaga 1750; mains AR$32-58; ⌚ lunch & dinner Mon-Sat**

Freud y Fahler, despite the name, isn't a high-concept eatery – the cozy, upscale corner spot offers a simple menu of gourmet Mediterranean-inspired and modern Argentine steaks, pastas, risottos, and salads. An added bonus for travelers with minimal Spanish language skills: the beautifully illustrated menu gives diners an idea of what you're ordering ahead of time. Thanks to a talented chef and a prime location, the art-gallery crowd often fills the petite space at lunchtime.

BELLA ITALIA Map p92 Italian $$

☎ **4802-4253; República Árabe Siria 3285; mains AR$32-48; ⌚ dinner Mon-Sat**

Located near Palermo Chico's residential apartments is this little Italian gem. Start with a cheese plate or olive 'tasting', then sink your teeth into the *tagliolini* with squid and scallops or the lemon ravioli with salmon. Treats like braised rabbit and grappa also line the menu. The popularity of the original Bella Italia is quickly being surpassed by the newer, more casual outpost in the same neighborhood, Bella Italia Grill & Bar (Segui 3760). The latter features slightly more affordable prices and lunch hours Tuesday to Sunday.

EL ÚLTIMO BESO Map p92 International $$

☎ **4832-7711; www.elultimobeso.com.ar; Nicaragua 4880; mains AR$32-45; ⌚ lunch & dinner Mon-Sat**

Walking into this sweet eatery, located in a romantic old house, is like walking into a feminine boutique. The menu is small and covers a few European-inspired dishes, which are a bit overpriced but tasty nonetheless. As is often the case in Palermo, you're here mainly for the atmosphere – the small spaces, covered terrace and little courtyard patio are hard to resist when you just want a break from that tiring shopping schedule.

BANGALORE Map p92 Indian $$

☎ **4779-2621; Humboldt 1416; mains AR$32-44; ⌚ 6pm-late**

Tucked away on the mezzanine above a happening English-style pub, this excellent little Indian restaurant focuses on well-prepared and delicious dishes like tandoori leg of lamb, pumpkin curry and *murg saag* (spiced chicken with spinach). The chefs are Basque, English and Argentine, bringing an interesting background to the mix. The bar itself is rollicking on weekend evenings; order the house specialty, a pitcher of gin and tonic, and join the party.

IL BALLO DEL MATTONE

Map p92 Italian $$

☎ **4776-4247; www.ilballo.tv; Gorriti 5737; mains AR$29-42; ⌚ lunch & dinner**

This pint-sized trattoria is the flagship location of a new Little Italy empire – a series of traditional pizzerias and Italian eateries, all run by the same owners – that's recently popped up in Palermo Hollywood. Squeeze in, if you can manage to get a table (you'll need reservations at night) and order from the chalkboard menu of homemade pasta. Then soak up the atmosphere: you might see artists with blue mohawks sharing a carafe of house wine, laid-back waiters serving espresso, and regulars with their tiny dogs dropping by to say hello. Wander around this section of Palermo, dubbed *'Pequeña Italia,'* to discover Il Ballo's lively sister locations.

NOVECENTO Map p92 Mediterranean $$

☎ **4778-1900; www.novecento.com; Av Báez 199; mains AR$28-48; ⌚ breakfast, lunch & dinner Mon-Fri, 11am-late Sat & Sun**

Full breakfasts (a rarity in BA) are served at this elegant corner restaurant, but the selection is limited to eggs benedict, salmon-topped bagels and – if you're lucky – waffles or chorizo-filled tortillas. Dinner offers fancier options like fried calamari, penne with wild mushrooms or grilled trout over risotto. The fine atmosphere is accented with pristine white tablecloths, soft music and romantic candlelight, and there's a good selection of dessert wines and after-dinner liqueurs to stretch out the evening.

LITTLE ROSE Map p92 Japanese $$

☎ 4833-9496; Armenia 1672; mains AR$28-45; 🕒 lunch & dinner Mon-Sat

Sashimi and sake are Little Rose's mainstays, but this is no minimalist sushi bar – the sultry candlelit interior is filled with mirrors, shadowy corners, and dreamy photographs. Step off the busy shopping street and into this otherworldly little restaurant for a romantic dinner date. Surprisingly, given the location, the value is fair here – Little Rose's portions are bigger than what you typically get at a sushi restaurant in BA, and the cocktails are well made every time.

MIRANDA Map p92 Parrilla $$

☎ 4771-4255; www.parrillamiranda.com; Costa Rica 5602; mains AR$28-40; 🕒 breakfast, lunch & dinner

Fashionable Miranda is the *parrilla* of choice for the breed of porteños who crave the classic grilled steaks and *chorizos* they grew up with – but who won't sacrifice style for red meat any day of the week. It's a fashionable, modern steakhouse with concrete walls, high ceilings and rustic wooden furniture, but high-quality grilled beef is the main attraction here. If you score a sidewalk table on a warm day, lunch doesn't get much better.

DON JULIO Map p92 Parrilla $$

☎ 4831-9564; cnr Guatemala & Gurruchaga; mains AR$28-36; 🕒 lunch & dinner

Classy service and fine wines add an upscale bent to this traditional corner steakhouse. Of course, the *bife de chorizo* is the main attraction at Don Julio, but the exposed-brick interior, dark-wood cutting boards, and leather placemats enhance the sensory experience, and the gourmet salads – served with a flourish by the uber-professional wait staff – are a treat.

BIO Map p92 Vegetarian $$

☎ 4774-3880; www.biorestaurant.com.ar; Humboldt 2199; mains AR$26-35; 🕒 lunch & dinner

The supremely health-conscious should make a beeline for this casual corner joint, which specializes in healthy, organic and vegetarian fare. Feed your body and soul with quinoa risotto, mushroom stir-fries and Mediterranean couscous with dried tomatoes. Be sure to order a delicious fresh juice blend, whipped up on the spot. Daily specials are available; reserve on weekends.

MUSEO EVITA RESTAURANTE

Map p92 Modern Argentine $$

☎ 4800-1599; www.museoevita.org; JM Gutierrez 3926; mains AR$22-45; 🕒 breakfast, lunch & dinner Mon-Sat, breakfast & lunch Sun

Fear not, tourists, this is not a corny 'theme' restaurant with Madonna's *Evita* soundtrack playing in the background. The antique building's charming tiled courtyard may be the city's prettiest spot for an alfresco lunch, and the cuisine is thoroughly sophisticated, too. Locals and visitors alike come for the gourmet risotto, steak, and grilled fish; on one side of the courtyard, a chef prepares sweet and savory crepes to order. The First Lady's biggest fans prefer to dine inside amid the Evita memorabilia.

LA DORITA Map p92 Parrilla $$

☎ 4773-0070; cnr Humboldt & Costa Rica; mains AR$22-42; 🕒 lunch & dinner

Simply put, back-to-basics La Dorita grills up well-priced steaks. The atmosphere is casual – local families feast on meat indoors where *fútbol* games are televised on a big screen, while outdoors, sidewalk tables are crowded with well-dressed couples kicking off a night on the town. The *parrilla* is so popular with locals that it's grown a bigger sibling, La Dorita Enfrente, on the same intersection. Order the house wine and a mini *parrillada* (grill) of three different cuts of beef.

ARTEMISIA Map p92 Vegetarian $$

☎ 4863-4242; www.artemisiaresto.com.ar; José Antonio Cabrera 3877; mains AR$22-38; 🕒 dinner Tue-Sat

The homey, vegetarian-friendly Artemisia is ideal for a low-key dinner of freshly baked brown bread, inventive tapas like zucchini bruschetta and mini caprese skewers, and heart-healthy wok dishes. Main courses are flavorful and creative – sample the polenta lasagna, salmon ravioli or veggies over green-pepper focaccia. There's organic wine, too, and highly recommended pitchers of fresh-squeezed ginger lemonade. A second location serving breakfast and lunch recently opened at Gorriti 5996, also in Palermo.

MEATLESS IN BUENOS AIRES

Argentine cuisine is internationally famous for its succulent grilled meats, but this doesn't mean vegetarians – or even vegans – are completely out of luck.

Most restaurants, including *parrillas,* serve a few items acceptable to most vegetarians, such as green salads, omelets, mashed potatoes, pizza and pasta (just make sure they're not topped with a meat sauce). *Pescado* (fish) and *mariscos* (seafood) are sometimes available for pescatarians. Key words to beware include *carne* (beef), *pollo* (chicken), *cerdo* (pork) and *cordero* (lamb), though all meat cuts are described in different words. *Sin carne* means 'without meat', and the phrase *soy vegetariano/a* ('I'm a vegetarian') will come in handy when explaining to an Argentine why in the world you don't eat their delicious steaks.

Luckily for non-meat eaters, vegetarian restaurants have become somewhat trendy in Buenos Aires recently. Close to the center, there's Pura Vida (p126); around Barrio Norte you'll find Bio (p137) and Artemisia (p137). Look for cool and casual Natural Deli (p138) in both Palermo and Recoleta. Free spirits with a taste for spices shouldn't miss Krishna (p139), and for that exclusive experience there's closed-door restaurant Casa Felix (see the boxed text, p135). In every neighborhood of the city, you'll find small but well-stocked health-food shops with extensive selections of bulk grains, whole-wheat pasta, dried fruit, nuts and bakery goods – great for snacks back in the hotel room.

LELÉ DE TROYA Map p92 International $$

☎ 4832-2726; www.leledetroya.com; Costa Rica 4901; mains AR$22-38; ⏲ lunch & dinner

As the name suggests (Lelé de Troya means 'Helen of Troy'), this eatery is aesthetically pleasing down to the last detail. Located in an antique house, each room is painted a different color – go for the sultry red room if you're on a romantic date – and the restaurant also boasts lovely sidewalk tables and a summer terrace that's ideal for kicking back with a glass of white on a warm day. Though you're mostly here for the atmosphere, the extensive menu offers decent sandwiches, steaks, pasta, pizza and risotto.

MARK'S DELI & COFFEEHOUSE Map p92 Deli $$

☎ 4832-6244; www.markspalermo.com; El Salvador 4701; mains AR$22-32; ⏲ 8:30am-9:30pm Mon-Sat, 10:30am-9pm Sun

If you're hankering for a pastrami sandwich, check out the huge chalkboard menu at this insanely popular cafe-deli. American-style sandwiches, fresh salads and tasty soups are beautiful and well prepared, and the luscious pastry case is hard to resist. On warm days the patio or sidewalk tables are like gold, while the modern interior is perfectly casual and hip. For a caffeine fix, order an iced coffee or double mocha.

OUI OUI Map p92 Cafe $

☎ 4778-9614; www.ouioui.com.ar; Nicaragua 6068; mains AR$18-28; ⏲ 8am-8pm Mon-Fri, 10am-8pm Sat & Sun

Pain au chocolat and shabby chic? *Oui.* This immensely popular French-style cafe produces the goods – dark coffee, buttery croissants, jars of tangy lemonade – and boasts a small and cozy rose-colored interior that's just as charming. Choose from creative salads, gourmet sandwiches and luscious pastries, just be sure to come early for breakfast to beat the porteña parade. A second location, Almacén Oui Oui (cnr Dorrego & Nicaragua) recently opened on the same block.

LAS CORTADERAS Map p92 Argentine $

☎ 4774-4709; Av Báez 444; mains AR$19-32; lunch & dinner Tue-Sun

Take a breather from the overcrowded heart of Las Cañitas' restaurant scene and head a couple of blocks north to this modern, casual and family-friendly spot. The menu won't pop your creative senses, but instead you'll get large portions of good pasta and meat dishes – try the *crepes de ricotta,* vegetarian lasagna or Patagonian lamb. Lots of salads are available, and a whole range of pastries tempt you in front.

NATURAL DELI Map p92 Deli $

☎ 4777-0372; www.natural-deli.com; Gorostiaga 1776; mains AR$18-32; ⏲ breakfast, lunch & dinner

A rarity in BA is this modern, organic deli offering delicious natural foods. Choose from the chicken breast and avocado sandwich, the tuna and mango wrap or marinated portabello mushrooms in balsamic vinegar. Salads are wonderfully fresh and sprinkled with a variety of creative ingredients, or go for a slice of vegetarian tart. You can add echinacea and ginseng to the healthy juices and *licuados*, and there's even a small health-food store for take-home treats. Look for a second location in Barrio Norte at Laprida 1672.

SOCIAL LA LECHUZA Map p92 Parrilla $

☎ 4773-2781; Uriarte 1980; mains AR$18-25; 🕑 lunch & dinner Wed-Sun, dinner Tue

A world away from its trendy Palermo Viejo neighbors, this classic joint holds on to tradition and offers a breath of fresh air from overpriced, over-hip restaurants. A gamut of funky art adorns the walls, from amateur owl paintings (*lechuza* means 'owl') to photos of Carlos Gardel and cheap cabaret posters. Traditionally prepared meats and pastas are served in abundant portions, but desserts like chocolate mousse and tiramisu are the house specialty – be sure to order soda in siphon bottles for the full old-time experience.

KRISHNA Map p92 Vegetarian Indian $

☎ 4833-4618; Malabia 1833; mains AR$17-25; 🕑 lunch & dinner Tue-Sun

Colorful, themed decor and low tables offer a vegetarian Indian food experience with a large dollop of hippyness. They're multireligious at this casual, eccentric eatery – you're likely to see Ganesh mixing it up with Jesus, a star of David and even Jimi Hendrix. Order the *thali* (side dishes with an Indian flat bread), *koftas* (balls of ground vegetables) or stuffed soya *milanesa*, and there's chai, mango lassi or alcohol-free beer to help wash it all down.

LAS CHOLAS Map p92 Argentine $

☎ 4899-0094; Arce 306; mains AR$14-25; 🕑 lunch & dinner

Las Cholas has found the golden rule of many successful restaurants: quality food, trendy design and bargain prices. This always-full, two-story corner eatery attracts the young and hip, and feeds them traditional Argentine foods like *locro* and *cazuela* (meat and veggie stews). The *parrilla* is also excellent, and the desserts can be exquisite – try the white-chocolate mousse. Expect a wait, rickety chairs and some slow service from the young, pretty waitstaff.

PALITOS Map p101 Chinese $$

☎ 4786-8566; Arribeños 2243; mains AR$18-32; 🕑 lunch & dinner Tue-Sun, dinner Mon

As the saying goes, 'the worse the decor, the better the food' – and this is spot on at this Taiwanese restaurant in Belgrano's Chinatown. Sift through the large menu and zoom in on the *pollo a los tres aromas* (garlic, ginger and basil chicken), the beef noodle soup, the fried noodles or any sweet-and-sour dish. Note: be prepared for Palitos' famously lackadaisical service. Wander the surrounding blocks for more traditional Chinese eateries; vegetarians can try nearby Siempre Verde (Map p101; Arribeños 2127).

CONFITERÍA ZURICH Map p101 Cafe $

☎ 4784-9808; Echeverría 2192; mains AR$16-30; 🕑 breakfast, lunch & dinner

Perfect for a midday break, this classic café offers suited waiters, an older crowd, professional service and sidewalk tables that scream for attention on a warm summer day. If you're peckish there are salads and sandwiches, or just nibble on some dainty croissants while you watch the world go by at the plaza across the way. Things are especially exciting when the weekend *feria* (street fair) is in full swing.

VILLA CRESPO, ONCE, CABALLITO & BOEDO

These neighborhoods have yet to be discovered by the tourist masses, but things are changing. Rents in Palermo Viejo are rising quickly, driving some new businesses to nearby Villa Crespo. Meanwhile, Boedo has a few traditional places that are just starting to be visited by foreigners looking for something different. And Once is a good place to hunt for ethnic foods with Jewish, Peruvian or Korean flavors.

BI WON Map p98 Asian $$

☎ 4372-1146; Junín 548; mains AR$30-55; 🕑 lunch & dinner Mon-Fri, dinner Sat

Bi Won might win the prize for the least fashionable interior design in the city – and the neighborhood's a little sketchy – but the traditional Korean food can't be beat. Go for the *bulgogi* (grill the meat yourself at the table), *bibimbap* (rice bowl with meat, veggies, egg and hot sauce – mix it all up) or *kim chee chigue* (kimchi soup with pork – for adventurous, spice-loving tongues only!) And don't forget to say *kamsamnida* (thank you) to your server at the end. Take a taxi here and away.

LICKING YOUR WAY THROUGH BA

Because of Argentina's Italian heritage, Argentine *helado* is comparable to the best ice cream anywhere in the world. Amble into a *heladería* (ice-cream shop), order up a cone (usually you pay first) and the creamy concoction will be artistically swept up into a mountainous peak and handed over with a small plastic spoon tucked in the side. Important: *granizado* means with chocolate flakes.

All types of *heladerías* offer their customers dozens of tempting flavors, from the conventional vanilla and *dulce de leche* variations to exotic fruits and other unexpected mixtures (*mate,* anyone?). In winter some *heladerías* close down, but during the hot Buenos Aires summer you'll find yourself among many sweet-toothed porteños standing in line waiting to dig into these delicious treats.

Here are some of the tastiest *heladerías* in town:

Dylan (Map p76; ☎ 0810-3333-9526; Péru 1086, San Telmo)

Freddo (Map p84; ☎ 0810-33-FREDDO; Av Santa Fe 1600, Retiro) Many branches; see www.freddo.com.ar.

Heladería Cadore (Map p72; ☎ 4374-3688; Av Corrientes 1695, Congreso)

Persicco (Map p92; ☎ 0810-333-7377; Salguero 2591, Palermo) Also at Migueletes 886, Las Cañitas (Map p92) and Vuelta de Obligado 2092, Belgrano (Map p101).

Una Altra Volta (Map p92; ☎ 4805-1818; Av del Libertador 3060, Palermo) Also at the corner of Av Quintana and Ayacucho, Recoleta (Map p87) and Av Santa Fe 1826, Barrio Norte (Map p87).

Vía Flaminia (Map p62; ☎ 4342-7737; Florida 121, Microcentro)

PAN Y ARTE Map p98 Argentine $

☎ 4957-6702; www.panyarte.com.ar; Av Boedo 878; mains AR$18-26; ⏲ breakfast, lunch & dinner

There's a wonderful old-time atmosphere at this bohemian eatery, which features a hippie waitstaff and organic bakery. Food ranges from the same old boring stuff (*milanesas,* spaghetti and pizza) to more interesting choices like *empanadas,* stuffed squash and vegan *picadas* (a plate of appetizers). The busy, generally non-touristy neighborhood is a plus, as is the live folk, piano and tango music that plays several times per week.

CAFÉ MARGOT Map p98 Argentine $

☎ 4957-0001; Av Boedo 857; mains AR$12-20; ⏲ breakfast, lunch & dinner

This classic cafe, one of the city's official *bares notables* (notable bars), is an off-the-beaten-path spot where you can relax with a platter of *picadas* (meat, cheese and olives) and a bottle of wine, or a frosty mug of artisan-crafted beer and a huge sandwich piled high with sliced turkey. The atmospheric main room is a bit snug; sidewalk tables are best for the claustrophobic.

SARKIS Map p98 Middle Eastern $

☎ 4772-4911; Thames 1101; mains AR$12-28; ⏲ lunch & dinner

It's not much to look at, but there's a good reason this long-standing Middle Eastern restaurant is still around – the food is fabulous, and it's wonderfully economical if you come with a group of friends and share several dishes. Start with the a hummus platter, *baquerones* (marinated sardines), *keppe crudo* (raw meat) or *parras rellenas* (stuffed grape leaves) – all are delicious. Follow up with kebabs, couscous with lentils or lamb in yogurt sauce.

BELGRANO

Unlike its neighbor Palermo, Belgrano tends more towards traditional Argentine fare than innovative cuisine. There are a few notable restaurants to try if you happen to make it up here, however, and if you like Chinese food, Buenos Aires' tiny Chinatown is worth checking out. Just remember that many places (not just restaurants) here are closed on Monday.

SUCRE Map p101 International $$$

☎ 4782-9082; www.sucrerestaurant.com.ar; Sucre 676; mains AR$42-65; ⏲ lunch & dinner

Sucre's ultra-elegant ambience features that modern look of high ceilings, wood floors, exposed pipes, metal ramparts and a gleaming open kitchen. The excellent, finely presented cuisine comes from a creative, international menu that changes every few months, but expect morsels like ginger-glazed salmon or grilled pork shoulder in lemon sauce. Check out the central bunker: a temperature-controlled, bomb-proof bodega.

BUDDHABA Map p101 Asian $$$

☎ 4706-2382; www.buddhaba.com.ar; Arribeños 2288; mains AR$35-48; lunch & dinner Tue-Sun

The fanciest restaurant in Belgrano's Chinatown is this pretty spot, which cooks up creative Chinese, Japanese, Thai and Vietnamese dishes. Order the shrimp in coconut milk, mixed-mushroom-and-veggie stir-fry or beef curry with tomatoes. The dining area is a slick, red lounge with moody music, and for extra quirkiness there's an Asian art gallery (1-7pm) upstairs and a bonsai 'deck' garden. Also open in the afternoon for tea service.

CONTIGO PERU Map p101 Peruvian $$

☎ 4780-3960; www.contigo-peru.com.ar; Echeverría 1627; mains AR$18-35; lunch & dinner Mon-Sat

The modern yet humble dining hall may not be much to look at, but you're not here for the atmosphere anyway. This institution of Peruvian cuisine has been around for years, serving up treats like garlic chicken, seafood with rice and – most notably – tasty *ceviche*. Don't walk away without ordering that most traditional of Peruvian drinks, the cinnamon-dusted pisco sour.

LOTUS NEO THAI Map p101 Thai $$

☎ 4783-7993; www.lotusneothai.com; Arribeños 2265; mains AR$30-45; lunch & dinner Tue-Sun, dinner Mon

A Las Cañitas institution that recently made the move to Barrio Chino, Lotus proudly claims to be the first Thai restaurant in Argentina. Kick back with the heady, mint-infused house cocktail at this blissful Thai eatery where painted lotus flowers climb the walls. The pad thai is properly made, and the duck curry is fantastic. Choose a low table surrounded with floor cushions or a traditional table for two in the antique dining room.

DRINKING

top picks

- **Le Bar** (p144)
- **878** (p150)
- **Milión** (p147)
- **Doppelgänger** (p146)
- **Gibraltar** (p146)
- **Mundo Bizarro** (p150)
- **La Puerta Roja** (p146)
- **Gran Bar Danzón** (p132)
- **Casa Cruz** (p149)
- **Las Violetas** (p153)

WHAT'S YOUR RECOMMENDATION? www.lonelyplanet.com/Buenos Aires

DRINKING

In a city that never sleeps, finding a good drink (or cup of tea) is as easy as walking down the street. Whether you're into 'trendy cocktail lounges, classic Irish pubs, atmospheric old cafes or serious wine bars, you'll find them all in Buenos Aires – sometimes all within a few blocks.

Porteños aren't big drinkers, but they do like to go out with friends and stay up late. Walk into any corner bar in the city and you'll see groups of friends sitting around a table, discussing philosophy while sipping from tiny white cups of espresso, or splitting a bottle of Quilmes (local beer), Malbec or *gaseosa* (soda) while laughing over Maradona's latest media drama. More fashionable cocktail bars and breweries draw more of a mixed crowd of partygoing tourists, style-conscious men trying to impress their dates, and groups of local girls toasting a birthday or special occasion.

In many cases, the line is blurred between bar and cafe: both usually stay open late, closing up shop at two or three in the morning, or 5am on weekends. Pretty much all of the bars and cafes serve beer, hard alcohol, cocktails and wine, plus coffee, juice, smoothies and a fair range of finger foods or main dishes. When in doubt, stick to the basics: because Argentines don't drink many cocktails, you're better off avoiding mixed drinks at most casual bars. Only order a martini at a place with a professional-looking bartender.

For more on BA's historic cafe culture, see the boxed text, (p151). For popular gay bars (and other gay venues) see the boxed text (p157); they're also among the reviews listed in this chapter.

BARS

Porteños love bars. At a local hole-in-the-wall, do as the natives do and order a classic *chopp* (mug) of Quilmes. No matter where you pull up a bar stool, you can never go wrong with a glass of Malbec or Torrontés. Keep in mind that in addition to the bars listed here, many of the city's upscale restaurants and hotels have lively bars well worth a visit. Younger travelers and backpackers looking to bar-hop in a group should check out the Buenos Aires Pub Crawl (www.pubcrawlba.com).

THE CENTER

Many watering holes in the center are Irish pub knock-offs that cater to the business crowd on weekdays. Because of this, some might close a bit earlier than in other neighborhoods, but the most popular ones stay packed all night long.

LA CIGALE Map p62

☎ 4312-8275; 25 de Mayo 722; 🕑 6pm-4am Mon-Fri, 9pm-late Sat

This long-running downtown lounge, sultry but laid-back, is very popular with both foreigners and porteños. There's live music most nights, with live bands on Thursday and DJs on Saturday. But it's most popular on 'French Tuesday', when electronica and exotic drinks draw the heavy crowds in. Happy hour runs from 6pm to 10pm weekdays, a good time to try an original cocktail or a couple of minty mojitos.

LE BAR Map p62

☎ 5219-0858; www.lebarbuenosaires.blogspot.com; Tucumán 422; 🕑 noon-2am Mon-Fri, from 8pm Sat

Provocative design, in-demand DJs, splashy art, and killer cocktails – Le Bar is the harbinger of downtown's nightlife renaissance. The antique four-story building was redone to resemble a fanciful European parlor with tear-drop lamps casting a sexy glow across the jewel-toned interior. Come late to knock back the passion fruit–tinged *Pasiónaria* cocktail on the rooftop terrace, or cozy up in futuristic dug-out seating on the 2nd floor.

NEW BRIGHTON Map p62

☎ 4322-1515; www.thenewbrightonsrl.com.ar; Sarmiento 645; 🕑 8am-late Mon-Sat

Though this historic gem is on the city's official list of *bares notables* (notable bars), it feels like the well-kept secret of refined local gentlemen who gather here after work. A doorman welcomes guests into the beautifully restored landmark where bartenders shake and stir drinks behind a polished wood bar and a pianist tickles

ARGENTINE WINE *David Labi*

You have to try hard to find a bad Argentine wine. Even a house cheapie in a metal jug from the scummiest *parrilla* (steakhouse) will surprise you with its drinkability. And among some 5000 labels produced by the world's fifth-biggest grape-squeezer, there is plenty to please the most particular palate.

The Argentine secret is in the irrigation. Techniques, inherited from aboriginal Huape Indians, channel melted Andean ice flow to create oases in the desert. In Europe artificial irrigation is prohibited, meaning that a good vintage was generally just a year with good weather. But in the New World, the tyranny of the heavens plays no part, and the location of vineyards in hot and arid climes has led to the optimum cultivation of over 50 varietals.

The most famous red is the Malbec, transformed in the Andean foothills beyond recognition from its origins as a sickly and second-class French grape; and the flagship white is Torrontés, a Spanish grape that has only really hit the bottle in Argentina. Other typical varietals such as Syrah, Cabernet – and even the delicate Pinot – are also produced in Argentina's 3000km of varied geography.

Mendoza is the viticulture capital, producing 60% of the country's wine, and it's the place to go for a tour of the big and little *bodegas* (wine cellars). Visit in March for the *vendimia* (grape harvest), when the whole province celebrates with a big festival. But don't restrict your consumption to just wine from Mendoza, or you will be missing many other exciting bottles that are popping out from every province.

Changes in social practices have seen domestic consumption fall from 90L per capita in the 1980s to around 30L now. But this also owes something to a more educated consumer drinking less and better wine. However, it's hard to imagine an afternoon *asado* (barbecue) without a gurgle of *vino tinto,* often quaffed with ice or soda to make it more refreshing. This might be sacrilege to you sophisticated connoisseurs; an Argentine would retort that it's not done to dilute the wine, but to purify the water.

So how to know which wines to try? They say there's a perfect Argentine wine for every occasion and a good *vinoteca* (wine boutique) will help you find it. There are over 150 dedicated wine shops in Buenos Aires, and this number is growing fast. You'll find plenty all over Palermo, Recoleta and San Telmo; in the center there's The Winery (p116), with many branches throughout BA. If you are willing to travel to the outskirts of the capital, however, you can find an excellent specialist in Vinoteca Borbore (☎ 4504-2425; www.bdv.com.ar; Av Mosconi 3654, Devoto), which stocks over 1500 labels. If you'd rather point and click to choose a few bottles, check out the fantastic wine delivery service 0800-VINO (☎ 4966-2500; www.0800-vino.com).

Supermarket selections are usually adequate, though you miss out on the tailored advice. Among the mainstay brands are Norton, Trapiche, Zuccardi and Santa Julia, with different lines to cater for every price range. Spend a bit more to try the elegant Rutini (from Bodega La Rural), or Luigi Bosca for a lesson in class.

Wine bars are still not very widespread and will mostly only be found among the trendy cobbles of Palermo. Big restaurants' lists tend to be rather conservative on an 'if it ain't broke…' basis, but that's bound to change as the education of the consumer continues in this exciting and rapidly developing market.

For a wine guide in Buenos Aires and beyond, contact Robertson Wine Tours (☎ 4772-5839; www.robertson winetours.com; Arevalo 2775).

the ivories on a baby grand. Order a classic cocktail (and enjoy the tray of elegant finger foods that comes with it).

CONGRESO & TRIBUNALES

This neighborhood is not known for its drinking holes, but there are at least a couple of friendly spots where you can toast the town while politicos scurry past on the sidewalks.

CRUZAT BEER HOUSE Map p72

☎ 6320-5344; www.cruzatba.com; Sarmiento 1617; ⏲ 10am-2am Mon-Thu, to 4am Fri & Sat

In wine-soaked Buenos Aires, Cruzat is as close as you can get to a German beer garden. Kick back on the shaded terrace and choose from a thick menu of craft beers from all over Argentina – look for El Bolsón (from Rio Negro), Antares (from Mar del Plata) and Gulmen (from Viedma.) There are also imported bottles from Belgium, Chile, Spain and Italy, and a beer-tasting option featuring a dozen mini draught beers.

LOS 36 BILLARES Map p72

☎ 4381-5696; www.los36billares.com.ar; Rivadavia 1265; ⏲ 8am-2am

Dating from 1894, this is one of the city's most historic bars. As its name implies, it's big on pool and billiard tables – both the back room and basement are full of men cuing up the racks of shuffling cards for a friendly poker game. Tango shows (from AR$25), highlighting different singers and dancers every night, are offered later in the evening (no shows on Monday). You can come by and order a drink at any time of day, taking in the old-school atmosphere.

SAN TELMO

San Telmo is gentrifying; fancy restaurants and bars are popping up with regularity, mixing it up with a few old classics. But it seems there's space for everyone, and this neighborhood has become very popular with locals, travelers and expats. For a couple more choices where you can grab a sandwich well into the night, see Bar El Federal (p131) and Bar Británico, p152.

647 DINNER CLUB Map p76

☎ 4331-3026; www.club647.com; Tacúari 647; 🕑 8pm-late Mon-Sat

This lavish Shanghai-style lounge boasts a talented barman and an experimental cocktail menu (try anything involving lychee fruit, or the refreshing house cocktail with sake, passionfruit, mint and a twist of lime). After-dinner drinks here are no bargain, especially by San Telmo standards – though on weeknights, two-for-one drink specials abound – and shelling out the pesos is worth it for a chance to feel like a rock star in a seductive space that calls to mind an otherwordly opium den.

BAR SEDDÓN Map p76

☎ 4342-3700; cnr Chile & Defensa; 🕑 6pm-late Tue-Sun

This laid-back corner bar, outfitted with black and white tiles and rustic wood tables and illuminated by the dramatic glow of hundreds of candles, is housed in an old restored pharmacy. Drop in for an icy *chopp* (mug of draught beer) or for a late-night glass of red – you'll keep good company with a neighborhood crowd.

DOPPELGÄNGER Map p76

☎ 4300-0201; www.doppelganger.com.ar; Av Juan de Garay 500; 🕑 7pm-late Tue-Fri, 8pm-late Sat

Mark our words: this cool, emerald-hued corner bar is one of the only places in Capital Federal where you can count on a perfectly mixed martini. That's because Doppelgänger, in homage to an immigrant tradition from the 1940s, specializes in vermouth cocktails. The atmosphere is calm and the lengthy menu is fascinating; the owners love to talk shop and will happily recommend a drink to suit your taste. Start with the journalist, a martini with a bitter orange twist, or channel Don Draper and go for the bar's bestseller – an old-fashioned.

GIBRALTAR Map p76

☎ 4362-5310; Peru 895; 🕑 6pm-4am

One of BA's classic expat pubs, the Gibraltar has a cozy atmosphere and an excellent bar counter for those traveling alone. It's also a great place for fairly authentic foreign cuisine – try the generous Thai, Indian or English dishes, or the sushi on Sunday. For a little friendly competition head to the pool table in the back, grabbing a well-priced pint of beer along the way.

LA PUERTA ROJA Map p76

☎ 4362-5649; www.lapuertaroja.com.ar; Chacabuco 733; 🕑 6pm-late

There's no sign, so ring the bell to get into this upstairs bar, which takes up several rooms in an old house. It has a cool, relaxed atmosphere (until the pub-crawl crowd shows up later on in the evening) with low lounge furniture in the main room and a pool table tucked behind. This is a traditional bar, so you won't find cosmopolitans or fruity cocktails on the menu – come for beer or a manly scotch on the rocks. Smokers can light up in the space overlooking the street – just be sure the windows are open.

M BUENOS AIRES Map p76

☎ 4331-3879; www.mbuenosaires.com.ar; Balcarce 433; snacks AR$8-12; 🕑 6pm-midnight Mon-Sat

New on the scene in San Telmo is this seductive cocktail bar and adjacent Japanese-Peruvian eatery. Framed by antique brick archways in one of the barrio's oldest buildings, M is a cool, cavernous space with velvet sofas and romantic low lighting. The sushi is tasty but costly; skip the dining room and just come to the bar for a glass of wine or a nightcap. The list of wines by the glass is fabulous. Try the fabulous Mendel Malbec – you can thank us later.

PRIDE CAFÉ Map p76

☎ 4300-6435; Balcarce 869; snacks AR$8-12; 🕑 10am-10pm Sun-Fri

This small contemporary cafe is especially swamped by cute gay men on Sunday during San Telmo's antiques fair, attracting them with homemade pastries, healthy snacks and 'queer coffee.' Sushi nights add interest, though you might also tuck yourself away, cocktail in hand, to peruse the foreign mags or watch DVDs on the small screen behind the counter. Wi-fi is available, and there's an annex down the street.

TERRITORIO Map p76

☎ 4300-9756; cnr Estados Unidos & Bolívar; 🕑 11am-3am

This moody, somewhat bohemian corner bar does *cerveza artesanal* (craft beer), wines by the glass, and appealing sandwiches and *picadas* platters featuring smoked trout, lamb, wild boar, goat cheese and homemade bread. There's only a pair of outdoor tables – if one's free when you're walking by, seize the moment to have a drink in the sunshine.

RETIRO

Retiro has a good range of bars, from Irish to upscale. Most are full of businessmen during the day and into the evening, and at night attract the traveler-expat crowd. For a sexy restaurant–wine bar there's Gran Bar Danzón (p132), while Dadá (p133) is also a good place for a cocktail, and Empire Thai (p132) offers more vodkas than you could possibly sample.

DRUID IN Map p84

☎ 4312-3688; Reconquista 1040; 🕑 noon-late Mon-Fri, 9pm-late Sat

Just half a block from the popular Kilkenny (p147) and sporting a more intimate and less crowded atmosphere is this modest Irish pub. A wide range of aged whiskeys, imported liquor, blended cocktails and more than 30 beers temper the pizza, sandwiches and British food that are served. There are live Scottish bagpipe and Celtic music on weekends.

FLUX BAR Map p84

☎ 5252-0258; www.fluxbar.com.ar; MT de Alvear 980; 🕑 7pm-2am Mon-Sat

Run by a friendly Englishman and his Russian partner, this unobtrusive basement gay bar is hetero-friendly – so everyone's more than welcome to come on down. The large, colorful space has a slightly artsy feel. Feeling adventurous? Try the Buenos Aires iced tea (made with Fernet, that popular Argentine mixer that's something of an acquired taste). Happy hour runs everyday from 7pm till 10pm.

KILKENNY Map p84

☎ 4312-7291; www.thekilkenny.com.ar; MT de Alvear 399; 🕑 5:30pm-late Mon-Fri, from 8pm Sat & Sun

Buenos Aires' most popular Irish bar has become, well, just too damn popular. Weekends are a crush and thumping music makes it hard to chat up your date, but the dark-woodsy atmosphere is congenial enough. Come early on weekdays if you want to score one of the cozy deep booths for easy conversation; there's also a smoking section on the 2nd floor if enough people want to light up. The pub has a good whiskey and beer selection on offer, too.

MARRIOTT PLAZA BAR Map p84

☎ 4318-3000; basement, Marriott Plaza Hotel, Florida 1005; 🕑 from 12pm

Don't let the name fool you: this refined subterranean cocktail lounge is a far cry from a typical hotel bar. The palatial century-old building, occupying an enviable square of real estate on the edge of Plaza San Martín, was designed by Alfred Zucker, the man responsible for St Patrick's Cathedral in New York. The hotel still boasts its original art-deco bar, cordial service and classic cocktails.

MILIÓN Map p84

☎ 4815-9925; www.milionargentina.com.ar; Paraná 1048; 🕑 6pm-2am Sun-Wed, to 3am Thu, 8pm-4am Fri & Sat

This elegant and very sexy bar takes up three floors of a renovated old mansion. The garden out back is a leafy paradise, overlooked by a solid balcony that holds the best seats in the house. Nearby marble steps are also an appealing place to lounge with a frozen mojito or frozen basil daiquiri, the tastiest cocktails on the menu (pay first, then good luck catching the bartender's eye!) Downstairs, the restaurant serves international dishes that are just so-so.

RECOLETA & BARRIO NORTE

HM Ortiz, across from Recoleta's famous cemetery, is a two-block strip of restaurants, cafes and bars. On warm sunny days most of them open up their fine outdoor front patios, perfect for a drink or meal and some people-watching.

BULLER BREWING COMPANY Map p87

☎ 4808-9061; www.bullerpub.com; RM Ortiz 1827; noon-late

Yes, it's a microbrewery in Buenos Aires, and in Recoleta, no less. Six kinds of beer are brewed on the premises, including a dry stout, a light lager and a honey beer with alcohol content ranging from 4.5% to 8.5%. There's a great outdoor patio in front and an extensive menu of snacks and sandwiches – try the Uruguayan-style *chivito* (a grilled steak sandwich with lettuce and tomato) or the amusingly named 'nibbles tower' of finger foods. There's a second location in Retiro at Paraguay 428.

CASABAR Map p87

☎ 4816-2712; Rodriguez Peña 1150; 5pm-late Mon-Fri, 9pm-late Sat, 7pm-late Sun

This recycled antique house turned cocktail bar offers a huge selection of spirits, a wider-than-usual range of microbrews, and a wine list stocked with higher-end bottles. You'll also find nachos and gourmet pub grub on the menu, plus generous happy-hour specials through to 11pm. Casabar is stylish but casual, with a funky mirrored interior, large LCD TVs screening soccer matches, and large windows looking out over the street.

SHAMROCK Map p87

☎ 4812-3584; Rodríguez Peña 1220; 6pm-4am Mon-Wed, to 6am Thu & Fri, 8pm-6am Sat

Rockin' during the 'longest' happy hour in town, which runs from 6pm to midnight daily, this contemporary Irish pub in Barrio Norte is decked out in dark wood and has a dim, moody atmosphere. DJs rule from Wednesday to Saturday, when the Basement Club (p158) opens up downstairs, usually around midnight.

PALERMO

You'll find Buenos Aires' hippest drinking scenes in and around Palermo, especially near Plaza Serrano in Palermo Viejo. Many restaurants in this neighborhood have good bars, including Bangalore (p136), Lelé de Troya (p138) and Olsen (p134). Palermo is also where you'll find a few gay and lesbian bars, mostly to the south near Av Córdoba.

Las Cañitas, another sub-neighborhood of Palermo, has a lively three blocks of nonstop restaurants, bars and discos, and is also worth a drop-in, especially later in the evening.

WINE TASTING 101

Big on wine? Head for a tasting to sample the grapes that have put Argentina on the map in recent years.

Casa Coupage (Map p92 ☎ 4777-9295 www.casacoupage.com.ar; Soler 5518) This upscale tasting is run by an Argentine couple, both sommeliers. The AR$200 price (per person) includes a gourmet food pairing.

Anuva Wines (☎ 4777-4661; www.anuvawines.com) Portland, Oregon, native Daniel Karlin organizes wine tastings – try five boutique vintages with food pairings. Best of all, he'll send your wines to the USA (BA's most affordable wine-shipping service) and can deliver within the city.

Nigel Tollerman (☎ 4966-2500; www.0800-vino.com) Easygoing wine tastings run by enthusiastic Brit Nigel Tollerman in his basement cellar. He'll also deliver fine-quality Argentine wines to your hotel, and has a premium-wine storage service.

ACABAR Map p92

☎ 4772-0845; Honduras 5733; 8pm-2am Sun-Thu, to 4am Fri & Sat

This is possibly the quirkiest restaurant-bar in town, at least in terms of design. A maze of more than a half-dozen rooms and spaces are decked out in mismatched chandeliers, funky furniture, clashing pastel colors and frilly wallpaper; it's a texture and pattern overload. It's also famous for having whole shelves dedicated to board games. Serves food earlier on.

ANTARES Map p92

☎ 4833-9611; www.cervezaantares.com; Armenia 1447; 7pm-4am

Thirsty for a decent *cerveza*? Look no further than this relaxed beer bar with a long, snaking bar, outdoor seating, and locally brewed ales, pilsners, lagers, barley wine and honey beer. Try a beer tasting, sample Antares' Brewmaster special-edition beer, or just enjoy the convivial atmosphere with a pint during happy hour (they're two for one from 7pm till 8pm). A second location has opened in Las Cañitas at Arévalo 2876.

BACH BAR Map p92

www.bach-bar.com.ar; Cabrera 4390; 11pm-late Wed-Sun

This small bar is most popular with lesbians, but plenty of guys make it here, too. The live drag shows on Wednesday and Thursday are downright raucous, and sultry dancing among the tables is not unheard of. There's a pre-dance vibe on Saturday and karaoke on Sunday; during the rest of the week local DJs play. A minimum consumption rule is often in place (Argentines aren't big drinkers) – just order a drink or two and you'll be fine.

BAR 6 Map p92

☎ 4833-6807; www.barseis.com; Armenia 1676; 🕑 8am-late Mon-Sat

A stylish neighborhood classic, Bar 6 is open all day – you can drop by for eggs and coffee in the morning or show up at night to lounge on a red-velvet couch with a bellini or a beer. The contemporary design, soaring ceilings, and foxy crowd make up for the indifferent service. When DJs start spinning, it's too loud for conversation, so come earlier if you're looking for a laid-back evening.

BULNES CLASS Map p92

☎ 4861-7492; Bulnes 1250; 🕑 7pm-2am Thu, 11pm-4am Fri & Sat

One of BA's most popular gay bars is this beautiful lounge with blood-red walls, hip white sofas and a white-draped booth. Both the staff and guests are young and handsome, the DJs are hot and it gets packed enough to draw lines outside. Good for 'after-office' and 'pre-dance' parties, and big on Halloween bashes.

CARNAL Map p92

☎ 4772-7582; Niceto Vega 5511; 🕑 9pm-late Tue-Sat

See and be seen – preferably in the open air with an icy vodka tonic in hand – on the rooftop terrace at Carnal. With its bamboo lounges and billowy curtains, the place can't be beat for a cool chill-out on a warm summer night. On Friday the reggae rocks, while Saturday means pop and '80s tunes, bringing a great-looking local crowd every weekend to this ever-popular watering hole.

CASA CRUZ Map p92

☎ 4833-1112; www.casacruz-restaurant.com; Uriarte 1658; 🕑 8:30pm-late Mon-Sat

This low-lit, drop-dead-gorgeous space is better known for its happening cocktail bar than for its cuisine (which can be hit or miss). Dress to the nines, then take a seat at the oval bar or lounge on the lobby's velvet sofas, mojito in hand, to observe a glamorous parade of actresses, athletes and investment bankers entering Casa Cruz through the massive bronze doorway.

CHUECA Map p92

☎ 4834-6373; www.chueca-restobar.com.ar; Honduras 5255; 🕑 9pm-late Wed-Sat

An exclusively gay restaurant-bar, Chueca offers an upscale experience in the stylish atmosphere of an old refurbished house. There are drag shows nearly every night, and on weekends 'pre-dance' events keep things lively up until 2am, when the clientele start thinking about hitting those nightclubs. Wednesday is *Chicas Chuecas* – for lesbians. There's a great little terrace upstairs; come early if you want dinner.

CONGO BAR Map p92

☎ 4833-5857; Honduras 5329; 🕑 8pm-3am Wed, to 4am Thu, to 5am Fri & Sat

The highlight at this trendy bar is the beautiful back patio – *the* place to be seen on hot summer nights, with its slick bar, leafy atmosphere and comfy wood booths. The music is great, too, with DJs spinning from Wednesday to Saturday, and inside there are elegant low lounges in creative spaces. A full food menu is available, along with strong cocktails.

HOME HOTEL Map p92

☎ 4778-1008; www.homebuenosaires.com; Honduras 5860; 🕑 12:30pm-late

Mixing up some of Palermo's best cocktails, Daniel Biber is a local legend at Home Hotel's intimate bar-restaurant. During the day you can relax in the grassy garden in full view of the slick infinity pool. At night, settle down at the polished cement bar for a signature house cocktail or a pour of one of 22 infused vodkas, carefully kept at -10°C. Friday evenings are livened up by DJ parties. Breakfast, lunch and evening tapas are available.

KIM Y NOVAK Map p92

☎ 4773-7521; Güemes 4900; 🕑 6pm-late Wed-Sun

This one of a kind, intimate and often off-the-wall corner bar has great *onda* (vibes). Come before 2am if you want to chat, because it really gets packed in the early hours – especially later in the week when the basement dance floor opens to an eclectic and energetic crowd. Strut your stuff any time on the stripper pole next to the counter, priming yourself with the *fruti jojo* (house drink) for extra confidence.

MUNDO BIZARRO Map p92

☎ 4773-1967; Serrano 1222; 🕒 8pm-late

Sporting the best neon sign in town is this red-lit, futuristically retro and stylish lounge bar. It's open pretty much all through the night on weekends, when everything from old-time American music to hip DJs to jazz stirs up the air waves. Thursday is ladies night (two for one, girls); for hungry party-goers, there's American-inspired bar food from burgers and shish kebabs to hot apple pie with ice cream.

SITGES Map p92

☎ 4861-3763; www.sitgesonline.com.ar; Av Córdoba 4119; 🕒 10:30pm-late Wed-Sun

Dangerously stuffed on a Saturday night, this mostly gay 'pre-disco' bar plays loud, beat-laden music for amorous crowds. On Sunday karaoke is king, on Wednesday and Thursday there's a drag and stripper show, and Friday means all-you-can-drink…really. And notice that phone at your table? If somebody across the room calls, they're interested. The action really gets going around 1am, even later on weekends.

SUGAR Map p92

☎ 4831-3276; www.sugarbuenosaires.com; Costa Rica 4619; 🕒 noon-1am

This lively expat watering hole brings in a youthful nightly crowd with bargain-priced drink specials, comfort food (chicken fingers, nachos, falafels, buffalo wings), and shindigs revolving around political and sporting events – any excuse for a party. The place is quiet early in the evening; Thursday, also known as ladies' night, always gets a little rowdy. On weekends, you can roll out of bed at noon and come here for eggs, waffles and mimosas.

UNICO Map p92

☎ 4775-6693; Honduras 5604; 🕒 8:30am-6am Mon-Fri, 8:30pm-6am Sat & Sun

If you like your bars loud and crowded, you'll love this classic corner magnet – still popular after all these years. It's not overly large, so on weekends people tend to spill out the door and onto the sidewalk tables and even the street. Thanks to its central location near popular restaurants and bars, many are passing through for a drink on their way to (or from) dinner – if you're feeling lazy, sandwiches and salads are also served here through the wee hours.

VAN KONING Map p92

☎ 4772-9909; www.vankoning.com; Av Báez 325; 🕒 7pm-late

Wonderfully rustic spaces make this Dutch-themed pub feel like the inside of a boat; after all, it's a 17th century–style seafaring theme complete with dark wood beams, flickering candles and blocky furniture. Bars on two floors serve 40 kinds of both local and imported brews, with Heineken, Guinness and Quilmes on draft. A magnet for expats; the first Wednesday of the month is Dutch night.

VILLA CRESPO, CABALLITO, ONCE & BOEDO

Villa Crespo, Boedo and neighboring areas are up-and-coming, mostly residential neighborhoods whose cheaper rents have attracted some interesting bars.

878 Map p98

☎ 4773-1098; Thames 878; 🕒 8pm-late

Hidden behind an unsigned door is this 'secret' bar – you have to ring the bell to get in, but it's hardly exclusive. Enter a wonderland of elegant low lounge furniture and red brick walls; if you're a whiskey lover, there are over 80 kinds to try. Tasty classic and original cocktails also lubricate the crowds of porteños and expats, happy to revel in the jazz, bossa nova and good old rock music playing on the speakers. It's located in a residential neighborhood a few blocks south of the Palermo Viejo border.

CASA BRANDON Map p98

☎ 4858-0610; www.brandongayday.com.ar; Luis María Drago 236; 🕒 Wed-Sun

Located a bit off the beaten path in Villa Crespo, this meeting spot is so much more than a bar. The concept at Casa Brandon is to promote art in the context of sexual diversity. There's an art gallery that showcases paintings and photographs, and you can watch movies or take in a live music performance. And for those who need a bit more excitement, there are karaoke and drag party nights. It also organizes the lively gay parties called Brandon Gay Day.

CERVECERÍA COSSAB Map p98

☎ 4925-2505; www.pubcossab.com.ar; Carlos Calvo 4199; 🕑 7pm-1am Wed-Thu, to 4am Fri, 9pm-4am Sat

Beer lovers unite, and head down to bohemian Boedo and this dedicated beer bar – a unique find for BA. Around 100 different tasty suds are represented, including 10 on tap and 80 varieties from around Argentina and many other countries (including Germany, Mexico and Canada). Delicious pizzas, cheese plates and sandwiches help you make a night of it – but for something out of the ordinary, try the *picada Patagonica* with smoked wild boar and venison.

CAFÉS

Cafés are an integral part of porteño life, and you shouldn't miss popping into one of these beloved hangouts to sip dainty cups of coffee with the locals. Many cafés are old classics that seem to take coffee drinkers back in time, especially those designated by the city government as *bares notables*. Others are contemporary or bohemian joints with sidewalk tables, perfect spots to take a load off while sightseeing or to delve into Borges' short stories at a corner table.

Most cafés serve all meals and everything in between (including a late-night snack). For a background on these legacies of Argentine social history, see the boxed text.

THE CENTER

The center has some of the oldest cafes in town, delightfully atmospheric venues that offer a welcome break while you're wandering around.

CAFÉ RICHMOND Map p62

☎ 4322-1341; Florida 468; 🕑 7am-10pm Mon-Sat

Feel like challenging the male locals to a billiards game or chess match? Then head to the basement of this very traditional cafe, which has been around since 1917. Better yet, just sink yourself into a leather chair upstairs and admire the Dutch chandeliers and English-style surroundings while sipping your hot chocolate – just like Jorge Luis Borges did. Borges didn't have the choice of 20 kinds of coffee, however.

CAFÉ TORTONI Map p62

☎ 4342-4328; www.cafetortoni.com.ar; Av de Mayo 825; 🕑 8am-3am Mon-Sat, to 1am Sun

Always cited as Buenos Aires' oldest and most famous cafe, the classic Tortoni has become so popular with foreigners in recent years that it's turned into something of a tourist trap. Still, it's practically an obligatory stop for any visitor to town: order a couple of *churros* (fried pastry dough) with your hot chocolate and forget about the inflated prices. Tortoni is truly a beautiful place, but it's not the only game in town. There are also up to four tango shows nightly (AR$80 to AR$100) – reserve ahead.

BUENOS AIRES' CAFÉS

Thanks to its European heritage, Buenos Aires has a serious café culture. Porteños will spend hours dawdling over a single *café cortado* (coffee with milk) and a couple of *medialunas* (croissants), discussing the economy, politics, recent loves lost or the nuances of that latest soccer play. Indeed, everything from business transactions to marriage proposals to revolutions has originated at the local corner cafe. It's hard to imagine Argentina functioning without this beloved traditional institution.

Some of BA's cafes have been around for over a hundred years, and many retain much of their original furniture, architectural details and rich atmosphere. They've always been the haunts of Argentina's politicians, activists, intellectuals, artists and old literary greats. London City (p152) boasts that Julio Cortázar wrote his masterpiece *The Prizes* at one of its tables, while Café Richmond (p151) says Jorge Luis Borges drank hot chocolate there. The most famous of them all, however, is the touristy Café Tortoni (p151), which was founded in 1858 and claims to be the oldest cafe in the country.

Most cafes have adapted to modern times by serving alcohol as well as coffee, and offer a surprisingly wide range of food and snacks; you can order a steak as easily as a *cortado*. A few even double as bookstores, or host live music, tango shows, poetry readings, films and other cultural events. So although they can transport you back in time, they'll still offer services keeping you in the present.

Cafes have long hours and are usually open from early morning to late at night, making them easy places to visit. And visit you should; sipping coffee and hanging out at one of these atmospheric cafes, perhaps on some lazy afternoon, is part of the Buenos Aires experience. At the very least, they're great for a late tea or a welcome break from all that walking you'll be doing.

LA PUERTO RICO Map p62

☎ 4331-2215; www.lapuertoricocafe.com.ar; Adolfo Alsina 416; ⏰ 7am-8pm Mon-Fri, 8am-12am Sat, noon-7pm Sun

One of the city's most historic cafes, La Puerto Rico has been going strong since 1887 but remains miraculously un-touristy. Located a block south of Plaza de Mayo, the place serves great coffee and pastries, the latter baked on the premises. Old photos on the walls hint at a rich past and the Spanish movies that have been filmed here. On weekends, tango, folklore and flamenco performances enliven the cafe: check the website for the line-up.

LONDON CITY Map p62

☎ 4342-9057; www.londoncitybar.com.ar; cnr Avs de Mayo & Perú; ⏰ 7am-10pm Mon-Fri, to 7pm Sat

After you've shopped your way down Florida, this classy cafe offers a welcome rest for those tired feet. It's been serving java enthusiasts for over 50 years, and claims to have been the spot where Julio Cortázar wrote his first novel. Your hardest work here, however, will most likely be choosing which pastry to try with your freshly brewed coffee before you continue up the busy pedestrian walkway of Florida.

CONGRESO & TRIBUNALES

This neighborhood offers several interesting cafes in which to relax, including many lesser-known spots that aren't listed here: take a stroll down the broad avenues of Congreso, especially along Av de Mayo between the Congreso building and Av 9 de Julio, and find your own spot to sit and read over a cup of coffee.

CAFÉ DE LOS ANGELITOS Map p72

☎ 4314-1121; www.cafedelosangelitos.com; cnr Rivadavia & Rincón; ⏰ 7am-2am Sun-Thu, to 3am Fri & Sat

Originally called Bar Rivadavia, this cafe was once the haunt of poets, musicians, even criminals, which is why a police commissioner jokingly called it *'los angelitos'* (the angels) in the early 1900s. Recently restored to its former glory, this historic cafe is now an elegant hangout for coffee or tea.

EL GATO NEGRO Map p72

☎ 4374-1730; www.elgatonegronet.com.ar; Av Corrientes 1669; ⏰ 9am-8pm Mon-Thu, to 11pm Fri, 3-11pm Sat

Tea-lined wooden cabinets and a spicy aroma welcome you to this pleasant little sipping paradise. Enjoy imported cups of coffee or tea, along with breakfast and dainty *sandwiches de miga* (thin, crustless sandwiches, traditionally eaten at tea time). Tea is sold by the pound, and a range of exotic herbs and spices are also on offer.

SAN TELMO

San Telmo is home to several historic cafes that have hardly changed over the years; older gentlemen still show up for their morning coffee and *medialunas*. To spend a few hours cafe-hopping, walk south along Defensa towards Parque Lezama, then loop around and walk north on Peru.

BAR BRITÁNICO Map p76

☎ 4361-2107; Brasil 399, cnr Defensa; ⏰ 24hr Wed-Sun, 8am-midnight Mon & Tue

A classic corner cafe on the edge of Parque Lezama, Bar Británico has an evocative old wooden interior and big glass windows that open to the street. Drop in for a *café cortado* (small espresso with milk) in the morning or a beer on a sunny afternoon.

BAR PLAZA DORREGO Map p76

☎ 4361-0141; Defensa 1098; ⏰ 8am-2am Sun-Thu, to 3am Fri & Sat

You can't beat the atmosphere at this traditional joint; sip your *submarino* (hot milk with chocolate) by a picture window and watch the world pass by, or grab a table on the busy plaza. Meanwhile, traditionally suited waiters, piped-in tango music, antique bottles and scribbled graffiti on walls and counters might take you back in time – at least until your steak sandwich lands on the table.

RETIRO

Retiro's a busy place full of businesspeople who need a break from work, so there are many cafes in the area that cater to them.

CAFÉ RETIRO Map p84

☎ 4516-0902; Retiro Station Lobby, Ramos Meija 1358; ⏰ 8:30am-9pm Mon-Sat

Catching a train out of town? Allow an extra half hour for coffee at this grand cafe in the main hall – the soaring ceilings, polished wood and bronze interior, and the bustling train station will make you feel like the star of a silent movie. One of the original fixtures of the station, built in 1915, the cafe has undergone a thorough restoration – the chandeliers twinkle beautifully at night. Look for jazz performances in the evening.

FLORIDA GARDEN Map p84

☎ 4312-7902; cnr Florida & Paraguay; 6:30am-midnight Mon-Fri, 7am-10pm Sat, 8am-10pm Sun

Usually full of businesspeople drinking up a storm of coffee, this two-story cafe – now sporting modern touches such as glass walls and copper-covered columns – was historically popular with politicians, artists and writers. In fact, Jorge Luis Borges and Pérez Célis (a famous Argentine painter) used to hang out here before the era of skinny lattes. The people-watching is excellent, both inside the cafe and out.

RECOLETA & BARRIO NORTE

There are also a few historical spots to linger in here. Otherwise tea lovers should head to Tea Connection (p133), while juice fans can visit Pura Vida (p138).

CLÁSICA Y MODERNA Map p87

☎ 4812-8707; www.clasicaymoderna.com; Av Callao 892; 8am-2am Mon-Sat, 5pm-2am Sun

Catering to the literary masses since 1938, this cozy and intimate bookstore-cafe continues to ooze history from its atmospheric brick walls. It's nicely lit, offers plenty of reading material and serves upscale meals. There are regular live performances of folk music, jazz, bossa nova and tango; Mercedes Sosa (may she rest in peace), Susana Rinaldi and Liza Minnelli have all chirped here.

LA BIELA Map p87

☎ 4804-0449; Av Quintana 600; 8am-3am Mon-Sat, 9am-3am Sun

A Recoleta institution, this classic landmark has been serving the porteño elite since the 1950s – when race-car champions used to frequent the place. The outdoor front terrace is unbeatable on a sunny afternoon, especially when the nearby weekend *feria* (street market) is in full swing. Just know that this privilege will cost 20% more.

VILLA CRESPO, ONCE, CABALLITO & BOEDO

As Palermo becomes more and more expensive, these traditionally blue-collar neighborhoods – east of the center and south of Palermo – are slowly gentrifying and attracting their own attention. Esquina Homero Manzi (p166) is a classic, and honors a famous poet and tango composer.

LAS VIOLETAS Map p98

☎ 4958-7387; Av Rivadavia 3899; 8am-2am Mon-Fri & Sun

Dating back to 1884, this historic coffeehouse was renovated in 2001 into the gorgeous place it is today. Lovely stained-glass windows and awnings, high ceilings, cream-colored Ionic columns and gilded details make this cafe possibly the most beautiful in the capital. Come for the luxurious afternoon tea – you might pretend to be royalty while reveling in your surroundings – and be sure to pick something up in the chocolate shop on the way out.

NIGHTLIFE

top picks

- **Cocoliche** (p158)
- **Basement Club** (p158)
- **Niceto Club** (p160)
- **La Trastienda** (p160)
- **Thelonious Club** (p161)
- **La Peña del Colorado** (p161)

NIGHTLIFE

Buenos Aires' nightlife is legendary all around the world. What else could you expect from a country where dinner rarely starts before 10pm? Clubbers especially will be in heaven here, as BA has spectacular nightclubs showcasing top-drawer international DJs. And the live-music scene is no slouch, either, with plenty of rock, blues, jazz and even folk-music venues spread throughout the city.

To help you get started, most newspapers have entertainment supplements published on Friday; the *Buenos Aires Herald*, an English-language publication, is particularly handy. The internet holds countless websites that detail BA's current activities; check www.whatsupbuenosaires.com for information in English. If you read Spanish, sort through www.vammos.com.ar and www.buenosaliens.com. Since nightlife venues come and go, it's worthwhile to ask around for the current hot spots during your tenure in town.

Massively popular annual event-parties include October's South American Music Conference (p159) and November's Creamfields (p159). For information on Latin and electronica music in BA, see p36.

CLUBBING

Thanks to its famous *boliches* (nightclubs), BA's nightlife is talked about all over South America. Every weekend – and even on some weeknights – the city's clubs come alive with beautiful people moving to electronic and house music, their faces illuminated in bright flashes as strobe lights pulse overhead. Many of the most impressive nightlife hot-spots are located in grandiose restored theaters, warehouses or factories – or perched on the banks of the Rio de la Plata where partygoers can watch the sun rise over the water as the festivities wind down. All have bouncers at the door keeping the masses in order and the riffraff out. If you have trouble getting in, politely play up your foreign accent – porteños love the exotic (though foreigners are getting pretty common in BA these days). It doesn't hurt to plan ahead and get your name 'on the list'; many of the bigger clubs offer an online reservation form through their websites.

Clubs are spread out over the city, with main clusters in the center and on the Costanera Norte. Very few clubs open before midnight, and the cool crowd generally doesn't show up before 2am, with the best nightclubs rocking on through dawn. How to handle the late-night scene like a porteño? Take a nap after dinner (and go easy on the booze, as the locals do, it will help you from tiring out too early). Don't dress up too much – the look is casual, cool, and urban, with half the crowd wearing jeans and brightly colored Converse high-tops.

Women usually pay less than men, and sometimes get in free. The price of admission sometimes includes a drink, and can skyrocket if a famous international DJ is spinning – your most economical choice is usually a *porrón* (bottle) of Quilmes. Some clubs offer dinners and shows before the dancing starts. Bring cash, as credit cards aren't often accepted.

ALSINA Map p62

☎ 4331-3231/1277; www.palacioalsina.com; Adolfo Alsina 940; Fri, Sat & Sun

Second only to Amerika as the capital's biggest gay magnet, Alsina's popular queer nights are Friday and Sunday (when a tea dance starts at 11pm to end the weekend). DJs crank up the house – a cavernous restored warehouse with a wonderfully gothic atmosphere – with dance, hip-hop and techno riffs. But on Saturday night, known as the 'Big One' (www.bigoneclub.com.ar), electronica entertains the mostly straight crowd. All nights are blessed with three floors of open balconies, chandeliers and thick drapes, along with plenty of pretty people.

AMERIKA Map p98

☎ 4865-4416; www.ameri-k.com.ar; Gascón 1040; Thu-Sun

BA's largest and feistiest gay nightclub, Amerika attracts all kinds of folks – but Fridays are especially popular with gays (check out the wild dark room). Saturday has a good mixed crowd and tends to be packed. The music is techno, dance, '90s and Latin, and despite the *canilla libre* (all-

GAY & LESBIAN BUENOS AIRES

There is a live and kicking gay scene in BA, and it's become even livelier since July 2010, when Argentina became Latin America's first country to legalize same-sex marriage (notably, eight years earlier, Argentina became the first country in the region to approve civil unions for same-sex couples). Politically and socially, Buenos Aires is LGBT-friendly; many say the city has outstripped Rio as South America's number one gay destination. November's gay pride parade, Marcha del Orgullo Gay (p22), rules the calendar of gay-oriented events, closely followed by an annual film festival (www.diversa.com.ar), a tango festival (www.festivaltangoqueer.com.ar) and periodic gay pride parties known as Brandon Gay Day (www.brandongayday.com.ar.) Let's not forget that the 2007 gay World Cup (www.iglfa2007.org) took place in BA.

Gay travelers will want to plan ahead of time to make the most of a visit to this forward-thinking capital. Gay websites in English include www.thegayguide.com.ar and buenosaires.queercity.info. Also look for free booklets such as *Gay Maps, La Otra Guía* and *The Ronda,* available at gay bars, hotels, tourist offices and some businesses. Even the city is distributing gay literature: magazines such as *Guapo* and *Imperio* can be bought at newsstands or picked up for free in tourist offices.

Gay-oriented guesthouses, cafes, and nightclubs are scattered around San Telmo, Barrio Norte and Palermo. For gay-friendly accommodation, see p187 and p188.

One traditional cruising area is at the intersection of Avs Santa Fe and Pueyrredón, where after midnight discount admission coupons get handed out on street corners (or check venues' websites). If you need to load yourself up on caffeine for the night to come, settle in at El Olmo (Map p92; ☎ 4821-5828), right at the intersection; it's a spot traditionally patronized by older gays, but everyone is welcome. To find out about the most current gay cruising spots or parties, ask the staff at any gay venue listed below.

For gay classes and *milongas,* visit Plaza Bohemia (p169), the Tuesday night *milonga* at Tango Queer (Map p76; www.tangoqueer.com; Belgrano 2259) – it's also at Perú 571 – and Lugar Gay (p188), a B&B which acts as a gay information center, organizing activities for guests and non-guests alike. Other resources include Grupo Nexo (☎ 4374-4484; www.nexo.org) and Comunidad Homosexual Argentina (CHA; ☎ 4361-6382; www.cha.org.ar).

Bars & Nightclubs

Buenos Aires is alive with enough gay and lesbian nightlife to keep you out all night long (and tomorrow night, and the night after that...) If you're in the mood to dance, Alsina (p156) and Amerika (p156) are BA's biggest gay magnets; otherwise, Glam (p158) is a casual yet very sexy club in an old mansion. If you're looking for some good drinking holes, we recommend Bach Bar (p148), Kim y Novak (p149), Bulnes Class (p149), Chueca (p149) and Sitges (p150) in Palermo; Pride Café (p146) in San Telmo; Casa Brandon (p150) in Villa Crespo, and Flux Bar (p147) in Retiro.

Need some sustenance to get you through the long night ahead? Gay-friendly restaurants include Empire Thai (p132), Rave (Map p92; ☎ 4833-7832; www.restaurantrave.com.ar; Gorriti 5092) and the adorable Goût Cafe (Map p87; ☎ 4825-8330; www.goutcafe.com.ar; Juncal 2124).

you-can-drink; except on Sunday), it's not completely insane – although the floors do get sticky. Three dance floors, large video screens and stripper shows keep things interesting.

ASIA DE CUBA Map p69

☎ 4894-1328; www.asiadecuba.com.ar; Pierina Dealessi 750, Puerto Madero Este; ⏲ nightly

An overpriced Puerto Madero restaurant by day, this beautiful spot turns into a flashy and snobby nightclub after midnight. The originally mixed and delightfully eclectic music ranges from old hits to disco to Latin house; it's a big draw for the dressy crowd, which is an even mix of tourists and Argentines. Breezy outside lounges offer romantic views of the *diques,* helping to make this one of BA's best clubs. Avoid the cover charge by grabbing dinner here beforehand.

AZÚCAR Map p98

☎ 4865-3103; www.azucarsalsa.com; Av Corrientes 3330; ⏲ Fri & Sat

The cha-cha-cha moves, neon lights and humid atmosphere might briefly take you to a more tropical locale than BA – but then a line dance brings you back to this slightly kitschy salsa club. It's a busy, energetic joint that has a good following, with plenty of salsa, rock and even belly-dancing classes available in the early evening. It's located diagonally across from the gorgeous Abasto mall.

BAHREIN Map p62

☎ 4314-8886; www.bahreinba.com; Lavalle 345; ⏲ Tue-Sat

Attracting a good share of BA's tattooed youth, Bahrein is a hugely popular downtown club housed in an old bank (check out the 'vault' in the basement.) On the ground floor is the lounge-like 'Funky Room,' complete with the bank's original wood fixtures and twinkling chandeliers, where resident DJs spin house music and electronica. Downstairs is the happening Xss discotheque, an impressive sound system, and a dance floor for hundreds.

BASEMENT CLUB Map p87

☎ 4812-3584; Rodriguez Peña 1220; ⏲ Thu-Sat
This cool but unpretentious subterranean club is known for first-rate DJ lineups, pounding house music, and a diverse young crowd. Thanks to the Shamrock (p148), the ever-popular Irish pub upstairs, the place sees plenty of traffic throughout the night – things get started a bit earlier on Thursday. Come at 3am to see the club in full swing, or just descend the stairs after enjoying a few pints at ground level.

CLUB ARÁOZ Map p92

☎ 4832-9751; www.clubaraoz.com.ar; Aráoz 2424; ⏲ Thu-Sat
Also known as 'Lost', this small club's finest hour is on Thursday, when hip-hop rules the roost and the regulars start break dancing around 2am (reggaeton comes on later in the evening). National and international DJs liven up the weekends. There's no dress code – a good thing, since it tends to get hot and sweaty in there. Very popular with young Americans, it's a great place to dance for hours and have a good time with friends – the drinks are wellpriced as well.

COCOLICHE Map p62

☎ 4342-9485; www.cocoliche.net; Rivadavia 878; ⏲ Fri & Sat
An effortlessly cool DJ club in BA is this electronic-music paradise, based in a bit run down old mansion. Strut in and be welcomed by a long bar and stiff cocktails; it's the downstairs basement, gritty and nearly always packed, that holds the main stage, a fantastic sound system and state-of-the-art light show. Breakbeat, drum and bass, reggaeton and electronic *cumbia* (Colombian music) entertain, and when you need a break go to the 2nd-floor chill-out room.

CROBAR Map p92

☎ 4778-1500; www.crobar.com; cnr Paseo de la Infanta Isabel & Marcelo Freyre; ⏲ Fri & Sat
One of the newer locations of the American club series (find others in Miami, Chicago, and Beijing), stylish Crobar remains, at least for the time being, the darling of BA's nightlife scene. Friday usually features international DJs mashing up the latest electronic selections, while Saturday tends to feature more commercial beats – check the website to see what's coming up. There's also a back room for those who prefer classic rock, '80s remixes and occasional live bands, while the main levels are strewn with mezzanines and catwalks that allow views from above.

EL LIVING Map p84

☎ 4811-4730; www.living.com.ar; MT de Alvear 1540; ⏲ Thu-Sat
Laid-back El Living (the Living Room) sticks to a decade-old formula: plush sofas, cheap whiskey sours, campy George Michael music videos projected onto a huge screen, and a young, cheerful crowd. Before 2am, dinner guests linger and most bar stools are empty, but you'll be squished between vintage Madonna fans and English punk enthusiasts when the '80s dance party gets going in the wee hours.

GLAM Map p92

☎ 4963-2521; www.glambsas.com.ar; Cabrera 3046; ⏲ Thu-Sat
Housed on three floors of an old mansion with tall brick hallways, this mazelike gay club still brings in a crowd of locals and travelers. The guys are young, good-looking and are here to dance and get to know each other better – there are no shows to distract, just casual lounges, pretty bars and free condoms at the door. Thursday and Saturday are the biggest nights here.

JET Map p58

☎ 4782-5599; www.jet-lounge.com.ar; Av Rafael Obligado 4801; ⏲ Fri & Sat
More of a fashionable lounge than a night club, Jet often serves as a precursor to high-class crowds that later will migrate to nearby late-night institution Pachá (p160). A long list of pricey drinks complements the food here (sushi is popular), while sexy couches look out over docks and sailboats. Expect attractive people, flattering lighting and good mainstream music.

LA SALSERA Map p98

☎ 4866-1829; www.lasalsera.com; Yatay 961; ⏲ Fri-Sun
Buenos Aires' first salsa and merengue club, La Salsera continues to be one of the city's

best spots for Caribbean beats. The scene is wonderfully energetic, and just about everyone is dancing and having fun. Upstairs it's much darker and more sedate – the place to go after you've worn yourself out from all that activity downstairs. There's also a chill-out garden, and salsa classes are available earlier on.

MALUCO BELEZA Map p72

☎ 4372-1737; www.malucobeleza.com.ar; Sarmiento 1728; ⏲ Wed & Fri-Sun

Located in an old mansion is this popular Brazilian *boliche*. It gets really packed with upbeat dancers moving to samba fusion music and others watching half-naked dancers writhing on the stage. For a more sedate atmosphere, climb the stairs where it's darker and more laid-back. If you're craving Brazilian cuisine, get here at 8pm on Wednesday when dinner (featuring *feijoada,* a bean and meat stew) and a show are on tap. You can even sign up for Axe or Zouk-Lambada dance classes.

MUSEUM Map p76

☎ 4543-3894; www.museumclub.com.ar; Perú 535; ⏲ Wed, Fri & Sat

This cavernous disco is best known for its Wednesday-night 'after-office' party,

ELECTRONICA IN BUENOS AIRES *Josh Hinden*

Buenos Aires might be known for its tango, but there is something else to keep you dancing until dawn in this late-night city that generally looks to Europe for its trends. Since 1990 the electronic-music scene of BA has grown to become a major force in the music world. Touting some of the world's best venues and biggest crowds, Buenos Aires is listed by many DJs as a favorite place to play.

One of the most internationally acclaimed homegrown DJs is Hernán Cattaneo, who began his professional career in the early '90s playing commercial clubs of the time, such as El Cielo and Cinema. Several years later he secured a residency for the Clubland night at Pachá (p160), where legend has it he was discovered and whisked off to international stardom by UK legend Paul Oakenfold. The success of Cattaneo and Pachá marked the beginning of a new era, when electronica emerged into mainstream pop culture.

Nowadays, when the weather warms up in spring, enormous events with up to 50,000 people take place, such as Creamfields (www.creamfieldsba.com) and the South American Music Conference (www.samc.net), while newer, smaller-scale festivals like Festival Ciudad Emergente (www.ciudademergente.gob.ar) pack venues with thousands of young people and feature electronica performances. In addition to these annual events, the club and underground scene is alive and well, although somewhat less kicking (and with good reason) due to stricter rules since the 2004 Cromagnon club tragedy in which almost 200 people lost their lives in a fire.

House music (referred to as *'punchi, punchi'* because of the relentless kick drum) is no longer the only option. You'll find a variety of sounds thanks to early diversification within Argentina's veteran underground DJ collective, DJ UNION, composed of Carla Tintore (www.carlatintore.com), Dr Trincado (www.drtrincado.com) and Diego Ro-k. Notoriously wild underground parties such as the Age of Communication and Ave Porco helped pave the way to a diverse underground tradition, which you can experience at Cocoliche (p158). For a mellower (and earlier) night of DJ-spun entertainment and killer cocktails, head for Le Bar (p144).

For years, the hottest party in town was Zizek at Niceto Club (p160); this self-touted 'urban beats club' features emerging hip-hop, dancehall, *cumbia* (Colombian music) and reggaeton, and their variations that range from grime to mashups. Thanks to great success, the Zizek outfit has been touring the Americas with regular stops back in Buenos Aires. Check www.zzkrecords.com for the latest news on this one-of-a-kind music experience.

The original DJ collectives and electronica parties have paved the way for another generation of musical stylings: whether it's progressive house (www.aldohaydar.com), breakbeat (www.babreaks.com), techno, IDM, deep house, drum and bass (www.djorange.com) or even experimental *cumbia,* Buenos Aires has it. Some of the DJs who experiment with styles are DJ Joven (http://djoven.blogspot.com) and Djs Pareja (www.djspareja.com.ar), the famous electronica twosome who spin a fusion of retro acid house techno and pop at clubs and parties around town; DJ Daleduro and his partner DJ Gone, who form the duo Groovedealers and do 2-step garage and dubstep; Franco Cinelli (www.francocinelli.com.ar), who plays minimal sounds and clicks; and Chancha Via Circuito (www.chanchaviacircuito.com), an experimental *cumbia* artist who got his start at Zizek.

A newer phenomenon on the BA electronica scene is chip music, 8-bit music made of obsolete videogame consoles, such as Commodore 64, Atari 2600 and Gameboy. A wave of DJs, such as Coleco Music (www.colecomusic.com.ar) and Neotericz, is now experimenting with this retro technology to create a new sound.

Most porteños turn to websites such as www.buenosaliens.com (in Spanish) to find out what's happening; www.whatsupbuenosaires.com caters more to tourists.

starting at 8pm, where fun-loving porteños throw back two-for-one drinks and dance their way over the midweek hump (read: it's a huge pick-up scene with younger suit-and-tie types outnumbering women four to one). It's a huge space with multiple levels, several bars, and funky light shows. Saturday nights, featuring house music, are quieter. Note the amazing building, an old factory designed by Gustave Eiffel – yes, the same one who built a Parisian landmark and gave it his own name.

NICETO CLUB Map p92

☎ 4779-9396; www.nicetoclub.com; Niceto Vega 5510; ⏲ Thu-Sat

One of the city's biggest crowd-pullers, the can't-miss event at Niceto Club is Thursday night's Club 69 (www.club69.com.ar), a subversive DJ extravaganza featuring gorgeously attired showgirls, dancing drag queens, futuristic video installations and off-the-wall performance art. On weekend nights, national and international spin masters take the booth to entertain lively crowds with blends of hip-hop, dancehall, electronic beats, cumbia, reggae, folklore and even aboriginal chants.

PACHÁ Map p58

☎ 4788-4280; www.pachabuenosaires.com; cnr Av Costanera Rafael Obligado & La Pampa; ⏲ Sat & some other nights, consult schedule, closed Jan

Famous guest DJs from countries as far-ranging as Israel and Germany spin tunes for the youthful, spruced-up (and sometimes snobbish) masses attracted by this huge and popular club inspired by the flagship Pachá's location in Ibiza. Laser lightshows and a great sound system make everyone happy. Saturday night is nicknamed 'Clubland'; don't come until after 4am. You'll have plenty of time to party away before heading to the terrace and watching the sun come up – bring your shades.

RUMI Map p101

☎ 4782-1307; www.rumiba.com.ar; Av Figueroa Alcorta 6442; ⏲ Wed-Sat

If you're looking for glamour, fashion and possible celebrity sightings, then ultracool Rumi is your mecca. Dress well and groom yourself impeccably to satisfy the picky bouncers, then enter into a wonderland of electronica, hip-hop and house beats. Famous DJs spin on Wednesday night's 'Be Happy' party, Thursday moves to a 70s soundtrack during 'Elegant Night,' Friday is the 'Back to Basics' dance party, and Saturday night brings in a crowd for the Latin-infused 'High Party.' If you want to make an evening of it, come to this upscale locale earlier for dinner first (starting at 9pm.)

LIVE MUSIC

There are some fine venues that only feature live music, but many theaters, cultural centers, bars and cafes also put on shows. For tango music performances, see the tango section in the Arts chapter (p164); Centro Cultural Torquato Tasso (p165) is an especially good choice.

ROCK, BLUES & JAZZ

Buenos Aires boasts a thriving rock-music scene. The following are smaller venues that showcase mostly local groups; when huge international stars come to town they tend to play soccer stadiums or Luna Park (see the boxed text, p171).

Blues and jazz aren't as popular as rock but still have their own loyal following. The restaurant-cafe Clásica y Moderna (p153) occasionally hosts jazz groups.

For more information on rock in Argentina see p35, and for blues and jazz see p36.

LA TRASTIENDA Map p76

☎ 5237-7200 via Ticketek; www.latrastienda.com; Balcarce 460; ⏲ nightly

This large, atmospheric theater welcomes over 700, features a well-stocked bar, and showcases national and international live-music acts. Look for headers such as Charlie Garcia, Divididos, José Gonzalez, Damien Rice and Conor Oberst. Get tickets at the office here or through Ticketek (www.ticketek.com.ar).

MITOS ARGENTINOS Map p76

☎ 4362-7810; www.mitosargentinos.com.ar; Humberto Primo 489; ⏲ Wed-Sun

This cozy old brick house in San Telmo has hosted rock groups for over a dozen years. It's not too big, with lots of tables, a perfectly sized stage and a small balcony above. Known for its tributes to *'rock nacional'* bands.

ND/ATENEO Map p84

☎ 4328-2888; www.ndateneo.com.ar; Paraguay 918; ⏲ nightly

This remodeled theater stages a wide variety of national and international acts of all genres, with emphasis on rock, jazz and folk music. Well organized with good acoustics and quality concerts, it also puts on films, theater and other artsy shows; in 2008 it hosted the Buenos Aires International Jazz Festival.

NOTORIOUS Map p87

☎ 4813-6888; www.notorious.com.ar; Av Callao 966; ⏲ nightly

This stylish, intimate joint is one of Buenos Aires' premier jazz venues. Up front you can sit at modern glass tables and listen to CDs before you buy them. In the back the restaurant-café (overlooking a verdant garden) hosts live jazz shows every night. Log on to the website for schedules.

THELONIOUS CLUB Map p92

☎ 4829-1562; www.theloniousclub.com.ar; Salguero 1884, 1st fl; ⏲ Tue-Sat

Up the stairs at this old mansion there's a bluesy, dimly lit jazz bar, with high brick ceilings and a good sound system. Come early to snag a seat and partake in the interesting menu and wide range of cocktails. Thelonious is known for its jazz lineups, with DJs entertaining into the early-morning hours.

FOLK

Música folklórica definitely has its place in Buenos Aires. There are several *peñas* (traditional music clubs) in the city, but other venues – such as Clásica y Moderna (p153) – occasionally host folk performances. For more information on folk music in Argentina, see p37.

LA PEÑA DEL COLORADO Map p92

☎ 4822-1038, www.lapeniadelcolorado.com; Güemes 3657; ⏲ nightly

Nightly folkloric shows are memorable at this rustic restaurant-bar, and afterwards audience members pick up nearby guitars to make their own entertainment (groups sing to each other in a sort of friendly competition). There's also tasty northern Argentine food on offer, including *locro* (a corn and meat stew), *chipá* (chewy cheese balls) and *humitas de Chala* (like tamales) – the spicy empanadas are excellent.

LOS CARDONES Map p92

☎ 4777-1112, www.cardones.com.ar; Borges 2180; ⏲ Wed-Sat

Come to this friendly, low-key *peña* for mellow guitar shows, audience-participatory jam sessions, hearty regional cuisine and free-flowing red wine. You'll likely see some real-life gauchos here, especially on weekends in winter when the countrymen come to town for the La Rural farm show. Check out the website for details on the current lineup.

THE ARTS

top picks

- **El Camarín de las Musas** (p170)
- **Centro Cultural Torquato Tasso** (p165)
- **Cuidad Cultural Konex** (p170)
- **Teatro Colón** (p71)
- **Salon Canning** (p169)

WHAT'S YOUR RECOMMENDATION? www.lonelyplanet.com/Buenos Aires

THE ARTS

What's a visit to Buenos Aires without going to a tango extravaganza? There are more shows than you can shake your booty at, from casual and dirt cheap (that is, street buskers) to footloose and fancy. Afterwards, consider keeping those toes on track with a tango class, then head to a *milonga* (tango hall) and put those moves to the test.

Love theater? Then take in a play – there are dozens of theater companies putting on excellent productions, be it singing, dancing, acting or all three. What about classical music? Yup, there are quite a few venues for that as well. And everyone likes going out to the movies – you'll find both independent films and recent blockbusters screening at classic old theaters or modern multiplexes. When it comes to artsy fun, you can find something to do every day of the week in this town.

To help you get started, see our listings in this chapter. And for current happenings, check www.whatsupbuenosaires.com, www.argentinaindependent.com or any of the many expat websites. You can also read the local newspapers – most are in Spanish and have entertainment supplements published on Friday; the *Buenos Aires Herald*'s 'Get Out' is in English.

DISCOUNT TICKETS & BOOKING

Major entertainment venues often require booking through Ticketek (☎ 5237-7200; www.ticketek.com.ar). The service charge is about 10% of the ticket price.

Carteleras (discount-ticket offices) along Av Corrientes sell a limited number of heavily discounted tickets for many entertainment events, such as movies, theater and tango shows, with savings of 20% to 50%. Buy tickets as far in advance as possible, but if you want to see a show or movie at short notice – especially at midweek – you can also drop by to check what's available.

Cartelera Baires (Map p72; www.cartelerabaires.com; Av Corrientes 1382; ⏲ 10am-9pm Mon & Tue, to 10pm Wed & Thu, to 11pm Fri, to midnight Sat, 2-9pm Sun) In Galería Apolo.

Cartelera Espectáculos (Map p62; ☎ 4322-4331; www.123info.com.ar; Lavalle 742; ⏲ noon-10pm Mon-Fri, to 11pm Sat, to 9pm Sun) Right on pedestrian Lavalle.

Cartelera Vea Más (Map p72; ☎ 6320-5319; ⏲ 10am-9pm Mon & Tue, to 10pm Wed-Fri, to 11pm Sat, 2-11pm Sun) In the Paseo La Plaza complex at Corrientes 1660, local 2.

TANGO

Once a furtive dance relegated to the red-light brothels of early 1900s Buenos Aires, tango has experienced great highs and lows throughout its volatile lifespan. These days, however, the sensual dance is back with a vengeance. Everyone from Seattle to Shanghai seems to be slinking their way down the parquet floor, trying to connect with their partner and memorize those elusive dance steps and rhythm that make the tango so damn hard to perfect. And many of them are jet-setting it to BA, creating their own pilgrimage to the city where the dance first began (speaking of which, keep an eye out for the screen adaptation of *Kiss and Tango*, with Sandra Bullock).

Tango's popularity is booming at both amateur and professional levels, and among all ages and classes. Traditional tango dancers will always be around, and can be seen at classic old *milongas*. There's no stopping evolution, however – nuevo tango, born in the late 1990s, was originally seeded by Ástor Piazzolla in the 1950s when he incorporated jazz and classical beats into traditional tango music. Dancers improvised new moves into their traditional base steps, utilizing a more open embrace and switching leads (among other things). Neo tango, the latest musical step in tango's changing landscape, fuses the dance with electronica for some decidedly nonstodgy beats that have done a superlative job of attracting the younger generation to this astounding dance. For more on tango and its history, see p34.

Also see the boxed text 'More Tango Information', p167.

SHOWS

If there's one thing Buenos Aires isn't short of, it's tango shows. Dozens of venues cater to this famous Argentine dance, and many of them are expensive, tourist-oriented spectacles that don't come close to what purists

TANGO HALL OF FAME *Anja Mutic*

- Carlos Di Sarli (1903–60) – Pianist, composer and orchestra leader
- Juan D'Arienzo (1900–76) – Violinist and orchestra leader
- Carlos Gardel (1890–1935) – Singer and actor
- Ástor Piazzolla (1921–92) – *Bandoneón* (accordionlike instrument) player and composer
- Roberto Goyeneche (1926–94) – Singer
- Aníbal Troilo (1914–75) – *Bandoneón* player, composer and orchestra leader
- Osvaldo Pugliese (1905–95) – Pianist, composer and orchestra leader
- Enrique Santos Discépolo (1901–51) – Composer and poet
- Homero Manzi (1907–51) – Lyricist and poet
- Horacio Salgán (b 1916) – Pianist, composer and orchestra leader
- Julio Sosa (1926–64) – Singer
- Eladia Blázquez (1931–2005) – Singer, pianist and composer
- Susana Rinaldi (b 1935) – Singer
- Adriana Varela (b 1952) – Singer

consider 'authentic' tango. These glamorized shows are still very entertaining and awe-inspiring, however, often showcasing amazing feats of grace and athleticism. They usually include various tango couples, an orchestra, a singer or two and possibly some folkloric musicians. All come with a dinner option, but the food can be hit or miss. VIP options mean a much higher price tag for better views and refreshments. Nearly all require advance reservations; some offer modest online discounts and pick-up from your hotel. And speaking of hotels, many will book tango shows for you – which is fine, since sometimes the price is similar to what you'd pay at the venue anyway.

More modest shows cost far less, and some are even free but require you to order a meal or drink at their restaurant. If you don't mind eating there this is a decent deal. Many *milongas* (see p167) also have good, affordable shows. For free (or donation) tango, head to San Telmo on a Sunday afternoon. Dancers do their thing in the middle of Plaza Dorrego, though you have to stake out a spot early to snag a good view. Another sure bet is weekends on El Caminito (p79) in La Boca; it's not quite as crowded here as in San Telmo. If you don't want to head so far south, however, see what's happening on Calle Florida in front of Galerías Pacíficos – there are sometimes dancers entertaining a crowd there, too. All of these buskers are quite good, so remember to toss some change into their hats.

One thing to note: nearly all tango shows are touristy by nature. They've been sensationalized to make them more exciting for observers. 'Authentic' tango (which happens at *milongas*) is a very subtle art, primarily done for the pleasure of the dancers. It's not something so much to be observed as experienced, and not nearly as interesting to the casual spectator. Going to a *milonga* just to watch isn't all that cool, either – folks are there to dance. So feel free to see a more flashy tango show and enjoy those spectacular high leg kicks – be wowed like the rest of the crowd.

If you like listening to live tango music, head to Centro Cultural Torquato Tasso (Map p76; ☎ 4307-6506; www.torquatotasso.com.ar; Defensa 1575). It's one of BA's best live-music venues, so don't expect any dancing.

Tango shows listed below are theatrical and a bit pricey – think Las Vegas. All offer a dinner option; dinner starts around 9pm, and shows around 10:30pm (most lasting about 1¼ hours).

COMPLEJO TANGO Map p98

☎ 4941-1119; www.complejotango.com.ar; Av Belgrano 2608; show AR$230, dinner & show AR$380

For those who wish to not only watch tango but also experience it, there's this classy venue in Balvanera. Should you choose to accept it, your first hour here is a free beginning tango lesson. Follow it up with a tasty dinner, then an excellent tango show – beware, however, as the performers go around towards the end, picking out audience members to dance with them (usually badly).

EL QUERANDÍ Map p62

☎ 5199-1770; www.querandi.com.ar; Perú 302; show AR$260, dinner & show AR$400

This large corner tango venue is also a an elegant restaurant boasting upscale atmosphere with dark-wood details. This show takes you through the evolution of tango, from its bordello origins to cabaret influences to *milongas* and modernism. It's more low-key tango dancing than other shows, so don't expect overly athletic moves from the dancers. One minus – an on-stage column blocks some views.

EL VIEJO ALMACÉN Map p76

☎ 4307-7388; www.viejoalmacen.com; cnr Balcarce & Independencia; show AR$220, dinner & show AR$400

One of Buenos Aires' longest-running shows (since 1969), this venue is a charming old building from the 1800s. An unmemorable dinner is served at a restaurant in the main building, then everyone heads across the small street to the theater, which tightly holds around 240 spectators. The show is a bit less sensationalized than similar shows, but is still pretty glitzy. Pluses include a folklore segment.

ESQUINA CARLOS GARDEL Map p98

☎ 4867-6363; www.esquinacarlosgardel.com.ar; Carlos Gardel 3200; show AR$295, dinner & show AR$420

One of the fanciest tango shows in town plays at this impressive 500-seat theater, an old cabaret right next to the lovely shopping mall Mercado de Abasto (p97). The Abasto neighborhood was once Carlos Gardel's old stomping ground, and he even hung out at this locale. The memorable show starts with a good film about the area, then goes on to highlight top-notch musicians and performers.

ESQUINA HOMERO MANZI Map p98

☎ 4957-8488; www.esquinahomeromanzi.com.ar; Av San Juan 3601; show AR$200, dinner & show AR$330

The best part about this tango venue is its location, right on the historic intersection of San Juan and Boedo. A completely remodeled historical cafe, Homero Manzi was named after one of Argentina's most famous tango lyricists. Today, this cafe – while still able to transport you back to the yonder days – mostly exists to be the vehicle for a glitzy tango show with capacity for 300 spectators. Nightly tango lessons offered before the show starts.

LA VENTANA Map p76

☎ 4334-1314; www.la-ventana.com.ar; Balcarce 431; show AR$220, dinner & show AR$420

The atmosphere at this long-running venue, located in an old converted building, will take you back in time. There are two salons, both with rustic brick walls and ceilings, and rough-hewn wood beams; one has an impressive stained-glass ceiling. A folklore show includes Andean musicians and a display of *boleadores* (balls on cords that gauchos used to tangle up prey). The tango show is also good, and there are 30 performers in total.

SEÑOR TANGO Map p58

☎ 4303-0231; www.senortango.com.ar; Vietes 1655; show AR$125, dinner & show AR$400

The most outrageous of them all, Señor Tango is the closest you'll get to a Las Vegas show in Buenos Aires. With dozens of performers, live horses, two tiers of balconies and an extended, hokey monologue (in Spanish) by the owner, this granddaddy of tango shows is – for good or bad – an unforgettable experience. Actual tango dancing is limited, as the show – a bit too long for many foreigners – covers the history of Argentina.

TANGO PORTEÑO Map p72

☎ 412-9400; www.tangoporteno.com.ar; Cerrito 570; show AR$130, dinner & show AR$390

One of the city's best shows takes place in this renovated and historical art deco theater, right in the center near Teatro Colón. Snippets of old footage are interspersed with plenty of athletic (and at times sensual) tango dancing. There's an interesting blindfold number, the orchestra is excellent and Juan Carlos Copes – a famous Argentine dancer in his time – usually makes a rug-cutting cameo. Tango class offered beforehand.

TANGO ROJO Map p69

☎ 5787-1536; www.rojotango.com; Faena Hotel & Universe, Martha Salotti 445; show AR$620, dinner & show AR$880

This sexy performance is the tango show to top all others – especially with its hefty price tag. Offering only 120 seats, the Faena's El Cabaret room is swathed in blood-red curtains and gilded furniture. The show itself loosely follows the history of tango, starting from its cabaret roots to the modern fusions of Ástor Piazzolla. The orchestra is first-rate, there are plenty of period costumes and even a brief (shock!) nudity scene.

For less fancy, more modest shows, there's the places following, or check out Los 36 Billares (p145).

More Tango Information…

Some of the most complete tango listings are in the many free tango booklets around town, including *El Tangauta* (www.eltanguata.com), *BA Tango* (www.batango.com) and *Diostango* (www.diostango.com). All have basic information on the city's *milongas,* classes, teachers and shows. They're often available at tango venues or tourist offices. Also, look for the tango map put out by the guesthouse Caserón Porteño (www.caseronporteno.com; also see p195).

For a very practical book on tango in BA, check out Sally Blake's *Happy Tango: Sallycat's Guide to Dancing in Buenos Aires.* It has great information on *milongas* – and how to dress for them, act in them and who you can expect to see – plus much more on the city's tango scene.

If you don't mind hiring a dance partner for classes or *milongas,* check out www.tangotaxidancers. There are many, many tango clothing and shoe stores in BA. For a tango museum, see p63.

BA has several accommodations catering to tango enthusiasts, including Caserón Porteño (Map p92) and Lina's Tango Guesthouse (p188). All offer on-site classes.

Finally, if you're in town in mid to late August, don't miss BA's tango festival (www.tangobuenosaires.gov.ar).

CAFÉ TORTONI Map p62

☎ 4342-4328; www.cafetortoni.com.ar; Av de Mayo 825; shows AR$80-100

Nightly tango shows take place at this very historic cafe, and they're either good (if you don't expect much) or bad (more slapstick cheesiness than actual tango dancing). The unmemorable food isn't included and is a bit overpriced, so consider eating elsewhere. If you come earlier for the cafe, don't expect great service – and if it's crowded you may have to line up outside before being let in. But we have to mention this popular, touristy café – it's BA's most famous, and still offers a beautiful atmosphere.

EL BALCÓN Map p76

☎ 4362-2354; www.elbalcondelaplaza.com.ar; Humberto Primo 461, 1st fl; shows free

If you're lucky enough to snag a balcony spot on a Sunday afternoon, you can watch both the tango show here *and* the antiques fair on Plaza Dorrego at the same time. This restaurant puts on free shows, but you do have to order some food – basic Argentine fare like empanadas, pasta and *parrilla* (mixed grill). Tango shows on Sunday only from 1:30pm to 7pm, with singing and folklore shows as well.

LA PUERTO RICO Map p62

☎ 4331-4178; www.lapuertoricocafe.com.ar; Alsina 416; Sat dinner show AR$250, Sun lunch show AR$130

One of Buenos Aires' most historic cafes offers a variety show of tango (dancers, singers, orchestra), flamenco (dance and singer) and folklore (gaucho fun). Shows start at 10pm on Saturday night and come with dinner. For a less expensive option consider the 2pm Sunday lunch show, which is only tango dancing with live orchestra (AR$130), and has an *a la carte* option (AR$30 plus food). For more on La Puerto Rico, see p152.

MILONGAS

Milongas are dance events where people strut their tango skills. The atmosphere at these events can be modern or historical, casual or traditional. Most have tango DJs that determine musical selections, but a few utilize live orchestras. The dance floor is surrounded by many tables and chairs, and this is where the subtle rules of code take place – determining who dances with whom. For more on tango etiquette, see p168.

Milongas start either in the afternoon and run until 11pm, or start at around midnight and run until the early-morning light (arrive late for the best action). They're affordable, with entry usually costing AR$15 to AR$30 per person. Classes are often offered before *milongas.*

For a unique outdoor experience, head to the bandstand at the Barrancas de Belgrano (Map p101), where the casual *milonga* 'La Glorieta' takes place on Saturday and Sunday evenings around 7pm. Free tango classes are given at 6pm.

CENTRO REGIÓN LEONESA Map p72

☎ 4304-5595; Humberto Primo 1462

Its famous Niño Bien *milonga* takes place on Thursday starting at 10:30pm and attracts a wide range of aficionados – including many tourists. Expect a beautiful atmosphere, a large ballroom and a good dance floor, but note it still gets very, very crowded. Take a taxi as it's a long way from the center.

TANGO AT A MILONGA

Not an easy dance to describe, tango needs to be seen and experienced for its full effect. Despite a long evolution from its origins, it still remains sensual and erotic. The upper bodies are traditionally held upright and close, with faces almost touching. The man's hand is pressed against the woman's back, guiding her, with their other hands held together and out. The lower body does most of the work. The woman swivels her hips, her legs alternating in short or wide sweeps and quick kicks, sometimes between the man's legs. The man guides, a complicated job since he must flow with the music, direct the woman, meld with her steps and avoid other dancers, all at once. He'll add his own fancy pivoting moves, and together the couple flows in communion with the music. Pauses and abrupt directional changes punctuate the dance. It's a serious business that takes a good amount of concentration so while dancing the pair often wear hard expressions. Smiling and chatting are reserved for the breaks between songs.

At a proper, established *milonga* (dance event), choosing an adequate partner involves many levels of hidden codes, rules and signals that dancers must follow. After all, no serious *bailarina* (female dancer; the male equivalent is a *bailarín*) wants to be caught out dancing with someone stepping on her toes (and expensive tango heels). In fact, some men considering asking an unknown woman to dance will do so only after the second song, not to be stuck for the three to five songs that make a session. These sessions (known as *tandas*) alternate between either tango, *vals* (the Argentine version of the waltz) or *milonga;* they're followed by a *cortina* (a short break when non-tango music is played). It's considered polite to dance an entire *tanda* with any partner, so if you are given a curt *gracias* after just one song, consider that partner unavailable for the rest of the night.

Your position in the area surrounding the dance floor can be critical. At some of the older *milongas,* the more established dancers have reserved tables. Ideally, you want to sit where you have easy access to the floor and to other dancers' line of sight. You may notice couples sitting farther back (they often dance just with each other), while singles sit right at the front. If a man comes into the room with a woman at his side, she is considered 'his' for the night. For couples to dance with others, they either enter the room separately, or the man signals his intent by asking another woman to the floor. Then 'his' woman becomes open for asking.

The signal to dance, known as *cabeceo,* involves a quick tilt of the head, eye contact and uplifted eyebrows. This can happen from way across the room. The woman to whom the *cabeceo* is directed either nods yes and smiles or pretends not to have noticed (a rejection). If she says yes the man gets up and escorts her to the floor. A hint: if you're at a *milonga* and don't want to dance with anyone, don't look around too much – you could be breaking some hearts.

So what is the appeal of the tango? Why is it that tango becomes so addictive, like an insidious drug? Could it be that it's just the 'vertical expression of a horizontal desire'? Experienced dancers will tell you this: the adrenaline rush you get from an excellent performance is like a successful conquest. Some days it lifts you up to exhilarating heights and other days it can bring you crashing down. You fall for the passion and beauty of the tango's movements, trying to attain a physical perfection that can never be fully realized. The best you can do is to make the journey as graceful and passionate as possible.

CONFITERÍA IDEAL p62

☎ 5265-8069; www.confiteriaideal.com; Suipacha 384, upstairs

This old classic (since 1912) is the mother of all historic tango halls, with many classes and *milongas* offered every single day – and pretty much continuously. Live orchestras often accompany dancers, the atmosphere is classic and the history rich. The actual cafe section could use a face-lift, as it's a bit dim, stodgy and impersonal, but it remains a Buenos Aires experience. Shows available. It featured in the film *The Tango Lesson*.

EL BESO Map p72

☎ 4953-2794; Riobamba 416

Another traditional and popular place, El Beso attracts some very good dancers – you should be very confident of your dancing skills if you come here. Located upstairs, it has very good music and a cozy feel, with a bar near the entrance.

GRICEL Map p98

☎ 4957-7157; www.clubgriceltango.com.ar; La Rioja 1180

This old classic (far from the center; take a taxi) often has big crowds, especially on Monday. It attracts an older, well-dressed clientele – along with plenty of tourists. There's a wonderful springy dance floor and occasionally live orchestras.

LA CATEDRAL Map p98

☎ 15-5325-1630; Sarmiento 4006

If tango can be youthful, trendy and hip, this is where you'll find it. The grungy warehouse space is very casual, with funky art on the walls, thrift-store furniture and dim atmospheric lighting. It's more like a young bohemian nightclub than anything else, and there's no implied dress code – you'll see plenty of jeans on the dancers. Great for cheap alcohol; the best-known *milongas* occur regularly on a Tuesday night.

PLAZA BOHEMIA Map p62

☎ 4300-3487; www.lamarshall.com.ar; Maipú 444

On Wednesday night the La Marshall *milonga* takes place here – and it's 'Tango Queer' (that's right, gay tango). Come at 10pm for a class, then at 11:30pm the *milonga* starts. No matter your sex, you can be asked to dance by a man or woman, and either lead or follow (make things clear beforehand!). Every orientation welcome; on Saturday La Marshall is held at Rivadavia 1392.

LA VIRUTA Map p92

☎ 4774-6357; www.lavirutatango.com; Armenia 1366

Popular basement venue. Good beginner tango classes are available before *milongas* – translating into many inexperienced dancers on the floor earlier on – so if you're an expert get here late (after 3:30am). Music can run the gamut from tango to rock to *cumbia* to salsa earlier in the evening, with more traditional tunes later. Tango shows also on offer.

SALON CANNING Map p92

☎ 4832-6753; www.parakultural.com.ar; Av Scalabrini Ortiz 1331

Some of BA's finest dancers (no wallflowers here) grace this traditional venue with its great dance floor. Well-known tango company Parakultural often stages good events here involving live music, tango DJs, singers and dancers. Expect big crowds and plenty of tourists.

SIN RUMBO off Map p58

☎ 4571-9577; Tamborini 6157

One of the oldest tango joints in BA, Sin Rumbo is considered the 'cathedral' of tango by those in the know – and has given rise to some famous tango dancers. It's a local place that attracts older professionals, and has a traditional black and white tile floor. Robert Duvall filmed his movie *Assassination Tango* here. Far from the center in Villa Urquiza; take a taxi.

CLASSES

Tango classes are available just about everywhere, from youth hostels to general dance academies (p170) to cultural centers (p225) to nearly all *milongas* (see p167). Even a few cafes and tango shows offer them. Costs are AR$20 to AR$50 in a group setting, and AR$200 AR$600 for a private session.

There are also several tango schools in town, such as Escuela Argentina de Tango (☎ 4312-4990; www.eatango.org). It has two locations: Map p84; Talcahuano 1052 and Map p62; San Martín 768 (the latter in Galerías Pacíficos).

Private teachers are also ubiquitous; there are so many good ones that it's best to ask someone you trust for a recommendation. And with so many foreigners flooding into Buenos Aires, many teach in English or other languages. Also see boxed text 'More Tango Information', p167.

FLAMENCO

With so many porteños boasting Spanish ancestry, its not surprising that there are a few flamenco venues in town. Most are located in Congreso's Spanish neighborhood, near the intersection of Salta and Av de Mayo.

ÁVILA BAR Map p72

☎ 4383-6974; Av de Mayo 1384; 🕑 Thu-Sat

Offering flamenco for many years now is this cozy little Spanish restaurant with good traditional food. Main dishes can include rabbit, paella and seafood stews. Shows have older, experienced dancers and cost AR$100 (drinks not included). They start around 10:30pm and reservations are a must.

CANTARES Map p72

☎ 4381-6965; www.cantarestablao.com.ar; Av Rivadavia 1180; 🕑 Thu-Sat

This flamenco venue, in the old Taberna Español, once hosted the Spanish poet Federico García Lorca. It's a small basement space with only 85 seats, providing a wonderfully intimate space for the highly authentic dances (AR$45 for just the show; AR$110 including food but not drinks). Flamenco classes available upstairs. Reserve in advance.

TIEMPO DE GITANOS Map p92

☎ 4776-6143; www.tiempodegitanos.com.ar; El Salvador 5575; 🕑 Wed-Sun

This venue in Palermo Hollywood offers good flamenco shows in an intimate restaurant setting. Classic Spanish foods like paella and tapas are offered. Dinner shows cost AR$90 to AR$140, depending on the night; drinks are extra. Reserve in advance.

OTHER DANCE STYLES

Buenos Aires has a few other dances to keep your toes twirling. Centro Cultural Ricardo Rojas (p225) has an especially wide selection of dance classes.

For salsa classes, try Latin clubs such as Azúcar (p157) and La Salsera (p158) – best of all, you can practice your moves later when the club doors open. La Viruta (p169) also has salsa classes, as does Dance & Move (Map p92; ☎ 4554-8991; www.dancemove.com.ar; Jorge Newberry 3663). For a more complete list see www.salsapower.com/cities/argentina.htm.

The best place to check out some Brazilian samba beats is Escuela Brasileña de Danzas (Map p92; ☎ 4963-6066; www.balaio.com.ar; Mansilla 2787), which also has capoeira classes. Learn flamenco at Cantares (p169).

For contemporary dance there's the alternative theater El Camarín de las Musas (Map p98; ☎ 4862-0655; www.elcamarindelasmusas.com.ar; Mario Bravo 960); Dance & Move (see above) also has interesting choices. Nearly all cultural centers (p225) also offer this art form.

THEATER

Traditionally, the center for theater has been Av Corrientes between Av 9 de Julio and Callao, but there are now dozens of venues all over the city. During the peak winter season, upwards of a hundred different events may take place, though you can find a good variety of shows any time during the year. The *Buenos Aires Herald* and other local newspapers are a good source for listings of major theater productions.

Many alternative (or 'off-Corrientes') theater companies and independent troupes receive relatively little attention from the mainstream media, but they're worth seeking out if you're looking for something different. See the boxed text for a list of these organizations. And if you read Spanish, www.alernativateatral.com is a good source for current nonmainstream performances.

Theater tickets are generally affordable, but check *carteleras* (discount-ticket offices; p164) for bargain seats. For more on the BA theater scene, see the Background chapter (p24).

TEATRO DE LA RIBERA Map p80

☎ 0800-333-5254; www.complejoteatral.gov.ar; Av Don Pedro de Mendoza 1821

This small, colorful theater, funded by famous Argentine painter Benito Quinquela

AVANT-GARDE THEATER

Get off the beaten play path and go for something out of the ordinary – there's plenty of choice in this creative city for unique and worthwhile theater. Most of these venues are located in BA's Abasto neighborhood.

Actors Studio Teatro (Map p98; ☎ 4983-9883; www.actors-studio.org; Díaz Vélez 3842) Offers new interpretations of old classics, along with cutting-edge productions in its 120-seat theater. Also has occasional acting classes.

Celcit (Map p62; ☎ 4342-1026; www.celcit.org.ar; Moreno 431) Standing for Centro Latinoamericano de Creación e Investigación Teatral, this venue features independent Latin American productions and offers plenty of workshops and classes.

Cuidad Cultural Konex (Map p98; ☎ 4864-3200; www.ciudadculturalkonex.org; Sarmiento 3131) This intrepid venue offers multidisciplinary performances that often fuse art, culture and technology. It's famous for its exhilarating Monday-night percussion shows (see p36).

El Camarín de las Musas (Map p98; ☎ 4862-0655; www.elcamarindelasmusas.com.ar; Mario Bravo 960) Offers contemporary dance, plays and theater. There are also workshops and classes available, and a trendy restaurant-cafe provides affordable snacks.

El Cubo (Map p98; ☎ 4963-2568; www.cuboabasto.com.ar; Pasaje Zelaya 3053) A hip, small Abasto space, it hosts gutsy theater pieces and offbeat performances such as queer musicals.

Espacio Callejón (Map p98; ☎ 4862-1167; www.espaciocallejon.blogspot.com; Humahuaca 3759) A small independent venue that showcases edgy new theater, music and dance, and offers a few classes (including 'clown' acting).

Teatro la Carbonera (Map p76; ☎ 4362-2651; Balcarce 998) Holds about a hundred people and presents mostly experimental theater, but also dabbles in musicals along with contemporary and theatrical dance.

LUNA PARK

If unique large-scale spectacles such as the Beijing Circus, the New York Ballet, the Philadelphia Philharmonic, Julio Iglesias or Tom Jones come to town, the dressing rooms of **Luna Park** (Map p62; ☎ 5279-5279; www.lunapark.com.ar; Av Madero 420) are probably their destination. Bordered by the thoroughfares of Lavalle, Bouchard, Av Corrientes and Madero, Luna Park was originally a boxing stadium built on the old grounds of the Pacific Railway. Finished in 1931, the venue gradually became the mecca of choice for public events needing large spaces. When Carlos Gardel died in a plane crash in 1935, his wake was held here for the thousands of grieving fans. In 1944, a relatively unknown actress named Eva Duarte first met general Juan Perón here during a benefit for the victims of an earthquake in San Juan province. And on November 7, 1989, no less than Diego Maradona was married here before 11,000 fans.

But Luna Park never forgot its roots; throughout its history 25 boxing titles have been decided within its walls. Many other sports, including volleyball, basketball and tennis, are also occasionally highlighted at this stadium, and productions such as fashion shows, ice-skating spectacles and mass religious baptisms have found their way here as well. With a capacity of 15,000 (Argentina's largest enclosed stadium), Luna Park can easily handle these crowds, which also come to see recent big-time performers such as Liza Minnelli, Luciano Pavarotti, Norah Jones, Ricky Martin, David Byrne and Chrissie Hynde.

Martín, was built in 1971 and holds nearly 650 seats. Check out the upright piano in the lobby; it was painted by Martín.

TEATRO DEL PUEBLO Map p62

☎ 4326-3606; www.teatrodelpueblo.org.ar; Diagonal Roque Saénz Peña 943

A smaller venue with two halls in the basement, this theater – one of the first independent theaters in Argentina – shows both classic and contemporary productions at affordable prices (about AR$50).

TEATRO SAN MARTÍN Map p72

☎ 0800-333-5254; www.teatrosanmartin.com.ar; Av Corrientes 1530

This major venue has several auditoriums (the largest seats over a thousand) and showcases international cinema, theater, dance and classical music, covering both conventional and more unusual events. It also has art galleries and often hosts impressive photography exhibitions.

TEATRO GRAN REX Map p62

☎ 4322-8000; Av Corrientes 857

A huge theater seating 3300, this place hosts myriad national and international musical productions, from Cyndi Lauper to Kenny G to Björk.

TEATRO PASEO LA PLAZA Map p72

☎ 6320-5350; www.paseolaplaza.com.ar; Av Corrientes 1660

Located in a small and pleasant outdoor shopping mall, this complex features several theater halls that run both classic and contemporary productions, including tango, theater and comedy.

TEATRO OPERA Map p62

☎ 4326-1335; Av Corrientes 860

This classic theater, which boasts an art-deco exterior, offers nearly 2000 seats and has performances that range from piano recitals to rock concerts to tango and ballet. It served many years as a movie cinema, later becoming a live theater venue.

TEATRO PRESIDENTE ALVEAR Map p72

☎ 4343-4245; www.complejoteatral.gov.ar; Av Corrientes 1659

Inaugurated in 1942 and named after an Argentine president whose wife sang opera, this theater holds over 700 and shows many musical productions, including ballet. Occasional free shows are on offer.

CLASSICAL MUSIC

Several venues in BA offer classical music concerts. To catch the local band, look up the Orquesta Filarmónica de Buenos Aires (www.ofba.org.ar), which plays at the Teatro Colón and often features guest conductors from throughout Latin America.

Teatro Colón (p71) is one of Buenos Aires' top entertainment venues; everyone who's anyone has played, acted, sung or danced here. The classical-music scene takes a break from December to February, and is best from June to August.

LA SCALA DE SAN TELMO Map p76

☎ 4362-1187; www.lascala.org.ar; Pasaje Guiffra 371

This small San Telmo venue, located in a refurbished colonial building, puts on classical and contemporary concerts that highlight piano, tango, musical comedies and other musical-related shows and workshops. Affordable or free admission.

TEATRO AVENIDA Map p72

☎ 4381-0662; www.balirica.org.ar; Av de Mayo 1222

In 1979 a fire closed down this beautiful 1906 theater for 15 years, but it was later restored to its former glory. Today the Avenida highlights Argentine productions, mostly classical music, ballet and flamenco. But its biggest strength is opera.

TEATRO COLISEO Map p84

☎ 4816-3789; www.fundacioncoliseo.com.ar; MT de Alvear 1125

Classical music, jazz, ballet, opera and symphony orchestras entertain at this theater most of the year, but a few surprises – such as Argentine-American rock star Kevin Johansen – occasionally show up.

CINEMA

Buenos Aires is full of cinemas, whether they be neon classics or slick modern multiplexes. The traditional cinema districts are along pedestrian Lavalle (west of Florida) and on Av Corrientes – both walking distance from downtown. Newer cinemas, however, aren't necessarily located in any one particular area – many are in shopping malls spread throughout the city. Not surprisingly, most newer places show international blockbusters, while quirkier underground flicks have to seek out less conventional venues.

Ticket prices are reasonable and most cinemas offer big discounts for matinees, midweek shows or first screenings of the day. There is usually a *trasnoche* (midnight or later showing) scheduled for Friday and Saturday night.

Check the *Buenos Aires Herald* (an English-language newspaper) for the original titles of English-language films. The entertainment sections of all the major newspapers will have movie listings as well, but be aware that Spanish translations of English-language film titles often don't translate directly. Except for children's films and cartoon features, which are dubbed, foreign films almost always appear in their original language with Spanish subtitles.

Cosmos-UBA (Map p72; ☎ 4953-5405; www.cosmosuba.wordpress.com; Av Corrientes 2046) and Sala Leopoldo Lugones (Map p72; ☎ 0800-333-5254; www.teatrosanmartin.com.ar/cine; Av Corrientes 1530) – in Teatro General San Martín – often show retrospectives, documentaries, foreign film cycles and art-house movies. Espacio INCAA (Map p72; ☎ 4371-3050; www.incaa.gov.ar; Av Rivadavia 1635) screens Ibero-American films only (essentially from Spanish- or Portuguese-speaking countries).

Some cultural centers (p225) have their own small cinemas, while places such as Alianza Francesa (p225) and British Arts Centre (p225) showcase movies in their respective languages.

See p41 for more about the Argentine film industry.

MEGA-MOVIE THEATERS

If you're looking for something a little bit more mainstream, the following multiplexes show blockbuster-style productions:

Atlas Cinemas (Map p62; ☎ 5032-8527; www.atlascines.com.ar; Lavalle 869)

Atlas Cines Patio Bullrich (Map p84; ☎ 5032-8527; www.atlascines.com.ar; Av del Libertador 750) In Patio Bullrich.

Cine Lorca 1 & 2 (Map p72; ☎ 4371-5017; Av Corrientes 1428)

Cinemark Puerto Madero (Map p69; ☎ 0800-222-2463; www.cinemark.com.ar; Av Alicía Moreau de Justo 1920)

Hoyts Abasto (Map p98; ☎ 4000-2923; www.hoyts.com.ar; Av Corrientes 3247) In the Mercado de Abasto.

Recoleta Mall (Map p87; cnr Junín & López) Check out this renovated mall next to Recoleta Cemetery – it will, hopefully, open in 2011.

SPORTS & ACTIVITIES

top picks

- **Attending a fútbol game** (p174)
- **Cycling in the Reserva Ecológica Costanera Sur** (p177)
- **Watching the world's best polo** (p176)
- **Splashing around at Parque Norte** (p177)
- **Being scrubbed at a day spa** (p179)

SPORTS & ACTIVITIES

When it comes to sports, only one thing really matters to most porteños – *fútbol* (aka soccer). Everyone has a team that they are loyal to until they die: if you go to a game, you'll witness passion to the human core. *Fútbol* here is so much more than the infamous reputation of its most notorious figure, Diego Maradona, who now spends most of his time avoiding drug scandals (see the boxed text).

Surprisingly enough, other spectator sports – and other sports stars – do exist in Buenos Aires. Basketball has gotten more popular since Argentina won Olympic gold at the 2004 summer games. Rugby attracted lots of attention in 2007, when the country placed a very respectable third in the Rugby World Cup. Horse racing attracts gamblers to Palermo's Hipódromo (racetrack), while polo and even *pato* (a kind of rugby on horseback) have their own modest followings.

Most porteños make an effort to look good, so many also participate in a variety of sports to help them along. Running, tennis and *fútbol* are all popular activities in Buenos Aires, both for health and fun. And when the weather is inclement, many turn to the city's numerous indoor health clubs. Other, less traditional indoor physical activities, such as yoga and Pilates, have become more mainstream.

SPECTATOR SPORTS

From *fútbol* and rugby to basketball and polo, watching sports is a great way for porteños to band together against rival teams and the world. Other than the sports mentioned here, boxing, tennis, field hockey, cricket and auto-racing (the Dakar Rally has been taking place in Argentina and Chile in recent years) also have their fans in BA.

SOCCER

Fútbol is a national obsession, and witnessing a live game is an integral part of the Buenos Aires experience. This is no amateur league – Argentina's national team won the World Cup in both 1978 and 1986 (one of only eight nations to have ever won the cup). The men's team also walked away with gold at the 2004 and 2008 summer Olympics. And Lionel Messi, currently Argentina's most famous *fútbol* player, won FIFA's World Player of the Year award in 2009.

Argentines are avid fans of the sport, and on game day (and there are many) you'll see TVs everywhere tuned to the soccer channels. Cheers erupt when goals are scored, and after a big win, cars sporting team flags go honking by – especially around the Obelisco.

Tickets for *entradas populares* (bleachers) cost around AR$50, while *plateas* (fixed seats) range from AR$70 to AR$120. Prices depend on the popularity of the game – the *súper clásico* between River and Boca commands rates many times that of normal and are hard to get without a special contact or connection. (By the way, this particular game – played at Boca's stadium – has been named by the *Observer* as the number-one sporting event to attend before you kick the bucket.)

As a foreigner (especially a lone woman), you'd do well to buy a seat in the *plateas;* the *populares* section is a real experience, but can get far too rowdy with its ceaseless standing, singing, drinking, jumping, pot smoking, robbing and fighting. It's also where the *barra brava* (the Argentine equivalent of football hooligans) sit.

Tickets are available at stadium box offices in the days before a game, or try www.ticketek.com.ar, which sells tickets to certain games. Scalping is also a possibility, and the most popular games sell out early. Some companies provide ticket, transportation and guide, such as Tangol (☎ 4312-7276; www.tangol.com). Expect to pay AR$360 to AR$600 for this service, much more for the *súper clásico*.

Games are nearly always safe, but don't carry anything to one that makes you stand out as a tourist. Keep cameras hidden, avoid wearing jewelry (even watches) and don't carry more money than you'll need that day. If it's sunny, take sun protection. Avoid wearing the visiting team's colors, and don't plan on eating there unless you like really bad junk food.

For more information on Argentine *fútbol*, see www.futbolargentino.com and www.afa.org.ar. Or check Daniel Schweimler's musings (via the team Argentina Juniors) at www.handofdan.com.

DIEGO MARADONA *Andy Symington*

Born in 1960 in abject poverty in a Buenos Aires shantytown, Maradona played his first professional game for Argentinos Juniors before his 16th birthday. Transferring to his beloved Boca Juniors, he continued to prosper. After a good showing at the 1982 World Cup, he moved to Europe to play for clubs in Barcelona and then Naples.

Here, his genius inspired unfashionable Napoli to two league titles, and in 1986 he single-handedly won the World Cup for a very average Argentina side. In the quarter-final against England, he scored a goal first with his hand – later saying the goal was scored partly by the hand of God – and then a second one with his feet, after a mesmerizing run through the flummoxed English defense that led to its being named the Goal of the Century by FIFA.

But the big time also ruined Diego. Earning huge sums of money, Maradona became addicted to cocaine and the high life. As his body began to feel the strain over the years, a succession of drug-related bans, lawsuits and weight issues meant that by his retirement in 1997 he had been a shadow of his former self for some years.

Since retiring, he has rarely been out of the news. Overdoses, heart attacks, detox, his own TV program and offbeat friendships – all par for the course in the Maradona circus. Then – unbelievably – someone in the Argentine Football Federation thought he'd be a suitable choice to manage the national team. Argentina just managed to qualify for the 2010 World Cup in South Africa (a triumphant Maradona was banned for a period after he suggested his critics could pleasure him orally), where they produced a couple of impressive performances before being tactically out-thought by Germany. Maradona's contract wasn't renewed, but he didn't go quietly – and Argentina awaits the next chapter in their torrid romance with him. But all the controversy and media moments are still substantially outweighed by those numerous touches of magic in the number 10 shirt that have sealed his immortality. To many Argentines, the hand of God and the hand of Maradona are one and the same.

The following are some of the clubs based in Buenos Aires:

Estadio Argentinos Juniors (Map p58; ☎ 4551-6887; www.argentinosjuniors.com.ar; Gavilán 2151)

Boca Juniors (Map p80; ☎ 4309-4700; www.boca-juniors.com.ar; La Bombonera, Brandsen 805)

Club Atlético Vélez Sársfield (Map p58; ☎ 4641-5663; www.velezsarsfield.com.ar; Juan B Justo 9200)

Club Deportivo Español (off Map p58; ☎ 4619-1516; www.cde.com.ar; Santiago de Compostela 3801)

Club Ferro Carril Oeste (Map p98; ☎ 4431-8282; www.ferrocarriloeste.org.ar; Avellaneda 1240)

Club Huracán (Map p58; ☎ 4911-0757; www.clubahuracan.com.ar; Av Amancio Alcorta 2544)

River Plate (Map p101; ☎ 4789-1200; www.cariverplate.com.ar; Av Figueroa Alcorta 7597)

San Lorenzo de Almagro (Map p58; ☎ 4918-8192; www.clubsanlorenzo.com.ar; Varela 2680)

BASKETBALL

The basketball scene in Buenos Aires has been picking up significantly since 2002, when Argentina's men's team played in the World Basketball Championship in Indianapolis. They only won silver, but made history by beating the US 'Dream Team' in international competition. Then, with a similar roster, they defeated the US squad again (along with Italy in the finals) to win gold in the 2004 summer Olympics – their first Olympic medal in basketball ever. No team had beaten the Americans in the Olympics since 1992, when pro basketball players were allowed to play. Argentina's best players are Emanuel 'Manu' Ginobili, Fabricio Oberto, Andrés Nocioni, Luis Scola and Carlos Delfino, all of whom have played for or currently play in the NBA.

Today BA has several major squads, the most popular being Boca Juniors. You can watch them play in La Boca at **Estadio Luis Conde** (La Bombonerita; Map p80; ☎ 4309-4748; www.bocajuniors.com.ar; Arzobispo Espinosa 600). Other popular basketball teams include Obras Sanitarias and Ferro Carril Oeste.

RUGBY

Rugby is getting more popular by the year in Argentina, in part because the country's national team – Los Pumas – has done well in past years. After placing third at the Rugby World Cup in 2007 (no mean feat), Los Pumas was rated the best rugby team in the Americas. However, they've never defeated the top two teams in the world, South Africa and New Zealand, keeping them just short of world-class status.

In Buenos Aires, the long-running **Club Atlético de San Isidro** (www.casi.org.ar) is the capital's best rugby team; in 1935 it gave birth to its own biggest rival, the **San Isidro Club** (www.sanisidroclub.com.ar).

Rugby season runs from April to October; contact the Unión de Rugby de Buenos Aires (☎ 4805-5858; www.urba.org.ar) for current happenings. Fanatics can visit the Museo de Rugby (☎ 4732-2547; www.museodelrugby.com; Juan Bautista de Lasalle 653) in San Isidro.

HORSE RACING

Races in BA are held at the Hipódromo Argentino (Map p92; ☎ 4778-2800; www.palermo.com.ar; Av del Libertador 4101), a grand building designed by French architect Fauré Dujarric that dates from 1908 and holds up to 100,000 spectators. The track is usually open Monday and weekends, but race times vary so check the schedule for exact times. The most important races take place in November, both here and at San Isidro's famous grass racetrack.

POLO

Add Argentina's history of gauchos and horses to its past British influence, and you'll understand why the best polo in the world is played right here. The country has dominated the sport for over 50 years, boasting most of polo's top players. Forget those British princes: the world's best player is considered to be the handsome Adolfo Cambiaso.

Matches take place in Buenos Aires from September to mid-November, culminating in the annual Campeonato Argentino Abierto de Polo (Argentine Open Polo Championship; p23), the world's most prestigious polo tournament. For current information, contact the Asociación Argentina de Polo (☎ 4777-6444; www.aapolo.com), which keeps a schedule of polo-related activities throughout the country.

PATO

Of gaucho origins, the polo-like game of *pato* (literally 'duck') takes its name from the original game-ball – a live duck encased in a leather bag. The unfortunate fowl has since been replaced by a ball with leather handles, and players no longer face serious injury in what was once a very violent sport.

For information on *pato* matches and tournaments (which usually take place 30km outside the city in the Campo Argentino de Pato) contact the Federación Argentina de Pato (☎ 4372-0180; www.pato.org.ar). The national championships (p23) occur in December, and are more centrally located in Palermo's polo grounds.

For polo camps (all outside BA) where you can learn to play yourself, check out www.poloelite.com, www.argentinapoloday.com.ar and www.lasofiapolo.info.

CAMPO ARGENTINO DE POLO

Map p92

cnr Av del Libertador & Av Dorrego

Just across from the Hipódromo Argentino in Palermo, this stadium holds up to 30,000 spectators and hosts polo's most important events (including the Argentine Open Polo Championship in November and December). Occasional music concerts are also held here. However, the northern suburb of Pilar has the highest density of polo clubs.

ACTIVITIES

Buenos Aires is a big concrete city, so you'll have to seek out the outdoor spots in which to work out. Extensive greenery in Palermo provides good areas for recreation, especially on weekends when the ring road around the rose garden is closed to motor vehicles. Recoleta also has grassy parks, but try to avoid the dog piles. Best of all is the Reserva Ecológica Costanera Sur (p70), an ecological paradise just east of Puerto Madero that might just make you forget you're in a big city; it's excellent for walks, runs, leisurely bike rides and even a bit of wildlife viewing.

An interesting sports complex for those seeking outdoor activities is **Perú Beach** (☎ 4793-5986; www.peru-beach.com.ar; Elcano 794; 8am-midnight). Short soccer fields, a covered roller rink, a freestanding climbing wall and water sports such as kite-surfing all bring in the crowds. In addition there's also a grassy lawn and outdoor tables for refreshments – great on a sunny day. It's more of a social scene than anything else, and families are welcome. Perú Beach is located in Acassuso, a suburb way north of Buenos Aires' center, just across from the Tren de la Costa's Barrancas station.

CYCLING

The city's new bike lanes are making cycling in the center a safer proposition, but there are better places in which to spin your wheels. Bike paths run along many roads in Parque 3 de Febrero (p92) – here, bicycle rentals are available in good weather on weekends, when the ring road is closed to motor vehicles. Look

DON'T JUST WATCH – PLAY FÚTBOL!

Inspired by watching professional *fútbol* teams play the game? Well, you can partake yourself – just contact Buenos Aires Fútbol Amigos (www.fcbafa.com) to join fellow travelers, expats and locals for some pick-up fun on the pitch. There's a modest charge for the experience, but *asados* (barbecues) often lie at the end of the *fútbol* rainbow – and the sporty memories can be priceless.

for rental companies along Av de la Infanta Isabel; four-wheeled pedal carts and in-line skates can also be rented.

For safe family cycling, head to Nuevo Circuito KDT in Palermo's Parque General Belgrano (Map p92; ☎ 4807-7700; Salguero 3450; entry AR$3). Here, Sprint Haupt (Map p92; ☎ 4804-2870; Salguero 3450; bike rental per hr AR$15-30; 9am-8:30pm Tue & Thu, to 7pm Wed, Fri, Sat & Sun) rents bicycles for use around a plain, 1250m-long concrete bike path (bring your passport). Helmets available. Look for the overpass parking lot, then go past the pedestrian bridge.

The Reserva Ecológica Costanera Sur (p70), on the eastern side of Puerto Madero along the coast, is green and tranquil and has some flat dirt roads that are great to bike on. Cheap bicycle rentals are available in good weather on weekends, just outside either entrance.

For information on cycling tours, see p229. And to read about BA's Critical Mass phenomenon, see p47.

GOLF

BA's most convenient course is the 18-hole **Campo Municipal de Golf** (Map p101; ☎ 4772-7261; Tornquist 6397; sunrise-sunset Tue-Sun); be sure to reserve your spot in advance. Practice your long shots at the **Costa Salguero Driving Range** (Map p92; ☎ 4805-4732; www.costasalguerogolf.com.ar; Avs Costanera R Obligado & Salguero), which also has a golf store, a cafe and a nine-hole, family-friendly course.

SWIMMING

Some upscale hotels have decent-sized pools, but they charge hefty prices for nonguests. The fee generally includes gym use, at least. Try the Panamericano Hotel & Resort (p182; day rate AR$250) or the Claridge Hotel (p182; day rate AR$210).

A more economical option is to find a health club with an indoor pool (see p178).

PARQUE NORTE Map p101

☎ 4787-1382; www.parquenorte.com; cnr Avs Cantilo & Guiraldes; admission Mon-Fri AR$35, Sat & Sun AR$50; 9am-10pm Mon-Fri, 8am-10pm Sat & Sun

Great for families is this large water park with huge shallow pools (perhaps 4 ft at their deepest), plus a large water slide and lots of umbrellas and lounge chairs (both cost extra). There are plenty of grassy areas in which to enjoy a picnic or *mate* (tea). Bring your own towels, and make sure you're clean – quick 'health' inspections are done to check for such unpleasantries as athlete's foot or lice.

TENNIS

Several places in BA offer courts, but not racquet rental. Bring your own from home if you're serious about getting in touch with the Nalbandian or del Potro inside you.

PARQUE GENERAL BELGRANO Map p92

☎ 4807-7879; Salguero 3450; entry AR$3, court hire per hr AR$20-25; 8am-9:30pm Mon-Fri, to 8pm Sat & Sun

Has eight clay courts. Floodlights at night cost AR$5 extra. You'll need your own equipment; call 48 hours in advance to reserve.

SALGUERO TENIS Map p92

☎ 4805-5144; Salguero 3350; per hr AR$75-87; 8am-midnight Mon-Fri, to 9pm Sat & Sun

Interestingly located between railroad tracks, with five clay courts. Sells balls; squash courts and tennis lessons are also available.

REAL HORSEBACK RIDING

If you want to get out of town for a few hours and hop on a horse, forget those touristy *estancias* (ranches) and check out Caballos a la Par (☎ 15-5248-3592, 4384-7013; www.caballos-alapar.com). Guided, private rides are given in a provincial park about an hour's drive from central Buenos Aires, and it's not just one of those 'follow-the-horse-in-front' deals. Adrian will take you around woodsy lanes and fields, and you'll have fun learning how to ride and even gallop on his fine horses.

HEALTH & FITNESS

BA has a good range of indoor gyms, many complete with modern equipment and pluses like indoor pools and spas. The yoga and Pilates movements have also become increasingly popular, with most gyms and even some cultural centers and health restaurants offering classes. Spa services are good, especially at international hotels that cater especially to foreigners. For dance classes, see p170.

Need more motivation to move? Then check out Boot Camp Buenos Aires (www.bootcampbuenosaires.com); if you thought group training sessions, then you're right.

GYMS

If you've never been to a gym in BA, on the first day you might be asked for a medical form from your doctor (so it's best to bring one just in case).

LE PARC Map p62

☎ 4311-9191; www.leparc.com; San Martín 645; day rate AR$60; 🕒 7am-11pm Mon-Fri, 10am-8pm Sat

Good, modern machines are centered around an open floor plan connected by catwalks and topped with a glass ceiling at this gym. There's a small indoor pool, a trendy cafe, a sports shop and a sauna; many classes are available. The sunny terrace is perfect for showing off your chiseled body.

MEGATLON Map p62

☎ 4322-7884; www.megatlon.com; Reconquista 335; day/week/month rates from AR$98/180/330; 🕒 6:30am-10pm Mon-Fri, 9am-5pm Sat

The king of BA's gyms has around 25 branches throughout the city, including another one in Barrio Norte (Map p87; Rodriguez Peña 1062); the Reconquista branch is conveniently located right in the center. Expect most or all gym services, including weights, aerobic machines, a sports and supplements shop, and a wide variety of classes. Some branches have an indoor pool and athletic courts for basketball, volleyball, handball and soccer; exact prices and hours vary by location.

SPORT CLUB Map p72

☎ 5199-1212; www.sportclub.com.ar; Bartolomé Mitre 1625; day rate AR$50; 🕒 7am-11pm Mon-Fri, 8am-7pm Sat

Great for muscle-popping weights and modern aerobic machines; exercising areas are spacious, and the rooftop sundeck is perfect for working on your tan. There are plenty of classes, including cycling workouts, an indoor lap pool and a café. Sport Club has around 20 locations in BA; some also have volleyball, basketball and soccer facilities.

YMCA Map p62

☎ 4311-4785; www.ymca.org.ar; Reconquista 439; day rate AR$50; 🕒 8am-9pm Mon-Fri, 10am-1:30pm Sat

Not very fancy, but not too expensive, either – and if you're a YMCA member from abroad just bring your card for a free month's membership. Expect typical weight and aerobic machines, plenty of classes and two pools (including one for the kiddies). Other services include massage and a sauna.

YOGA & PILATES

Nearly all gyms offer yoga and Pilates classes, but there are several specialty centers for each of these as well. Many cultural

YOGA IN THE PARK?

And now for something completely different – Eco Yoga Park (☎ 4901-0744; 15-6507-0577; www.ecoyogapark.com), located about 1½ hours west of Buenos Aires, near Lújan.

Run by friendly Hare Krishnas, this pretty countryside retreat comes complete with grassy lawns, eco-built cabañas, organic vegetable garden, yoga studio, art shop and meditation hall shaped like a giant beehive. The tiny restaurant serves vegetarian meals, much of it from the garden, and easy yoga classes are offered daily. Accommodations are all in rustic but comfortable hostel-type bunks. Other than doing perhaps some volunteer work and taking part in the yoga and meditation activities, there's not much to do except relax.

All religious denominations are welcome to stay the night (AR$130 including meals; AR$60 if you do volunteer work four hours per day). There are just a few rules: no alcoholic drinks, drugs, smoking or meat-eating allowed on premises. A small price to pay for some peace and quiet.

SOLVE THOSE HAIR PROBLEMS – IN ENGLISH

More comfortable with an English-speaking expat when describing exactly how to wax your privates? Then check out Fancy Fingers and Lady Gardens (www.ladygardens.net), run by a UK-born Aussie woman who also does mani- and pedicures.

And if you want to describe your haircut in English terms, head to BA Hairdresser (www.gatanegro1.wordpress.com), where Irishwoman Terri Or can style your locks without mistaking 'give me a mini-cut' for 'give me a mohawk'.

centers (p225) have affordable yoga, as do some health-oriented restaurants like Natural Deli (see p138) – sometimes with tai chi and meditation, too.

If your Spanish is limited, try Buena Onda Yoga (☎ 15-5423-7103; www.buenaondyoga.com) or Happy Sun Yoga (☎ 15-5179-1871; www.happysunyoga.com), both taught by English-speaking expat women.

CENTRO VALLETIERRA Map p92

☎ 4833-6724; www.valletierra.com; Costa Rica 4562

This slick Palermo Viejo studio offers a variety of yoga classes, including Hatha, Kundalini and Ashtanga; some instructors speak English. There are also meditation classes, and seven kinds of massage (AR$160 per hr) are offered, reserve ahead. Facilities are beautiful and Zen-like. Check the website for schedules.

TAMARA DI TELLA PILATES Map p87

☎ 4813-1216; www.tamaraditella.com; cnr Juncal & R Peña; per class AR$70, 4 classes AR$250

This well-known 'Pilates Queen' has over a dozen branches throughout Buenos Aires and other major cities in Argentina and even all around the world. Facilities are modern, and private instructors are also available. Ask about 'tango pilates' – it's kind of what you'd expect.

VIDA NATURAL Map p92

☎ 4826-1695; www.vidanatural.com.ar; Charcas 2852; 4 classes AR$150

This naturalistic center, located in a beautiful old house with wood floors, offers Ashtanga, Hatha and Iyengar yoga. Therapeutic massage, breathing classes, meditation, Pilates, tai chi and harmonizing Tibetan bowls are also available.

MARTIAL ARTS & CLIMBING

If you feel like climbing outdoors (but not on real rock – that's a bit far away), check out Perú Beach (p176). It has a wall, but it's geared more towards a family and social crowd than true climbers.

BOULDER Map p92

☎ 4779-2825; www.elboulder.com.ar; Arce 730; day rate AR$15, shoe & harness rental AR$5 each; 🕑 3-10pm Mon, Wed & Fri, 1-10pm Tue & Thu, 3-9pm Sat

Located in Palermo's Las Cañitas area, Boulder is a small climbing gym with a small bouldering cave. Classes are available, along with occasional field trips. A downstairs store sells new equipment and buys good used equipment.

KURATA DOJO Map p92

☎ 4774-4409; www.federacionaikikai.org.ar; JSM de Oro 2254; 1 class AR$25; 🕑 6-9pm Mon-Fri, noon-1pm Sat

This good Aikido school in Palermo Viejo was started by a Japanese *sensei* (teacher). You don't need any experience to start with, and people of any age can train in Aikido. Costs depend on how many classes you attend per week.

YMCA Map p62

☎ 4311-4785; www.ymca.org.ar; Reconquista 439

Those looking to karate their way through Buenos Aires can check out the YMCA. There are also classes in kickboxing and Muay Thai; costs and hours vary so call ahead.

DAY SPAS

There's nothing quite like pampering yourself at a spa after a hard day's sightseeing. Luckily enough, BA has a few good ones to choose from. Prices and services can vary widely, so ask beforehand.

Some of the best day spas in town are at fine hotels such as the Palacio Duhau – Park Hyatt (p190), Four Seasons Buenos Aires (p189), Panamericano, Claridge and Home Hotel (Map p92; ☎ 4778-1008; homebuenosaires.com).

SER SPA Map p92

☎ 4807-4688; www.aguaclubspa.com; Cerviño 3626; 🕒 7:30am-10:30pm Mon-Fri, 11am-9pm Sat

Services at this Palermo spa include several kinds of massage, reflexology sessions and skin treatments (including facials). Feeling itchy? Go for an exfoliating body scrub. Other services include yoga, Pilates, and a small gym; there's also a great rooftop area in which to relax.

ESPACIO OXIVITAL Map p92

☎ 4775-0010; www.espacioxivital.com.ar; Nicaragua 4959; 🕒 10am-8pm Mon-Sat

Beautiful spa with clean, relaxing spaces in which to enjoy your facial, skin peel or mani/pedicure. Types of massage include deep tissue, Shiatzu, 'bioenergetic' and stone. Also does pore extractions, and beauty treatments using ultrasonic and electrotherapy (don't be shocked, now). Humid and dry saunas, along with Jacuzzi.

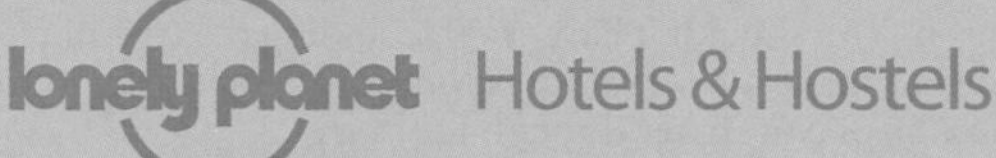

Want more sleeping recommendations than we could ever pack into this little ol' book? Craving more detail – including extended reviews and photographs? Want to read reviews by other travelers and be able to post your own? Just make your way over to **lonelyplanet.com/hotels** and check out our thorough list of independent reviews, then reserve your room simply and securely.

SLEEPING

top picks

- **Palacio Duhau – Park Hyatt** (p190)
- **Art Suites** (p192)
- **Casa Calma** (p190)
- **Magnolia Hotel** (p193)
- **Garden B&B** (p187)
- **Mine Hotel** (p193)
- **Cocker B&B** (p187)

SLEEPING

Buenos Aires' huge tourist boom, which began in 2002 after the Argentine peso plummeted, has seen the city's accommodation options increase exponentially to keep up with demand. There's a good range of international five-star hotels, such as Hilton, Park Hyatt and Four Seasons. Budget and midrange hotels are common, and many have upgraded their facilities. Boutique hotels and intimate guesthouses have mushroomed in neighborhoods like San Telmo and Palermo, and hostels are a dime a dozen. You shouldn't have trouble finding the type of place you're looking for, but it's a good idea to make a reservation beforehand – especially during any holidays or the busy summer months of November through February.

Many places will help you with transportation to and from the airport if you reserve ahead of time. The most expensive hotels will take credit cards, but cheaper places may not (or may levy a surcharge for them). Some kind of breakfast, whether it be continental or buffet, is included at most hotels, guesthouses and hostels; the same goes for internet access, wi-fi and air-con. It's always a good idea to ask beforehand if you need any amenity or service in particular.

Smoking is not generally allowed in any pubic hotel spaces, though some hotels have smoking rooms. Boutique hotels, guesthouses and hostels usually only allow smoking in their outside spaces.

The following accommodations are listed from most expensive to most affordable. For more information see p223.

THE CENTER

Buenos Aires' center, being right in the middle of things, has the most business-type accommodations in the city. Towards the north you'll be close to the popular pedestrian streets of Florida and Lavalle, as well as the neighborhoods of Retiro and Recoleta (and their upscale boutiques). The Plaza de Mayo area contains the bustling banking district and many historic buildings, and is within walking distance to San Telmo. During the day the whole area is very busy, but nights are much calmer as businesspeople flee the center after work. Don't expect creative cuisine in this area – for that you'll have to head to Palermo.

PANAMERICANO HOTEL & RESORT

Map p62 Hotel $$$

☎ 4348-5000; www.panamericano.travel; Carlos Pellegrini 551; d AR$1360; ; Línea C Carlos Pellegrini

Your finest moment at this five-star hotel will likely be looking down on Av 9 de Julio from the 23rd-floor solarium, fresh from a dip in the pool. The 360 good-sized rooms are elegant, boasting ultramodern touches like designer toilets, electric curtain openers and safe boxes large enough for laptops (including a plug for them, too). Also on the premises are the highly regarded restaurant Tomo I, golf-course simulators and an atmospheric smoking pub. Book online for big discounts.

562 NOGARÓ BUENOS AIRES

Map p62 Hotel $$$

☎ 4331-0091; www.562buenosaires.com; Av Julio Roca 562; d AR$905; ; Línea E Bolívar

Elegant and sophisticated designs and earth-tone colors make this four-star hotel a hip, upscale choice in the Plaza de Mayo area. The good-sized rooms aren't super luxurious but rather simple, elegant and atmospherically lit, featuring hardwood floors and contemporary flavor. There's no restaurant, but the lobby bar will at least keep you hydrated.

CLARIDGE HOTEL Map p62 Hotel $$$

☎ 4314-2020; www.claridge.com.ar; Tucumán 535; d AR$640; ; Línea B Florida

One of downtown BA's oldest and finest hotels, the Claridge also features a relatively grand entrance and lobby for the area,

BOOK YOUR STAY ONLINE

For more accommodation reviews by Lonely Planet authors, check out hotels.lonelyplanet.com/argentina You'll find independent reviews, as well as recommendations on the best places to stay. Best of all, you can book online.

PRICE GUIDE

Buenos Aires is still decent value compared to the USA or Europe. Inflation has increased steadily over the last few years, however, and will likely continue to do so. To avoid sticker shock, double check the rates in this guidebook before reserving.

Many of the prices we list – particularly for the four- or five-star hotels – are the rack or high-season rates for November through January. During holidays such as Easter or Christmas, prices can skyrocket; plan ahead if you want to avoid these times. Some places lower their rates during slow periods, while others don't. But whatever the season, you don't always have to pay the official posted rate.

Your best bet for getting a cheaper price is to book in advance. You can do this via most hotels' websites. Calling ahead and talking to a salesperson with the power to negotiate prices can also be fruitful, especially if you plan on staying more than a few days. Note that most hotels at higher echelons add a 21% room tax; if you don't want a surprise, ask if this tax is included in the prices you're quoted.

$$$	over AR$600 a night
$$	AR$275-600 a night
$	under AR$275 a night

where space is at a premium. Standard rooms, with their tiny baths, aren't as fancy as you'd think, so go for a suite (some with balcony and Jacuzzi) if you want something special. The spa and pool are the best part

HOTEL LAFAYETTE Map p62 Hotel $$

☎ 4393-9081; www.lafayettehotel.com.ar; Reconquista 546; d AR$550; ; Línea B Florida

Spacious, elegant rooms are on offer at this fine downtown hotel on the pedestrian street Florida. The bathrooms are small but efficient, while double-paned windows guarantee peace and quiet. Hotel amenities include a sauna and gym, a nice restaurant, and a fancy lobby with plant atrium, fireplace and sofas. Buffet breakfast; book ahead for the best rates.

GRAND KING HOTEL Map p62 Hotel $$

☎ 4393-4012; www.grandking.com.ar; Lavalle 560; d AR$520; ; Línea B Florida

As you enter the Grand King you'll notice the strange ramp system in the lobby (but it works well enough as a practical design element). Not only do you get a conveniently central and quiet location on pedestrian Lavalle, but you'll also be sleeping in beautifully contemporary rooms painted in muted colors and boasting flat-panel TVs (in the superiors, at least).

GRAN HOTEL ARGENTINO Map p62 Hotel $$

☎ 4334-4001; www.hotel-argentino.com.ar; Carlos Pellegrini 37; d AR$350; ; Línea C Av de Mayo

This modest, semi-art nouveau hotel, situated on busy Pellegrini, boasts very nice, modern and tasteful rooms. Get a suite on a higher floor, facing Av 9 de Julio, for good views and lots of light – it's also not as loud up there. There's a restaurant on the 7th floor. A decent deal for the central location.

HOTEL CARSSON Map p62 Hotel $$

☎ 4131-3800; www.hotelcarsson.com.ar; Viamonte 650; d AR$300-400; ; Línea C Lavalle

Walk down the long, stately hallway to the center of the block and this quiet, central hotel, which offers great value for its four-star services and location. Old-time, classic decor is the game here, from the elegant lobby to the simpler but very comfortable rooms – all with writing desks, and some with chandeliers. There's also a conference salon for business travelers.

HOTEL FACÓN GRANDE Map p62 Hotel $$

☎ 4312-6360; www.hotelfacongrande.com; Reconquista 645; s/d AR$300/340; ; Línea B Florida

For those seeking a touch of the country in Buenos Aires, there's this (slightly) gaucho-themed hotel. The lobby is decorated in rustic furniture and traditional textiles, and rooms are modern and comfortable. The location on pedestrian Reconquista is good and there's an intimate vibe that's rare in similar-sized hotels. Get a top-floor room for views out toward Puerto Madero. Overall, a good deal for the price.

GRAN HOTEL HISPANO Map p62 Hotel $

4345-2020; www.hhispano.com.ar; Av de Mayo 861; s/d AR$225/270; ; Línea A Piedras

The tiny stairway lobby here isn't an impressive start, but upstairs there's a sweet atrium area with covered patio. Rooms are carpeted and comfortable; those in front are the biggest, and those on the top floor command the most light. There's also a pleasant outside sun terrace. It's a popular, well-tended place in a central location, so be sure to reserve ahead. There's a 10% cash discount.

HOTEL AVENIDA Map p62 Hotel $

4331-4341; www.hotelav.com.ar; Av de Mayo 623; s/d AR$190/250; ; Línea A Peru

Just 34 plain but efficient rooms greet you at this friendly place. There's a pleasant breakfast area and the location is great, right near Plaza de Mayo. Get a back room for more peace and quiet; the front ones have nice balconies (except for the 4th floor) but are noisy.

CLAN HOUSE Map p62 Hostel $

4331-4448; www.bedandbreakfastclan.com.ar; Adolfo Alsina 917; dm AR$45, s/d AR$140/160; ; Línea C Moreno

More like a fancy guesthouse with dorm rooms, this interesting place offers a dozen comfy rooms, each with its own bathroom. They're all a bit different from each other, though most don't have windows and only a few overlook the terrace. Three have their own bathrooms across the hallway and cost a bit less. There's kitchen access, coffee and tea all day, and tasteful design touches like the scooter-mounted reception desk.

V & S HOSTEL CLUB Map p62 Hostel $

4322-0994; www.hostelclub.com; Viamonte 887; dm AR$52-84, d AR$264; ; Línea C Lavalle

Still one of the best in town, this attractive hostel is actually located in a pleasant older building. There's a large-screen TV in the cozy common space, which is a kitchen-dining and lobby area, perfect for easy socializing. Dorms are good-sized and each has its own bathroom. The hotel-quality doubles are exceptionally classy, and the whole place has a tasteful atmosphere and good security – as well as a great, central location.

HOTEL MAIPÚ Map p62 Hotel $

4322-5142; Maipú 735; s/d AR$110/130, without bathroom AR$90/110; Línea C Lavalle

Head on up the old marble staircase into the gloomy, tiled hallway. Your senses will tingle at the faded glory of this classic old building, once owned by the Anchorenas, a very wealthy and aristocratic Argentine family. Lovely original tiles and high ceilings add charm to these budget lodgings, while new mattresses, cable TV and a convenient location are other pluses. There's no breakfast, but it's an inexpensive and clean place.

PUERTO MADERO

There are hardly any hotels in Puerto Madero, a relatively new, upscale neighborhood that lies just east of the center. Buildings here are either old warehouses that have been converted into fancy restaurants, offices and lofts, or they're brand-new apartment high-rises.

Public transport doesn't reach Puerto Madero, but the nearest Subte line is three blocks away, and many buses run along Av Leandro N Alem/Paseo Colón.

FAENA HOTEL + UNIVERSE Map p69 Hotel $$$

4010-9000; www.faenahotelanduniverse.com; Martha Salotti 445; d AR$1880-3400;

Located in a renovated Puerto Madero storage mill, this Philippe Starke–designed boutique fantasy is more than just a place to stay. Traipse through the plush main hallway, lined with two top-notch restaurants, a sultry lounge, basement cabaret and – outside – a slick swimming pool. On arrival, guests are given a personal valet and cell phone (there's no reception counter), and taken to luxurious rooms that feature claw-foot beds, etched-mirror entertainment centers and glass-walled bathrooms. On the premises are also a Turkish bath and spa services. For an out-of-this-world experience, there's no topping the Faena.

CONGRESO & TRIBUNALES

The Congreso and Tribunales area contains many of the city's older theaters, cinemas and cultural centers. Lively Av Corrientes

top picks

SPECIALTY STAYS

- Best hotel restaurant (p182) Panamericano's Tomo I
- Best roof garden (p187) The Cocker B&B
- Best hotel pool (p182) Panamericano
- Best eco-consciousness (p190) and p195) Casa Calma and Eco Pampa Hostel
- Best courtyard (p190) Palacio Duhau – Park Hyatt
- Best tango guesthouse (p167) Caserón Porteño
- Best fantasy stay (p184) Faena Hotel + Universe

has many modest shops, services and bookstores, and was BA's original theater district. The Plaza de Congreso area is always moving, sometimes with mostly peaceful public demonstrations. Generally, this area is not quite as packed as in the Center and has a less business-and-touristy flavor, but still bustles day and night.

NOVOTEL HOTEL Map p72 Hotel $$

☎ 4370-9540; www.novotel.com; Av Corrientes 1334; d AR$580; ; Línea B Uruguay

Smack in the middle of Corrientes' entertainment district is this large, contemporary French chain hotel. Unsurprisingly so, it's tastefully designed, and the lobby area is a slick affair. Head out to the back and find paradise – a beautiful deck surrounding the pools – one for adults and one for the kiddies – and a living wall of vegetation (plus the bar) providing serenity. Upstairs, comfortable rooms have unique showers with glass on two opposite sides, plus a fun colored-light system (leave it to the French). This Novotel is family friendly, offering kid discounts, a playroom and Xbox rental.

LA CAYETANA Map p72 Hotel $$

☎ 4383-2230; www.lacayetanahotel.com.ar; México 1330; d AR$480-720; ; Línea E Independencia

Located south of Congreso in Montserrat, this is a beautiful 1850s guesthouse offering 11 simple, colorful rooms, all decorated differently with rustic yet upscale furniture. One of the bigger ones has a loft. They all surround three lovely outdoor patios, which are accented with original tiles and leafy plants – the last one has a grassy garden. Breakfast is also special, with goodies like fresh fruit, yogurt and eggs to order. It's a quiet little paradise in an up-and-coming neighborhood.

LOFT Y ARTE Map p72 Apartments $$

☎ 4115-1770; www.loftyarte.com.ar; Hipólito Yrigoyen 1194; d AR$320-500; ; Línea A Lima

If you want your own roomy spaces, good security and great service, you can't beat this fancy spot. The nearly two dozen contemporary and elegantly furnished apartments come with kitchenette, cute dining area and daily cleaning service; some have airy lofts. All are different and tastefully decorated. It's a great deal and they're popular, so reserve ahead (no walk-ins).

HOTEL LYON Map p72 Hotel Apartments $$

☎ 4372-0100; www.hotel-lyon.com.ar; Riobamba 251; d/q AR$330/450; ; Línea B Callao

If you're a traveling family or group, this place is for you. The two- and three-bedroom apartments available here are no-frills but very spacious, and all include entry halls, large bathrooms and separate dining areas with fridges (but unfortunately no kitchens). Up to five people can be accommodated in each apartment. Reserve ahead as this place fills up quickly.

HOTEL DE LOS DOS CONGRESOS Map p72 Hotel $$

☎ 4372-0466; www.hoteldoscongresos.com; Av Rivadavia 1777; s/d AR$300/330; ; Línea A Congreso

Within spitting distance of the Palacio del Congreso is this modern hotel with attractive midrange rooms. For something special, snag a suite (AR$400) – they come with views and Jacuzzi, and some have a spiral staircase to a loft. The lobby and tiled halls are nice, too, with a scratch here and there – but for the price and location, this place is a fairly good deal.

LIVIN' RESIDENCE Map p72 Apartments $$

☎ 5258-0300; www.livinresidence.com; Viamonte 1815; studios AR$300, 1-bedroom apt AR$370, 2-bedroom apt AR$520; ; Línea D Callao

One of the better deals in town, especially if you're traveling in a group, are these studio and one- or two-bedroom apartments.

All have that simple, contemporary feel, with tasteful furniture, flat TVs, small kitchens and balconies. There's a tiny rooftop terrace with Jacuzzi, *asado* (barbecue) and nearby gym room – with views. Breakfast costs extra. Security is good, and there are discounts available for stays of over a week. Reserve ahead.

HOTEL IBIS Map p72 Hotel $$

☎ 5300-5555; www.ibishotel.com; Hipólito Yrigoyen 1592; r AR$280; ; Línea A Saénz Peña

This modern hotel is popular, and it's no wonder; prices are low and the location is great, right on Plaza del Congreso. Rooms are small but neat and practical, and the shiny lobby connects with a comfy café/restaurant. Minuses include showers only (no bathtubs), but snag a room with a window to the front and you can soak in the views rather than the tub. Breakfast costs extra. There's another branch at Corrientes 1344.

LOS PATIOS DE MONTSERRAT

Map p72 Guesthouse $$

☎ 4361-3328; www.hotelpatios.com; Alsina 1144; r AR$220-300; ; Línea C Moreno

One of BA's hidden jewels is this beautiful and centrally located stay, run by a friendly American-Argentine couple. The remodeled building is now defined by large atrium-like covered patios, surrounded by very spacious, high-ceilinged rooms (four with private bath). The floors are wood and original tile, and there are artsy touches here and there. Decor everywhere is minimal, emphasizing the spaces. And on Saturday, tango classes are given in the huge salon, which doubles as the breakfast room. If you're looking for space to relax in after a busy day in BA, this is your spot.

HOTEL CHILE Map p72 Hotel $

☎ 4381-6363; www.hotelchilebsas.com.ar; Av de Mayo 1297; s/d AR$220/250; ; Línea A Lima

An oldie but still a goodie, this popular standby offers an art-nouveau facade outside and around 50 decent budget rooms inside. Corner rooms are largest and have the best balconies and views, but are noisy and have only fans. Inside rooms come with air-con and are darker and more peaceful. The hotel is well located on busy Av de Mayo; reserve ahead.

NUEVO HOTEL CALLAO Map p72 Hotel $

☎ 4374-3861; www.hotelcallao.com.ar; Av Callao 292; s/d AR$200/240; ; Línea B Callao

The rooms at this attractive hotel are spacious, comfortable and modern, and many have balconies looking out over busy Av Callao. Two are bigger and rounded, located in the cupola edge of the building – these cost AR$20 more but have more expansive views and make you feel special. Inside rooms are darker but still reasonably sized, and avoid the street noise.

HOTEL MARBELLA Map p72 Hotel $

☎ 4383-8566; www.hotelmarbella.com.ar; Av de Mayo 1261; s/d AR$180/230, apt AR$290; ; Línea A Lima

The rooms at this hotel are basic but clean – if you can stand a bit of traffic noise, try to secure one with a balcony. More spacious (and more expensive) rooms are available, and there's a good, modern bar-restaurant where breakfast is served. From here it's an easy tramp to either Plaza del Congreso or Plaza de Mayo. Pay in cash and save 10%.

HOTEL TURILUZ SA Map p72 Hotel $

☎ 4374-9112; Av Callao 164; s/d AR$150/200; ; Línea A Congreso

The singles are small with open showers that get everything wet, but rooms in general are basic and neat and come with tasteful decor. The security is good and the lobby sparkles; this is excellent value and a popular choice in Congreso, and probably the only hotel in this book without a website. Book ahead.

GRAN HOTEL ORIENTAL Map p72 Hotel $

☎ 4951-6427; ghoriental@hotmail.com; Bartolomé Mitre 1840; s/d AR$120/160; ; Línea A Congreso

Despite its name this hotel is not grand, but it is good – and an absolute deal. Downstairs rooms are a bit dark (get one upstairs) and showers in general are small, but the simple, high-ceilinged rooms are comfortable enough for non-fussy travelers – just don't expect many services. The tiled lobby and hallways are long and narrow, and there are a few old touches that add some personality.

HOSTEL ESTACION BUENOS AIRES

Map p72 Hostel $

☎ 4381-0734; www.hostelestacionbuenosaires.com; Solís 458; dm AR$48, s AR$148, d AR$140-168; ; Línea A Congreso

If you're looking for a cheap stay in Congreso, this hostel might fit the bill. It's located in an old *casa chorizo,* a house shaped like a 'sausage' – long and thin. All rooms are located along a long, tiled hallway, so bring earplugs as noises can travel easily down the way. The rooms themselves are nice and comfortable enough – decent dorms hold four to six beds and three of the four private rooms have their own bathroom. There's also a long rooftop area for *asados* and hanging out.

SAN TELMO

South of the center, San Telmo has some of the most traditional atmosphere in Buenos Aires. Buildings are more charming and historical, and less modern than in the center, and tend to be only a few stories high. Many restaurants and fancy boutiques have opened here in recent years, and there are some good bars, tango venues and other nightspots for entertainment. Most accommodation options here are hostels, guesthouses or boutique hotels.

If you're looking to house up to eight people for a week minimum, check out www.playinbuenosaires.com – and reserve well in advance.

GARDEN B&B Map p76 Guesthouse $$$

☎ 4300-3455; www.gardenbuenosaires.com; Piedras 1677; d AR$600-700; ; 29

One of BA's most beautiful stays is this B&B, run by an American woman. Four rooms and two suites fill a lovely old rambling house, lined with covered outdoor hallways and vegetation. Wood-floored rooms all have high ceilings and are decorated in a simple, tasteful style; all have private bathroom. Suites are larger, with a living area. There's a gorgeous back garden with raised metal pond. You can hang out with your fellows in the living room, and the full homemade breakfast is a treat. It's a little paradise that you'd never guess existed as you walk in from San Telmo's gritty outskirts.

AXEL HOTEL Map p76 Hotel $$$

☎ 4136-9393; www.axelhotels.com; Venezuela 649; r AR$560-640; ; Línea E Belgrano

BA's first four-star gay hotel is certainly a showpiece – the lobby boasts a multistory wall fountain and if you look up the central area you'll see right through the clear bottom of the top-floor swimming pool and towards the sky. Stairways are also glassy (watch that vertigo), and rooms are as contemporary as you can imagine, with acid-concrete floors and glass-wall bathrooms. There's a large, decked-out back garden with another (outdoor) pool, two bar-lounges, a restaurant, saunas, Jacuzzis and a gym. It's hetero-friendly to boot.

RIBERA SUR HOTEL

Map p76 Boutique Hotel $$

☎ 4361-7398; www.riberasurhotel.com.ar; Av Paseo Colón 1145; d AR$450-520; ; 64, 152

OK, so its location essentially sucks – Av Paseo Colón is an industrial avenue, a multi-lane byway constantly spewing roadside pollution and producing noise heard blocks away. And here is where this beautiful, serene boutique hotel calls home. What were they *thinking*? Perhaps it's that contrasting edginess that inspired the location scouts. Once ensconced inside, you'd never know that snarling jungle of craziness lies outside the elegant entrance. Reception looks down to a peaceful lobby bar below, there's a small pretty pool in the loungey back patio and the rooms themselves are pretty slick. It's like a little paradise – and now you know why it's so affordable.

COCKER B&B Map p76 Guesthouse $$

☎ 4362-8451; www.thecocker.com; Juan de Garay 458; d AR$360-440; ; 29

Possibly BA's most tastefully refurbished old home is this exceptional San Telmo B&B. The street outside seems unlikely to offer such a paradise, but after you climb the stairs to the 2nd floor you'll be surrounded by contemporary touches, from the grand piano in the living room to the elegant dining nook in back. Four lovely rooms are available, but the best feature is likely the lush rooftop terraces – go up to the very top for San Telmo views and occasional summer movies screened against a wall. Yoga classes available; reservations mandatory. Run by expats.

LO DE RICK Map p76 Guesthouse $$

www.loderick.com; s/d AR$340/400;

Owned by an Englishman is this beautiful guesthouse with a handful of very comfortable and pleasant rooms – they're not luxurious, but that's not the point here. Guests meet each other every morning (for the filling breakfast) at the large rectangular table in the dining room, a tastefully furnished common space shared by the owner's two dogs and two cats. There's also a large rooftop terrace and several patios in which to hang out. No walk-ins; telephone and address given with email reservation notification.

BOHEMIA BUENOS AIRES

Map p76 Hotel $$

☎ 4115-2561; www.bohemiabuenosaires.com.ar; Perú 845; r AR$340; ; Línea C Independencia

With its slight upscale-motel feel, this little San Telmo cherry offers just over a dozen simple and neat rooms, most good-sized if a bit antiseptic with their white-tiled floors. At least the linens are nice and bright. None of the rooms have bathtubs, so instead of taking a soak enjoy the peaceful grassy backyard and small interior patios. The breakfast buffet is a plus, especially as it's located in the airy back room. A decent deal for its convenient San Telmo location.

LUGAR GAY Map p76 Guesthouse $

☎ 4300-4747; www.lugargay.com.ar; Defensa 1120; dm AR$100, s AR$180-240, d AR$240-360; ; 29

Head up a long flight of stairs to this intimate guesthouse, where only gay men can book a stay. Just four of the eight small but elegant rooms have a private bathroom, but most boast stunning views of the pretty church out back. It's a maze of catwalks, spiral staircases and sunny terraces (nude sunbathing welcome), plus there's a tango salon and a tiny cafe. Two Jacuzzis – one indoor, one out – translate into fun nights, and even if you don't book a stay they'll give out information on BA's gay scene. Afternoon snacks and wine are complimentary, as is a closet kitchenette.

POSADA DE LA LUNA

Map p76 Guesthouse $$

☎ 4343-0911; www.posadaluna.com; Perú 565; s/d AR$200/280; ; Línea E Belgrano

Want an intimate stay? Then head to this charming, family-run guesthouse located in an old historical house. The five stylish, high-ceilinged rooms – which lie along a tiled patio hallway decorated with potted plants – boast wooden floors and high ceilings, along with modern comforts like air-con and TV. At the back there's a modest terrace and even a small Jacuzzi room tucked into the basement. Casual living room in which to hang out; friendly dog on premises.

LINA'S TANGO GUESTHOUSE

Map p76 Guesthouse $

☎ 4361-6817; www.linatango.com; Estados Unidos 780; s AR$200-240, d AR$300; ; Línea C Independencia

For a homey stay with a tango twist, consider this humble spot. Five simple rooms are available (nearly all with private bath) and there's a kitchen for guests to use. A casual inner courtyard doubles as tango salon when the weather is good, and there's an upstairs common room as well. Plenty of tango information, from events to *milongas* to shows, is also on tap – great for those who want to immerse themselves in the dance.

NOSTER BAYRES Map p76 Hotel $

☎ 4361-3341; www.nosterbayres.com.ar; Brasil 459; s AR$160-220, d AR$200-260; ; 29

If you're looking for one of San Telmo's most inexpensive (while decent) hotels, you've just found one. Only eight rooms are available at this homely place, which could almost be interesting – yet it seems to be missing something, perhaps a bit of light and air downstairs? The lobby is a bit cold, with a bleak breakfast area. At least the wood-floored, high-ceilinged, slightly artsy rooms are OK – especially if you get a window or luck out with a balcony. But why complain? The location is fine, and it's cheap.

LIVING DANGEROUSLY

Like to live on the edge? Then stay at a studio or apartment in La Boca – likely the only places for tourists to rent in this neighborhood. This colorful, 10-unit block is located a half-block west of Av Almirante Brown, the main thoroughfare, so it's a reasonably busy and safe area (see the location of Patios de la Boca on Map p80).

But it's La Boca – why stay there? Well, they're not expensive (studios AR$200, two-bedroom flats AR$300, long-term discounts) – and it's something different. Perhaps an opportunity to get to know a rough, blue-collar neighborhood and slowly become a local. Though you should still be careful about looking like a tourist around here. Curious? Then check out www.patiosdelaboca.blogspot.com.

CIRCUS HOSTEL Map p76 Hostel $

☎ 4878-7786; www.hostelcircus.com; Chacabuco 1020; dm AR$80, r AR$200; ; Línea C Independencia

Here's a first for even Buenos Aires – a boutique hostel. From the trendy lounge in front to the timber deck–surrounded wading pool in back (which doubles as a large Jacuzzi), this hostel exudes a certain slickness. Both dorms and private rooms are decked out with simple, contemporary furniture and all sport their own bathrooms. With all five floors connected by elevator you won't have to get a bead of sweat on your hip backpack as you head down to the pool table. One apartment with kitchen and terrace available (AR$360).

ARKA HOSTEL Map p76 Hostel $

☎ 4361-9789; www.arkasantelmo.com; Bolivar 893; dm AR$80, s/d AR$100/200; ; 29

A spiffed-up version of your usual run-of-the-mill backpacker joint, this intimate hostel features a glass ceiling in the bar lounge and small but neat dorms (up to three people in each, max). All rooms (even private ones) share bathrooms. The highlight of this joint is the rooftop terrace, which feels more like a restaurant than a common area, with slatted wooden deck and fancy container plants. Yoga, meditation and massages available.

TELMO TANGO HOSTEL Map p76 Hostel $

☎ 4361-5808; www.hostelmotango.com; Chacabuco 679; dm AR$55, s/d AR$120/190; ; Línea E Belgrano

Located in a nice old building with original touches, this hostel doesn't really have large dorms – they're basically shared doubles or private rooms for two to four people. Also unusual is that there's no kitchen, just a place to heat up beverages. Two beautiful original rooms are available in front, which have two to four beds each and awesome balconies, but otherwise all rooms are small and basic. It's a tranquil place and not for party types; nice rooftop terrace.

LA GURDA HOSTEL Map p76 Hostel $

☎ 4362-0701; www.alagurdahostel.com.ar; Bolivar 920; dm AR$50, r AR$165; ; 29

A very intimate hostel, La Gurda is a homey, laid-back house with comfortable rooms, a small enclosed patio and cozy living-room area. There are two private rooms (each with its own bathroom) and three- or four-bed dorms – the whole place only holds about 16 people total. The best part is its location – right in the middle of San Telmo's action, and next to Mercado San Telmo. Owned by a couple of young Argentines.

AYRES PORTEÑOS HOSTEL
Map p76 Hostel $

☎ 4300-7314; www.ayresportenos.com.ar; Perú 708; dm AR$45, s/d AR$105/165; ; Línea C Independencia

One of San Telmo's larger hostels, Ayres is located in an old house with dark halls. What saves it from mediocrity is the artwork – all of the rooms have their doors painted with colorful figures – often Argentine icons. Many rooms have windows, balconies and good mattresses, but all share outside bathrooms. Dorms tend to have single beds rather than bunks, and there are a large number of private rooms (14) to choose from. There's also a bright TV lounge at the top floor, plus roof terrace with *asado*. Don't bother trying to cook, however, unless you like ridiculously tiny kitchens.

RETIRO

Retiro is a great, central place to be, *if* you can afford it – many of BA's most expensive hotels, along with some of its richest inhabitants, are settled in here. Close by are leafy Plaza San Martín, the Retiro train and bus stations, and many upscale stores and business services. Ritzy Recoleta is to the north and the busy Microcentro is to the south – both just a short and pleasant stroll away.

FOUR SEASONS BUENOS AIRES
Map p84 Hotel $$$

☎ 4321-1200; www.fourseasons.com/buenosaires; Posadas 1086; d from AR$1980; ; 67

No surprise here – Buenos Aires' Four Seasons offers all the perks that define a five-star hotel, such as great service and white terry-cloth robes. Rooms are large and beautiful, with contemporary furnishings and decorations, and the finest suites are located in an old, luxurious mansion next door. There's also a gorgeous spa, an outdoor, heated swimming pool, an international restaurant and a business center.

CASA CALMA Map p84 Boutique Hotel $$$

☎ 5199-2800; www.casacalma.com.ar; Suipacha 1015; d AR$650-1100; ; Línea C San Martín

Those with stuffed wallets and of an eco-conscious mind now have their perfect hideaway in BA – Casa Calma. This little luxurious gem does its part by using eco-certified wood in its building and outside greenery to adjust the hotel's temperatures. It recycles what it can and offers guests organic towels, bulk toiletries and even two bamboo bicycles to rent. But it's so gorgeous you wouldn't know any of this. Rooms are beautifully pristine and relaxing (some even have sauna or Jacuzzi), with Zen-like baths and serene atmosphere. It's a world away from outside the front door, where BA noisily buzzes by.

ELEVAGE HOTEL Map p84 Hotel $$

☎ 4891-8000; www.elevage.com.ar; Maipú 960; d AR$560; ; Línea C San Martín

The best thing about this four-star hotel is its location, steps from Plaza San Martín and Calle Florida. The rooms aren't bad either – mostly good sized and classically decorated, with all the services you'd imagine at this level. The swimming pool is small but sweet, an especially wonderful treat you'll appreciate during BA's stifling summers. Other pluses include a cozy basement bar (with occasional live music) and friendly staff.

DAZZLER HOTEL Map p84 Hotel $$

☎ 4816-5005; www.dazzlerlibertad.com; Libertad 902; d AR$480; ; Línea D Tribunales

They're big on glass at this modern hotel; the lobby is nearly surrounded by the stuff, which lets in a lot of traffic noise. Most of the nice, decently sized rooms have a whole wall of glass as well (double-paned at least), providing light and a great view over leafy Plaza Libertad. It's a comfortable spot, with a pleasant 2nd-floor restaurant, and is well situated near the Microcentro and Recoleta. Ask for available discounts when booking, or check the website.

HOTEL PRINCIPADO Map p84 Hotel $$

☎ 4313-3022; www.principado.com.ar; Paraguay 481; d AR$440; ; Línea C San Martín

A relatively affordable stay in Retiro is this modest hotel, which features good, clean and rather bland midrange rooms with outdated furniture, in a very central location. Most of the typical hotel and room services are on tap, including a minibar, safety box, hairdryer and business center.

HOTEL CENTRAL CÓRDOBA Map p84 Hotel $

☎ 4311-1175; www.hotelcentralcordoba.com.ar; San Martín 1021; s AR$170, d AR$190-220; ; Línea C San Martín

Possibly Retiro's most affordable hotel is the Central Córdoba. Halls are outdated, but rooms are neat and feature desk areas and tiled floors, even while they don't leave much space to move around. Ask for an inside room if you want quiet, an outside room if you want a balcony. The location is spot on – the Kilkenny (p147) bar is within easy staggering distance – and it's very popular, so it's best to book ahead.

RECOLETA & BARRIO NORTE

Most of the accommodations in Recoleta (Barrio Norte is more of a sub-neighborhood) are expensive, and what cheap hotels there are tend to be full much of the time. Buildings here are grand and beautiful, befitting the city's richest barrio, and you'll be close to Recoleta's famous cemetery, along with its lovely parks, museums and boutiques.

PALACIO DUHAU – PARK HYATT Map p87 Hotel $$$

☎ 5171-1234; www.buenosaires.park.hyatt.com; Av Alvear 1661; d AR$3132; ; 130

One of the loveliest new hotels in Buenos Aires, the Park Hyatt takes up a city block and consists of two wings – a building on Av Posadas and the Palacio Duhau, a renovated mansion on Av Alvear. In between is a gorgeously terraced, grassy garden with fountains and patios, which the palace's large restaurant balcony overlooks. Rooms are – unsurprisingly – luxuriously wonderful, and swanky amenities include a fine spa, indoor pool, a wine and cheese bar, an art gallery, even a tea house. Service is excellent.

ALVEAR PALACE HOTEL Map p87 Hotel $$$

☎ 4808-2100; www.alvearpalace.com; Av Alvear 1891; d from AR$1920; ; 130

Ask any local to name the classiest, most traditional hotel in Buenos Aires, and

APARTMENTS ONLINE

Many foreigners visiting Buenos Aires love the city so much that they want to stay longer and find an apartment. But snagging a pad isn't as easy as it could be; renters often need to commit to two years and nearly always need a local's bond to guarantee monthly payments – nearly impossible for most foreigners.

To cater to foreign demand, dozens of apartment websites have popped up in the city in recent years. These sites charge significantly more for their properties than locals would pay but don't demand those pesky requirements, either. You can view pictures of rental properties, along with prices and amenities. Usually the photos match what you will get, but not always; if you'd like someone to check out an apartment before you rent it, Madi Lang at www.bacultralconcierge.com can make sure the place isn't on a busy street, in an outlying neighborhood or near a construction site.

- www.adelsur.com
- www.alojargentina.com.ar
- www.apartmentsba.com
- www.barts.com
- www.buenosaires.en.craigslist.org/apa
- www.buenosaireshabitat.com
- www.friendlyapartments.com
- www.oasisba.com
- www.roomargentina.com
- www.santelmoloft.com
- www.stayinbuenosaires.com
- www.tucasargentina.com
- www.yourhomeinargentina.com.ar
- Here's a good one if you're just looking for a room: www.spareroomsba.com

If you want to take the ultimate step and purchase property, do your research carefully as the laws work differently in BA than in many Western countries. Get advice from other foreigners who have purchased; ask on forums at expat websites. Or consider using the services of a company like www.maisonbuenosaires.com, who can help you jump through the right hoops and cut the bureaucracy. For more information on moving to Buenos Aires, see the boxed text on p234.

they'll surely name the Alvear Palace. Old world sophistication and superior service will help erase the trials of that long 1st-class flight into town, while the bathtub Jacuzzi, Hermès toiletries and Egyptian-cotton bed sheets aid your trip into dreamland. There are also three fine restaurants, an elegant tea room, a cigar bar, a spa and an indoor swimming pool, as well as butler service.

CASASUR ART HOTEL Map p87 Hotel $$$

☎ 4515-0085; www.casasurhotel.com; Av Callao 1823; d AR$1240-1680; ; 59

Certainly one of the finest stays in Recoleta is this gorgeous newcomer in the five-star scene. CasaSur calls itself an 'art hotel' mostly because it's close to BA's finest art galleries. It might look like a gallery too – shiny marble floors, cowhide-covered ottomans, beautiful floral vases – and that's just the lobby. Rooms are bathed in earth colors, fluffy bed linens and dark wood floors – plus boast all the modern conveniences like iPod docks and flat TVs. It's the kind of place where the staff wear black suits. There are also spa services, afternoon tea and a French-influenced restaurant. How could you not have a nice stay?

AYRES DE RECOLETA

Map p87 Apartments $$

☎ 4801-0505; www.ayresderecoleta.com; Uriburu 1756; studios AR$560; ; 59

Perfect for those looking for more than just a pretty room, these studio apartments are the bomb. All come with king-size beds (or two twins), brown-and-white color scheme and classy decoration. You'll also get a kitchenette, and though they're a bit too insubstantial to do any real cooking, they're perfect for beverages or heating up leftover takeout. There's even a small indoor pool with Jacuzzi on the premises. And the location can't be beat – you're within spitting distance of Recoleta cemetery.

HOTEL PLAZA FRANCIA

Map p87 Hotel Suites $$

☎ 4804-9631; www.hotelplazafrancia.com; E Schiaffino 2189; d AR$532-620; ; 67

A good choice for a mid- to high-range hotel, the Plaza Francia's best feature are the views from the front-facing, upper-floor rooms. Gaze past Recoleta's Parque Thays all the way to the Río de la Plata, or watch the planes land at Aeroparque. It's located on noisy Av del Libertador, but windows are double-paned for peace. Rooms are decent (though a bit outdated, with small bathrooms) for the location and price, and services are good. Reserve ahead.

ART SUITES Map p87 Apartments $$

☎ 4821-6800; www.artsuites.com.ar; Azcuénaga 1465; d AR$440-720; ; Línea D Pueyrredón

Fifteen luxurious, very modern and spacious apartments are on offer at this very exclusive spot. All are bright, with minimalist decor, full kitchens or kitchenettes, sunny balconies and slick, hip furniture. Windows are double-paned for quiet, staff speak English well, security is excellent and there's even a daily cleaning service. Long-term discounts are available, but reserve way in advance, as this is not a place to just show up to without warning. An annex has more apartments.

PRINCE HOTEL Map p87 Hotel $$

☎ 4811-8004; www.princehotel.com.ar; Arenales 1627; s/d AR$240/320; ; Línea D Callao

If you must stay in Recoleta and have a thin wallet, consider the Prince Hotel. Slightly misnamed (a prince would not likely stay here), this cheap stay offers older halls and very small interior rooms (the exterior ones are a bit larger) – but at least they're tastefully decorated, and some even come with balcony. Services will obviously be limited, but for the location you can't complain. Be sure to check out the ancient metal elevator.

GUIDO PALACE HOTEL Map p87 Hotel $

☎ 4812-0341; www.guidopalace.com.ar; Guido 1780; s/d AR$260/270; ; 59

Modest accommodations can be found at this humble hotel, which offers 46 plain but comfortable rooms at decent prices. You'd basically just stay here to be rubbing shoulders with the rich in ritzy Recoleta, because there's not much to the place other than its great location. There *is* a small dining area for breakfast – but treat yourself and get it taken up to your room, along with the daily paper.

RECOLETA GUEST HOUSE

Map p87 Guesthouse $

☎ 4803-5474; www.recoletaguesthouse.com; Laprida 1821; s/d AR$180/260; ; Línea D Pueyrredón

This pleasant family-run guesthouse is a great deal for the location. It's in an atmospheric older neo-Tudor-style building close to public transportation and Recoleta's cemetery. The five homey, good rooms all come with their own bathroom and there's a nice living room area for you to relax and meet fellow boarders or chat with your hosts. Be sure to make a reservation – no walk-ins allowed. Some English is spoken.

LUCO B&B Map p87 Hotel $

☎ 4961-5675; www.lucobnb.com.ar; Av Córdoba 2409; dm AR$70, s AR$180-260, d AR$220-300; ; Línea D Facultad de Medicina

This is an unusual place, located at the very edge of Barrio Norte, on a crowded and noisy avenue usually full of students from the nearby university. Not typical Recoleta or Barrio Norte, but at least it's a bustling, energetic area. It's a rather spartan place that offers 22 simple and tidy rooms, with a few colors to make things interesting; if you want TV, get a suite. There's even a three-bed dorm room. It's not a true B&B – there is breakfast, but it's not special and certainly not served by the owner. There are also long-term rooms available.

PETIT RECOLETA HOSTEL

Map p87 Hostel $

☎ 4823-3848; www.petitrecoleta.com; Uriburu 1183; dm AR$56-64, d AR$160-220; ; Línea D Facultad de Medicina

It's hardly a stunner as far as hostels go, but you can't beat this cheapie's price and location. Common spaces include an interior patio, small TV room and larger pool-table area. Rooms are a mix of old and new, and there's a decent casual vibe. Out of the dozen rooms only one has air-con. Long-term tenants are usually loitering around (two-month minimum, AR$1200 to AR$1400 per month).

PALERMO

Despite being a slight trek from the center, Palermo is the top choice for many travelers. Not only is it full of extensive parklands – which are great for weekend jaunts and sporting activities – but you'll have heaps of cutting-edge restaurants, designer boutiques and hip dance clubs at your door. Many of these places are located in the extensive sub-neighborhood of Palermo Viejo, which is further subdivided into Palermo Soho and Palermo Hollywood. All are connected to the center by bus or Subte.

MAGNOLIA HOTEL

Map p92 Boutique Hotel $$$

☎ 4867-4900; www.magnoliahotel.com.ar; J Àlvarez 1746; s AR$480, d AR$720-960; ; Línea D Scalabrini Ortíz

One of Buenos Aires' finest stays is this classy boutique hotel, located in a gorgeously restored old house. Its eight impeccably groomed rooms are bathed in muted colors and fitted with elegant furniture, and all offer flat TVs. Common spaces are beautiful, and the rooftop terrace is strewn with cushy lounges – perfect for relaxing after a hard day of walking the nearby streets of Palermo. Other pluses include a welcome drink and good breakfast.

OWN HOTEL

Map p92 Boutique Hotel $$$

☎ 4772-8100; www.ownhotels.com; Cabrera 5556; d from AR$640; ; 111

One of the largest boutique hotels in town – with 16 rooms – is this modern and hip construction on the southern edge of Palermo Hollywood. It's a good place with friendly staff and very contemporary design. Rooms are spacious and most of them bright; some have a balcony. Nice touches include robes and 500-thread count Egyptian-cotton bed linens. You'd better be cozy with your partner, however – the sinks are located outside the bathrooms, in the sleeping area. For those into the finer things in life, an art gallery lives on the ground floor and there's a bar-lounge in the lobby.

MINE HOTEL

Map p92 Hotel $$$

☎ 4832-1100; www.minehotel.com; Gorriti 4770; d AR$640-860; ; 55

This Palermo charmer is a beautiful and very hip boutique hotel. The 20 rooms (in three classes) are good sized; some come with Jacuzzi and balcony and all have a desk and natural decor touches. Get one overlooking the highlight of the hotel – the peaceful backyard, which comes complete with small wading pool and lounging area. There's a small bistro where you can enjoy the buffet breakfast, and Mine even attempts to be somewhat eco-friendly (reusing towels, low-energy bulbs, recycling).

DUQUE HOTEL

Map p92 Boutique Hotel $$$

☎ 4832-0312; www.duquehotel.com; Guatemala 4364; s AR$480, d AR$560-720; ; Línea D Scalabrini Ortíz

More upscale than most boutique hotels around is this elegant charmer, located just outside the trendiest parts of Palermo Soho – which might suit some people just fine. Each of the 14 rooms are lovely and well designed, though some can be a bit small – go for a superior or deluxe if you need more space to stretch out. Pluses include use of a large Jacuzzi and sauna, rental bikes, buffet breakfast, afternoon tea with pastries and great little garden in back with a tiny pool. Massages available in the basement spa.

PALERMITANO

Map p92 Boutique Hotel $$$

☎ 4897-2100; www.palermitano.biz; Uriarte 1648; d AR$560-660; ; 39, 55

Located pretty much smack in the middle of Palermo's nightlife is this well-located boutique hotel. Rooms here are tastefully decorated in contemporary style, but standard ones are a bit small – at least having one wall made of glass keeps claustrophobia away. Big plus: the full breakfast here is served all day, and they'll even bring it to your door. And pretty unusual for Buenos Aires is their small rooftop terrace with wading pool. Things should get even better when the ground-floor restaurant, a branch of the Peruvian joint Sipan, opens up.

POSADA PALERMO

Map p92 Guesthouse $$

☎ 4826-8792; www.posadapalermo.com; Salguero 1655; s/d AR$440/500; ; Línea D Bulnes

This pleasant B&B offers something that truly makes it a bed and breakfast – a good and full breakfast, including homemade jams and yogurt. The seven simple yet comfortable rooms are all different (there's even a pillow 'menu') – all were designed

LONG-TERM GUESTHOUSES

Any hotel (eg Luco, see p192), hostel (eg Petit Recoleta Hostel, see p192) or guesthouse listed in this guidebook should significantly discount a long-term stay; negotiate this in advance. Sleeping at a guesthouse that specializes in week- or month-long stays is often a more intimate experience, however. Below are a few that operate in BA; only monthly rates are listed, but many rent by the week also.

Casa de Plata (Map p72; ☎ 4953-3950; nelifernandez2003@yahoo.es; Av Corrientes 2092, 4th fl; monthly r AR$1200-1600) Homey, airy place with seven good rooms, all with balcony. Nice old touches to the house; a small kitchen is available. Mature renters preferred.

Casa Los Angelitos (Map p98; ☎ 4954-4079; www.casalosangelitos.com; Hipólito Yrigoyen 2178; monthly r AR$1420-1900) Gorgeous old house with seven simple rooms around outdoor patios. The two on the top floor (each with their own bathroom) are the most private. Good large kitchen.

La Casa de Marina (Map p76; ☎ 15-6945-2415; www.lacasademarina.com.ar; monthly r AR$1000-1800) Four rooms, two of them tiny, are available at this small but pleasant San Telmo guesthouse; all share bathrooms and a kitchen. Address given upon reservation.

Ke Viva el Mundo (Map p92; ☎ 4864-7691, 15-5990-1905; kevivaelmundo@yahoo.com.ar; monthly r AR$2000-3500) Very casual spot for young, backpacker types only who like a laid-back atmosphere and are OK with the weekly *asado* parties held on the rooftop. Nine simple rooms with lots of common spaces. Cat on premises; reservations mandatory.

If you're interested in spending time with a host family, check out www.coret.com.ar, which offers private rooms in Montserrat and San Telmo. Shared rooms are cheaper, and meals cost extra. You can also look for a room at www.spareroomsba.com or www.buenosaires.en.craigslist.org/roo. Address is given upon reservation.

by one of the owners, an architect. Best of all is likely the leafy backyard patio, a little paradise on a warm day, and the multilevel breakfast-living area is also a great hangout. Allergics beware: pets on the premises.

NOA NOA LOFTS

Map p92 Boutique Apartments $$

☎ 4776-4546; www.noanoalofts.com.ar; Bonpland 1549; d AR$480-720; ; 111

If you need a lot of space and like minimalist decor, then head over here. Just 10 'lofts' (apartments with kitchenettes) are available, some with their own Jacuzzi and all with either a patio or a balcony. The floors are polished concrete and one wall is made of glass – bring earplugs if your room faces the street. There's also a small backyard area with tiny pool. Up to four people can stay in each apartment; avoid the ground-floor one across from the office, unless you don't care about privacy.

RENDEZVOUS HOTEL Map p92 Hotel $$

☎ 3964-5222; www.rendezvoushotel.com.ar; Bonpland 1484; d AR$440-620; ; 111

One of Palermo's most interesting boutique hotels is in this beautiful, four-story French-style building. The owner (also French) is a serious feng shui practitioner, and integrated its principles into his hotel. Each of the 11 rooms is unique, different – one room is dashed out in red and brown, with modern furnishings; another has purple accents and antiques. One even boasts its own private balcony with outdoor Jacuzzi. Wine tastings happen in the downstairs bistro (extra charge), and the location is close to Palermo's nightlife scene.

CASA LAS CAÑITAS

Map p92 Boutique Hotel $$

☎ 4771-3878; www.casalascanitas.com; Huergo 283; r AR$420-640; ; Línea D Ministro Carranza

With nine small but lovely rooms, this boutique hotel offers a hip stay and a fabulous location just a block away from Las Cañitas' bustling nightlife. Room 9 is the nicest – it comes with attached patio. There's a tiny, two-seat bar in the fancy lobby, behind which is the breakfast area and the hotel's highlight – a small but pleasant, grassy backyard with barbecue, sundeck, outdoor shower and Jacuzzi.

RUGANTINO HOTEL Map p92 Hotel $$

☎ 4773-2891; www.rugantinohotel.com; Uriarte 1844; d AR$340-420; ; Línea D Palermo

Here is a wonderfully small and intimate hotel in the middle of Palermo, located in a 1920s building and run by an Italian family. Various tiny terraces and catwalks connect the eight simple but beautiful rooms, all decked out in hardwood floors and modern styling – combined with a few antiques. The climbing vine-greenery in the small central courtyard well is soothing, and you can expect espresso for breakfast – no surprise given your hosts' ancestry.

ABODE Map p92 Guesthouse $$

☎ 4774-0818; www.abodebuenosaires.com; d AR$300-360; ; Línea D Palermo

Run by an expat couple, who live on the premises, is this very intimate and homey guesthouse. Each of the four simple yet comfortable rooms comes with its own bathroom, and the largest one comes with balcony (AR$460). The highlight: a wonderfully relaxing rooftop terrace, where you can enjoy your full English breakfast. Well located in Palermo Soho, four blocks from Plaza Serrano. By reservation only; no walk-ins (you'll get the address when you reserve). Friendly dog on premises.

HOTEL COSTA RICA Map p92 Hotel $$

☎ 4864-7390; www.hotelcostarica.com.ar; Costa Rica 4137; d AR$280-600; ; Línea D Scalabrini Ortíz

There aren't many large hotels in Palermo, but the Costa Rica, with 30 rooms, manages to retain a sense of intimacy – the cozy bar and patio area in the lobby really help. It's run by a Frenchman, who has installed contemporary details like slick, raised sinks and modern decor while keeping some of the building's original details, like its tall doors. Tiled hallways are narrow and plain, but there's a spacious rooftop patio for sunny lounging. To save a few pesos, go for the cheaper rooms with shared bathrooms.

LIVIAN GUESTHOUSE

Map p92 Guesthouse $$

☎ 4862-8841; www.livianguesthouse.com; Palestina 1184; d AR$280-460; ; 106, 160

Located in a lovely old building in an untouristy section of Palermo is this chill, unpretentious guesthouse. There are only eight pretty rooms on offer, and half are en suite; the others either share bathrooms or have their private bathroom down the hall (one even has its own small terrace). There's a nice back deck and patio garden for all to enjoy. A large two-bedroom downstairs apartment is available; it holds up to five people (price starts at AR$480 for two).

CASERÓN PORTEÑO

Map p92 Guesthouse $$

☎ 4554-6336; www.caseronporteno.com; Ciudad de la Paz 344; s AR$200-300, d AR$260-380; ; Línea D Olleros

Catering especially to tango dancers is this fine guesthouse with 10 simple but tastefully furnished rooms. All have private bathrooms, but four have them located outside the actual rooms. Behind the lush garden there's a small dance studio where classes take place, while other common spaces include a relaxing rooftop terrace and a kitchen for guest use. Plenty of tango information is available. The location is in a non-touristy residential neighborhood; four-night minimum stay in high season.

CHE LULU GUESTHOUSE

Map p92 Guesthouse $

☎ 4772-0289; www.chelulu.com; Emilio Zolá 5185; dm AR$80, d AR$180-220, d with bathroom AR$280; ; Línea D Palermo

One of BA's original boutique guesthouses, Che Lulu offers an upscale but unpretentious atmosphere dotted with artistic touches. Each of the eight small, simple and colorful rooms sports a different size and theme, and all but two share bathrooms. Sophisticated backpackers can opt for the cozy attic dorm, which sleeps five. There are a couple of cute patios and a comfortable main common space. To find Che Lulu, just look for its bright-red paint job – a homage to BA's old red-light district, which used to run just a half-block away.

ECO PAMPA HOSTEL Map p92 Hostel $

☎ 4831-2435; www.hostelpampa.com; Guatemala 4778; dm AR$60, s/d AR$220/300; ; Línea D Plaza Italia

Buenos Aires' first green hostel is this causal spot sporting vintage-recycled furniture, low-energy light bulbs and recycling system. The rooftop is home to a small veggie garden, compost pile and solar panels. Dorms are good sized, with six to eight beds, and each of the eight private rooms comes with bathroom, air-con and flat TV. It's a good place that donates some of its proceeds to local organizations; there's another branch further north in Belgrano (off Map p92; Iberá 2858).

REINA MADRE HOSTEL

Map p92 Hostel $

☎ 4962-5553; www.hostelreinamadre.com.ar; Anchorena 1118; dm AR$60, s/d AR$140/180; ; Línea D Pueyrredón

Here's a wonderful hostel option located on the fringe of Recoleta in an interesting neighborhood that is crammed full of students (there's a university nearby). It's a family-run place, which means it's clean and safe – but it also has a great youthful vibe. The old building has plenty of personality, with high ceilings and original tiles, and all rooms are comfortable and modern (and share outside bathrooms). There's a bright hall area and kitchen, plus a wood-deck rooftop with *asado* area. A great stay.

OLD FRIENDS HOSTEL Map p92 Hostel $

☎ 4833-4056; www.oldfriends.com.ar; Lavalleja 1352; dm AR$50, d AR$130-160; ; 106, 160

This very casual hostel is so cool, they even make their own beer – and might possibly treat you to one when you walk in the door. Old Friends would be best for a summer stay, as the exterior spaces are great – open courtyard, a relaxing back deck and great rooftop terrace. All around are examples of graffiti art, and the intimacy here is a plus – as are the free bike rentals. It's in a non-touristy area on the edge of Palermo – but still within walking distance of its trendiness.

BAIT HOSTEL Map p92 Hostel $

☎ 4774-2859; www.baitba.com; El Salvador 5115; dm AR$45, d AR$140-175; ; 39, 55

For those who care more about good vibes than fancy atmosphere, there's this intimate, laid-back hostel. Reception is at the upstairs bar–common room area, which gives you an idea of the casualness here. There's also a downstairs patio for weekly *asados* and live music events on the weekend. Dorms have privacy curtains. There are seven private rooms, two with attached bathroom, for those who need more space.

VILLA CRESPO, ONCE, CABALLITO & BOEDO

With the popularity of Palermo raising property values and rents, some places to stay have popped up in the more blue-collar, historical, artsy or even 'bohemian' neighborhoods to the south. This large area is a good choice if you want to 'go local' and don't mind being a bit further from the main sights (but not *too* far away). Public transport is good – and there probably won't be another tourist in sight.

RACÓ DE BUENOS AIRES

Map p98 Boutique Hotel $$

☎ 3530-6075; www.racodebuenosaires.com.ar; Yapeyú 271; d AR$400-800; ; Línea A Castro Barros

If you like staying far from the tourist hordes but within the comforts of a high-end boutique hotel, then this Italian-designed building is your paradise. The 12 lovely rooms here all come with different styling, from virgin white classic to subdued masculinity to animal print. All are spacious and have wood floors, high ceilings and modern bathrooms. There's a small plant-strewn patio for breakfast and a basement wine bar for evening tastings. And you're just a few blocks from the Subte, which will have you downtown in minutes.

QUERIDO B&B Map p98 B&B $$

☎ 4854-6297; www.queridobuenosaires.com; Juan Ramirez de Velazco 934; s/d AR$360-380; ; Línea B Malabia

Run by a friendly and helpful Brazilian-English couple is this homey yet modern B&B. It's located in a non-touristy neighborhood, but within easy walking distance to Palermo's hip restaurants, shops and bars. The eight clean rooms are small but comfortable, and all have private bathrooms; ask for an inside 'courtyard' room for more quiet. There's a living room in which to meet fellow travelers, a little gravel patio in back for fresh air and even an elevator if you don't feel like stair-climbing. Nice continental breakfast, too.

SOCO HOTEL Map p98 Boutique Hotel $$

☎ 4864-2032; www.socohotels.com; Lavalle 3119; d AR$300-380; ; Línea B Carlos Gardel

Abasto is a wonderfully diverse neighborhood – Jews, Koreans and Peruvians all mingle here. It's also home to one of BA's most bustling street markets, plus one of its highest-end shopping malls, both within blocks of each other. You'll experience it all just outside your doorstep at Soco, located in a classic old building. There are just eight rooms here, most spacious affairs with wood floors, high ceilings and bold decor. All are different and come with modern bathrooms. Strangely enough, there's also a kitchen available for guest use, but it's industrial like and in the bleak basement – not a place you want to hang out. Eat out in Abasto instead.

GENTE DEL SUR HOSTEL

Map p98 Hostel $

☎ 4864-3731; www.gentedelsurhostel.com; Salguero 717; dm AR$64-76, s/d AR$140/280; ; Línea B Medrano

In the middle of BA's alternative-theater district is this clean and modern hostel. It's not your typical backpacker hostel – students are more likely to stay here than grungies – so it tends to be quieter and have a bit less personality. However, the furniture is high quality (think good mattresses) and all bunks have their own lights and shelves – a thoughtful little detail. Private rooms are quite nice, and there's an elevator to the rooftop terrace–TV room–barbecue area. Service is good and efficient, as you can imagine.

LA MENESUNDA Map p98 Hostel $

☎ 4957-0946; www.lamenesundahostel.com.ar; Boedo 742; dm AR$45, d AR$145-185; ; Línea E Boedo

This hostel is located in bohemian Boedo, a great choice for those who don't mind being in a less touristy yet still vibrant part of the city. It's on a busy avenue, but in the middle of the block – traffic noise isn't an issue. A long hallway opens up to a pleasant patio area surrounded by two floors of spacious dorms and large private rooms. Nearby is the artsy TV lounge and large kitchen, and upstairs is another smaller, tiled patio with barbecue and potted plants.

DAY TRIPS

DAY TRIPS

Buenos Aires can occupy many enjoyable days' worth of your hard-earned vacation, but when you tire of the big city's noise, concrete and busyness there's a handful of destinations within a few hours' travel that will sweep you into completely different worlds. After all, porteños themselves eagerly take the opportunity to get away from their beloved city on long weekend stretches, but do so especially during their summer vacations – when Buenos Aires resembles Paris in summertime, and it's mainly the overheated tourists dragging their way through the hot and humid streets.

Most of the following trips can be done in a day, but a few are best for in-depth exploration if you have the time to spare. Among your getaway choices you can take a laid-back boat ride along the murky estuaries of Tigre's backwaters, find peaceful town walks in San Isidro or San Antonio de Areco, wander through Colonia's fine colonial architecture or join the summertime hordes at Punta del Este's sunny beaches. Montevideo (Uruguay's capital) sports its own style but is a much less frenetic city than BA, while Luján is a must for those interested in the Christian religion. For more information on the mind-blowing Cataratas de Iguazú – which are not to be missed if you have even the smallest chance of visiting them – see p203.

NATURE

Your best bet for peaceful greenery and riverside views is the delta surrounding Tigre (p200). Only an hour or so away from the center of Buenos Aires, this city provides easy access to the tranquil waterways of the spreading Delta del Paraná. There are no roads in this watery region; instead you'll find boat trips that access summer getaway homes and peaceful nature walks.

CITIES & TOWNS

San Isidro (p204), just north of BA's center, is an upscale suburb offering historical buildings and calm neighborhoods. The devotional center of Luján (p205) to the west provides an interesting look into the Catholic heart of Argentina, while Buenos Aires province's gaucho hub is the serene village of San Antonio de Areco (p206). Montevideo (p212) is Uruguay's capital and lies across the Río de la Plata, but it's easily accessible from downtown BA by ferry; it has a smaller-city feel, a distinct vibe and plenty of old European architecture worth checking out. Also in Uruguay and equally accessible is Colonia (p209), a pleasant little colonial gem with cobbled streets and charming buildings.

BEACHES

Punta del Este (p215) is the ritzy beach destination for many summering Argentines, providing plenty of sun, sand and stars – celebrities, that is. It fills to the brim January through March, when most porteños flee overheated Buenos Aires, but is much calmer (and less expensive) outside these peak months.

TIGRE & THE DELTA

Only an hour's drive from BA, tranquil Tigre and its huge river delta make a popular weekend getaway for cement-weary porteños. And while Tigre itself is a pleasant enough riverside town, it's really the swampy waterways that everyone is after. Latte-colored waters – rich with iron from the jungle streams flowing from inland Argentina – alongside reedy shores are far from any stereotypical paradise, but there are a few surprises here. Boat rides into the delta offer peeks at local houses and colonial mansions, or you can just get off and explore some nature trails. All along the shores are signs of water-related activity, from sailing, kayaking and canoeing to sculling and even wakeboarding.

Tigre itself is easily walkable and holds some worthy attractions. Check out the Puerto de Frutos (Sarmiento 160; 🕐 10am-6pm), where housewares, furniture, wicker baskets, dried flowers, plants and a whole lot of kitsch are sold. Friday to Sunday is best, when a large crafts fair sets up; there are several restaurants too. To reach the market from the Tren de la Costa's Delta station, walk past the casino back down the tracks and turn left at the stoplight. There's a tourist office at the entrance to the port.

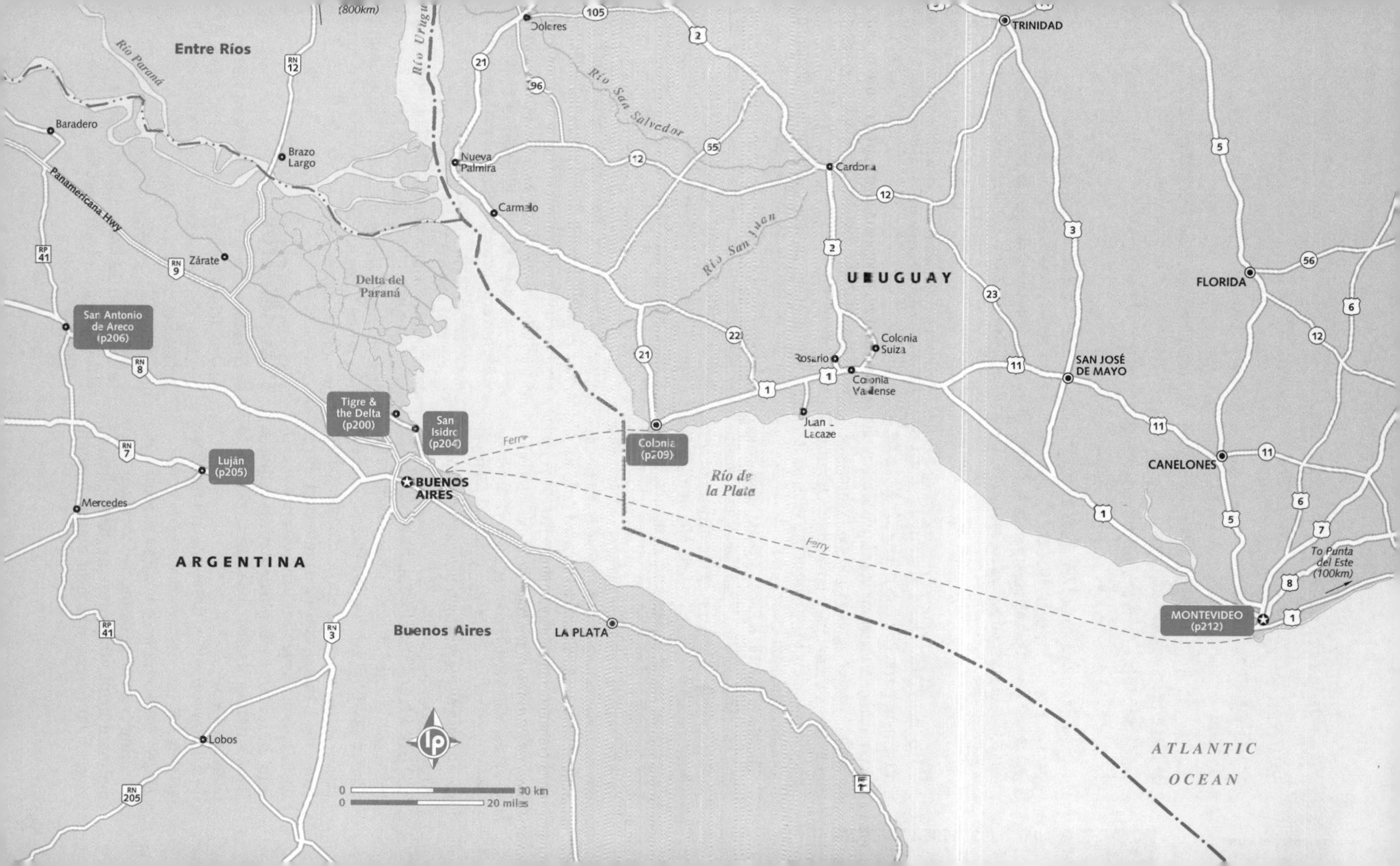

Entre Ríos
Río Paraná
Baradero
Brazo Largo
Panamericana Hwy
Zárate
Delta del Paraná
San Antonio de Areco (p206)
Tigre & the Delta (p200)
San Isidro (p204)
Luján (p205)
Mercedes
BUENOS AIRES
ARGENTINA
Buenos Aires
LA PLATA
Lobos
Dolores
Nueva Palmira
Carmelo
Río San Salvador
Río San Juan
Cardona
TRINIDAD
URUGUAY
Colonia Suiza
Rosario
Colonia Valdense
Juan L Lacaze
Colonia (p209)
Río de la Plata
Ferry
SAN JOSÉ DE MAYO
FLORIDA
CANELONES
MONTEVIDEO (p212)
To Punta del Este (100km)
ATLANTIC OCEAN
(800km)
0 30 km
0 20 miles

TRANSPORTATION: TIGRE & THE DELTA

Distance from Buenos Aires 35km.

Direction Northwest.

Travel time by public transportation One to 1½ hours.

Boat Sturla Viajes (☎ 4731-1300; www.sturlaviajes.com.ar) has a 6:30pm boat to Tigre (AR$18, 70 minutes, Monday to Friday only, reservations mandatory) that leaves from Grierson 400 in Puerto Madero.

Bus 60 (most 60 buses go to Tigre, but double check with the driver).

Car Take the Panamericana highway northwards to *ramal* (branch) Tigre.

Train From Estación Retiro you can take a train straight to Tigre (AR$1.35, one hour). The best way to reach Tigre, however, is via the Tren de la Costa (AR$14; www.trendelacosta.com.ar) – a pleasant electric train with attractive stations and views. This train line starts in the suburb of Olivos; to get there, take a train from Retiro station and get off at the Mitre station, then cross the bridge to the Tren de la Costa. Buses 59, 60 and 152 also go to the Tren de la Costa.

Also near the Delta station is Tigre's amusement park, Parque de la Costa (☎ 4002-6000; www.parquedelacosta.com.ar; admission AR$40-60). There are roller coasters, games and everything else that makes a theme park enjoyable. Opening hours vary widely throughout the year, so it's a good idea to call beforehand.

The Museo Naval de la Nación (☎ 4749-0608; Paseo Victorica 602; admission AR$3; 8:30am-5:30pm Mon-Fri, 10:30am-6:30pm Sat & Sun) traces the history of the Argentine navy with an eclectic mix of historical photos, model boats and airplanes, artillery displays and pickled sea critters. The Museo de la Reconquista (☎ 4512-4496; Padre Castañeda 470; admission free; 10am-6pm Wed-Sun) was the house where Viceroy Liniers coordinated resistance to the British invasions of the early 19th century; it's mildly interesting. Boat buffs can also visit the Museo Histórico Prefectura Naval Argentina (☎ 4749-6161; Liniers 1264; admission free; 10am-noon & 2-6pm Wed-Sun), which has exhibits on the Argentine coast guard.

Tigre's fanciest museum, however, is the Museo de Arte Tigre (☎ 4512-4528; Paseo Victorica 972; admission AR$5; 9am-7pm Wed-Fri, noon-7pm Sat & Sun). Located in an old social club that dates from 1912, this beautiful art museum showcases famous Argentine artists from the 19th and 20th centuries, plus rotating exhibits. The building itself is beautiful enough to warrant a visit.

And for something different, visit the Museo del Mate (☎ 4506-9594; www.elmuseodelmate.com; Lavalle 289; admission AR$10; 10am-6pm Wed-Sun). Celebrating everything connected to Argentina's national drink, this museum has collected over 2000 pieces, which of course include the *mates* (drinking receptacles) themselves – check out the ones especially made for blind people. You can also watch a short video and – in the pleasant garden out back – sample the concoction itself.

The waterways of the delta offer a glimpse into how the locals live here, along peaceful canals with boats as their only means of transportation. Frequent commuter launches (round trip AR$20 to AR$30) depart from Estación Fluvial (situated behind the tourist office) for various destinations in the delta. A popular destination is the neighborhood of Tres Bocas, a half-hour boat ride from Tigre, where you can take residential walks on slender paths connected by bridges over narrow channels. There are several restaurants and accommodation options here. The Rama Negra area has a quieter and more natural setting with fewer services, but is located an hour's boat ride away.

Several companies offer inexpensive boat tours (AR$25-60), but commuter launches give you flexibility if you want to go for a stroll or stop for lunch at one of the delta's restaurants. For rental bikes see Tigre Hostel p204; it rents to nonguests.

INFORMATION

Bonanza Deltaventura (☎ 4728-1674; www.deltaventura.com) Offers adventures that include walks, canoe trips, bike rides, horseback rides and *asados* (barbecues). It also has overnight stays; see p204.

Deltasur Ecoturismo (☎ 4553-8827; www.deltasurecoturismo.com.ar) Check out the Unesco biosphere reserve of the Paraná, located within the delta, with this eco-sensitive organization.

Selkñam Canoas (☎ 4731-4325; www.selknamcanoas.com.ar) Off-the-beaten-path watery tours in wooden Canadian-style canoes, including moonlight and custom outings.

Tangol's Tigre Tour (☎ 4312-7276; www.tangol.com) Full-day tour that includes transport from BA's center to Tigre (via train) and back (via boat), along with an optional kayak tour.

Tourist Office (☎ 4512-4497; www.vivitigre.gov.ar; 8am-6pm) Located behind McDonald's; will help you sort out the complex delta region. There are other tourist offices at the Puerto de Frutos entrance, near the Museo de Arte Tigre and at the train station.

EATING

Tigre's cuisine is not cutting edge, but it can be atmospheric – stroll Paseo Victorica, the city's pleasant riverside avenue, for the nicest options. Out on the Delta are several waterside choices, especially in the residential Tres Bocas area, a 30-minute boat ride away.

Il Novo María del Luján (☎ 4731-9613; mains AR$40-65; Paseo Victorica 611; breakfast, lunch & dinner) A good choice for an upscale meal of typical Argentine fare, this beautiful, large restaurant also has a great patio boasting full river views – surprisingly, the only restaurant in Tigre to do so.

Un Lugar (☎ 4749-0698; www.parrillaunlugar.com.ar; mains AR$38-60; Lavalle 369; lunch & dinner Tue-Sun) Some of Tigre's best grilled meats can be found at this new *parrilla* (steakhouse), which is run by four friends. There's comfortable indoor seating, but on warm days the place to be is on the sidewalk patio out front. Homemade pastas available, along with occasional live music.

Boulevard Saenz Peña (☎ 5197-4776; Blvd Saenz Peña 1400; mains AR$38-42; 9am-7pm Wed-Sat) For Tigre, this creative new eatery is a breath of fresh air. Not only is the food delicious (granola and yogurt for breakfast, gourmet sandwiches and salads for lunch, luscious pastries for teatime), but everything in the restaurant is for sale, from rustic tables and chairs to all the decor. A cute outside patio is a plus in warm weather.

Over in the Tres Bocas area, within the Delta, is **La Riviera** (☎ 4728-0177; mains AR$25-50; 10am-7pm). With relaxing sunny patios and river views, this is a scenic spot to kick back. Just beyond is **El Remanso** (☎ 4728-0575; 10am-6pm) and further inland is **El Hornero** (☎ 4728-0325; noon-5pm).

A 50-minute boat ride away from Tigre is **El Gato Blanco** (☎ 4728-0390; www.gato-blanco.com; mains AR$40-64 noon-6pm), the biggest restaurant in the delta. It boasts an international and Argentine menu for adults, and a play structure for the kids. **Beixa Flor** (☎ 15-6990-0730, www.beixaflor.com.ar; mains AR$50-60) is another good delta restaurant about a 30 minute boat ride from Tigre, offering great homemade pasta; reservations mandatory.

VISITING IGUAZÚ FALLS

Many visitors to Buenos Aires tour the city and then take a side trip to one of the most spectacular sites in South America: Iguazú Falls. If you have an extra couple of days it's definitely worth the time and money. Just remember that it's much warmer and more tropical there than in BA, and that in January and February the heat and humidity can be overwhelming.

Iguazú Falls straddles the Argentina–Brazil border, and some of the most stunning views are from the Brazilian side, so you shouldn't miss them. As for Brazilian visas, if you are from the US, Canada or Australia, you officially need a visa to enter Brazil. Western Europeans do not. Brazilian visas aren't cheap, and getting one may take some time, so plan ahead.

Here are some approximate prices for transportation and package deals available:

- One-way bus ticket from BA to Puerto Iguazú: AR$370, 19 hours
- One-way airplane ticket from BA to Puerto Iguazú: AR$750
- Sample bus package – roundtrip bus fare, transfers, guided tour and two night stay: AR$2000 to AR$2500 (per person, double occupancy). Brazilian visa and national park admission not included.
- Sample airplane package – roundtrip airfare, airport transfers, guided tour and two-night stay AR$2200 to AR$2700 (per person, double occupancy). Brazilian visa and national park admission not included.

During July, on holiday weekends and during Semana Santa (Easter week) you should plan way ahead or be prepared to pay premium prices. For a list of travel agencies that organize tickets or tours to Iguazú, see p232.

For general information on Iguazú, see the Casa de Misiones tourist office (Map p84; ☎ 4317-3700; Santa Fe 989; 8am-6pm Mon-Fri).

SLEEPING

Tigre

The following places are in the city of Tigre itself. For all accommodations in the region, book ahead on weekends and holidays (when prices can rise significantly).

Tigre Hostel (☎ 4749-4034; www.tigrehostel.com.ar; Av San Martín 190; dm AR$60, d AR$200-300;) This HI-affiliated hostel is in two parts: the main building is in an old mansion with spacious, private rooms and a great large garden with deck. Across the street is another building with dorms. Both are cool places and have kitchens. HI discount; prices 25% higher on Friday and Saturday nights. Rental bikes available.

Casona La Ruchi (☎ 4749-2499; www.casonalaruchi.com.ar; Lavalle 557; d AR$240;) This family-run B&B is in a beautiful mansion that's showing its age (it was built in 1893). All four of the romantic bedrooms have balconies, and all share bathrooms with original tiled floors. There's a pool and a large garden out back; two dogs roam the premises.

Hotel Villa Victoria (☎ 4731-2281; www.hotelvillavictoria.com; Av Liniers 566; r Sun-Fri AR$280-480, Sat AR$380-670;) Run by an Argentine-Swedish family, this boutique hotel is more like an upscale guesthouse. Only six simple yet elegant rooms are available, and there's a clay tennis court and pool out back. Swedish, French and English spoken.

The Delta

The huge delta region is dotted with dozens of accommodation possibilities: camping, B&Bs, cabanas, beach resorts and even activity-oriented places. The further out you are, the more peace and quiet you'll experience. Since places are relatively hard to reach (guests generally arrive by boat), the majority provide meal services, which are not always included in the price – be sure to ask. Children are welcome at some places but not at others. Bring mosquito repellent.

The Tigre tourist office has photos and information on all these places, and many are listed on its website at www.vivitigre.gov.ar. If you have a large group, check out www.deltaescape.blogspot.com.

Alpenhaus (☎ 4731-4526; www.alpenhaus.com.ar; d Mon-Thu AR$390-460, Fri & Sat AR$860-960;) A 60-minute boat ride from Tigre, this German-themed *hostería* (inn) offers modern, two-bedroom alpine-style cabanas, along with more modest but still pleasant rooms. There's a great pool and grassy lounging areas. Yoga, sauna, Jacuzzi, massage and facials available.

Bonanza Deltaventura (☎ 4728-1674; www.deltaventura.com; per person AR$485;) A 60-minute boat ride from Tigre. Best of those who like activities is this casual house with four simple yet comfortable rooms, all of which share bathrooms. You can ride horses, go on canoe trips, hike around or just relax on a small beach nearby. There's also table tennis and a soccer pitch. All meals and activities included; English spoken.

Los Pecanes (☎ 4728-1932; www.hosterialospecanes.com; r Mon-Thu AR$265-460, Fri & Sat AR$320-540) A 90-minute boat ride from Tigre. You'll feel at home in this friendly, family-run B&B with just three simple but comfortable guest rooms. The meals are homemade (these are not included in the price), and there are hummingbirds to watch. English and French are spoken.

Puerto Carpincho (☎ 4728-2966; www.puertocarpincho.com; d Mon-Thu AR$440-530, Fri & Sat AR$960-1160;) A 30-minute boat ride away, in the busier Tres Bocas area. Nine simple but tasteful rooms, all with balcony; some lead down to the sunny pool. There's no restaurant, but El Hornero (p204) is right next door.

La Becasina Lodge (☎ 4328-2687; www.labecasina.com; d AR$960;) A 90-minute boat ride from Tigre. For luxury, this beautiful place will do. The 15 private, stilted guest rooms are lovely, each with a nice bathtub and private deck overlooking the river. It's expensive, but the atmosphere is romantic and the pool area is lovely.

SAN ISIDRO

About 22km north of Buenos Aires is peaceful and residential San Isidro, a charming suburb of cobblestone streets lined with graceful buildings. The historic center is at Plaza Mitre, with its beautiful neo-Gothic cathedral; on weekends the area buzzes with a crafts fair. There's a tourist office (☎ 4512-3209; Ituzaingo 608; 8am-5pm Mon-Fri, 10am-6pm Sat & Sun) at the plaza near Av Libertador.

A stroll through the rambling neighborhood streets behind the cathedral will turn up some luxurious mansions (as well as more modest houses) and the occasional view over toward the coast. Close by is also the Tren de la Costa's San Isidro station, with a fashionable outdoor shopping mall to explore.

TRANSPORTATION: SAN ISIDRO

Distance from Buenos Aires 22km.

Direction Northwest.

Travel time 45 minutes to one hour.

Bus 168 drops you on Av del Libertador a couple of blocks from Quinta Pueyrredón.

Car Take the Panamericana Norte, or go up Av del Libertador all the way from Recoleta.

Train The best way to reach San Isidro is via the Tren de la Costa (www.trendelacosta.com.ar), which starts in the suburb of Olivos (get to the Tren de la Costa via buses 59, 60 or 152). The Mitre train line from Estación Retiro (downtown) also reaches Olivos.

Once owned by Argentine icon General Pueyrredón, the Museo Histórico Municipal General Pueyrredón (☎ 4512-3131; Rivera Indarte 48; admission free; 🕒 2-6pm Tue & Thu, 3-7pm Sat & Sun) is an old colonial house set on spacious grounds with faraway views of the Río de la Plata. Don't miss the *algarrobo* (carob) tree under which Pueyrredón and San Martín strategized against the Spanish. To get here from the cathedral, follow Av Libertador five blocks, turn left on Peña and after two blocks turn right onto Rivera Indarte.

Even more glamorous is the Unesco-owned Villa Ocampo (☎ 4732-4988; www.villaocampo.org; Elortondo 1837; admission Thu & Fri AR$10, Sat & Sun AR$15; 🕒 12:30-6pm Thu-Sun), a wonderfully restored mansion and reminder of a bygone era. Victoria Ocampo was a writer, publisher and intellectual who dallied with the literary likes of Borges, Cortázar, Sabato and Camus. The gardens are lovely here and there's a cafe. Daily tours at 4pm.

If you decide to spend the night in San Isidro try Hotel del Casco (☎ 4732-3993; www.hoteldelcasco.com.ar; Av del Libertador 16170; d from AR$640;), located in a gorgeous 1892 mansion. An atrium lobby, period furnishings and a lovely courtyard are all part of the charm.

LUJÁN

Luján (population 80,000) is a sleepy riverside town that once a year overflows with pilgrims making their way to Argentina's most important shrine. It's worth visiting any time, though, for its gracious Spanish-style paved square and the imposing neo-Gothic cathedral, as well as a couple of interesting museums. The riverside area is lined with restaurants and barbecue stands selling *choripán* (spicy sausage sandwiches); you can rent boats for a paddle on the river and on festival days there are games and rides. The chairlift carrying sightseers over the grubby river is an oddly charming touch.

On the first Saturday in October, thousands of Catholics walk to Luján from Buenos Aires' barrio of Liniers (65km away!) – up to an 18-hour trek. Other large gatherings occur on May 8 (the Virgin's Day), the first weekend in August (the colorful Peregrinación Boliviana), the last weekend in September (the 'gaucho' pilgrimage – watch for horses) and December 8 (Immaculate Conception Day).

INFORMATION

Area code (☎ 02323)

Oficina de Turismo (☎ 427-082; San Martín 1, edificio La Cúpola; 🕒 9am-6pm) Near the river at the west end of Lavalle.

SIGHTS

Luján's striking French Gothic basilica, the Basílica Nuestra Señora de Luján (☎ 420-058; cnr San Martín & 9 de Julio) is home to the Virgencita (see p206) and the heart of this deeply religious town. The statue of the virgin, which dates from 1630, sits in the high chamber behind the main altar. Masses take place in the basilica several times a day, mostly morning and evening.

Another place you shouldn't miss is the gorgeous, colonial-era Complejo Museográfico Enrique Udaondo (☎ 420-245; cnr Lavalle & Padre Salvaire; admission AR$1; 🕒 11:30am-5:30pm Wed-Fri, 10:30am-6pm Sat & Sun). This colonial complex (and

TRANSPORTATION: LUJÁN

Distance from Buenos Aires 65km.

Direction West.

Travel time 1½ to two hours by car.

Bus Transportes Atlántida (57) leaves every 30 minutes from Plaza Italia in Palermo (AR$10.50).

Car Drive west on RN 7.

Train Daily departures from Estación Once in Buenos Aires, but change trains in Moreno (AR$5).

ex-prison) has exhibitions showcasing the exploits of General José de San Martín and Juan Manuel de Rosas, as well as beautiful *mate* ware, horse gear, guitars and other gaucho paraphernalia. The pretty patios and gardens are in themselves worth a look.

The nearby Museo de Transporte (☎ 420-245; cnr Lavalle & Padre Salvaire; admission AR$1; 11:30am-5:30pm Wed-Fri, 10:30am-6pm Sat & Sun) displays a steam locomotive, a hydroplane that was used to cross the Atlantic in 1926 and some fantastic, horse-drawn carriages. The most offbeat exhibits, however, are the stuffed and scruffy remains of Gato and Mancha, the hardy Argentine *criollo* horses ridden by adventurer AF Tschiffely from Buenos Aires to Washington, DC, from 1925 to 1928.

Luján also boasts a leafy, elevated riverside area full of restaurants and more shops, and leisurely paddleboat rides are available.

EATING

Pilgrims won't go hungry in Luján – the central parts of San Martín, 9 de Julio and the riverfront are all lined with restaurants.

Cervecería Berlin (☎ 426-767; San Martín 151; mains AR$20-30; 11am-1am Sun-Thu, to 3am Fri & Sat) With tables on its small front deck, this is a good choice on a warm day. Food isn't fancy – burgers, sandwiches and waffles – but there are plenty of drinks.

Café La Basilica (☎ 428-376; San Martín 101; mains AR$30-60; 8am-8pm Sun-Thu, to 1am Fri & Sat) This classic old corner bar offers satisfying meals of homemade pastas and grilled meats. There's English translation on the menu.

L'Eau Vive (☎ 421-774; Constitución 2112; 3-course menu AR$55; lunch & dinner Tue-Sat, lunch Sun) Two kilometers from the center you'll find this excellent French restaurant run by Carmelite nuns from around the world; make sure to reserve ahead. Taxis here cost around AR$10, or take bus 501 from the center.

LA VIRGENCITA

According to legend, in 1630 an ox-drawn wagon containing a small terra-cotta statue of the Virgin Mary suddenly got stuck on the road and would not budge until the image was removed. The wagon was heading to Santiago del Estero, but the devoted owner took this pause as a sign and built a chapel on the site – which today is the city of Luján. 'La Virgencita' soon became Argentina's patron saint.

SLEEPING

Rates drop significantly during the week, and reservations are recommended on weekends and holidays.

Hostel Estación Lujan (☎ 429-101; www.estacionlujanhostel.com.ar; 9 de Julio 978; dm AR$60, d AR$180;) This small, modern hostel is just steps from the basilica. There are four clean rooms (dorms and privates), some with balcony, plus kitchen use and a large common area.

Hotel del Virrey (☎ 420-797; www.hoteldelvirreylujan.com.ar; San Martín 129; d AR$240;) Right near the basilica is this modern hotel offering 18 small but good rooms.

Hotel Hoxón (☎ 429-970; www.hotelhoxon.com.ar; 9 de Julio 760; s/d AR$180/285;) The best and biggest in town, with modern, clean and comfortable rooms. Superior rooms are carpeted and come with fridge and air-con, while the swimming pool (the only one in town) has a raised sundeck.

SAN ANTONIO DE ARECO

Nestled in lush farmlands, San Antonio de Areco is one of the prettiest towns in the pampas. An easy drive from the capital, it welcomes many day-tripping porteños, who come for the peaceful atmosphere and the picturesque colonial streets. The town dates from the early 18th century and to this day it preserves a great deal of the *criollo* (creole) and gaucho traditions, especially among its artisans, who produce very fine silverwork and saddlery. By day, men don the traditional *boina* (a kind of gaucho beret), while in the evenings locals head to the *peña*, a party with folk music and dancing.

Areco's compact center and quiet streets are very walkable. Around the Plaza Ruiz de Arellano, named in honor of the town's founding *estanciero* (rancher), are several historic buildings, including the Iglesia Parroquial (parish church) and the Casa de los Martínez, the site of the main house of the original Ruiz de Arellano *estancia* (cattle ranch).

The Puente Viejo (old bridge; built 1857) across the Río Areco follows the original cart road to northern Argentina. Once a toll crossing, it's now a pedestrian bridge leading to San Antonio's main attraction, the Museo Gauchesco Ricardo Güiraldes (☎ 455-839; cnr R Güiraldes & Sosa; admission AR$10; 11am-5pm Wed-Mon). This park-like gaucho-land features restored or fabricated

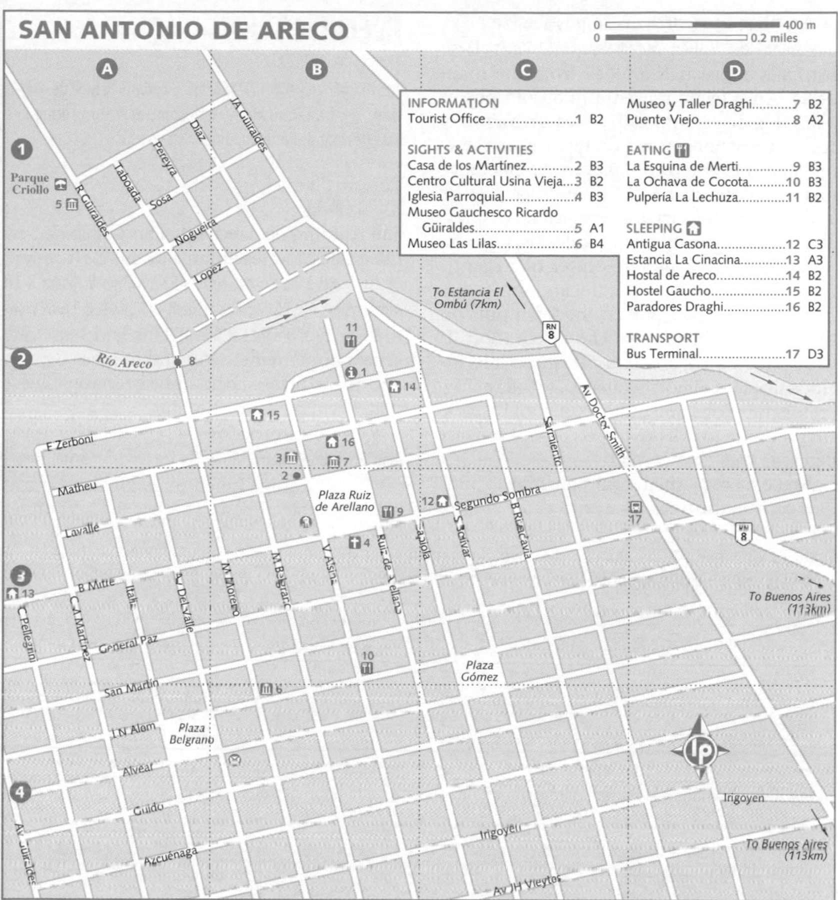

buildings that include an old flour mill, a recreated tavern and a colonial-style chapel. The main deal is a 20th-century reproduction of an 18th-century *casco* (ranch house), which holds lots of gorgeous horse gear and various works of gauchesco art. Two rooms are dedicated to Güiraldes himself.

A newcomer to town is pretty **Museo las Lilas** (☎ 456-425, www.museolaslilas.org; Moreno 279; admission AR$20; ⌚ 10am-8pm Thu-Sun Sep 21-May 25, to 6pm Thu-Sun May 26-Sep 20), a courtyard museum that displays the famous Argentine painter Florencio Molina Campos' work. Campos is to Argentines what Norman Rockwell is to Americans, a folk artist with wide-ranging appeal whose themes are based on comical caricatures.

The small **Museo y Taller Draghi** (☎ 454-219; Lavalle 387; admission AR$10; ⌚ 10am-1pm & 3:30-7:30pm Mon-Sat, 10am-1pm Sun) highlights an exceptional collection of silver *facones* (gaucho knives), beautiful horse gear and intricate *mate* paraphernalia. It's mainly the workshop of Juan José Draghi and family, however, so guided tours are given.

TRANSPORTATION: SAN ANTONIO DE ARECO

Distance from Buenos Aires 113km.

Direction West.

Travel time Two hours.

Bus Frequent buses (AR$30) from Retiro bus station drop you five blocks from the center of town.

Car Take RN8 west to *ramal* (branch) Pilar.

Another site worth visiting is the Centro Cultural Usina Vieja (V Alsina 660; admission AR$1.50; 11am-5pm Tue-Sun), just half a block from the main plaza. An eclectic museum in an old power plant that dates from 1901, it features a funky collection of ancient radios, typewriters, sewing machines and record players. Farm equipment, sculptures, an old-time grocery store and even a small airplane are also on display, as are rotating exhibits of local artists' work.

Areco is the symbolic center of Argentina's vestigial cowboy culture, and on Día de la Tradición in mid-November, the town puts on the country's biggest gaucho celebration. If you're in the area, don't miss it: attractions include displays of horsemanship, folk dancing, craft exhibitions and guided tours of historic sites. Be sure to call the tourist office for exact dates, as they change yearly.

Areco is best visited from Thursday to Sunday; early in the week many places are closed.

INFORMATION

Area code (02326)

Tourist office (453-165; cnr E Zerboni & Ruiz de Arellano; 8am-7pm Mon-Fri, to 8pm Sat & Sun) Located in a white, stand-alone building in the park.

EATING

San Antonio de Areco has a host of character-filled cafes and restaurants to choose from.

La Ochava de Cocota (452-176; cnr V Alsina & LN Alem; mains AR$25-50; 7:30am-2:30pm & 6-11pm Wed-Fri & Mon, to midnight Sat & Sun) This laid-back cafe serves homemade cakes and quiches by day, and turns into a cocktail bar serving cheese plates and pizzas by night.

Pulpería La Lechuza (454-542, near cnr Ruiz de Arellano & E Zerboni; mains AR$25-50; lunch Sat & Sun, dinner Sat) Enjoy a huge lunch of *empanadas* (meat and vegetable pies) and barbecued beef under

HISTORIC ESTANCIAS

One of the best ways to enjoy the wide-open spaces of Argentina is to visit an *estancia,* or cattle ranch (some more 'authentic' than others). The late-19th-century belle époque saw wealthy landowning families build up their country ranches with lavish, often fanciful homes, which they used as country retreats.

Today these establishments cater to tourists with *días de campo* – day tours that include large *asado* (barbecue) lunches, horseback rides, folk shows and, often, swimming facilities. Most also have overnight stays, which offer a longer glimpse into Argentina's history on the pampas.

El Ombú (off Map p207; in Buenos Aires 4737-0436; www.estanciaelombu.com) Just outside San Antonio de Areco, this working *estancia* offers nine rooms and the opportunity to watch gauchos do their stuff.

El Roble (in Buenos Aires 11-6899-9785; www.insidethepampas.com) Not far from Luján is this small but excellent working estancia with just two rooms for an exclusive group. Unique horse-riding opportunities; well run by an English-Argentine couple.

Juan Gerónimo (02221-481-414; www.juangeronimo.com.ar) There's excellent horseback riding and bird-watching at this working cattle farm, located within a Unesco world biosphere reserve about two hours from Buenos Aires.

La Candelaria (02227-424-404; www.estanciacandelaria.com) Located about 1½hr from Buenos Aires. Special for its castle and manicured grounds designed by Charles Thays (he did many of BA's public parks). Polo matches often held here.

La Cinacina (Map p207; in Buenos Aires 5252-1414; www.lacinacina.com.ar) Right on the edge of San Antonio de Areco's center, this historic (though touristy) *estancia* offers comfortable lodgings in a pretty park setting. Gaucho shows on offer.

La Margarita (in Buenos Aires 4951-0638; www.estancialamargarita.com) Old *estancia* from 1870 and located in Tapalqué, about 100 miles southwest of BA. Unique in that it offers a self-catering option, which makes your stay more self-sufficient and affordable.

La Oriental (in Buenos Aires 15-5146-5210; www.estancia-laoriental.com) More authentic than luxurious is this lovely *estancia* three hours from Buenos Aires. Activities include fishing or windsurfing in a nearby lagoon. Attentive owner.

San Antonio's tourist office has more information on *estancias,* as does Buenos Aires' Secretaría de Turismo de la Nación (Map p84; 4312-2232; Av Santa Fe 883). Online you can check www.estanciasargentinas.com.

the trees, or grab a *choripán* (spicy sausage sandwich) and go and enjoy it by the riverbank. It's opposite the tourist office.

La Esquina de Merti (☎ 456-705; Ruiz de Arellano 147; snacks AR$8-20, mains AR$24-45; 9am-1am) This is Areco's only restaurant that doesn't close in the afternoons; luckily it has great old atmosphere. Offers typical fare at mealtimes, with mostly sandwiches and *empanadas* for teatime.

SLEEPING

While San Antonio is popular as a day trip out of Buenos Aires, it's worth hanging around, as there are some lovely places to stay.

Paradores Draghi (☎ 454-219; www.paradoresdraghi.com.ar; reception at Lavalle 387; d AR$320;) Five large, gorgeous rooms (two with kitchenette) are available at this tranquil place. There's a grassy garden with beautiful pool, greenhouse breakfast room and two patios in which to relax.

Antigua Casona (☎ 456-600; www.antiguacasona.com; Segundo Sombra 495; d AR$300) This restored traditional home offers five high-ceilinged, rustically decorated rooms set around brick patios. Bike rentals available.

Hostal de Areco (☎ 456-118; www.hostaldeareco.com.ar; Zapiola 25; d Mon-Fri AR$180, Sat & Sun AR$220;) Clustered with two other hotels, which aren't as personable but do have pools, this place has a pleasant salon and nice grassy garden in the back.

Hostel Gaucho (☎ 453-625; www.hostelgaucho.com.ar; Zerboni 308; dm AR$60, d Mon-Fri AR$160, Sat & Sun AR$180;) This is Areco's only hostel, and it's a good one. Dorms and rooms are small but fine, and there's a grassy garden in the back. Bike rentals and tours available.

COLONIA

Colonia (officially Colonia del Sacramento) is an irresistibly picturesque town in neighboring Uruguay whose colonial-era Barrio Histórico is a Unesco World Heritage Site. Pretty rows of sycamores offer protection from the summer heat, and the Río de la Plata provides a venue for spectacular sunsets. Colonia's charm and its proximity to Buenos Aires draw thousands of Argentine visitors, and if you're short on time you can visit here comfortably on a day trip.

The city's heart – and main tourist attraction – is the Barrio Histórico, a historical neighborhood full of colonial architecture. The most dramatic way to enter is via the reconstructed 1745 city gate, the Portón de Campo, on Calle Manuel Lobo. A short distance west is Plaza Mayor 25 de Mayo, from which the narrow, roughly cobbled Calle de los Suspiros (Street of Sighs), lined with tile-and-stucco colonial houses, runs south almost to the water.

TRANSPORTATION: COLONIA

Distance from Buenos Aires 60km.

Direction East.

Travel time One to three hours by ferry.

Boat Buquebus and Colonia Express have many daily ferries between Buenos Aires & Colonia (AR$140 to AR$200; advance discounts available). For more details see p219.

A single Ur$50 ticket covers admission to Colonia's seven most major historical sights. All keep the same hours (11:15am to 4:45pm), but opening days vary as noted. Around Plaza Mayor are the following four attractions.

Museo Portugués (Plaza Mayor 25 de Mayo 180; closed Wed) holds Portuguese relics including porcelain, furniture, maps and the old stone shield that once adorned the Portón de Campo. Museo Municipal (Comercio 77; closed Tue) houses an eclectic collection of treasures, including a whale skeleton, an enormous rudder from a shipwreck and a scale model of Colonia c 1762. Casa Nacarello (Comercio 67; closed Tue) is one of the prettiest colonial homes in town, with period furniture, thick, whitewashed walls, wavy glass, original lintels and a nice courtyard. Archivo Regional (Misiones de los Tapes 115; closed Sat & Sun) contains historical documents and a bookstore.

Off the southwest corner of the Plaza Mayor are the ruins of the 17th-century Convento de San Francisco, within which stands the 19th-century faro (lighthouse; admission Ur$30; 11am-8pm). The lighthouse provides an excellent view of the old town.

Head to the west end of Misiones de los Tapes to the dinky Museo del Azulejo (cnr Misiones de los Tapes & Paseo de San Gabriel; closed Wed), a 17th-century house with a sampling of colonial tile work. From here, walk north two blocks, then inland to the Museo Indígena (Comercio s/n; closed Thu), which houses a collection of Charrúa (the indigenous people of Uruguay) stone tools and exhibits on indigenous history.

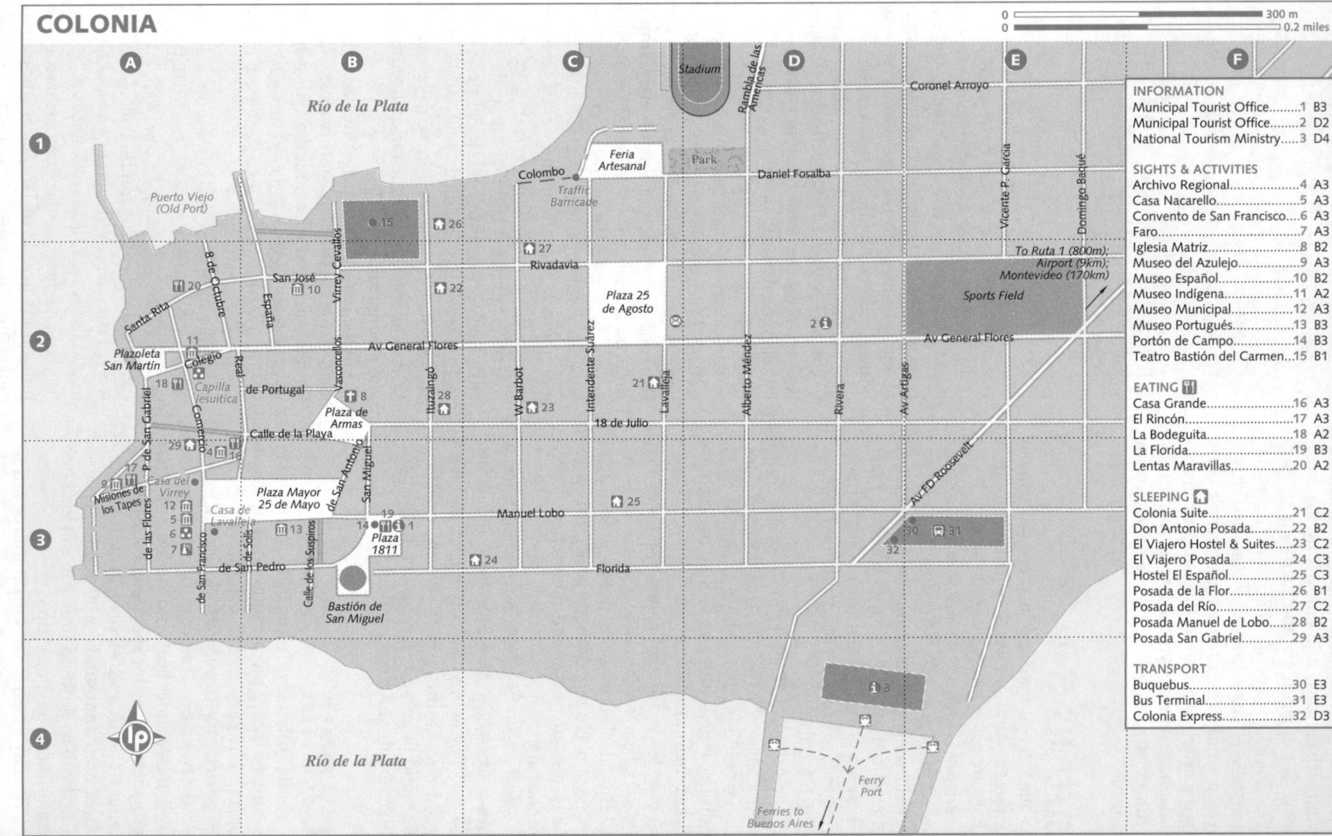
COLONIA
0 300 m
0 0.2 miles
Río de la Plata
Puerto Viejo (Old Port)
Stadium
Park
Feria Artesanal
Traffic Barricade
Plaza 25 de Agosto
Sports Field
To Ruta 1 (800m); Airport (9km); Montevideo (170km)
Plazoleta San Martín
Capilla Jesuítica
Plaza de Armas
Plaza Mayor 25 de Mayo
Casa del Virrey
Casa de Lavalleja
Misiones de los Tapes
Plaza 1811
Bastión de San Miguel
Ferry Port
Ferries to Buenos Aires
Coronel Arroyo
Rambla de las Americas
Colombo
Daniel Fosalba
Vicente P. García
Domingo Baqué
Rivadavia
San José
Santa Rita
8 de Octubre
España
Virrey Cevallos
Av General Flores
Colegio
Real
de Portugal
Vasconcellos
Ituzaingó
W Barbot
Intendente Suárez
Lavalleja
Alberto Méndez
Rivera
Av Artigas
18 de Julio
Calle de la Playa
P de San Gabriel
Comercio
de San Antonio
San Miguel
Av FD Roosevelt
de las Flores
de San Francisco
de Solís
Calle de los Suspiros
de San Pedro
Manuel Lobo
Florida
INFORMATION
Municipal Tourist Office.........1 B3
Municipal Tourist Office.........2 D2
National Tourism Ministry.....3 D4
SIGHTS & ACTIVITIES
Archivo Regional..................4 A3
Casa Nacarello.......................5 A3
Convento de San Francisco....6 A3
Faro...7 A3
Iglesia Matriz..........................8 B2
Museo del Azulejo.................9 A3
Museo Español....................10 B2
Museo Indígena...................11 A2
Museo Municipal.................12 A3
Museo Portugués.................13 B3
Portón de Campo.................14 B3
Teatro Bastión del Carmen..15 B1
EATING
Casa Grande........................16 A3
El Rincón..............................17 A3
La Bodeguita........................18 A2
La Florida............................19 B3
Lentas Maravillas.................20 A2
SLEEPING
Colonia Suite........................21 C2
Don Antonio Posada............22 B2
El Viajero Hostel & Suites.....23 C2
El Viajero Posada.................24 C3
Hostel El Español.................25 C3
Posada de la Flor.................26 B1
Posada del Río.....................27 C2
Posada Manuel de Lobo......28 B2
Posada San Gabriel.............29 A3
TRANSPORT
Buquebus.............................30 E3
Bus Terminal........................31 E3
Colonia Express....................32 D3

Heading east on Av General Flores and then a block further north brings you near the Museo Español (San José 164), which had exhibitions of replica colonial pottery, clothing and maps; it was closed at research time but, hopefully, will be open during your visit. At the north end of nearby Calle España is the Puerto Viejo, the old port, now a yacht harbor. One block east, the Teatro Bastión del Carmen (cnr Calle del Virrey Cevallos & Rivadavia; closed Mon) is a theater and gallery complex that incorporates part of the city's ancient fortifications. The huge chimney is newer, dating from the 1880s.

Situated south a couple of blocks is the Plaza de Armas, also known as Plaza Manuel Lobo. The Iglesia Matriz, begun in 1680, is Uruguay's oldest church, though it has been completely rebuilt twice. The plaza also holds the foundations of a house dating from Portuguese times.

INFORMATION

Municipal Tourist Office (4522-6141; Centro (cnr Av General Flores & Rivera); 9am-7pm, to 8pm summer); there's also a hotel office (4522-7302; 11am-7pm) that will help you find accommodation.

Municipal Tourist Office (4522-8506; Manuel Lobo sñ; 9am-6pm, to 7pm Dec-Mar) Located just outside the old town gate.

National Tourism Ministry (4522-4897; www.turismo.gub.uy) Inside the ferry terminal.

EATING

Colonia has a good range of restaurants to choose from.

La Florida (94-293036; www.restorantlaflorida.com; Florida 215; mains Ur$400-500; 1-4pm Thu-Tue, 9pm-1am Sat) For trivia buffs: this cute antique-decorated house, now housing Colonia's best restaurant, was once a brothel. For gourmets: chef Carlos Bidanchon whips up both traditional and creative international dishes with only fresh and seasonal ingredients; expect delicious productions like shrimp risotto, rack of lamb, or mussels in a blue cheese and curry sauce. Reserve for Saturday dinner.

La Bodeguita (4522-5329; Comercio 167; meals Ur$220-330; lunch & dinner Mon-Fri, lunch Sat & Sun) Nab a table out back on the sunny, two-level deck and soak up the sweeping river views while drinking sangria or munching on La Bodeguita's trademark pizza.

Casa Grande (4522-8371; www.casagrandebistro.com; Misiones de las Tapas 174; mains Ur$200-360; 10am-midnight) This upscale restaurant specializes in Italian homemade pastas (the chef is from Italy) but also serves good meat and fish dishes. Romantic street tables near Plaza Major are a plus.

El Rincón (99-675202; Misiones de los Tapes 41; mains Ur$200-300; noon-5pm Thu-Tue) El Rincón is best enjoyed on a sunny weekend afternoon, lounging out back under a big tree between stone and stucco walls or watching the riverfront scene. Order the *parrillada* (mixed grill) here.

Lentas Maravillas (4522-0636; Santa Rita 61; mains Ur$120-280; 3-9pm Mon-Fri, 4-11pm Sat, noon-9pm Sun) Colonia's best hangout is this cozy spot that's more like a living room than an eatery. Owner Maggie Molnar's book collection is open for browsing, and there are serene views to the grassy garden (which also offers tables) and river beyond. The food – casual gourmet and excellent. Wi-fi available.

SLEEPING

Some hotels charge higher rates Friday through Sunday. From December to March reserve ahead.

Colonia Suite (9851-8966; www.coloniaste.net; Lavalleja 169; ste Ur$3100-3700;) Colonia's best intimate stay are these three gorgeous suites. All are very spacious, boasting tasteful yet comfortable decor with fine rustic touches like exposed-brick walls and open-beam ceilings. The homemade breakfast is prepared by your English-speaking host; reservations only.

Don Antonio Posada (4522-5344; www.posadadonantonio.com; Ituzangó 232; r Ur$1900-3400;) If you're looking for an atmospheric dip in a pool, this upscale hotel is your ticket to cool.

LIFE IN THE COUNTRYSIDE

Want to get away from it all but still have some affordable fun? Check into El Galope Hostel (99-105985; www.elgalope.com.uy; Km 114.5, Ruta 1; dm Ur$400, d Ur$1400), a farm about 50 minutes by bus outside Colonia. You can take nature walks, ride horses, go for a bike ride and hang out by the fireplace with a bottle of wine, all in the peaceful Uruguayan countryside. Its owners, Mónica and Miguel, are friendly and helpful, and are experienced international travelers who speak English, Spanish, French and German. HI discounts; some activities cost extra.

Terraced patios make for a classic and romantic old feel, and the rooms (choose from four classes) are bright and comfortable.

Posada Manuel de Lobo (☎ 4522-2463; www.posadamanueldelobo.com; Ituzaingó 160; r Ur$2000-3000;) The historical charms of this 150-year-old house include heavy wooden furniture, antique tile work, beamed ceilings, brick walls, fountains, and twin patios out back. There are only eight rooms (suites have Jacuzzis) and owner Paco is friendly.

Posada San Gabriel (☎ 4522-3283; www.posadasangabriel.com.uy; Comercio 127; r Ur$1430-1540;) This sweet little *posada* (inn) with stone walls and brass beds has only six rooms – the two upstairs ones sport river views and are more expensive. Reserve ahead as it's popular.

Posada de la Flor (☎ 4523-0794; www.posada-delaflor.com.ar; Ituzaingó 268; r Ur$1300-1660;) Serenely situated on a sycamore-lined street dead-ending onto a small beach, the Flor's biggest draws are a wonderfully leafy central courtyard and an upstairs terrace overlooking the river.

Posada del Río (☎ 4522-3002; www.posadadelrio.com.uy; Washington Barbot 258; s/d Ur$800/1400;) This peaceful place on a dead-end street offers 12 nice, comfortable and remodeled rooms. The small upstairs breakfast room has partial river views, and there's a nice little patio downstairs.

El Viajero Hostel & Suites (☎ 4522-2683; www.elviajerohostels.com; Washington Barbot 164; dm Ur$340-360, d Ur$1200;) Here's a decent hostel in an old house, with a back patio (overlooked by the bright private rooms) and pleasant rooftop terrace. Rental bikes are available. Better yet is their nearby posada (☎ 4522-8645; Florida 269; d Ur$1600), which offers more upscale ambience and fine rooms around a pretty courtyard.

CROSSING INTO URUGUAY

Traveling from Buenos Aires into Uruguay is fairly easy and straightforward, but you'll need a valid passport. Nationals of Western Europe, the USA, Canada, Australia and New Zealand will receive a tourist card on entry, valid for 90 days. Other nationals may require visas. Check the current visa situation for your stay.

Uruguay's unit of currency is the peso (Ur$), but US dollars and Argentine pesos are widely accepted for tourist services. Uruguay's telephone country code is ☎ 598. The country is one hour ahead of Argentina, but daylight saving may affect time differences.

Hostel El Español (☎ 4523-0759; www.hostelespaniol.com; Calle Manuel Lobo 377; dm Ur$240-260, d with shared/private bathroom Ur$650/800;) Popular with young Latin Americans, this old hostel's dark common areas are redeemed by a sunny patio out back. Dorms have four to 10 beds and rental bikes are available. Hostel club members (from Hi, HoLa and Minihostels) get 10% off.

MONTEVIDEO

Uruguay's capital and by far its largest city, Montevideo is a vibrant, eclectic place with a rich cultural life. In the historic downtown business district, art deco and neoclassical buildings jostle for space alongside grimy, worn-out skyscrapers, while in Ciudad Vieja – the heart of historic Montevideo – old buildings are being restored to make room for boldly painted cafes, hostels and galleries. Meanwhile, the city's music, theater, art and club scenes continue to thrive, from elegant older theaters and cozy little tango bars to modern beachfront discos.

Montevideo's key commercial and entertainment area is Av 18 de Julio, but its functional center is Plaza Independencia. It's here that you'll find the somber yet dramatic Mausoleo de Artigas, which celebrates the achievements of Uruguay's independence hero. The underground mausoleum is smack in the middle of the plaza; look for stairs underneath the statue of Artigas on horseback.

Just off the plaza is the elegant Teatro Solís (☎ 1950-3323; www.teatrosolis.org.uy; Buenos Aires 678), Montevideo's premier performance space. First opened in 1856 and completely renovated during the past decade, it has superb acoustics and hosts music festivals, concerts, ballet, opera and plays. From December to March, tours are given Tuesday to Friday and Sunday at 11am, noon and 5pm; on Saturday there's an extra tour at 1pm (in other months tour hours vary). They cost Ur$20 in Spanish and Ur$40 in English; Wednesday they're free but in Spanish only.

Three blocks east of the plaza, the Museo del Gaucho y de la Moneda (☎ 2900-8764; 18 de Julio 998; admission free; 10am-5pm Mon-Fri) eloquently conveys the deep attachment and interdependent relationship between gauchos, their animals and the land. The excellent collection features artifacts from Uruguay's gaucho history, including horse gear, silver work and *mate* gourds and *bombillas* (drinking straws) in whimsical designs.

TRANSPORTATION: MONTEVIDEO

Distance from Buenos Aires 220km.

Direction East.

Travel time By air 35 minutes; by ferry 2½ to three hours.

Airplane Daily flights with Pluna and Aerolíneas (AR$520).

Bus Daily buses from Retiro bus station (AR$830, eight hours).

Boat Buquebus has high-speed ferries with daily departures to Montevideo (AR$430, three hours). There are also bus-ferry combinations via Colonia (AR$240 to AR$320, four to six hours). Colonia Express has fewer options but is less expensive; for more details see p219.

Vestiges of Montevideo's 19th-century neoclassical buildings still exist in Ciudad Vieja, the city's picturesque historic neighborhood. Many museums are located in this area, including the Casa Rivera (☎ 2915-1051; Rincón 437; 🕑 11am-5pm Mon-Fri, 10am-3pm Sat), former home of Uruguay's first president. The collection of paintings, documents, furniture and artifacts traces Uruguayan history from indigenous roots through independence. A couple of blocks away is the Museo de Artes Decorativas (☎ 2915-1101; 25 de Mayo 376; 🕑 12:30-6pm Tue-Sat, 2-6pm Sun), a wealthy merchant's residence dating from 1810. Free guided tours of the palatial building and its exquisite furnishings are given (in Spanish) between 2pm and 5pm from Wednesday to Friday.

Over by the waterfront, the Museo del Carnaval (☎ 2916-5493; Rambla 25 de Agosto 218; 🕑 11am-5pm Tue-Sun) houses a wonderful collection of costumes, drums, masks, recordings and photos documenting the 100-plus-year history of Montevideo's Carnaval. Nearby, the Mercado del Puerto is a wrought-iron superstructure from 1868, sheltering a gaggle of reasonably priced *parrillas*. Especially on Saturday afternoons, it's a lively and colorful spot where artists, craftspeople and street musicians hang out.

East of downtown, La Rambla – Montevideo's long coastal promenade – is one of the city's defining elements, connecting downtown to the eastern beach communities of Punta Carretas, Pocitos, Buceo and Carrasco. This is Montevideo's social hub on Sunday afternoon, when the place is packed with locals cradling thermoses of *mate* and socializing with friends.

INFORMATION

Municipal tourist office (☎ 2916-8434; cnr Rambla 25 de Agosto & Maciel; 🕑 11am-5pm) Located near the port in Ciudad Vieja; a more central branch might return to the cnr of Av 18 de Julio & Ejido.

National Tourism Ministry Ciudad Vieja (☎ 1885-111; www.turismo.gub.uy; cnr Rambla 25 de Agosto & Yacaré; 🕑 9am-6pm Mon-Fri); Carrasco airport (☎ 2604-0386; 🕑 8am-10pm); Tres Cruces bus terminal (☎ 2409-7399; cnr Bulevar Artigas & Av Italia; 🕑 8am-10pm)

Bicicletería Sur (☎ 2901-0792; Alquiles Lanza 1100; 9am-1pm, 3-7pm Mon-Sat) Rents bicycles for your *rambla* (riverfront boardwalk) adventure.

EATING

Montevideo's restaurants are largely unpretentious and offer excellent value.

Ciudad Vieja

The classic area for restaurants in Montevideo is Mercado del Puerto on the Ciudad Vieja waterfront. The densely packed *parrillas* here cater to every budget and serve up huge steaks.

Café Roldós (☎ 2915-1520; Mercado del Puerto; sandwiches Ur$45; 🕑 9am-6pm) This historic spot has been pouring its famous *medio y medio* – a refreshing concoction of half wine, half sparkling wine – since 1886. Throw in a tasty sandwich and you've got a meal!

Shawarma Ashot (☎ 2900-7250; Zelmar Michelini 1295; Ur$75-130; 🕑 11am-5pm Mon-Fri) Very casual joint serving up tasty falafels and other Middle Eastern treats; get the lamb shawarma on Friday.

Cervecería Matriz (☎ 2916-1582; Sarandi 582; mains Ur$160-335; 🕑 breakfast, lunch & dinner) Join the crowds enjoying beer and *chivitos* (Uruguay's national sandwich and cholesterol bomb) under the trees on picturesque Plaza Constitución. You'll also find pizza on the menu.

CIUDAD VIEJA WARNING

While Montevideo is pretty sedate by Latin American standards, exercise caution as in any large city. Wallet and purse snatchings are not uncommon in the Ciudad Vieja, and it's wise to avoid Mercado del Puerto at night. If you want to report a crime, contact the Tourist Police (☎ 2403-6123).

CENTRO

Los Leños Uruguayos (☎ 2900-2285; San José 909; mains Ur$145-360; 11:30am-3:30pm & 5:30pm-midnight) A firm favorite with the business set, this restaurant has a nice salad bar and there's always a big rack of meat roasting up front. The *menu ejecutivo* (set menu; Ur$240) includes the *cubierto* (cover charge; Ur$34 to Ur$42), main dish, dessert and coffee.

Ruffino Pizza y Pasta (☎ 2908-3384; San José 1166; mains Ur$160-310; lunch & dinner Mon-Fri, dinner Sat, lunch Sun) Deservedly popular for Sunday lunch, Ruffino serves good homemade Italian pizza and pasta. Try its Caruso (mushroom and cream) sauce, a uniquely Uruguayan specialty created for Italian tenor Enrico Caruso during his 1915 visit to Montevideo.

El Rincón de los Poetas (☎ 2908-5345; San José 1312; mains Ur$150-200; lunch & dinner Mon-Sat) Featuring the classic Uruguayan trinity of pasta, pizza and, of course, grilled meat, this eatery epitomizes the Mercado de la Abundancia's cozy, relaxed ambience.

La Vegetariana (☎ 2902-3178; Yí 1369; meals Ur$150; lunch & dinner Mon-Sat, lunch Sun) Grab a plate and help yourself from the steam trays, salad bar and dessert table – it's not fine dining, but it's one of the few truly veggie options in this meat-crazed country.

SLEEPING

Montevideo's burgeoning hostel scene is a dream come true for budget travelers with competition keeping the quality high.

Ciudad Vieja

Posada al Sur (☎ 2916-5287; www.posadaalsur.com.uy; Pérez Castellano 1424; dm Ur$360, s Ur$900-1200, d Ur$1000-1300, apt Ur$1500;) A few blocks above Mercado del Puerto, this lovingly restored older building has a six-bed dorm room and three private rooms (two share bathrooms). It's also green-themed – there are solar panels on the roof, and proceeds help support an eco-tourism business. Nice rooftop terrace and bike rentals available.

Hotel Palacio (☎ 2916-3612; www.hotelpalacio.com.uy; Bartolomé Mitre 1364; r Ur$780-900) A palace it's not, but rather an ancient hotel with sagging beds, antique furniture and a vintage elevator. Try for one of the two 6th-floor rooms; there are good views of the Ciudad Vieja from the large balconies.

Centro

Radisson Victoria Plaza (☎ 2902-0111; www.radisson.com/montevideouy; Plaza Independencia 759; s/d Ur$4800/5200, ste Ur$5600;) A true five-star hotel, with luxurious rooms, a semi-Olympic (25m) swimming pool and remarkable city views from the 25th-floor restaurant. The central location on Plaza Independencia can't be beat.

Hotel Embajador (☎ 2902-0012; www.hotelembajador.com; San José 1212; s/d from Ur$1380/1780, ste Ur$3700;) The four-star Embajador offers comfortable accommodation without a monster price tag. Rooms are good sized, but if you really want space go for the huge suites with Jacuzzi tubs. There's a rooftop pool, sauna, small gym and plenty of other amenities.

Hotel Lancaster (☎ 2902-1054; www.lancasterhotel.com.uy; Plaza Cagancha 1334; s/d from Ur$1100/1280;) This centrally located three-star on Plaza Cagancha is good value. The halls are a bit dingy and the rooms somewhat plain, but at least they're clean and comfortable – and many of the bigger ones sport views of the square in front.

El Viajero Hostel & Suites Centro (☎ 2908-2913; www.elviajerodowntown.com; Soriano 1093; dm Ur$340, d Ur$1400;) This colorful hostel is located in a charming old building; its best feature could be the sunny patio in back, a great hangout spot. Dorms here are good sized and each of the eight private rooms has its own bathroom. A bright lobby, bike rentals and the occasional *asado* are pluses. HI discount is 15%; there's another branch in Ciudad Vieja (☎ 2915-6192, Ituzaingo 1436).

Red Hostel (☎ 2908-8514; www.redhostel.com; San José 1406; dm/s/d Ur$320/700/1080;) The bright-orange walls and the roof deck, plants and natural light pouring in through stained-glass skylights make this Montevideo's cheeriest hostel. The staff are energetic and friendly, and even though the TV room and kitchen could be a tad bigger, it's highly recommended overall.

Montevideo Hostel (☎ 2908-1324; www.montevideohostel.com.uy; Canelones 935; dm Ur$300;) With musical instruments strewn here and there, a cellar bar, a nice fireplace and a spiral staircase connecting all three levels of the spacious central common area, this older hostel remains one of Montevideo's best budget options. There's also a ping-pong table in the basement, a rooftop terrace and bike rentals available. HI discount.

PUNTA DEL ESTE

Punta del Este – with its many beaches, elegant seaside homes, yacht harbor, high-rise apartment buildings, pricey hotels and glitzy restaurants – is one of South America's most glamorous resorts and easily the most expensive place in Uruguay. Extremely popular with Argentines (especially in January and February) and Brazilians, Punta suffered a period of decline during the Uruguayan and Argentine recessions, but has come back with a vengeance. Celebrity-watchers have a full-time job here: Punta has hosted the likes of Ralph Lauren, soccer star Zinedine Zidane, and Metallica's lead singer, James Hetfield.

Punta's center is very walkable – you can stroll from one end to the other in under half an hour. Av Gorlero, the city's main drag, is just 10 blocks long and offers the biggest concentration of touristy shops, services and casual eateries.

Beaches are the area's main attraction, however. Punta is at the rocky tip of a V-shaped peninsula edged with sandy ribbons. Close to the center and on the Río de la Plata side of the peninsula is Playa Mansa, whose calm sands attract families and low key beachgoers. Playa Brava is on the east side but less than a five-minute walk away; it has a more active crowd and boasts fierce waves that claim a few lives each year, so be careful when swimming here.

Punta's best beaches are a short bus ride away. Stretching up to the northeast is a run of sand that ends 10km away at La Barra, a small hamlet where the rich and good-looking come to party and preen themselves. Disco clubs, restaurants and shops service the trendy crowds.

Heading up on the northwest side of the peninsula is another stretch of beaches that ends 15km away at Punta Ballena, whose main tourist attraction is Casapueblo (☎ 578-041; admission Ur$120; ⌚ 10am-sunset), a free-form, neo-Mediterranean structure covered in white stucco and boasting unforgettable views. It's a gallery inspired by Uruguayan artist and adventurer Carlos Páez Vilaró (Uruguay's best-known artist), and next door is a unique hotel and cafe-bar. To get here, walk 2km from the junction where non-direct Montevideo buses (like Cot or Copsa) stop.

TRANSPORTATION: PUNTA DEL ESTE

Distance from Buenos Aires 360km.

Direction East.

Travel time By air 45 minutes; by bus 10 hours.

Airplane Daily flights with Aerolíneas; Pluna only in high seasons (AR$800).

Bus Frequent buses from Montevideo (AR$30, two hours), with connections to Retiro in Buenos Aires.

Boat Bus-boat combinations available with Buquebus (p219) via Colonia (AR$260) or Montevideo (AR$380).

INFORMATION

Centro de Hoteles y Restaurantes (☎ 4244-0512; www.puntadelestehoteles.com; Plaza Artigas; ⌚ 8am-midnight Dec-Mar, 10am-6pm Apr-Nov) Helps with hotel bookings.

Centro de Informes (☎ 4244-6519; www.maldonado.gub.uy, cnr Calle 31 & La Rambla; ⌚ 8am-midnight Dec-Mar, 10am-6pm Mar-Nov) Other branches at Plaza Artigas and at the bus terminal.

National Tourism Ministry (☎ 4244-1218; www.turismo.gub.uy; Gorlero 942; ⌚ 10am-1:30pm & 4:30-8pm Dec-Mar, 10am-5pm Mon-Sat, noon-4pm Sun Apr-Nov)

EATING

Punta has mostly expensive eateries and boasts excellent seafood restaurants. Hours listed below are more limited April to November, when some places open only on weekends.

Lo de Tere (☎ 4244-0492; www.lotdetere.com; Rambla Artigas & Calle 21; mains Ur$450-890; ⌚ lunch & dinner) Even with early-bird discounts (there's even one for women dining alone!) Lo de Tere is hard on the wallet, but it's hard to get finer food in Punta. Expect international choices like panzerotti stuffed with duck and the famous rack of lamb. The harbor views are a plus.

Il Baretto (☎ 4244-5565; www.ilbarettopunta.com; cnr Calles 9 & 10; mains Ur$320-520; ⌚ breakfast, lunch & dinner Mon-Sat, lunch & dinner Sun) Il Baretto's colorful menu features some of the best pasta in Punta – try their homemade fish ravioli or salmon *en croûte*; there's good pizza too. Live music Friday and Saturday nights.

Virazón (☎ 4244-3924; www.virazon.com.uy; Rambla Artigas & Calle 28; mains Ur$300-570; ⌚ breakfast, lunch & dinner) Grab a spot on the beachside deck, and have fun watching the waiters try to look dignified as they cross the street with loaded trays. There's something for everyone here – meats, seafood, pastas, salads and even a few sushi choices.

Baby Gouda Deli Café (☎ 4277-1874; Km 161, Ruta 10, La Barra; mains Ur$250-450; ⌚ lunch & dinner) Sit back with other trendsetters at this cool restaurant with inviting outdoor deck, and nibble on the limited menu of gourmet sandwiches, salads and pastas. It's on the main drag in La Barra, a 20-minute bus ride away from Punta's center.

La Fonda del Pesca (☎ 4244-9165; Calle 29 btwn Gorlero & Calle 24; mains Ur$180-250; 7am-4am) A vividly painted hole-in-the-wall specializing in fish, La Fonda also serves up plenty of local color (literally), and owner-chef Pesca often makes appearances from the kitchen. Pastas, meats and homemade desserts too.

Chivitería Marcos (☎ 4244-9932; Rambla Artigas btwn Calles 12 & 14; chivitos Ur$180; 11am-4am) Montevideo based Marcos earned its fame building mega-sandwiches to order. Just tell the *chivito*-sculptor behind the counter which of the 12 toppings and seven sauces you want, then try to balance the thing back to your table.

El Milagro (☎ 4244-3866; Calle 17 btwn Calles 22 & 24; mains Ur$100-195; lunch & dinner) This humble *chivitería* (Uruguayan sandwich shop) and pizzeria is about as affordable as things get in Punta. It has a cheap *menu del día* and – surprisingly enough – no cover charge. Also good for burgers, hot dogs and pasta.

SLEEPING

From Christmas through January (when reservations are mandatory), Punta is jammed with people and prices are astronomical. From June to August Punta is a ghost town; places that stay open lower their prices considerably.

Prices below are for the shoulder months of November, early December and February, though everyone has their own idea of the seasons. Check ahead to get exact prices.

Casapueblo (☎ 4257-8611; www.clubhotel.com.ar; Punta Ballena, Maldonando; r from UR$4200) Over in Punta Ballena is this unique, large stucco building flowing down a hillside to the ocean. All rooms have a terrace with partial or full ocean views, and there are maze-like hallways and stairs everywhere. The outdoor pool is heavenly – there's also an indoor pool. It's a great stay, but you'll need your own transport unless you like walking – the nearest bus stop is 2km away. Reserve ahead; five-night minimum December 23 to February 28.

La Posta del Cangrejo (☎ 4277-0021; www.lapostadelcangrejo.com; Ruta 10, La Barra; d from Ur$4000) Over in La Barra, a 20-minute bus ride from Punta's center is this beachside hotel. It's a multi-level, almost labyrinthine building with whitewashed adobe walls, excellent French-influenced restaurant and poolside terrace. Some rooms have patios with sea view, but if you want lots of space get an upstairs suite – they're huge, with two bathrooms, fireplace, Jacuzzi and separate TV room.

Hotel Concorde (☎ 4244-4800; www.hotelconcorde.com.uy; Calle 9 717; d from Ur$2700) This remodeled three-star hotel offers good rooms (some with kitchenette) and a pleasant pool area out back. It's well located near the yacht harbor and many restaurants. Four-person apartments also available (Ur$5000).

Bonne Étoile (☎ 4244-0301; www.hotelbonneetoile.com; Calle 20 btwn Calles 23 & 25; d Ur$2600-3000) Don't be scared off by the black-and-white, antiseptic lobby – the rooms, despite being a bit outdated, are decent and spacious, and some even boast river views. It's in a 1940s beach house adjoining a more modern six-story tower. Air-con costs extra.

Days Inn (☎ 4244-7116; www.daysinnhotels.com.uy; cnr Calle 28 & Gorlero; d Ur$2400-3200) American travelers can be comforted by this US-based chain of popular hotels. Rooms are nice, clean and have typical amenities like safes and minibars; some boast sea views. There's a rooftop lounging area and indoor pool. Also on Playa Mansa at Rambla Williman, parada 3.

Hotel Tanger (☎ 4244-1333; www.hoteltanger.com; Calle 31 btwn Calles 18 & 20; d Ur$2200) Just a block from the bus terminal is this family-run hotel with spacious, comfortable rooms. Suites and apartments are bright, and some boast Jacuzzi and ocean views. There are two pools – one on the rooftop, and another indoors.

Tas D'Viaje Hostel (☎ 4244-8789; www.tasdviaje.com; Calle 24 btwn 28 & 29; dm Ur$600, d Ur$1600) Punta's best vibe hostel is this newcomer a block from Playa Brava. It has wonderful spaces for relaxing, including a small patio in front, a comfortable living room and – best of all – a garden out back with *parrilla*, bar and hammocks. Bicycle and surfboard rentals, plus surfing lessons.

1949 Hostel (☎ 4244-0719; www.1949hostel.com; cnr Calles 30 & 18; dm Ur$600-800) This hostel's best feature is the hangout spots out front, boasting hammocks and partial water views. Low points are the small kitchen, and crowded dorms (though in winter they turn into private rooms). There is also surfboard rentals.

El Viajero Brava Beach Hostel (☎ 4248-0331; www.elviajerohostels.com; cnr Av Francia y Charrúa; dm Ur$500, d Ur$2000) Bearing all the trademarks of the popular Viajero chain is this good and colorful hostel. It's on a noisy street corner, but conveniently close to the bus station as well as the waves and nightlife of Playa Brava. Bike rentals, surfing lessons and Hi discounts.

TRANSPORTATION

Argentina is a big country, and most people fly into Buenos Aires to get there. You can bus into the capital from neighboring countries, but this nearly always involves overnight trips. Uruguay is the exception, as it's just across the Río de la Plata (a huge river estuary) and a relatively short boat or plane ride away.

BA is a large, modern city with good public transportation options, but walking is really the best way to see the sights. The main downtown area is small enough that you could walk from one end to the other in about a half-hour. For longer distances, most people get around by bus, Subte (BA's subway system) or taxi. Driving is recommended for the suicidal only.

Tickets for flights, tours and rail can be booked online at www.lonelyplanet.com/travel_services.

AIR

BA is Argentina's international gateway and easily accessible from North America, Europe and Australasia, as well as most other capital cities in South America. Aerolíneas Argentinas and Lan are the main regional airlines at the moment, but Argentine airlines are in constant flux and come and go very frequently. Even airline offices will often move. Always check current travel information during your tenure here.

THINGS CHANGE...

The information in this chapter is particularly vulnerable to change. Check directly with the airline or a travel agent to make sure you understand how a fare (and ticket you may buy) works and be aware of the security requirements for international travel. Shop carefully. The details given in this chapter should be regarded as pointers and are not a substitute for your own careful, up-to-date research.

Airlines

Aerolíneas Argentinas (Map p62; ☎ 0810-222-86527; www.aerolineas.com; Perú 2).

Air Canada (Map p62; ☎ 4327-3640; www.aircanada.ca; Av Córdoba 656)

Air France (Map p62; ☎ 4317-4700; www.airfrance.com.ar; San Martín 344, 23rd fl)

Alitalia (Map p62; ☎ 0810-777-2548; www.alitalia.com; San Martín 344, 23rd fl)

American Airlines (Map p84; www.aa.com; ☎ 4318-1111; Av Santa Fe 881)

British Airways (Map p84; ☎ 0800-222-0075; www.britishairways.com; Av del Libertador 498, 13th fl)

Continental (Map p62; ☎ 0800 333 0425; www.continental.com; Carlos Pellegrini 529)

CLIMATE CHANGE & TRAVEL

Climate change is a serious threat to the ecosystems that humans rely upon, and air travel is the fastest-growing contributor to the problem. Lonely Planet regards travel, overall, as a global benefit, but believes we all have a responsibility to limit our personal impact on global warming.

Flying & Climate Change

Pretty much every form of motor transport generates CO_2 (the main cause of human-induced climate change) but planes are far and away the worst offenders, not just because of the sheer distances they allow us to travel, but because they release greenhouse gases high into the atmosphere. The statistics are frightening: two people taking a return flight between Europe and the US will contribute as much to climate change as an average household's gas and electricity consumption over a whole year.

Carbon Offset Schemes

Climatecare.org and other websites use 'carbon calculators' that allow travelers to offset the greenhouse gases they are responsible for with contributions to energy-saving projects and other climate-friendly initiatives in the developing world – including projects in India, Honduras, Kazakhstan and Uganda.

Lonely Planet, together with Rough Guides and other concerned partners in the travel industry, supports the carbon offset scheme run by climatecare.org. Lonely Planet offsets all of its staff and author travel.

For more information check out our website: www.lonelyplanet.com.

Delta (Map p84; www.delta.com; ☎ 0800-666-0133; Santa Fe 887)

KLM (Map p62; ☎ 4317-4711; www.klm.com; San Martín 344, 23d fl)

Lan (Map p84; ☎ 4378-2222; www.lan.com; Cerrito 866)

Líneas Aéreas del Estado (LADE; Map p76; ☎ 0810-810-5233; www.lade.com.ar; Perú 714)

Swissair (Map p84; ☎ 4319-0000; www.swiss.com; Av Santa Fe 846, 1st fl)

Transportes Aéreos de Mercosur (TAM; Map p84; ☎ 0810-333-3333; www.tam.com.py, in Spanish; Cerrito 1026)

United Airlines (☎ 0810-777-8648; www.united.com.ar) Located only at airport.

AIRPORTS

Ezeiza

Almost all international flights arrive at Buenos Aires' Ezeiza airport (EZE; officially Aeropuerto Internacional Ministro Pistarini), about 35km south of the center. Ezeiza is a modern airport with decent services like ATMs, restaurants, bookstore, pharmacy, duty-free shops and a small post office (9am-5pm Mon-Fri, to noon Sat, mailbox open 24hr). There's also an overpriced *locutorio* (open 24 hours) with telephone cabins and internet access. Wi-fi is only available at La Pausa Restaurant, upstairs. For more on arriving in Ezeiza, see the boxed text, p218.

Flight information, in English and Spanish, is available by calling ☎ 5480-6111 or accessing www.aa2000.com.ar.

If you're alone, the best way to and from Ezeiza is taking a shuttle with transfer companies such as Manuel Tienda León (MTL; Map p84; ☎ 4315-5115; www.tiendaleon.com.ar; Av Eduardo Madero 1299). You'll see its stand immediately as you exit customs, in the transport 'lobby' area. Shuttles cost AR$50 per person to the city center, run all day and night and take 40 to 60 minutes, depending on traffic. They'll deposit you either at the MTL office (from where you can take a taxi) or at some limited central addresses. Tickets are reservable online.

Another shuttle service, directed at independent travelers, is Hostel Shuttle (☎ 4511-8723; www.hostelshuttle.com.ar). Cost is AR$55 per person. Check the website for a schedule and drop-off destinations (only certain hostels), and try to book ahead. You can also try www.minibusezeiza.com.ar.

If taking a taxi, avoid MTL's taxi service – overpriced at AR$186. Instead, go past the transport 'lobby' area outside customs, walk past the taxi touts, and you'll see the freestanding city taxi stand (blue sign saying 'Taxi Ezeiza'; ☎ 5480-889; www.taxiezeiza.com.ar). It charges AR$150 to the center. To save even more pesos, head a few feet outside the building and look for the yellow taxi stand, which charges AR$138.

For a special treat, reserve a luxury car from Silver Star Car (☎ 15-6826-8876; www.silverstarcar.com);

EZEIZA ARRIVAL & DEPARTURE TIPS

When arriving at Ezeiza, citizens from several countries have to pay a 'reciprocity fee' (*tasa de reciprocidad*). This is equal to what Argentines are charged for visas to visit those countries. These fees are US$100 for Australians (good for one year), US$140 for Americans (good for 10 years) and US$75 for Canadians (per entry – sucks, eh?). Aeroparque also requires this fee, but there is no fee if entering Argentina via other airports or borders. This situation is likely to change, however.

To change money at Ezeiza, don't use a *cambio* (exchange house) unless you know the current exchange rates. Better rates are generally found at the local bank branch; after exiting customs, pass the rows of transport booths, go outside the doors into the reception hall and veer sharply to the right to find Banco de la Nación's small office. Its rates are identical to downtown offices, there's an ATM and it's open 24 hours, though long lines are common. There's another ATM nearby, next to Farmacity, and yet another way beyond, at the airline counters.

If you want to take a taxi into town, head outside this same transport booth area (taxis are a bit overpriced here), past the folks at reception and – avoiding any taxi tout – find the city's official taxi stand (a blue sign that says 'Taxi Ezeiza'). In late 2010 it charged AR$150 to the center, including tolls. For shuttle or bus information, see under 'Airports, Ezeiza.'

There's a tourist information booth (24hr) just beyond the city's taxi stand.

When leaving Buenos Aires, get to Ezeiza at least two hours (or more) before your international flight out; security and immigration lines can be very long (and be aware that traffic can be bad even *getting* to Ezeiza). Also, even when you get past main security there may be bag checks at the gate, and neither food nor liquids may be allowed onto airplanes. Eat and drink up before boarding.

you'll be driven by native English speakers to the destination of your choice (AR$375, up to four passengers).

Finally, if you're *really* on a penny-pinching budget, take public bus 8, which costs AR$2.50 (in late 2010) and can take up to two hours to reach the Plaza de Mayo area. Catch it outside the Aerolíneas Argentinas terminal (Terminal B), a 200m walk from the international terminal. You'll need coins; there's a Banco de la Nación just outside customs.

Aeroparque

Most domestic flights use Aeroparque airport (officially Aeroparque Jorge Newbery; ☎ 5480-6111; www.aa2000.com.ar), a short distance from downtown Buenos Aires. Manual Tienda Leõn does transfers from Ezeiza to Aeroparque for AR$50. To get from Aeroparque to the center, take public bus 33 or 45 (don't cross the street; take them going south). MTL also has shuttles to the center for AR$18; taxis cost around AR$40.

BICYCLE

Buenos Aires is generally not the best city to cycle around. Traffic is dangerous, hardly respectful toward cyclists, and the biggest vehicle wins the right of way – with bikes being low on the transport totem pole.

However, things are getting better. New bike lanes were installed in 2010, when a bike share program also went in (geared towards locals). Critical Mass, an international bike awareness movement, is alive in BA (see p47). Every day there seem to be more cyclists on the streets – but even so, BA has a long way to go to be seen as a 'bike friendly' city. For more information on the changing bike scene in BA, see p47.

The city's best places for two-wheeled exploration are Palermo's parks (p90) and the Reserva Ecológica Costanera Sur (p70); on weekends you can rent bikes at these places. You can also join city bike tours, which include bicycle and guide (see p229). For more information see p176.

BOAT

There's a regular ferry service to and from Colonia and Montevideo, both in Uruguay. Most ferries leave from the Buquebus terminal (Map p84; ☎ 4316-6500; www.buquebus.com; Av Antártida Argentina 821); there's another Buquebus office at Av Córdoba 879. Colonia Express (Map p84; ☎ 4317-4100; www.coloniaexpress.com; Córdoba 753) is cheaper than Buquebus but has fewer departures, and its terminal is in an ugly, industrial neighborhood near La Boca.

Both companies have many more launches in the busy summer season; book online in advance for discounts. For more information, see p209 and p213.

BUS

Buenos Aires has a huge and complex bus system. If you want to get to know it better you'll have to buy a *Guia T* – it's sold at any newsstand, but get the pocket version (less than AR$10). It details hundreds of the city's bus routes. Just look at the grids to find out where you are and where you're going, and find a matching bus number. You can also check www.xcolectivo.com.ar for an online version. And if you know your present location, destination and some Spanish, use www.comoviajo.com (click on 'Comó ir En Colectivo, Tren o Subte') to punch in your coordinates and get the nearest bus, train or Subte line. For information (in English) on how to get to your destination on city buses, check out http://www.omnilineas.com/argentina/buenos-aires/city-bus/.

Most bus routes (but not all) run 24 hours; there are fewer buses at night. For a guide to some popular bus routes, see the boxed text p220.

Save your change like it's gold; local buses do not take bills. Bus ticket machines on board will give you small change from your coins. Rides around town are very cheap (most are AR$1.25); just mention your destination to the driver and he'll cue the machine. Seats up front are offered to the elderly, pregnant women and those with young children.

If you're arriving into Buenos Aires at Retiro bus terminal, don't try to sort out the local bus system – there are way too many bus

EASY BUS TICKETS

You can buy nearly any long-distance bus ticket without taking a special trip to Retiro bus station. Use the practical booking services of Omnilíneas (Map p62; ☎ 4326-3924; www.omnilineas.com; Maipú 459, 10D), started by an expat German. Just reserve and buy your ticket over the website, and either print it out at home or pick it up at the office. Prices are the same as at Retiro bus station, and English is spoken.

HANDY BUS ROUTES

Route	Bus
Microcentro to Palermo Viejo	111
Microcentro to Plaza Italia (in Palermo)	29, 59, 64
Once to Plaza de Mayo to La Boca	64
Plaza de Mayo to Ezeiza airport (placard says 'Ezeiza')	8
Plaza Italia to Microcentro to San Telmo	29
Plaza Italia to La Boca via Retiro & Plaza de Mayo	152, 29
Plaza Italia to Recoleta to Microcentro to Constitución	59
Plaza San Martín to Aeroparque airport	33, 45
Recoleta to Congreso to San Telmo to La Boca	39
Retiro to Plaza de Mayo to San Telmo	22

lines outside. It's worth spending a few pesos to take a *remise* (radio taxi) directly to your destination. There are two small *remise* booths near bus slots 8 and 9 that are open 24 hours.

And remember to keep an eye on your bags at this station!

CAR & MOTORCYCLE

Anyone considering driving in Buenos Aires should know that most local drivers are reckless, aggressive and even willfully dangerous. They'll ignore speed limits, road signs, road lines and often traffic signals. They'll tailgate you mercilessly and honk even before signals turn green. Buses are a nightmare to reckon with, potholes are everywhere, traffic is a nightmare and parking is too. Pedestrians haphazardly cross the road (seeming to beg to be run over at times).

Reconsider your need to have a car in this city: public transportation will often get you anywhere faster, cheaper and with much less stress. And you won't have to worry about the police, who have a habit of stopping cars to check for violations, while subtly asking for *coimas* (bribes). If this happens to you when you weren't doing anything illegal, insist on contacting your embassy – too much trouble for some officers.

Driving

Driving outside BA is another story. Drivers are still crazy, but there are fewer of them, and you'll have more flexibility in your travels. If you drive in Argentina – especially in your own car – it may be worth joining the Automóvil Club Argentino (ACA), which has many nationwide offices. ACA recognizes members of overseas affiliates, such as the American Automobile Association (AAA), and often grants them similar privileges including discounts on maps, accommodations, camping, tours and other services. For more information contact the **ACA head office** (Map p92; ☎ 4802-6061; www.aca.org.ar; Av del Libertador 1850).

Rental

If you want to rent a car, expect to pay AR$200 to AR$400 per day (it may be worth trying to make a reservation with one of the major international agencies in your home country, as these can sometimes guarantee stable rates). You'll need to be at least 21 years of age and have a valid driver's license; having an international driver's license wouldn't be a bad idea, though you don't necessarily need one. A credit card and passport are also necessary.

Avis (Map p84; ☎ 4378-9640; www.avis.com; Cerrito 1535)

Hertz (Map p84; ☎ 4816-8001; www.milletrentacar.com.ar; Paraguay 1138)

RETIRO BUS TERMINAL

If you're heading out of town you'll probably have to visit BA's modern Retiro bus terminal (also known simply as 'Retiro'; Map p84; www.tebasa.com.ar). It's 400m long, three floors high and has slots for 75 buses. The bottom floor is for cargo shipments and luggage storage, the top for purchasing tickets, and the middle for everything else. There's an **information booth** (☎ 4310-0700) that provides general bus information and schedules, plus a **tourist office** (🕑 7:30am-2pm Mon-Fri) near Puente 3 on the main floor, under bus counter 105. Other services include telephone offices (some with internet access), restaurants, cafes and dozens of small stores.

You can buy a ticket to practically anywhere in Argentina and departures are fairly frequent to the most popular destinations. Reservations are not necessary except during peak summer and winter holiday seasons.

WATCH THAT POCKET!

When traveling on BA's crowded bus or Subte lines, watch for pickpockets. They can be well-dressed, men or women, often with a coat slung over their arm to hide nefarious activities going on near your bag or pocket. Occasionally there are several of them, working as a team, and they'll try to shove or distract you. The best thing to do is not look like a tourist, keep you wallet well ensconced in your front pocket, wedge your purse under your arm and wear your backpack in front – like the locals do. Don't make yourself an easy target and they'll move on – and you might not even notice they exist.

New Way (Map p84; ☎ 4515-0331; www.new-wayrenta car.com.ar; MT de Alvear 773)

Transitar (Map p72; ☎ 4115-4585; www.transit-ar.com; Cerrito 270, oficina 8)

For motorcycle rentals, be at least 25 years of age and head to Motocare (☎ 4761-2696; www.moto care.com.ar/rental; Echeverría 738, Vicente López). Honda Transalps 650 cost AR$440 per day with a five-day minimum (they're cheaper by the month). Bring your own helmet and riding gear. Crossing into Chile, Uruguay, Paraguay and Brazil is allowed. If you buy a motorcycle here you can negotiate to sell it back, possibly saving money in the long term.

SUBTE (UNDERGROUND)

BA's Subte (www.subte.com.ar) opened in 1913 and is the quickest way to get around the city, though it can get mighty hot and crowded during rush hour. It consists of *líneas* (lines) A, B, C, D, E and H. Four parallel lines run from downtown to the capital's western and northern outskirts, while *Línea* C runs north–south and connects the two major train stations of Retiro and Constitución. *Línea* H runs from Once south to Av Caseros, with plans to expand it from Retiro to Nuevo Pompeya.

One-ride magnetic cards for the Subte cost AR$1.10. To save time and hassle buy several rides, since queues can get backed up (especially during rush hour). If you're planning on staying in BA for a while, the Monedero (www .monedero.com.ar) is a convenient, rechargeable card that negates the need for coins.

Trains operate from 5am to around 11pm Monday to Saturday and 8am to around 10:30pm on Sunday and holidays, so don't rely on the Subte to get you home after dinner. Service is frequent on weekdays; on weekends you'll wait longer. At some stations platforms are on opposite sides, so be sure of your direction *before* passing through the turnstiles.

The oldest Subte line, *Línea* A, offers a tarnished reminder of the city's elegant past, with its tiled stations and vintage wooden trams – though newer cars are slowly being added as ridership increases.

TAXI & REMISE

Buenos Aires' very numerous (about 40,000) and cheap taxis are conspicuous by their black-and-yellow paint jobs. In early 2011 meters started at AR$5.90 during the day and AR$6.90 at night (10pm to 6am). They click every 200m (or every minute of waiting time). Make sure that the meter's set to the current price when you start your ride. Drivers do not expect a big tip, but it's customary to let them keep small change. Taxis looking for passengers will have a red light lit on the upper right corner of their windshield.

Most cab drivers are honest workers making a living, but there are a few bad apples in the bunch. Try not to give them large bills; not only will they usually not have change, but there have been many cases where the driver quickly and deftly replaces a larger bill with a smaller (or fake) one. One solution is to state how much you are giving them and ask if they have change for it ('*¿Tiene usted cambio de un veinte?*' – 'Do you have any change for a 20?').

Be wary of receiving counterfeit bills; at night have the driver turn on the light (or *luz*) so you can carefully check your change (look for a watermark on bills). They'll do the same with your bills. And make sure you get the right change.

Try to have an idea of where you're going or you might be taking the 'scenic' route (though also be aware there are many one-way streets in BA, and your route to one place may be quite different on the way back). A good way to give the impression that you know where you're going is to give the taxi driver an intersection rather than a specific address. Also, if you are obviously a tourist going to or from a touristy spot, it's not a good idea to ask how much the fare is; this makes quoting an upped price tempting, rather than using the meter. And try not to take a taxi right outside a tourist spot or after you've withdrawn money from an ATM – walk a block or two and flag one down instead.

HELPFUL TRAIN INFORMATION

Destination(s)	Station	Contact
Belgrano, San Isidro, Tigre, Rosario	Retiro	Trenes de Buenos Aires (TBA, Mitre line; ☎ 0800-333-3822; www.tbanet.com.ar)
To the southern suburbs and La Plata	Constitución	Metropolitano (Roca line; no contact information)
Bahía Blanca and Atlantic beach towns	Constitución	Ferrobaires (☎ 4304-0028; www.ferrobaires.gba.gov.ar)
To the southwestern suburbs and Luján	Once	Trenes de Buenos Aires (TBA, Sarmiento line; ☎ 0800-333-3822; www.tbanet.com.ar)

Finally, make an attempt to snag an 'official' taxi. These are usually marked by a roof light and license number printed on the doors; the words *radio taxi* are usually a good sign. Official drivers must display their license on the back of their seat or dashboard; you can write down the taxi's number and agency telephone in case you have problems with the ride or forgot something.

Most porteños will recommend you call a *remise* instead of hailing cabs off the street. A *remise* looks like a regular car and doesn't have a meter. It costs a bit more than a street taxi but is considered more secure, since an established company sends them out. Most hotels and restaurants will call a *remise* for you; expect a short wait for them to show up.

TRAIN

Trains connect Buenos Aires' center to its suburbs and nearby provinces. They're best for commuters and only occasionally useful for tourists. Several private companies run different train lines; train stations are all served by Subte.

TRAM

In July 2007 Buenos Aires inaugurated a new light-rail system in Puerto Madero, called the Tranvía del Este. It's currently 2km long and has only four stops, with plans extend the line from Retiro to Constitución. It's cheap to ride, but consider skipping it – stroll on Puerto Madero's lovely cobbled lanes instead.

DIRECTORY

ACCOMMODATIONS

In Buenos Aires the average three-star double room with bathroom costs around US$80, with seasonal variations (highest in summer, from November to February, with peak rates during holidays like Christmas, New Year's and Easter). Generally we've quoted rack rates for hotels, and these tend to be higher than the discounted rates many hotels will give. Booking online can save you quite a bit, but if you're already there feel free to ask a hotel for its 'best rate' – and negotiate politely.

The accommodations listings in the Sleeping chapter (p182) are ordered by neighborhood, from most expensive to least expensive. For long-term guesthouses see p194. For a list of websites that rent out apartments to foreigners see p191.

BUSINESS HOURS

Office business hours run from 8am to 5pm; there can be a little variance, though. Banks can close as early as 4pm. Stores and places like travel offices will stay open later, sometimes as late as 9pm.

Restaurants are generally open daily from noon to 3:30pm for lunch and 8pm to midnight for dinner; they'll stay open later on Friday and Saturday. In this book, we detail exact opening hours for restaurants only when they deviate from these standard hours.

Cafes are often open from morning to night without a break. Bars will open in the evening and stay open all night long. In the center, however, they cater to the business crowd, so most will be open during the day and close relatively early at night.

CHILDREN

Although it's a megalopolis, Buenos Aires is remarkably child-friendly. Once children are old enough to cross the street safely and find their way back home, porteño parents will send unaccompanied preadolescents on errands or on visits to friends or neighbors. While most visiting parents are not likely to do this, they can usually count on their children's safety in public places, though it's always a good idea to keep an eye on them.

This is also a country where people frequently touch each other, so your children may be patted on the head.

Porteños can be helpful on public transportation. Often someone will give up a seat for a parent and young child. Baby strollers on the crowded and uneven sidewalks of BA's downtown center are a liability, however; consider a baby carrier instead.

Basic restaurants provide a wide selection of food suitable for children (like vegetables, pasta, meat, chicken and fish), and a few even have children's menus. Waiters are accustomed to providing extra plates and cutlery for little tykes, though you may not always find booster seats. Don't forget to take the kids out for ice cream – it's a real Argentine treat!

Poorly maintained public bathrooms lacking baby-changing facilities or countertop space are common. Always carry toilet paper and wet wipes.

Buenos Aires' numerous plazas and public parks, many with playgrounds, are popular gathering spots for families, the most attractive are the wide open spaces of Palermo, including a nearby zoo. For more suggestions on where to take the little ones see p91.

Lonely Planet's *Travel with Children* is a handy general reference guide.

CLIMATE

If they don't know it already, travelers from the northern hemisphere will soon realize that the southern hemisphere's seasons are completely reversed. Summer runs December to February; fall is March to May; winter is June to August; and spring is September to November.

Buenos Aires' climate is generally pleasant, with an annual rainfall of about 1000mm. The changeable spring, hot and humid summer and mild fall resemble New York City's seasons, but winter temperatures are moderated by the South Atlantic and – for a city with a relatively low latitude (34° 37' S) – are more comparable to Los Angeles, Sydney or Cape Town.

Frosts are uncommon, and the lowest temperature ever recorded is -5.4°C (22.3°F). Snowfall is rare, but in 2007 a storm left the city covered in a thick layer of white – something that hadn't happened since 1918.

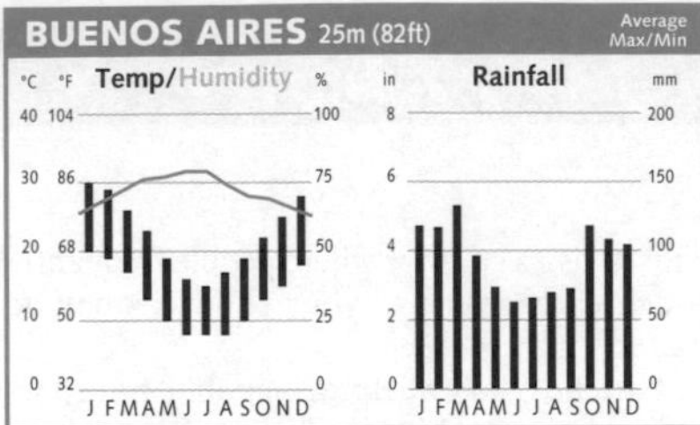

CONCIERGE SERVICE

BA Cultural Concierge (☎ 15-5457-2035; www.baculturalconcierge.com) Madi Lang will help you plan itineraries, arrange airport transport, get a cell phone, run errands, reserve theater tickets, scout out a potential apartment and do a thousand other things for your trip to run smoothly.

COURSES

Visitors have opportunities to study almost anything in BA, from Spanish to cooking to tango, see p169. For other styles of dance, see p170. For yoga, see p178. Most cultural centers (p225) offer a variety of classes at affordable rates.

Language

BA has become a major destination for students of Spanish. Good institutes are opening up all the time and private teachers are a dime a dozen. Cultural centers (see p224) also offer language classes; the Centro Cultural Ricardo Rojas has an especially good range of offerings, from Korean to Russian to Yiddish.

For something different, contact Español Andando (☎ 5278-9886; www.espanol-andando.com.ar). You'll walk around town with a guide, learning Spanish by interacting with *porteños* on the street. Or try Spanglish (www.spanglishexchange.com), set up like speed dating; you'll speak five minutes in English and five in Spanish, then switch partners (and it's a bit of a pickup scene too). Also, check out their 'beerlingual' trivia nights www.beerlingual.com).

Following are just a few language institutes. All organize social activities, private classes and (usually) volunteer opportunities. Homestay programs are also available, but often cost more than finding a place yourself (see p191). Check websites for fees and schedules.

Academia Buenos Aires (Map p62; ☎ 4345-5954; www.academiabuenosaires.com; Hipólito Yrigoyen 571, 4th fl) Highly regarded school that pushes you to achieve. Specialty courses & free workshops for students.

DWS (Map p98; ☎ 4773-1379; www.danielawasser.com.ar; Av Córdoba 4382) Friendly institute with good vibe and free internet computers.

Expanish (Map p62; ☎ 5252-3040; www.expanish.com; Juan D Perón 700) Excellent school with modern facilities and proven teaching ideals.

One on One (Map p72; ☎ 3528-4452; www.oneononeargentina.com; Rodriguez Peña 617, 4th fl) Tiny school with tailor-made courses.

Rayuela (Map p76; ☎ 4300-2010; www.spanish-argentina.com.ar; Chacabuco 852, 1st fl No11) Friendly, small school in a nice old San Telmo building. Full immersion, fun activities and free *mate*.

University of Buenos Aires (UBA; Map p62; ☎ 4343-5981; www.idiomas.filo.uba.ar; 25 de Mayo 221) Regular and intensive, long-term classes (one to four months). Italian, German, French, Portuguese and Japanese are also taught. Cheap and great for serious students, but classrooms can be run-down.

VOS (Map p84; ☎ 4812-1140; www.vosbuenosaires.com; MT de Alvear 1459) Very welcoming institute located just outside Recoleta.

Vamos (Map p92; ☎ 5352-0001; www.vamospanish.com; Coronel Díaz 1736) Has specialty courses for expats, busy travelers (the 'crash' course) & students over 55. Eco-conscious – recycles, does food drives & gets involved with local charities.

Cooking

Taking cooking classes in small groups or private classes are probably the best option for short-term visitors who don't speak Spanish. There are several options in Buenos Aires, a few with expat chefs who have their own 'closed door' restaurant (see p135).

A Little Saigon (☎ 15-6056-8823; www.alittlesaigon.com/class) American-Vietnamese Chef Thuy Lam will instruct you on how to make authentic Vietnamese cuisine from old family recipes (think *pho*, that amazing beef noodle soup).

Cooking with Teresita (☎ 4293-5992; www.try2cook.com) Learn to cook cuisine from Argentina, such as *asados* (barbecues) and empanadas; she'll also take you to local markets.

Dan Perlman (dan@saltshaker.net; www.saltshaker.net/class-schedule) Ex–New Yorker Dan Perlman teaches Italian, Mediterranean, Asian and vegetarian classes.

Norma Soued (☎ 15-4470-2267; www.argentinecookingclasses.com) Will teach you to make typical Argentine cuisine like empanadas, traditional stews and *alfajores*.

If you have time, speak Spanish and are considering making cooking a profession, try the highly regarded Instituto Argentino de Gastronomía (IAG; Map p87; ☎ 4816-1414; www.iag.com.ar; Montevideo 968) or Mausi Sebess (☎ 4791-4355; www.mausisebess.com; Maipú 594), located in BA's suburb of Vicente López.

CULTURAL CENTERS

Buenos Aires has good cultural centers offering all sorts of art exhibitions, classes and events.

Centro Cultural Borges (Map p62; ☎ 5555-5359; www.ccborges.org.ar; Viamonte & San Martín) One of the best cultural centers in BA, with inexpensive but high-quality art exhibitions and galleries, cinema, music, lectures, classes and workshops. Tango lessons are also available.

Centro Cultural de la Cooperación (Map p72; ☎ 5077-8000; www.centrocultural.coop; Av Corrientes 1543) A modern center offering theatre, cinema, music, dance, expositions and workshops. On weekends it sometimes has children's puppet shows or other kids' events. Also on the premises is a slick cafe and bookstore.

Centro Cultural Recoleta (Map p87; ☎ 4803-1040; www.centroculturalrecoleta.org; Junín 1930) This large cultural center offers many free or inexpensive events, including art exhibitions, a science museum for kids and occasional outdoor film screenings on summer evenings.

Centro Cultural Ricardo Rojas (Map p72; ☎ 4954-5523; www.rojas.uba.ar; Av Corrientes 2038) This popular and exceptionally good cultural center has a wide range of affordable classes, including tango, belly dancing, percussion, photography, life drawing, Greek mythology, film analysis and even clown acting. Exotic language classes, too.

Centro Cultural San Martín (Map p72; ☎ 4374-1251; www.ccgsm.gov.ar; Sarmiento 1551) One of Buenos Aires' best resources, this large cultural center has free or inexpensive galleries, music, films, lectures, art exhibitions, classes and workshops.

Ciudad Cultural Konex (Map p98; ☎ 4864-3200; www.ciudadculturalkonex.org; Sarmiento 3131) Cutting-edge cultural center offering multidisciplinary performances that often fuse art, culture and technology. Amazing Monday night percussion shows.

There are also several foreign cultural centers in the Microcentro, such as the Instituto Cultural Argentino-Norteamericano (Map p62; ☎ 5382-1500; www.icana.org.ar; Maipú 672) which has Spanish classes; the Alianza Francesa (Map p62; ☎ 4322-0068; www.alianzafrancesa.org.ar; Av Córdoba 946) which concentrates on French-themed instruction and arts; and the Instituto Goethe (Map p62; ☎ 4318-5600; www.goethe.de/hs/bue; Av Corrientes 319) which offers German-language instruction, lectures, films and even concerts. All have good libraries in their respective languages.

The British Arts Centre (Map p84; ☎ 4393-6941; www.britishartscentre.org.ar; Suipacha 1333) has well-priced theater, films, music and workshops (among other things) in English and Spanish.

Backpackers should consider joining the South American Explorers (www.saexplorers.org). Annual membership costs US$60, but SAE offers a small library, guidebooks for sale, mail service, luggage storage, discounts and plenty of information about travel in South America (including other travelers' 'trip reports').

CUSTOMS REGULATIONS

Argentine officials are generally courteous and reasonable toward tourists. Electronic items, including laptops, cameras and cell phones, can be brought into the country duty free, provided they are not intended for resale. If you have a lot of electronic equipment, however, it may be useful to have a typed list of the items you are carrying (including serial numbers) or a pile of purchase receipts.

Depending on where you have been, officials focus on different things. Travelers south-bound from the central Andean countries may be searched for drugs, and those from bordering countries will have fruit and vegetables confiscated.

DISCOUNT CARDS

Travelers of any age can obtain a Hostelling International card (AR$64) at any HI hostel (www.hostels.org.ar) or at their tiny HI office in Retiro (Map p84; ☎ 4511-8723; www.hitravel.com.ar; Av Florida 835, main fl). With this card you can obtain discounts at any HI hostel in Argentina, usually 10% to 15% off regular prices.

International Student Identity Cards (ISIC; AR$44) are also sold here; you'll need current student ID.

For non-HI hostels, check out minihostels (www.minihostels.com), a network of quality, 'good vibe' hostels throughout Argentina and expanding to other places in Central and South America. The HoLa (www.holahostels.com) card works in a similar way for a different network of hostels.

Travelers over the age of 60 can sometimes obtain senior-citizen discounts on museum admissions and the like. Usually a passport with date of birth is sufficient evidence of age.

ELECTRICITY

Argentina's electric current operates on 220V, 50 Hertz. There are two types of electric plugs: either two rounded prongs (as in Europe) or three angled flat prongs (as in Australia). See www.kropla.com/electric2.htm for details. Adapters are readily available from almost any *ferretería* (hardware store), or visit a travel store before hitting the road.

Most electronic equipment (such as cameras, pdas, telephones, computers and laptops) are dual/multi-voltage, but if you're bringing in something that's not, use a voltage converter or you might short out your device.

EMBASSIES

Some countries have both an embassy and a consulate in Buenos Aires, but only the most central location is listed here.

Australia (Map p92; ☎ 4779-3500; Villanueva 1400, Belgrano)

Canada (Map p92; ☎ 4808-1000; Tagle 2828, Palermo)

France (Map p84; ☎ 4515-6900; Basavilvaso 1253, Retiro)

Germany (Map p92; ☎ 4778-2500; Villanueva 1055, Belgrano)

Italy (Map p84; ☎ 4114-4800; Reconquista 572, Retiro)

Spain (Map p87; ☎ 4814-9100; Guido 1770, Recoleta)

UK (Map p92; ☎ 4808-2200; Dr Luis Agote 2412, Recoleta)

USA (Map p92; ☎ 5777-4533; Colombia 4300, Palermo)

EMERGENCY

Ambulance ☎ 107

Police ☎ 101, 911

Fire ☎ 100

Tourist Police (Comisaría del Turista; Map p62; ☎ 4346-5748, 0800-999-5000; Av Corrientes 436; 24hr) Provides interpreters; helps victims of robberies and rip-offs.

GAY & LESBIAN TRAVELERS

Argentina is a strongly Catholic country with heavy elements of machismo. In Buenos Aires, however, there is a palpable acceptance of homosexuality. In fact, gay tourism has become so popular that BA is now South America's top gay destination. For more information on the gay community and its nightspots, see the boxed text p157.

Argentine men are more physically demonstrative than their North American and European counterparts, so behaviors such as kissing on the cheek in greeting or a vigorous embrace are considered innocuous even to those who express unease with homosexuals. Lesbians walking hand-in-hand should generally attract little attention, since heterosexual Argentine women sometimes do so, but this would be very conspicuous behavior for males. If you are in any doubt, it's better to be discreet.

HOLIDAYS

Government offices and businesses are closed on the numerous national holidays. If a holiday falls midweek, it's often bumped to the nearest Monday; if it falls on a Tuesday or Thursday, then the in-between Monday or Friday are taken as holidays.

Public transportation options are more limited on holidays, when you should reserve tickets far in advance. Hotel booking should also be done ahead of time. See p20 for a list of fun festivals in the city.

January 1 Año Nuevo; New Year's Day.

February/March Carnaval – dates vary; a Monday and Tuesday become holidays.

March 24 Día de la Memoria; anniversary of the day that started the 1976 dictatorship and subsequent Dirty War.

March/April Semana Santa (Easter week) – dates vary; most businesses close on Good 'Thursday' and Good Friday; major travel week.

April 2 Día de las Malvinas; honors the fallen Argentine soldiers from the Islas Malvinas (Falkland Islands) war in 1829.

May 1 Día del Trabajor; Labor Day.

May 25 Día de la Revolución de Mayo; commemorates the 1810 revolution against Spain.

June 20 Día de la Bandera (Flag Day); anniversary of death of Manuel Belgrano, creator of Argentina's flag and military leader.

July 9 Día de la Independencia; Independence Day.

August (third Monday in August) Día del Libertador San Martín; marks the anniversary of José de San Martín's death (1778–1850).

October 12 (celebrated on a Monday in October) Día del Respeto a la Diversidad Cultural; a day to respect cultural diversity.

November 20 (celebrated on a Monday in November) Día de la Soberanía Nacional; Day of national sovereignty.

December 8 Día de la Concepción Inmaculada; celebrates the immaculate conception of the Virgin Mary.

December 25 Navidad; Christmas Day.

Note that Christmas Eve and New Year's Day are treated as semi-holidays, and you will find some businesses closed for the latter half of those days.

INSURANCE

A travel-insurance policy to cover theft, loss and medical problems is a good idea. Some policies offer a range of lower and higher medical-expense options; the higher ones are chiefly for countries such as the USA, which has extremely high medical costs. There is a wide variety of policies available, so read the small print.

Some policies specifically exclude 'dangerous activities,' which can include scuba diving, motorcycling and even trekking. Check that the policy you're considering covers ambulances and an emergency flight home.

INTERNET ACCESS

Buenos Aires is definitely online. Internet cafés and *locutorios* (telephone offices) with internet access are very common everywhere in the center; you can often find one by just walking a few blocks in any direction. Rates are very cheap at about AR$5 per hour, and connections are quick. To find the @ (*arroba*) symbol, try holding down the Alt key and typing 64. Or ask the attendant '*¿Cómo se hace la arroba?*' ('How do you make the @ sign?').

Nearly all hotels have wi-fi or in-room internet connections for guests traveling with their own laptops, and the fancier ones also feature 'business centers' with one or more computers. Many hostels provide free internet to guests. Also, many cafés and restaurants (even McDonald's) offer free wi-fi.

For a list of recommended internet resources, see p23.

NEED AN OFFICE – FOR AN HOUR OR A DAY?

The brainchild of one of BA's many expat entrepeneurs, Areatres (Map p92; ☎ 5353-0333; www.areatresworkplace.com; Malabia 1720) is a secure working office where you can rent a desk, cubicle, office or meeting room. There are fax and copy services, complete internet and wi-fi connections, networking social events, a business lounge, a large presentation room and even a Zen-like patio at the back for the stress-prone. Facilities are cutting-edge – it's like you never left Silicon Valley. It's even eco-conscious. It's also at Humboldt 2032.

LAUNDRY

There are many *lavanderías* (laundries) in the city, and they're pretty affordable – about AR$12 to wash/dry a load. Most are closed on Sunday. Many hotels also have laundry services.

LIBRARIES

The best library for English speaking travelers is Biblioteca Lincoln (Map p62; ☎ 5382-1536; www.bcl.edu.ar; Maipú 672; ⏲ 10am-8pm Mon-Wed, 10am-6pm Thu-Fri), inside the Instituto Cultural Argentino-Norteamericano. And while you can't check out materials – unless you become a member – you can sit in a quiet, comfortable environment and read the *New York Times*, along with English-language books and magazines (some available in digital format).

The Alianza Francesa (p225) and Instituto Goethe (p225) also have foreign libraries.

The Biblioteca Nacional (Map p92; ☎ 4806-9764; www.bn.gov.ar; Agüero 2502; ⏲ 9am-9pm Mon-Fri, noon-7pm Sat & Sun) is in a can't-miss, ugly, mushroomlike building and offers books in Spanish along with the occasional literary event and concert.

MAPS

Free BA maps are available at your hotel or any tourist office. More detailed maps are sold at newspaper kiosks and bookstores.

The Automóvil Club Argentino (ACA; Map p92; ☎ 4802-6061; www.aca.org.ar; Av del Libertador 1850) publishes excellent road maps. There are many ACA branches throughout BA and Argentina. Bring your auto-club card from home for map discounts.

Geography nerds will adore the topographic maps available from the Instituto Geográfico Militar (Map p92; ☎ 4576-5576; www.igm.gov.ar; Cabildo 381, Palermo, Buenos Aires; ⏲ 8am-2pm Mon-Fri).

MEDICAL SERVICES

Highly regarded hospitals include Hospital Italiano (Map p98; ☎ 4959-0800; www.hospitalitaliano.org.ar; Gascón 450) and Hospital Británico (Map p58;

(☎ 4304-1081; www.hospitalbritanico.org.ar; Perdriel 74). The latter has a more central clinic for consultations only in Barrio Norte (Map p84; ☎ 4812-0040; MT de Alvear 1573); call for an appointment. Another popular medical facility is Swiss Medical (Map p92; ☎ 0810-333-8876; www.swissmedical.com.ar; cnr Santa Fe & Scalabrini Ortiz), with various branches around town.

For more personalized medical care with English-speaking doctors and dentists, contact Medicalls (☎ 4823-5999, 15-5156-8384; www.medicalls.com.ar). It's open 24 hours and makes house (or hotel) calls. Dental Argentina (Map p87; ☎ 4828-0821; www.dental-argentina.com.ar; Laprida 1621 2B) provides modern facilities and good dental services with English-speaking professionals.

For information on plastic surgery in Buenos Aires, see p51.

Pharmacies

Pharmacies are common in Buenos Aires. The biggest chain is Farmacity (www.farmacity.com), with dozens of branches throughout the city; they're modern, bright and well stocked with sundries. They have a prescription counter and some are open 24 hours. It's hard to miss their blue-and-orange color theme.

MONEY

Argentina's unit of currency is the peso (AR$). Prices in this book are quoted in Argentine pesos unless otherwise noted. See the inside front cover for exchange rates. Also see p23 for information on costs.

Banks and *cambios* (foreign-exchange offices) are common in the city center; banks have longer lines and more limited opening hours but may offer better rates. A good *cambio* to try is Alhec (Map p84; ☎ 4316-5000; Paraguay 641; 🕓 10am-4:30pm Mon-Fri).

For international transfers Western Union has many branches in BA, including an office near Retiro (Map p84; ☎ 0800-800-3030; www.westernunion.com; Av Córdoba 975; 🕓 9am-8pm Mon-Fri, till 2pm Sat).

Carrying cash, ATM and credit cards is the way to go in Argentina.

CASH

Notes come in denominations of 2, 5, 10, 20, 50 and 100 pesos. One peso equals 100 centavos; coins come in denominations of 5, 10, 25 and 50 centavos, and 1 peso. The $ sign in front of a price is usually used to signify pesos, so this should be the case unless otherwise marked.

Don't be dismayed if you receive dirty and hopelessly tattered banknotes; they will still be accepted everywhere. Some banks refuse worn or defaced US dollars, however, so make sure you arrive in Buenos Aires with pristine bills. In a pinch, American Express (p229) will probably change your older or written-on bills, and you don't have to be a member (but you will have to wait in line).

Counterfeiting of both local and US bills has become something of a problem in recent years, and merchants are very careful when accepting large denominations. You should be, too; look for a clear watermark or running thread on the largest bills, and be especially careful when receiving change in dark nightclubs or taxis (for more on taxi money tips, see p221).

Getting change from large denominations is usually a problem, especially for small purchases. Large supermarkets and restaurants are your best bet. Always keep a stash of change with you, both in small bills and coins; when you need coins for the bus you'll find *kioscos* (small stores or newspaper stands) might not have enough to give out.

ATMs

ATMs (*cajeros automáticos*) are everywhere in BA and the handiest way to get money. ATMs dispense only Argentine pesos and can be used for cash advances on major credit cards. There's often an English translation option if you don't read Spanish.

There may be limits per withdrawal (in 2010 it was about AR$1200), but you may be able to withdraw several times per day – just beware of per-transaction fees. To avoid having a fistful of large-denomination bills, withdraw odd amounts like 590 pesos.

Also, a small fee is charged on ATM transactions by the *local* bank (not including charges by your home bank, which are extra). Note that this is a *per transaction* fee, so consider taking out your maximum allowed limit – if you feel safe doing so.

Credit Cards

Many tourist services, larger stores, hotels and restaurants take credit cards such as Visa and MasterCard, especially for big purchases. Be aware, however, that some businesses add a *recargo* (surcharge) of up to 10% to credit-card purchases; ask ahead of time if this is the case. Some lower-end hotels and private businesses will not accept credit cards, and tips can't usually be added to credit-card bills at restaurants.

The following local representatives can help you replace lost or stolen cards:

American Express (Map p84; ☎ 4310-3000; Arenales 707)

MasterCard (Map p62; ☎ 4340-5656; Perú 151)

Visa (Map p72; ☎ 4379-3400; Av Corrientes 1437, basement)

Traveler's Checks

Traveler's checks are very impractical in Argentina, and even in BA it's hard to change them. Only the fancier hotels and a few banks and *cambios* will take them, and they'll charge a very hefty commission. Stores will *not* change them.

American Express checks can be cashed without commission at its central office (see above) from 10am to 4pm Monday to Friday, though you won't quite get the best rate. Outside BA it's almost impossible to change traveler's checks. If you do decide to bring some, get them in US dollars.

ORGANIZED TOURS

There are plenty of organized tours, from the large tourist bus variety to more intimate car trips to guided bike rides to straight-up walks. Other than the following listings, see also Travel Agencies (p232); most of these broker a wide variety of excellent offerings, from Jewish sights to helicopter rides to night strolls.

The city of Buenos Aires organizes free monthly tours (☎ 4114-5791) from April to December, with themes ranging from art to historic bars to particular neighborhoods. Stop by any government tourist information office (p232) for a schedule.

If you have an MP3 player (such as an iPod) and are self-sufficient, check out www.MPTours.com. You can download unique self-guided tours and maps of BA neighborhoods for US$4.99 each, walking, stopping and listening at your leisure. The city also has good downloads (www.bue.gov.ar/audioguia; both in English and Spanish) and they're free, but not quite as offbeat or 'local' feeling.

The Gay Guide (www.thegayguide.com.ar) helps gay travelers with city tours (and much more).

All companies listed following offer tours in English and possibly other languages; some companies listed under 'Group Tours' also do private tours

Group Tours

Anda Responsible Travel (☎ 3221-0833; www.andatravel.com.ar) Most notable for its La Boca tour, which introduces travelers to local organizations working towards improving the lives of its citizens.

BA Free Tour (☎ 15-6395-3000; www.bafreetour.com) Free (actually, donation) walking tours given by enthusiastic young guides who love their city. Even if you can't give anything you're welcome to join.

Bike it (☎ 5218-1641; www.bikeit.com.ar) Get out of BA: Head to the northern suburbs on a train, then bike through San Isidro to Tigre (where you can get in a canoe).

Biking Buenos Aires (☎ 6208-2176; www.bikingbuenosaires.com) Friendly American guys that take you on their north or south tour of Buenos Aires. Bike rentals available; bike sales in the future.

Buenos Aires Bus (☎ 5239-5160; www.buenosairesbus.com) Hop-on, hop-off topless bus with a dozen stops. Runs every 30 minutes at designated stops (see website).

Cultour (☎ 15-6365-6892; www.cultour.com.ar) Good tours run by teachers and students from UBA (University of Buenos Aires). Prepare to learn the historical and cultural facets of Buenos Aires.

Fileteado Porteño Tour (☎ 3959-0054; www.054online.com – click on 'guias' then 'agencias de viaje') Visit colorfully stylized buildings, painted with Argentina's famous *fileteado* designs (see p44).

Graffitimundo (☎ 3683-3219; www.graffitimundo.com) Expat-run tours of some of BA's best graffiti, by those in the know. Learn artists' history and the local culture of graffiti. Stencil workshops too.

Private Tours

BA Local (☎ 4870-5506; www.balocal.com) Expats specializing in shopping, art and off-the-beaten-path (or just regular city) tours.

Buenos Tours (☎ 3221-1048; www.buenostours.com) Well-run city tours guided by friendly, knowledgeable and responsible local expats. Great website too.

Seriema Nature Tours(☎ 4312-6345; www.seriematours.com) They'll do nature tours to all South America, but around BA the most popular outings are to Costanera Sur and Otamendi Nature Reserve.

Sylvia Zapiola (☎ 4822-1187, 15-3555-3639; sylviazapiola@gmail.com) Feisty Argentine and professional guide who does general city orientation tours and special services like airport pickups.

PHOTOGRAPHY

Many photo stores can transfer images from your digital camera's card to CD, and it's not expensive. You can also get them printed out. Dinosaurs will be happy to know that they can buy and develop print or slide film at affordable rates.

POST

The more-or-less reliable Correo Argentino (www.correoargentino.com.ar) is the government postal service, with numerous branches scattered throughout BA. Essential overseas mail should be sent *certificado* (registered). For international parcels weighing over 2kg, take a copy of your passport and go to the Correo Internacional (Map p84; ☎ 4316-1777; Av Antártida Argentina; 10am-5pm Mon-Fri) near the Retiro bus station. Check the website for all prices.

If a package is being sent to you, expect to wait awhile for it to turn up within the system (or to receive notice of its arrival). Unless you have a permanent address, your parcel will likely end up at the Correo Internacional. To collect the package you'll have to wait – first to get it and then to have it checked by customs. There might also be a small holding fee, charged per day. Don't expect any valuables to make it through.

Privately run international and national services are available. Federal Express (Map p62; ☎ 0810-333-3339; www.fedex.com) has its central branch at Maipú 753. Another choice is DHL International (Map p84; ☎ 4344-4000; www.dhl.com.ar; Av Córdoba 783). OCA (www.oca.com.ar) and Andreani (www.andreani.com.ar) are good for domestic packages; both have various locations around town.

SAFETY

Buenos Aires is generally pretty safe. You can comfortably walk around at all hours of the night in many places, even as a lone woman. People stay out very late, and there's almost always somebody else walking on any one street at any hour of the night. (Some areas where you should be careful at night, however, are around Constitución's train station, the eastern border of San Telmo, and La Boca – where, outside tourist streets, you should be careful even during the day).

Like all big cities, BA claims its share of problems. The economic crisis of 1999–2001 plunged a lot of people into poverty, and street crime has subsequently risen. As a tourist you're much more likely to be a target of petty crimes like pick-pocketing and bag-snatching than armed robbery or kidnapping. Be careful on crowded buses and on the Subte (see p221), and don't put your bag down without your foot through the strap (especially at sidewalk cafes), and even then keep a close eye on it. Also watch out for *motochorros,* or two men on motorcycles who snatch wallets or bags.

> **THE OLD MUSTARD TRICK**
>
> It's one of the oldest tricks in the book. You're in a tourist hot spot like Plaza de Mayo, minding your own business, and suddenly a man or woman tells you there are 'bird droppings' (or whatever) on your clothing. While this kind stranger takes out their surprisingly handy tissues to clean you up, their friend is cleaning out your pockets or stealing your bag.
>
> If anyone stops you and points out any dirty substance on your person, immediately grab your belongings and start walking away fast. Deal with washing up later.

Minor nuisances include lack of respect shown by cars toward pedestrians, lax pollution controls and high noise levels. Many Argentines are heavy smokers, and you can't help but be exposed to it on the street (smoking is banned in most restaurants, bars and public transport). For dealing with taxis, see p221. There's also a tourist police that can help (see p226).

Using your head is good advice anywhere: don't flash any wealth (including expensive jewelry), don't stagger around drunk, always be aware of your surroundings and look like you know exactly where you're going (even if you don't). And realize that if you're reasonably careful, the closest thing to annoyance you'll experience is being shortchanged, tripping on loose sidewalk tiles, stepping on the ubiquitous dog pile or getting flattened by a crazy bus driver. Watch your step.

Police

You're hardly likely to get involved with the local police if you follow the law. If you drive a car, however, officers are not above petty harassment. So-called safety campaigns often result in motorists receiving citations for minor equipment violations (such as a malfunctioning turn signal) that carry fines. In most cases, corrupt officers will settle for less expensive *coimas* (bribes), but this requires considerable caution and tact. A discreet hint that you intend to contact your consulate may minimize or eliminate such problems – often the police count on foreigners' ignorance of Argentine law. Another tactic, whether you know Spanish or not, is to pretend you don't understand what an officer is saying.

For tourist police information, see under Tourist Information, p232.

TAXES & REFUNDS

One of Argentina's primary state revenue-earners is the 21% value-added tax known as the Impuesto de Valor Agregado (IVA). Under limited circumstances, foreign visitors may obtain IVA refunds on purchases of Argentine products upon departing the country. A 'Tax Free' window decal (in English) identifies participants in this program, but always check that the shop is part of the tax-free program before making your purchase.

You can obtain tax refunds on purchases of AR$70 or more made at one of these participating stores. To do so, present your passport to the merchant, who will make out an invoice for you. On leaving the country keep the purchased items in your carry-on baggage; a customs official will check them. And be sure to leave yourself a bit of extra time at the airport to get this done.

TELEPHONE

Two companies, Telecom and Telefónica, split the city's telephone services. Competition has sprouted up, however, and cheap international services are available. Inexpensive phone cards can be bought at *kioscos*, allowing you to call home for relatively cheap. Making international calls over the internet using Skype is another cheap option; many internet cafés have this system in place.

The easiest way to make a local or international phone call is to find a *locutorio*, a small telephone office (sometimes marked *telecentro*) with private booths from which you make your calls and then pay at the register. There's a *locutorio* on practically every other block. They cost just a bit more than street phones, but here you can sit down, you won't run out of coins and it's much quieter. Street phones require coins or *tarjetas telefónicas* (magnetic phone cards available at many kiosks). You'll only be able to speak for a limited time before you get cut off, so carry enough credit. When making international calls from *locutorios* ask about off-peak discount hours, which generally apply after 10pm and on weekends.

Landlines in BA have eight-digit numbers. When calling a cell phone you'll need to dial ☎ 15 before the eight-digit number. If you're calling a BA number from somewhere else in Argentina, you'll need to dial ☎ 011 first. When calling BA from *outside* Argentina, first dial your country's international access code, then ☎ 54 11 and the eight-digit number. When calling cell phones from outside Argentina, dial your country's international access code, then ☎ 54 9 11 and then the eight-digit number, leaving out the 15. Toll-free numbers in BA have a 0800 before a seven-digit number.

Faxes are cheap and widely available at most *locutorios* and internet cafes. For emergency telephone numbers see p226.

Cell Phones

It's best to bring your own unlocked tri- or quad-band GSM cell phone to BA, then buy a SIM chip (around AR$15; you'll get a local number) and get top-up credits (or *carga virtual*) as needed. You can also buy cell phones that use SIM chips for around AR$200; these usually include some credits for your first batch of calls. Be careful renting phones as they're not usually a better deal than outright buying a cell phone.

If you plan to travel with a smart phone, prepare yourself beforehand – you may need to purchase an international plan to avoid being hit by a huge bill with roaming costs. This is a fast-changing field so check the current situation before you travel; a useful website is www.kropla.com.

TIME

Argentina is three hours behind GMT and generally does not observe daylight saving time (though this situation can easily change). Many porteños use the 24-hour clock to differentiate between am and pm.

TIPPING

In restaurants it's customary to tip about 10% of the bill. Some Argentines just leave leftover change, but generally if you can afford to eat out you can afford to tip. Note that tips can't be added to credit-card bills, so carry cash for this purpose.

Taxi drivers don't expect tips, but it's usual to round up to the nearest peso if the difference isn't much.

TOILETS

Public toilets in BA are generally decent and often stocked with toilet paper (carry some anyway), but soap and towels are rarer. If you're looking for a bathroom while walking around, note that the largest shopping malls (such as Galerías Pacífico) always have public bathrooms available, but in a pinch you can always walk into a McDonald's or large cafe.

Some may find bidets a novelty; they are those strange shallow, ceramic bowls with knobs and a drain, often accompanying toilets in hotel bathrooms. They are meant for between-shower cleanings of nether regions. Turn knobs slowly, or you may end up spraying yourself or the ceiling.

TOURIST INFORMATION

The Secretaría de Turismo de la Nación (Map p84; ☎ 4312-2232; www.turismo.gov.ar; Av Santa Fe 883; 9am-5pm Mon-Fri) dispenses information on Buenos Aires, but focuses on Argentina as a whole.

The Tourist Police (Comisaría del Turista; Map p62; ☎ 4346-5748; 0800-999-5000; turista@policiafederal.gov.ar; Av Corrientes 436; 24hr) can provide interpreters and helps victims of robberies and rip-offs.

There's a tourist kiosk at Ezeiza airport (24 hrs) and another one at Retiro bus station (Map p84; 7:30am-2pm Mon-Fri) near Puente 3 on the main floor, under bus counter 105.

There are several tourist offices and kiosks in Buenos Aires. Note that hours vary depending on the season and number of volunteers. The official tourism site of Buenos Aires is www.bue.gov.ar and the government site is www.buenosaires.gov.ar.

Plaza San Martín (Map p84; Av Florida & MT de Alvear)

Florida (Map p62; Av Florida & Diagonal Norte)

Puerto Madero (Map p69; Dique 4) Especially good for getting-to-Uruguay information.

Recoleta (Map p87; Av Quintana 596)

Another excellent source of information and generally indispensable resource is South American Explorers (www.saexplorers.org), which maintains a clubhouse in Buenos Aires (see p235).

TRAVEL AGENCIES

The following agencies all arrange group or private tours in BA and Argentina, and the staff speak English. For more on city tours, see p229.

Anda Responsible Travel (Map p92; ☎ 3221-0833; www.andatravel.com.ar) Organizes tours around BA & Argentina with a 'sustainable' focus in mind, by introducing travelers to local communities, fair trade organizations & social projects.

Say Hueque (Map p62; ☎ 5199-2517; www.sayhueque.com; Viamonte 749, 6th fl) This friendly, traveler-oriented agency will not only make the usual air, bus and hotel reservations, but also offers BA city tours and adventure trips all around Argentina. Also in Palermo at Thames 2062 (Map p92) and in San Telmo at Chile 557 (Map p76).

Tangol (Map p84; ☎ 4312-7276; www.tangol.com; Florida 971, ste 31) Do-all agency that offers city tours, tango shows, guides to fútbol games, hotel reservations, Spanish classes, air tickets and country-wide packages. Also offers unusual activities including helicopter tours and skydiving. Also in San Telmo at Defensa 831 (Map p76).

Wow Argentina (Map p84; ☎ 5239-3019; www.wowargentina.com; Av Santa Fe 882, 12F) This small, knowledgeable and detail-oriented agency caters to middle and upper-class clientele, offering excellent, professional services. Complete itineraries to Iguazú, Mendoza, Salta and Patagonia, along with tours around Buenos Aires.

TRAVELERS WITH DISABILITIES

Negotiating Buenos Aires as a disabled traveler is not the easiest of tasks. City sidewalks are narrow, busy and dotted with many broken tiles. Not every corner has a ramp, and traffic is ruthless when it comes to pedestrians (and wheelchair-users). A few buses do have *piso bajo* (they 'kneel' and have extra-large spaces), but the Subte (subway) does not cater to the mobility-impaired.

International hotel chains often have wheelchair-accessible rooms, as do other less fancy hotels – accessibility laws have changed for the better over the last few years. Some restaurants and many important tourist sights have ramps, but BA is sorely lacking in wheelchair-accessible bathrooms – although the city's shopping malls usually have at least one, restaurants don't often have the appropriate installations.

In Buenos Aires, QRV Transportes Especiales (☎ 011-4306-6635, 15-6863-9555; www.qrvtransportes.com.ar) offers private transport and city tours in vans fully equipped for wheelchair users. BA Cultural Concierge (www.baculturalconcierge.com) offers service for low-mobility travelers, by helping with errands. Or you could head to

BA with a company like Accessible Journeys (www.disabilitytravel.com), which has tours and cruises in South America – including one that includes Buenos Aires.

Other than the use of brail on ATMs little effort has been dedicated to bettering accessibility for the blind. Stoplights are rarely equipped with sound alerts. The Biblioteca Argentina Para Ciegos (BAC; Argentine Library for the Blind; ☎ 4981-0137; www.bac.org.ar; Lezica 3909, Buenos Aires) maintains a brail collection of over 3000 books, as well as other resources.

VISAS & ENTRY FEES

Nationals of the USA, Canada, most Western European countries, Australia and New Zealand do not need visas to visit Argentina, but check current regulations. Most foreigners receive a 90-day visa upon arrival.

To get yourself a 90-day extension (AR$300), visit the Dirección Nacional de Migraciones (Immigration office; Map p84; ☎ 4317-0200; www.migraciones.gov.ar; Av Antártida Argentina 1355; 8am-1pm Mon-Fri). Set aside some time, as there are lines and this process can take an hour or two. Get your extension the same week your visa expires. Overstaying your visa (AR$300) costs as much as an extension, but it's also much more stressful – and the rules can change quickly.

Another option if you're staying more than three months is to cross into Colonia or Montevideo (both in Uruguay; Colonia can be an easy day trip) and return with a new three-month visa. This strategy is most sensible if you are from a country that does not require a visa to enter Uruguay.

Americans, Australians and Canadians need to pay a reciprocity fee (*tasa de reciprocidad*) when arriving at Ezeiza and Aeroparque. These are significant fees; for more information see 'Ezeiza Arrival and Departure Tips', p223.

WOMEN TRAVELERS

Buenos Aires is a modern, sophisticated city, and women travelers – even those traveling alone – should not encounter many difficulties. Men do pay more overt attention to women in Argentina, however, and a little open-mindedness might be in order. Argentina's machismo culture is, after all, alive and well.

A few men feel the need to comment on a woman's attractiveness. This often happens when you're walking alone and pass by a man; it will never occur when you're with another man. Comments usually include whistles or *piropos*, which many Argentine males consider the art of complimenting a woman. *Piropos* are often vulgar, although a few can be poetic. Much as you may want to kick them where it counts, the best thing to do is completely ignore the comments. After all, many porteñas are used to getting these 'compliments,' and most men don't necessarily mean to be insulting; they're just doing what is socially acceptable in Argentina.

On the plus side of machismo, expect men to hold a door open for you and let you enter first, including getting on buses; this gives you a better chance at grabbing an empty seat, so get in there quick.

WORK

Unless you have a special skill, business, and/or speak Spanish, it's hard to find work other than teaching English – or perhaps putting time in at a hostel or expat bar. And it's good to realize that you're not likely to get rich doing these things.

Working out of an institute, native English-speakers can earn around AR$30 to AR$35 per hour (and you aren't paid for prep time or travel time, which can add another hour or two for each hour of teaching). Twenty hours a week of actual teaching is about enough for most people. Frustrations include dealing with unpleasant institutes, time spent cashing checks at the bank, classes being spread throughout the day and cancelled classes. Institute turn-over is high and most people don't teach for more than a year.

A TEFL certification can certainly help but isn't mandatory for all jobs. You'll make more money teaching private students, but it takes time to gain a client base. And you should take into account slow periods like December through February, when many locals leave town on summer vacation.

Finding an English-teaching job shouldn't be too difficult – there are plenty of porteños who want to learn, so many English-language institutes have popped up. Check the classified section of the *Buenos Aires Herald* for leads, call up the institutes or visit expat bars and websites and start networking. March is when institutes are ramping up their courses, so it's the best time to find work. Many teachers work on tourist visas (which is not a big deal), heading over to Uruguay every three months for a new visa or visiting the immigration office (see Visas) for a visa extension.

MOVING TO BUENOS AIRES *Kristie Robinson*

Due to the relatively low cost of living, rent and property prices, coupled with a society that resembles more Paris than Mexico City, Buenos Aires has seen an unprecedented influx of foreigners who want to live in the city for an extended period of time. This already-strong community of new and old expats keep in touch via blogs, forums, magazines and events dedicated to bringing people together. Here are some of the most important things to know if you want to be a wanna-be porteño!

Visas

Many people wishing to live in Buenos Aires simply arrive with a three-month tourist visa, which they renew every three months by traveling to Uruguay. Another option is to go to the Dirección Nacional de Migraciones (immigration office; see p233) and apply for a three-month extension. This extension can only be done once without leaving the country, so in theory a person could stay indefinitely in Buenos Aires while only having to go to Uruguay twice a year.

Getting a long-stay visa has become easier, as the government recently introduced a simplified work visa. The company hiring foreign employees writes a letter of employment, then the employee simply takes this document to the immigration office and applies for a one-year renewable work visa. It's best to check with your consulate about current changes on this front.

Work

It's generally pretty hard to find a paying job in Buenos Aires. Some of the ones that are available are in call centers, commission-based jobs and paid internships, but the most common job available is teaching English. Most people seeking this kind of employment have a TEFL or TEOFL certificate (see www.ebc-tefl-course.com if you don't), but you can obtain work without one – though you may be paid less. For work opportunities check out the *Buenos Aires Herald* classifieds and www.buenosaires.craigslist.com. Most jobs are paid in cash, but the Buenos Aires government is trying to combat this with advertising campaigns and work visas. If you are self-employed or want to start your own business you can apply for a CUIT business number, which allows you to issue invoices. To obtain this you will need to visit your closest Administración Federal de Ingresos Públicos (AFIP; www.afip.gov.ar) office and present your passport.

For more on working in BA see p233.

Renting

If you're a foreigner, you'll find it hard to get a long-term lease on an apartment without a *garantía* – an Argentine citizen willing to guarantee that you will pay your bills and expenses. Without this, there are a few things you could do; offer to pay six months' rent upfront, look at renting a room in an established house, or pay a little extra for a short-term rental through an agency. At the time of printing, the average renting price for foreigners was roughly AR$1300 a month for a room and AR$2800 for a studio apartment.

To find a place, check the Spanish newspapers *Clarín* (www.inmuebles.clarin.com) or *La Nación* (www.classificados.lanacion.com.ar); for English speakers there's the *Buenos Aires Herald* (no on-line listings).

Plenty of apartments websites cater to foreigners; see boxed text p191 for a list.

Buying

Buying a property in Buenos Aires is relatively easy. You'll need your passport, a CDI certificate and lots of money – in cash! A CDI certificate can easily be obtained through your closest Administración Federal de Ingresos Públicos (AFIP; www.afip.gov.ar) office for free. Having large amounts of money in cash can be daunting, but international bank transfers make it easier. Be aware that there are tax laws, rights and responsibilities that should be thoroughly investigated before buying any property. There are many websites for buying houses, but it may be better to read the various expat forums and contact people who have already bought in Buenos Aires (see 'Meeting People').

English-Language Media

There are three main publications in English that will help you settle into Buenos Aires. The *Buenos Aires Herald* (www.buenosairesherald.com) is available at most *kioscos*. And the free *Argentina Independent* (www.argentinaindependent.com) is a fortnightly publication that is more features-based and has a great events listings section.

Bank Accounts

Opening a bank account is not easy for a person with only a tourist visa. If you're staying for a year or less, it's often less hassle-free to just use your ATM card from back home and take the transaction fee hits. However, it might be possible to do limited banking in Buenos Aires via your home bank – *if* it has branches in BA. But depending on your skills of persuasion and who you talk to at the bank, you may also be able to open an account in the capital. Just put on your ambassador hat, spruce up your Spanish and bring as much paperwork as you can: Photo ID, property title, lease contract, bills in your name and a CDI certificate (a government-issued tax identity number). All will help persuade the bank employee to let you establish a BA nest egg.

Cell Phones

Generally there are two different plans available for cell phones: a monthly plan and a pay-as-you-go plan. The monthly plans are hard to get as you are required to have a DNI (Argentina's national identity document) or evidence of permanent residency. The pay-as-you-go plans are easy, cheap and only require a passport. The main companies are Personal (www.personal.com.ar), Movistar (www.movistar.com.ar) and Claro (www.claroargentina.com). There isn't much difference in service or price between them, and they all offer a free text-message service through their websites. For more on cell phones in BA see p231.

Meeting People

You may want to be in touch with the Buenos Aires expat community, which is quite large and welcoming. Other than expat bars, there are several places to check:

BA Expats (www.baexpats.com) Lots of information on Buenos Aires, plus hosts a forum for members' questions.

BAIN (www.bainnewcomers.com) A group of expats that gets together for a variety of events.

BANewcomers (http://groups.yahoo.com/group/BANewcomers) Yahoo newsgroup; good place to throw out questions to expats in Argentina.

Club Europeo (www.clubeuropeo) Bringing together the social clubs of most of the European embassies in Buenos Aires, they host weekly drinks, social events and language lessons.

Expat Connection (www.expat-connection.com) An online company which runs events for both expats and locals. Check its online calendar for its next event.

South American Explorers Club (www.saexplorers.org) A member-based travellers' hub and resource center which hosts events, offers luggage storage and travel information.

Useful Websites

For more useful websites on Buenos Aires, see p23.

Argentina Residency & Citizenship Advisors (ARCA; www.argentinaresidency.com) Helps foreigners obtain legal residency & citizenship.

Just Landed (www.justlanded.com/english/Argentina) More info for expats.

Some Rules for Living like a Local

- Never give out your loose change to anybody. Guard it with your life!
- Always complain about the weather – 'too cold in winter, too hot in summer'.
- Put your cell phone on speaker and use it like a walkie-talkie on the streets.
- Never go out before 2am on a Friday night, and never come home before 4am.
- Don't ask why the electricity and water are out; just accept it with a shrug and go take a walk until services return!

Kristie Robinson is a journalist who has been living in Buenos Aires for five years, and is founder and editor of The Argentina Independent.

For general job listings check www.buenosaires.en.craigslist.org. You can also try posting on expat website forums like www.baexpats.org. For volunteer opportunities, see below.

Doing Business

Personal relationships are very important for getting things done in Argentina, so take time to get to know your business contacts. Setting up an appointment beforehand is always better than cold-calling. Always start a conversation with small talk about your family or sporting events, and be wary of political talk.

In social circumstances Argentines always kiss each other on the cheek in greeting, but if you're meeting a business contact for the first time a handshake is best. Dress conservatively and be prompt (though your Argentine contact will usually be a bit late).

Most business in Argentina is done in Spanish, and legal papers in a foreign language are generally translated into Spanish by a certified public translator. Think about printing your business cards in Spanish as well as English. If you're an American, say you're from 'los Estados Unidos' (the United States) rather than 'America' (some Argentines consider themselves 'American' also – *South* American).

Most four- or five-star hotels have business centers and meeting rooms. For general business hours, see p223. For work visas there's the immigration office (see Visas p234). Finally, the commercial service department at your embassy in Buenos Aires is a good first resource for general business dealings in Argentina.

Volunteering

There are plenty of volunteer opportunities in Buenos Aires, from food banks to working with kids in *villas miserias*. Some ask for just your time, or a modest fee – and some charge hundreds of dollars (with likely a low percentage of money going directly to those in need). Before choosing an organization, it's good to talk to other volunteers about their experiences.

Argentine organizations include:

Centro Conviven (www.conviven.org.ar) Helps kids in villas.

L.I.F.E (www.lifeargentina.org) More help for kids in villas.

Unión de los Pibes (www.uniondelospibes.blogspot.com) Kids in need.

Eco Yoga Park (see p178) One-of-a-kind.

Fundación Banco de Alimentos (www.bancodealimentos.org.ar) Short-term, simple work at a food bank.

Habitat for Humanity Argentina (www.hpha.org.ar) Building communities.

WWOOF Argentina (www.wwoofargentina.com) Organic farming in Argentina.

You can also use the referral service provided by:

Anda Responsible Travel (www.andatravel.com.ar) Local travel agency supporting local communities.

Foundation for Sustainable Development (www.fsdinternational.org) Nourishes grassroots programs worldwide.

Volunteer South America (www.volunteersouthamerica.net) List of NGOs.

Voluntario Global (www.voluntarioglobal.org.ar) Community volunteering.

Voluntarios sin fronteras (www.voluntariossf.org.ar) All kinds of volunteering.

Writers can consider penning articles for the *Argentina Independent* (www.argentinaindependent.com), or interning at the *Buenos Aires Herald* (www.buenosaireshelald.com). There's also the South American Explorers Club (see p235).

LANGUAGE

Spanish is Argentina's official language, and you can make your stay in Buenos Aires a whole lot more rewarding simply by learning a little lingo before you go. You'll find that locals genuinely appreciate travelers trying their language, no matter how muddled you may think you sound. It's not difficult to pick up a few basic phrases, but even better is undertaking a language course once you're there.

Argentines normally refer to the Spanish language as *castellano* rather than *español*. In addition to their flamboyance, an Argentine's Italian-accented Spanish pronunciation and other language quirks such as the use of vos for tu (you) and the pronunciation of the letters ll and y as 'sh', identify them throughout Latin America and abroad. The speech of Buenos Aires in particular also abounds with words and phrases from the colorful slang known as *lunfardo*. Although you shouldn't use *lunfardo* words unless you are confident that you know their every implication (especially in formal situations), it's good to be aware of some of the more common everyday usages.

If you want a more extensive introduction to Spanish than what we've included here, pick up a copy of Lonely Planet's comprehensive and user friendly *Latin American Spanish Phrasebook*.

SOCIAL

Meeting People

Hi!	¡Hola!
Bye!	¡Chau!
Please.	Por favor.
Thank you (very much).	(Muchas) Gracias.
Yes.	Sí.
No.	No.
Excuse me.	Permiso.
Sorry.	Perdón.
Pardon?	¿Cómo?
Do you speak English?	¿Hablá inglés?
Does anyone speak English?	¿Hay alguien que hable inglés?
I understand.	Entiendo.
I don't understand.	No entiendo.
Could you please ...?	¿Puede ..., por favor?
repeat that	repetirlo
speak more slowly	hablar más despacio
write it down	escribirlo

Going Out

What's there to do in the evenings?	¿Qué se puede hacer a la noche?
Is there anything to do ...?	¿Hay algo para hacer ...?
in (Palermo Viejo)	en (Palermo Viejo)
this weekend	este fin de semana
today	hoy
tonight	esta noche
Where are the ...?	¿Dónde hay ...?
clubs	boliches
gay venues	lugares para gays
places to eat	lugares para comer
pubs	pubs
Is there a local entertainment guide?	¿Hay una guía de entretenimiento de la zona?

PRACTICAL

Question Words

How?	¿Cómo?
How many?	¿Cuántos? (m) ¿Cuántas? (f)
How much is it?	¿Cuánto cuesta?
What?	¿Qué?
When?	¿Cuándo?
Where?	¿Dónde?
Which?	¿Cuál? (sg) ¿Cuáles? (pl)
Who?	¿Quién? (sg) ¿Quiénes? (pl)
Why?	¿Por qué?

Numbers & Amounts

0	cero
1	uno
2	dos
3	tres
4	cuatro
5	cinco
6	seis
7	siete
8	ocho
9	nueve
10	diez
11	once
12	doce
13	trece
14	catorce
15	quince
16	dieciséis
17	diecisiete
18	dieciocho
19	diecinueve
20	veinte
21	veintiuno
22	veintidos
30	treinta
31	treinta y uno
32	treinta y dos
40	cuarenta
50	cincuenta
60	sesenta
70	setenta
80	ochenta
90	noventa
100	cien
200	doscientos
1000	mil
2000	dos mil

Days

Monday	lunes
Tuesday	martes
Wednesday	miércoles
Thursday	jueves
Friday	viernes
Saturday	sábado
Sunday	domingo

Banking

Where's the nearest ATM?	¿Dónde está el cajero automático más cercano?
Where's the nearest foreign exchange office?	¿Dónde está la oficina de cambio más cercana?

LUNFARDO

Below are are some of the spicier *lunfardo* (slang) terms that you may hear on the streets of Buenos Aires.

boliche – disco, nightclub
boludo – jerk, idiot; often used in a friendly fashion between good friends, but a deep insult to a stranger
bondi – bus
buena onda – good vibes
carajo – bloody hell
chabón/chabona – guy/girl (term of endearment)
che – hey
fiaca – laziness
guita – money
macanudo – great, fabulous
mango – one peso
masa – a great, cool thing
mina – woman
morfar – eat
pendejo – idiot
pibe/piba – cool young guy/girl
piola – cool, clever
pucho – cigarette
re – very, as in *re interestante* (very interesting)

che boludo – the most *porteño* phrase on earth; ask a friendly local youth to explain
diez puntos – OK, cool, fine (literally '10 points')
Le faltan un par de jugadores. – He's not playing with a full deck. (literally 'He's a couple of players short of a team.')
Me mataste. – I have no idea. (literally 'You killed me.')
¡Ponete las pilas! – Get on with it! (literally 'Put the batteries in!')

I'd like to change ...	Quisiera cambiar ...
cash	dinero en efectivo
money	dinero
traveler's checks	cheques de viajero
Do you accept ...?	¿Aceptan ...?
credit cards	tarjetas de crédito
debit cards	tarjetas de débito

Post

Where's the post office?	¿Dónde está el correo?
I want to send a ...	Quiero enviar ...
parcel	un paquete
postcard	una postal
I want to buy ...	Quiero comprar ...
a stamp	una estampilla
an envelope	un sobre

Phone & Cell Phones

I want to ...	Quiero ...
buy a phonecard	comprar una tarjeta telefónica
make a call (to ...)	hacer una llamada (a ...)
make a collect call	hacer una llamada con cobro revertido
I'd like a/an ...	Quiero ...
adaptor plug	un adaptador
cell phone for hire	un celular para alquilar
charger for my cell phone	un cargador para mi celular
prepaid cell phone	un celular pagado por adelantado
SIM card for your network	una tarjeta SIM para su red

Internet

Where's can I use the internet?	¿Dónde puedo usar internet?
I'd like to ...	Quiero ...
check my email	chequear mi email
get online	usar internet

Transportation

What time does the ... leave?	¿A qué hora sale el ...?
boat	barco
bus	colectivo
plane	avión
train	tren
What time's the ... (bus)?	¿A qué hora es el ... (colectivo)?
first	primer
last	último
next	próximo
Is this taxi available?	¿Está disponible este taxi?
Please put the meter on.	Por favor, ponga el taxímetro/reloj.
How much is it to ...?	¿Cuánto cuesta ir a ...?
Please take me (to this address).	Por favor, lléveme (a esta dirección).

FOOD

breakfast	desayuno
lunch	almuerzo
dinner	cena
snack	snack
to drink	tomar
to eat	comer
Can you recommend a ...?	¿Puede recomendar ...?
bar	un bar
café	un café
coffee bar	una cafetería
restaurant	un restaurante
Is the service charge included in the bill?	¿El precio en el menu incluye el servicio de cubierto?

EMERGENCIES

Help	¡Ayuda!
It's an emergency!	¡Es una emergencia!
Call ...!	¡Llame a ...!
a doctor	un médico
an ambulance	una ambulancia
the police	la policía
Could you help me, please?	¿Me puede ayudar, por favor?
Where's the police station?	¿Dónde está la policía?

HEALTH

Where's the nearest ...?	¿Dónde está ... más cercano/a? (m/f)
(night) pharmacy	la farmacia (de turno) (f)
dentist	el dentista (m)
doctor	el médico (m)
hospital	el hospital (m)
I'm sick.	Estoy enfermo/a. (m/f)
I need a doctor (who speaks English).	Necesito un médico (que hable inglés).
I have (a) ...	Tengo ...
diarrhoea	diarrea
fever	fiebre
headache	dolor de cabeza
pain (here)	dolor (acá)
I'm allergic to ...	Soy alérgico/a ... (m/f)
antibiotics	a los antibióticos
nuts	a las frutas secas
peanuts	al maní
penicillin	a la penicilina
seafood	al marisco

GLOSSARY

alfajor – two flat, soft cookies filled with *dulce de leche* and covered in chocolate or meringue
arbolito – literally 'little tree'; a street moneychanger
argentinidad – rather nebulous concept of Argentine national identity, often associated with extreme nationalistic feelings
asado – famously Argentine barbecue, often held on a family outing in summer
autopista – freeway or motorway

bandoneón – accordion-like instrument used in tango music
bárbaro – local word meaning 'wonderful' or 'great'
barras bravas – violent soccer fans; the Argentine equivalent of Britain's football hooligans
barrio – neighborhood or borough of the city
boliche – a *lunfardo* term for nightclub
bombilla – silvery straw with built-in filter, used for drinking *mate*
boquenses – inhabitants of La Boca
bronca – anger, frustration

cabeceo – invitation to dance tango which involves a quick tilt of the head, eye contact and uplifted eyebrows
cabildo – colonial town council
café cortado – espresso with steamed milk added (macchiato)
cajero automático – automatic teller machine (ATM)
cambio – see *casa de cambio*
candombe – Afro-Uruguayan, percussion-based musical form that enjoys some popularity in Buenos Aires, especially at Carnaval
canilla libre – all-you-can-drink
característica – telephone area code
cartelera – discount ticket agency offering great bargains on tickets to cinemas, tango shows and other performances
cartoneros – people who pick through garbage looking for recyclables
casa de cambio – foreign-exchange house, often simply called a *cambio*
castellano – Spanish (the language)
caudillo – 'strongman'; the term was applied to Argentina's iron-fisted rulers of the 19th century
cebador – designated *mate* server
cerveza – beer
chacarera – traditional Argentine style of folk music, typically performed on the *bombo* (a small Andean drum) and guitar
chamamé – musical form originating in Corrientes province, derived from a blend of Eastern European, indigenous and African styles
chimichurri – spicy marinade for meat, usually made of parsley, garlic, spices and olive oil
chopp – glass of draft beer
choripán – spicy sausage sandwich
coima – bribe
colectivo – local bus
confitería – shop that serves mostly sandwiches and hamburgers
conventillo – a tenement that housed immigrants in older neighborhoods of Buenos Aires and Montevideo
costanera – seaside, riverside or lakeside road
cubierto – in restaurants, this is the cover charge you pay for utensil use and bread
criollo – in the colonial period, an American-born Spaniard; the term now commonly describes any Argentine of European descent; also describes the feral cattle and horses of the Pampas

desaparecido – 'disappeared one'; a victim of the 1976–83 Argentine dictatorship
despelote – mess, fiasco; often used when describing the current government (see *porquería*)
dique – water dike
dulce de leche – Argentina's national sweet, found in many desserts and snacks: a type of thick, liquid caramel, milky and creamy

empanada – meat or vegetable pie; popular Argentine snack
estancia – historically speaking, an extensive grazing estate, either for cattle or sheep, under a dominating *estanciero* or manager with a dependent resident labor force of gauchos; now often destinations for tourists for recreational activities such as riding, tennis and swimming, either for weekend escapes or extended stays

facturas – pastries; also a receipt
feria – street fair or street market

gauchesco/a – relating to the romantic image of the gaucho
genial – wonderful, great, fine

heladería – ice-cream shop

ida – one-way
ida y vuelta – round-trip
iglesia – church
interno – telephone extension; often abbreviated 'int'
IVA – *impuesto de valor agregado*, or value-added tax; often added to restaurant or hotel bills in Argentina

kiosco – small store or newspaper stand

locro – corn and meat stew
locutorio – private long-distance telephone office that usually offers fax and internet services as well

lunfardo – street slang of Buenos Aires, with origins in immigrant neighborhoods at the turn of the century

mango – slang for peso (like the US 'buck' for dollar)
mate – shortened form of *yerba mate*, Argentina's popular tea; also refers to the gourd used for drinking it
milonga – tango dance event
minuta – in a restaurant or *confitería*, a short order such as spaghetti or schnitzel
murga – Spanish for 'racket' or 'din'; also a *rioplatense* performance style of African and Spanish origins. *La murga porteña* is another term for Buenos Aires' Carnaval festivities.

nafta – gasoline or petrol

paisanos – country folk
Pampas – grassy plains that stretch east of the Andes
parada – bus stop
parrillada – a mixed grill of steak and other beef cuts and a restaurant specializing in such dishes
parrilla – a restaurant specializing in *parrillada*
paseaperros – professional dog walker in Buenos Aires
pato – a traditional ball game played on horseback
peatonal – pedestrian mall, usually in the downtown area
peña – club that hosts informal folk music gatherings
piqueteros – picketers (political street protestors carrying signs), who often stop traffic while marching in a public place (such as Plaza de Mayo)
piropo – sexist remark, ranging in tone from complimentary and relatively innocuous to rude and offensive
porteño/a – inhabitant of Buenos Aires
porquería – fiasco, trash, mess; often used when describing the government (see *despelote*)
propina – tip (gratuity)
puchero – soup combining vegetables and meats, served with rice
puerto – port

quilombo – mess, chaos

recargo – an additional charge (such as for use of a credit card)
reloj – local word commonly used for *taxímetro* (taxi meter)
remise – a call taxi; they look like regular cars and collect a fixed fare
rioplatense – describes anything native to the Río de la Plata region
ruta – highway, route

sandwiches de miga – thin crustless sandwiches, traditionally eaten at tea time
spiedo – spit; an alternative to the *parrilla*
Subte – the Buenos Aires underground railway

tarjeta telefónica – magnetic telephone card
tenedor libre – literally 'free fork,' an 'all-you-can-eat' restaurant; less commonly known as *diente libre* ('free tooth')
trucho – bogus; widely used by Argentines to describe things that are not what they appear to be

villa miseria – shantytown, also often simply called *villa*
viveza criolla – sly foxiness, a valued quality for some Argentines

yerba mate – 'Paraguayan tea' (*Ilex paraguariensis*), which Argentines consume in very large amounts; see also *mate*

BEHIND THE SCENES

THIS BOOK

This 6th edition of Buenos Aires was written by Sandra Bao and Bridget Gleeson. The previous three editions were also written by Sandra Bao. This guidebook was commissioned in Lonely Planet's Oakland office, and produced by the following:

Commissioning Editors Kathleen Munnelly, Catherine Craddock-Carillo, Nora Gregory

Coordinating Editors Jocelyn Harewood, Jeanette Wall

Coordinating Cartographer Tom Webster

Coordinating Layout Designer Frank Deim

Managing Editors Brigitte Ellemor, Bruce Evans

Managing Cartographers Shahara Ahmed, Alison Lyall

Managing Layout Designer Celia Wood

Assisting Editor Sarah Bailey

Assisting Cartographer Jennifer Johnston

Cover Research Brendan Dempsey

Internal Image Research Sabrina Dalbesio

Language Content Annelies Mertens, Branislava Vladislavljevic

Thanks to Melanie Dankel, Jane Hart, Yvonne Kirk, Lisa Knights

Cover photographs
Rear of bus in Plaza Constitucio, Buenos Aires, Argentina, South America, Damien Simonis/LPI (top); Painted facades near Museo Casa Carlos Gardel, Buenos Aires, Argentina, South America, Krzysztof Dydynski/LPI (bottom).

All images are copyright of the photographer unless otherwise indicated. Many of the images in this guide are available for licensing from Lonely Planet Images: www.lonelyplanetimages.com.

THANKS

SANDRA BAO

I'm grateful for the support of my colleague Bridget Gleeson, and excellent commissioning editor (and supermom) Kathleen Munnelly. This book wouldn't be the fine thing that it is without the help from Angela McCallum and Kristie Robinson, and thanks also to Andy Symington and Marina Charles for their input. Sally Blake is my tango connection, while Romina MacGibbon offered invaluable insight to Buenos Aires' eco-green scene (or lack thereof). Plenty of *besos y abrazos* to Phil Appleton, Sam Frommer, Graciela Guzmán, Amalia Holub, Madi Lang, Lucas Markowiecki, Jed Rothenburg and Sylvia Zapiola for all the tips and fun times. Thanks especially to my godmother Elsa for her always-welcoming hospitality and home made meals. Finally, lots of love to my husband Ben Greensfelder for keeping the house from burning down (though a bit untidy, sorry honey) while I was gone for five weeks during research.

BRIDGET GLEESON

As usual, it's been a pleasure to work with Sandra Bao and Kathleen Munnelly at Lonely Planet. I'm grateful to my friends and professional acquaintances in Buenos Aires; your suggestions make my work better and your active social lives inspire me to get out and try the new restaurants and bars for myself. Special thanks to my sister Liz for her willingness to meet me at a café, even at a moment's notice, and to Rodolfo for his constant support. Thanks, finally, to the Lonely Planet readers I've met on the road – your passion for adventure pushes me to be better and reminds me why I wanted to be a travel writer.

OUR READERS

Many thanks to the travelers who used the last edition and wrote to us with helpful hints, useful advice and interesting anecdotes:

Carlos Abela, Jessie Akin, Emanuela Appetiti, David Barber, Charleyne Biondi, Bernard Breen, Steve Brosnan, John

OUR STORY

A beat-up old car, a few dollars in the pocket and a sense of adventure. In 1972 that's all Tony and Maureen Wheeler needed for the trip of a lifetime – across Europe and Asia overland to Australia. It took several months, and at the end – broke but inspired – they sat at their kitchen table writing and stapling together their first travel guide, Across Asia on the Cheap. Within a week they'd sold 1500 copies. Lonely Planet was born.

Today, Lonely Planet has offices in Melbourne, London and Oakland, with more than 600 staff and writers. We share Tony's belief that 'a great guidebook should do three things: inform, educate and amuse'.

SEND US YOUR FEEDBACK

We love to hear from travelers – your comments keep us on our toes and help make our books better. Our well-traveled team reads every word on what you loved or loathed about this book. Although we cannot reply individually to postal submissions, we always guarantee that your feedback goes straight to the appropriate authors, in time for the next edition. Each person who sends us information is thanked in the next edition and the most useful submissions are rewarded with a free book.

To send us your updates – and find out about Lonely Planet events, newsletters and travel news – visit our award-winning website: lonelyplanet.com/contact.

Note: We may edit, reproduce and incorporate your comments in Lonely Planet products such as guidebooks, websites and digital products, so let us know if you don't want your comments reproduced or your name acknowledged. For a copy of our privacy policy visit lonelyplanet.com/privacy.

Burger, Alex Burke, Richard Case, Bianca Celestin, Aneesa Chaudhry, Ray Duncan, Richard Ferguson, Lilian Gentile, Andy Goldschmidt, Peter Goll, Ben Herman, Amador Hernandez, Tony Hutton, Rich Jabs, Anne Jaumees, Antje Kalinauskas, Bart Keersmaekers, Antje König, Ricardo Krieger, Anna Lyndon, Scott Molinaroli, Olaf Moon, Bryce Newman, James Patrick Higgins, Christoph Poutiers, Christophe Poutiers, Pat Roberts, Diogo Rodrigues, Diana Swartz, Arno Thuis, Andre V, Tomarchio Vasta Gianluca, Richard Villegas, Salome Weis, Shawn Whatley, Marcos Zuazu

Horhay??

ACKNOWLEDGMENTS

Buenos Aires Subte Map © Metrovías 2010

Artisan Fair

Wine Tasting

Tango

Proa – La Boca

Museum ... MALBA

Library

Theater / History museums

Walking tours

Notes

Notes

Notes

Notes

Notes

INDEX

See also separate indexes for:

ARTS

CINEMAS

CLASSICAL MUSIC

FLAMENCO

MILONGAS

STADIUMS

TANGO SHOWS

THEATERS

NOTABLE BUILDINGS

PARKS & GARDENS

THEME PARKS

SLEEPING

APARTMENTS

B&BS

ESTANCIAS

GUESTHOUSES

HOSTELS

HOTELS

000 map pages
000 photographs

POSADAS

SPORTS & ACTIVITIES

DAY SPAS

GOLF

GYMS

MARTIAL ARTS & CLIMBING

POLO

SOCCER

SWIMMING

TENNIS

YOGA & PILATES

TOP PICKS

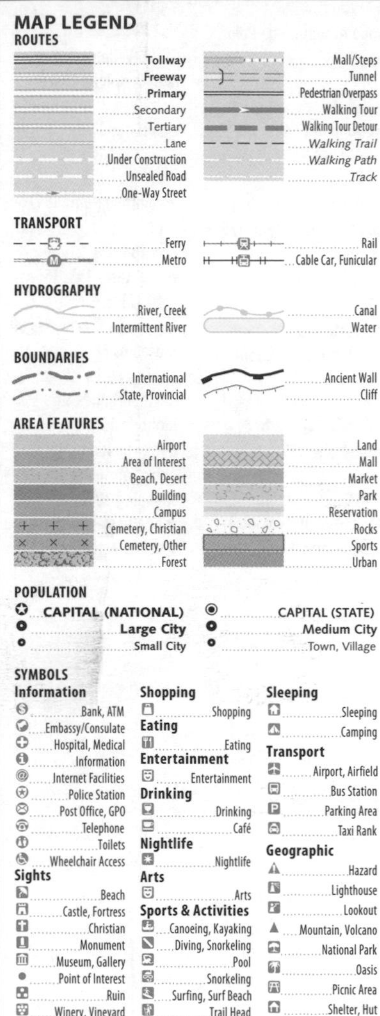

Although the authors and Lonely Planet have taken all reasonable care in preparing this book, we make no warranty about the accuracy or completeness of its content and, to the maximum extent permitted, disclaim all liability arising from its use.

Published by Lonely Planet Publications Pty Ltd
ABN 36 005 607 983

Australia (Head Office)
Locked Bag 1, Footscray, Victoria 3011,
☎03 8379 8000, fax 03 8379 8111

USA 150 Linden St, Oakland, CA 94607,
☎510 250 6400, toll free 800 275 8555,
fax 510 893 8572

UK 2nd fl, 186 City Rd, London, EC1V 2NT,
☎020 7106 2100, fax 020 7106 2101

Contact talk2us@lonelyplanet.com
lonelyplanet.com/contact

© Lonely Planet 2011
Photographs © as indicated 2011

All rights reserved. No part of this publication may be copied, stored in a retrieval system, or transmitted in any form by any means, electronic, mechanical, recording or otherwise, except brief extracts for the purpose of review, and no part of this publication may be sold or hired, without the written permission of the publisher.

10 9 8 7 6 5 4 3 2 1

6th edition
ISBN: 978 1 74179 578 3
Printed in China

Lonely Planet and the Lonely Planet logo are trademarks of Lonely Planet and are registered in the US Patent and Trademark Office and in other countries.

Lonely Planet does not allow its name or logo to be appropriated by commercial establishments, such as retailers, restaurants or hotels. Please let us know of any misuses: lonelyplanet.com/ip.